PROGRAMMING STRUCTURES

VOLUME I

Machines and Programs

PROGRAMMING STRUCTURES

VOLUME I

Machines and Programs

Jan Hext

PRENTICE HALL

New York   London   Toronto   Sydney   Tokyo

Typeset by Jan Hext and Deblaere Typesetting Pty Ltd

Printed and bound in Australia by
Macarthur Press Sales Pty Limited, Parramatta, NSW

Cover design and artwork by Tan Teong Eng

1 2 3 4 5 93 91 92 91 90

   ISBN 0 7248 0940 6. (paperback)
   ISBN 0-13-730391-2 (hardback)

National Library of Australia
Cataloguing-in-Publication Data

Hext, J. B. (Jan B.).
   Programming Structures. Volume 1. Machines and programs.

   Includes index.
   ISBN 0 7248 0940 6.

   1. Programming (Electronic computers). I. Title.
   II. Title: Machines and programs.

005.1'028

Library of Congress
Cataloguing-in-Publication Data

Hext, J. B., 1938–
   Programming structures.

   Includes index.
   Contents: v. 1. Machines and programs.
   1. Electronic digital computers – Programming. 2. Data structures
   (Computer science) 3. Structured programming. I. Title.
QA76.6.H49   1987   005.1   87-18693
ISBN 0-13-730391-2 (v. 1)

Prentice Hall, Inc., *Englewood Cliffs, New Jersey*
Prentice Hall Canada, Inc., *Toronto*
Prentice Hall Hispanoamericana, S.A., *Mexico*
Prentice Hall of India Private Ltd, *New Delhi*
Prentice Hall International, Inc., *London*
Prentice Hall of Japan, Inc., *Tokyo*
Prentice Hall of Southeast Asia Pty Ltd, *Singapore*
Editora Prentice Hall do Brasil Ltda, *Rio de Janeiro*

 PRENTICE HALL

A division of Simon & Schuster

To

Margaret

τῇ πολυτίμῳ μαργαρίτῃ μου

CONTENTS

4   SCALAR TYPES

5   MACHINE ARCHITECTURE

6   SEQUENCES, LANGUAGES, AND GRAMMARS

7   STRAIGHTLINE PROGRAMS

8   SEQUENTIAL CONTROL STRUCTURES

9   PROCEDURES AND FUNCTIONS

10   OBJECTS AND PROCESSES

PREFACE

'In all ages wherein learning has flourished, complaint hath been made of the itch of writing, and the multitude of worthless books wherewith importunate scribes have pestered the world. *Scribimus indocti doctique* and *tenet insanabile multos scribendi cacoethes*.'

Those words were written in 1691 by the distinguished scientist John Ray, a Fellow of the Royal Society and a contemporary of Isaac Newton at Trinity College, Cambridge. He wrote them in the introduction to his book *The Wisdom of God Manifest in the Works of the Creation* and, being sensitive to the charge that the book might 'incur the censure of a superfluous piece', proceeded to make a detailed apology for presenting it to the world. He offered five excuses, including the claim that it contained 'some considerations new and untouched by others' and that, compared with similar books, its 'manner of delivery and expression may be more suitable to some mens apprehension, and facile to their understanding'. Even if no-one else read the book, he hoped that his friends would benefit from it. But he need not have been so modest. The book was a best-seller and ran to seventeen editions.

Three hundred years later, the itch of writing is as great as ever and the complaint can still be made about importunate scribes who pester the world with a multitude of worthless books. Like John Ray, this particular scribe is sensitive to the charge that he may have written a 'superfluous piece'. Indeed, if this book is continued into Volumes II and III, as planned, there may be three superfluous pieces. So what excuses can he offer? What justification is there for producing a three-volume work on the subject of programming structures?

My apology must be set in the context of the entire computing phenomenon. It is scarcely 40 years since the first stored-program computer came into operation, and 30 since computing began to emerge as an accepted academic discipline. Yet in that brief span of time computers have developed at a rate that is without precedent in human history. People working in the field have had little time to catch their breath. There is always something newer, cheaper, faster, and more attractive coming on the scene. Today's knowledge is better than yesterday's, and tomorrow's promises to be even better. It has been a time of glorious adolescence, with all the energy, exuberance, and exhilaration of that phase of life.

As part of the growth to maturity, this book takes a pause from the onward rush and attempts to put some of our knowledge into order. It is written in the belief that there is now a core of material with which computer science students and practising programmers should be familiar, and that there is a need to present it in a way that is 'facile to their understanding'. True, there are many books and journals where this material has been well described by 'the most learned men of our time', including Dr Knuth, Dr Dijkstra, Mr Strachey late of Oxon and, to name no more, his successor Dr Hoare. Nevertheless, there may yet be some value in bringing the particulars together into a single framework, so sparing 'those fastidious readers who are not willing to take the pains to seek them out'.

The material in question is summarized by the title of the three volumes — *Programming Structures*. I am indebted to Fred Brooks for first alerting me to the fundamental importance of this topic. He did so in 1966 at a conference in Canberra (though he has probably forgotten the lunch we had together), at a time when I was struggling to organize my first course on programming. The wisdom of his advice was borne out in the 1970s by the way in which structured programming became a topic of heated debate and data structures an area of lively research. It was during those years that these volumes began to take shape and the first drafts were written. The 1980s have seen several quests for better ways of programming — functional programming, logic programming, object-oriented programming, and so on. Generally speaking, though, they have not overthrown the principles that had been established earlier. The core material has been augmented in several ways, but it has not radically changed.

The three volumes develop the material in a way that can be described, broadly speaking, as 'bottom-up'. This one lays the foundations by reviewing a wide range of basic concepts, including sets, bit patterns, numbers, sequences, and conventional machine organization. It then focuses on program structures, starting with simple, straightline programs and working through to fully parallel ones. The second volume deals with fundamental data structures, moving in similar fashion from the machine-oriented ones, such as arrays, to the more abstract ones, such as queues and trees. Building on these, the third volume explores the structures that are needed for the all-important area of information storage and retrieval. The progression is reasonably well-ordered. However, it does not follow a single straight line, nor need it be read in that way. The presentation is designed for people who already have some background in the field — typically, those who have learnt to program in a language such as Pascal. If they wish to explore a topic further, they can go direct to the relevant chapter, referring to earlier parts only as the fancy takes them.

In the development of the material, one of the hardest problems has been the choice of a programming language. Early on, I enjoyed the great leap forward that was provided by ALGOL 60. Fred Brooks urged me to study APL, which I did, learning much from it. Then, after a brief spell with BCPL, I spent several years with Pascal, and to some extent SIMULA 67, gaining great pleasure from their progressive data structures and control structures. Finally, though, I settled on Ada. The choice carries a risk because Ada, like APL, has been the subject of considerable prejudice and even hostility. Now that it is widely available, I hope that its qualities will be more readily appreciated. For myself, I enjoy using it and admire its designers for their achievement. Of course, it is not a panacea for all our programming ills and so I have drawn on other languages where appropriate, including those mentioned above. Nevertheless, Ada provides a common thread to all the volumes. I hope that its authorities will excuse me for adding the symbols '≤', '≥', and '≠' to its repertoire.

Another problem that has resolved itself over the years is the preparation and production of the text. In this I have been greatly helped by the facilities of the Unix operating system. I have used troff and tbl, together with a preprocessor that simplifies the input and a postprocessor that turns the output into Postscript. The latter became available at the eleventh hour and has been extremely useful for the final formatting and printing. I am grateful to the designers of these three systems — Unix, Troff, and Postscript — for the tools that they have created, and also to my colleagues Peter Dumbrell, Michael Homsey, and Martin Foord for maintaining our local versions and patiently answering all my cries for help.

It is a pleasure to acknowledge various forms of help from many other people as well. Foremost among them is my wife Margaret, whose patience, loyalty, support, and encouragement have meant so much to me in all the time that these volumes have been slowly (oh, so slowly!) taking shape. This volume is dedicated to her — an inadequate expression of appreciation and gratitude to a wonderful companion in life. At a rather different level, I am grateful to the University of Sydney in the 1970s and to Macquarie University in the 1980s for supporting my writing even when the promise was so long in fulfillment. They did not press me to churn out other publications nor to take up research of more immediate economic relevance. In some parts of our western society this academic freedom is being gradually eroded and can no longer be taken for granted.

Over the years, many people have read drafts of various chapters and contributed to their improvement. I am particularly grateful to my brother George for his detailed and perceptive comments on many of the early ones. Several groups of students have also provided valuable feedback. Then there were the reviewers, especially John Warner, whose constructive advice prompted some major improvements to this volume. Next came Richard Dahl, whose copy editing cured me of some bad writing habits. Following him, James Stephenson ran a fine comb through the penultimate draft, removing detailed errors that the rest of us had missed. Then Tan Teong Eng added his creative touch by designing the cover and the chapter headings. Overseeing it all have been Ian MacArthur and Fiona Marcar of Prentice Hall Australia, who have patiently allowed me to pursue my foibles, even when deadlines were long past. To all these people I express my sincere thanks, hoping that they will derive some pleasure from the book that they have helped to produce.

Jan Hext
Macquarie University

April 1989

SETS

1.1   THE RELEVANCE OF SETS

Sets are well known for their importance in mathematics. Indeed, the modern curriculum thrusts them upon every aspiring or perspiring student from an early age, usually at the expense of more traditional topics. 'What is the cardinality of the set of one-digit numerals?' asks a certain textbook of all its ten-year-old readers, and gives the answer 9. One weeps as much for the pomposity of the question as for the deficiency of the answer. In any case, if these ten-year-olds grow up to be cashiers, clerks, farmers, engineers, or even politicians, how many of them will ever make use of set theory? Perhaps they echo the hopes of Henri Poincaré (1854–1912) that 'later generations will see set theory as a disease from which they have recovered'.

And what about computer programmers? In the ranks of industry, there are very few for whom set theory looms at all large. It is true that many of them are concerned with handling sets of data, and so in one sense their work can be described as a continual round of set processing. Nevertheless, looking at the programming languages that they use, we seldom find any mention of sets or any provision of conventional set operations. Why should this be so?

The answer is that the sets of mathematics differ from those of programming in two significant ways. First, the items in a mathematical set must all be distinct. Thus the expression $\{7, 4, 6\}$ denotes a three-element set but $\{7, 4, 7\}$ does not. From an abstract point of view this is entirely reasonable. After all, the number 7 is a unique entity and cannot belong twice to the same set any more than Charlie Brown can belong twice to the same baseball team. But in the world of computing, this ideal does not necessarily apply. Sets of data can have duplicate values whether we like it or not. The expression $\{7, 4, 7\}$ has two instances of 7 and it is no use pretending otherwise. If Charlie Brown appears twice in the mailing list for a magazine, he will receive two copies of the magazine. To emphasize this important difference, sets that can have duplicate values are sometimes called *multisets*. In the computing literature they are also known as *bags*. If the term catches on, we can look forward to studies in the theory of bags and to erudite monographs on bag processing. But so far its acceptance has been rather muted.

The second point of difference is that a mathematical set is, in general, an *unordered* collection of items. For example, the sets $\{a, b, c\}$, $\{b, a, c\}$, and $\{c, b, a\}$ are all identical. By contrast, a collection of items in the memory of a computer has an ordering imposed on it, namely the order of the physical or logical representation. In general, this ordering cannot be ignored since it may be important to the algorithm that uses it.

Because of these two factors, a mathematical set is not one of the structures that occur 'naturally' in computer programming. What, then, is its importance for the study of programming structures? The answer is twofold. First, the concepts and definitions of set theory underlie the more theoretical aspects of programming. They are therefore important if the subject is to be treated with any degree of rigor. Second, in many areas of application — especially those relating to databases — sets of the mathematical kind have great practical relevance. Their implementation by means of more 'natural' structures constitutes a major part of the programmer's craft.

So sets present a paradox. On the one hand, they are the primitive data structure on which much of the theory depends. On the other hand, the lack of a convenient representation causes most programming languages to ignore them. They pervade everything we do and yet we seldom notice them. In response to the paradox, this chapter brings sets temporarily into focus, giving a brief review of their basic features and of associated concepts. After that, they will slip into the background, making brief appearances only when needed. Not until Volume III, in the final chapter on databases, will they return to full prominence.

1.2   SET OPERATIONS

A set S can be regarded as a structure on which a *membership* operation is defined. For any item x, this is an operation $x \in S$ that yields a value either true or false. If it is true, we say that x is a *member* of S or an *element* of S, and that x *belongs* to S. This simple definition provides a good conceptual basis on which to build. There are problems if sets are allowed to be members of themselves — problems that also occur with functions that can take themselves as arguments (see Exercise 2). But for the time being we shall sidestep these issues and shall assume that the basic idea is coherent and well understood.

The *cardinality* of a set, sometimes written as $|S|$, is the number of members of S. A set is *finite* if it has a finite number of members, otherwise it is *infinite*.

There are, in principle, two ways of describing a set: the first by *extension* and the second by *intension*. The former lists the members explicitly, usually enclosing them in curly brackets. For example, the colors of the rainbow can be described as the set:

$$\{\, red, \ orange, \ yellow, \ green, \ blue, \ indigo, \ violet \,\}$$

The alternative is to write an expression of the form:

$$\{\ x \quad | \quad P(x)\ \}$$

This denotes the set comprising all items x that satisfy the property P. The notation has the advantage that it can handle infinite sets. For example, the expression

$$\{\ x \quad | \quad prime(x)\ \}$$

denotes the set of all prime numbers. To indicate that x must belong to a larger set T, we can extend the notation by writing:

$$\{\ x : T \quad | \quad P(x)\ \}$$

In mathematics, T is known as the *universe* from which the set is drawn, but in the context of programming it is usually called the element's *type*.

A set S1 is a *subset* of S if every member of S1 is also a member of S. It is a *proper subset* if it is a subset of S but not identical to S; that is, at least one member of S is excluded. The former relation is written as $S1 \subseteq S$ and the latter as $S1 \subset S$.

The *null* set, or *empty* set, is the set with no members. It can be written as { } or as the special symbol $\varnothing$. It has the property that, for every item x, $x \in$ { } is *false*. It is a proper subset of every other set.

The *powerset* of S is the set of all its subsets. For example, if S is {a, b, c}, its power-set is:

$$\{ \{a, b, c\}, \ \{b, c\}, \ \{c, a\}, \ \{a, b\}, \ \{a\}, \ \{b\}, \ \{c\}, \ \varnothing \}$$

This has eight members, including S itself and the empty set. In general, a subset is formed by making a binary (two-valued) decision on each element — whether to include it or not. It follows that if S has n members, it has 2^n possible subsets; in other words, its powerset has 2^n members. Accordingly, its powerset is sometimes written as 2^S and it satisfies the relation:

$$|2^S| \ = \ 2^{|S|}$$

For any sets S, S1, and S2, with base type T, there are three common operations for constructing other sets. The first is set *complement*, denoted by $\overline{S}$, which gives the elements *not* in S:

$$\overline{S} \quad \equiv \quad \{ \ x : T \ \mid \ x \notin S \ \}$$

The second is set *union*, denoted by $S1 \cup S2$, which gives the elements in S1 *or* S2 (or both):

$$S1 \cup S2 \quad \equiv \quad \{ \ x : T \ \mid \ x \in S1 \quad or \quad x \in S2 \ \}$$

The third is set *intersection*, denoted by $S1 \cap S2$, which gives the elements in S1 *and* S2:

$$S1 \cap S2 \quad \equiv \quad \{ \ x : T \ \mid \ x \in S1 \quad and \quad x \in S2 \ \}$$

For example, if the universe is the set of letters {a, b, c, d}, with S = {a}, S1 = {a, b}, and S2 = {b, c}, the operations produce the following results:

$$\overline{S} \quad = \quad \{ \ b, \ c, \ d \ \}$$
$$S1 \cup S2 \quad = \quad \{ \ a, \ b, \ c \ \}$$
$$S1 \cap S2 \quad = \quad \{ \ b \ \}$$

Several other operations can be defined, but these are the most common. (For set difference and symmetric set difference, see Exercise 3).

Two sets S1 and S2 are said to be *disjoint* if they have no elements in common ($S1 \cap S2 = \varnothing$). The sets S1, S2, ... Sk are *mutually disjoint* if each pair is disjoint. A *partition* of S is a set of mutually disjoint non-empty subsets whose union equals S.

1.3 RELATIONS BETWEEN SETS

If S and T are two sets, their *Cartesian product* $S \times T$ is the set of ordered pairs (x, y) with x belonging to S and y belonging to T:

$$S \times T \quad \equiv \quad \{ \ (x, y) \ \mid \ x \in S, \ y \in T \ \}$$

For example, the product of $\{0, 1\}$ and $\{a, b, c\}$ is the set:

$$\{(0,a), \ (0,b), \ (0,c), \ (1,a), \ (1,b), \ (1,c)\}$$

The name 'set product' reflects the fact that the cardinality of $S \times T$ is $|S| \times |T|$: that is, the size of the product is the product of the sizes.

The definition can be extended to an arbitrary number of sets, $S1, \ldots Sn$:

$$S1 \ \times \ \ldots \ \times \ Sn \ \ \equiv \ \ \{ \ (x_1, \ \ldots \ x_n) \ \mid \ x_i \in \ Si, \ i = 1 \ldots n \}$$

The term $(x_1, \ldots x_n)$ is called an *n-tuple* and the items x_i are its *components*. An n-tuple differs from a set in that its components are ordered and they need not be distinct. As mentioned in Section 1.1, this brings them nearer to the structures that occur 'naturally' in a computer.

A *binary relation* on the sets S and T is a subset of $S \times T$. For example, if S is the set $\{Ben, Pat\}$ and T is the set $\{golf, music, drama\}$, a possible relation is:

$$\{ \ (Ben, music), \ (Pat, golf), \ (Pat, music) \ \}$$

The relation might have the significance 'is interested in'; thus Ben is interested in music, Pat is interested in golf, and so on. But it could equally well mean 'enjoys' or 'is good at' or 'spends all their money on' — mathematically, it would still be the same. The relation can be denoted by an operator ρ (say) with $x \rho y$ being the condition that (x, y) belongs to the subset.

More generally, a *relation* on the sets $S1, \ldots, Sn$ is any subset of the product $S1 \times \ldots \times Sn$, and n is its *degree*. For example, if S1 is a set of customers, S2 a set of businesses, and S3 the set of positive integers, there could be a relation of degree three with the significance 'x owes y the sum of z dollars'. Relations of this kind are of great practical importance, especially in the field of relational databases.

If S and T are sets, a *function* is a relation, f say, that relates each element of S to exactly one element of T. It is expressed by the notation:

$$f \ : \ S \ \ \rightarrow \ \ T$$

f is sometimes called a *mapping* of S into T. The set S is the *domain* of f and T is its *range*. If x is an element of S, it can be used as an *argument* of f and its corresponding element in T is denoted by $f(x)$. The situation can be generalized to the case where S is a product $S1 \times \ldots \times Sn$. The function f then takes an n-tuple $(x_1, \ldots x_n)$ as its argument and the expression $f(x_1, \ldots x_n)$ denotes the corresponding member of T. The expression can also be interpreted as the application of f to n separate arguments, in which case f is called an *n-ary* or *n-adic* function.

A *nondeterministic* function is a relation, f say, that relates each element of S to one *or more* elements of T. The *image* of x is the set of elements to which x is related and the expression $f(x)$ can be interpreted either as the image of x or as a value that is drawn nondeterministically from that set. The concept is important for the formal description of nondeterministic programs.

1.4 RELATIONS ON A SINGLE SET

An important kind of relation is one that exists between a set S and itself — that is, a binary relation on the product S×S. It can be described simply as a relation 'on S'. For example, if S is a set of people, it could be a relation x ρ y signifying 'x likes y', or 'x is a cousin of y', or 'x employs y'. The following are some examples from other contexts:

1. The elements are places in a city; x ρ y means that there is a street leading from x to y.

2. The elements are species in an ecological system; x ρ y means that x feeds on y.

3. The elements are names of telephone subscribers; x ρ y means that x precedes y in the alphabetic listing.

4. The elements are jobs which are part of a large project; x ρ y means that x must be completed before y can be started.

5. The elements are procedures that are defined in a computer program; x ρ y means that the definition of x contains a call of y.

6. The elements are categories in a BNF grammar (see Section 6.14); x ρ y means that there is a production of the form x ::= y . . . .

The relation $\bar{\rho}$ is the *complement* of ρ: that is, x $\bar{\rho}$ y holds if x ρ y does *not* hold.
  A relation on S×S can be characterized by a number of important properties:

- It is *reflexive* if x ρ x for every element x ∈ S; it is *irreflexive* if x $\bar{\rho}$ x for every element x ∈ S.

- It is *symmetric* if x ρ y implies y ρ x for all pairs x, y ∈ S; it is *antisymmetric* if x ρ y implies y $\bar{\rho}$ x for all x ≠ y.

- It is *transitive* if x ρ y and y ρ z implies x ρ z for all x, y, z ∈ S.

The properties can be illustrated by considering relations on the set of integers:

  '=' is reflexive, symmetric, and transitive;
  '≠' is irreflexive and symmetric;
  '<' is irreflexive, antisymmetric, and transitive;
  '≤' is reflexive and transitive.

Note that irreflexive is not the same as non-reflexive; nor is antisymmetric the same as non-symmetric.
  If a relation x ρ y is reflexive, symmetric, and transitive, it is called an *equivalence* relation, implying that x and y are in some sense 'equivalent'. It partitions S into disjoint subsets, known as *equivalence classes*, with the property that x and y belong to the same class if and only if they are equivalent. The '=' relation on the integers provides a rather trivial example, each subset having only one element. A more interesting example is the relation 'has the same remainder when divided by q', which partitions the integers into q

subsets: the subsets are called *residue classes* and members of the same class are said to be 'equivalent modulo q'. For example, the integers 0 to 15 have the following residue classes modulo 4:

$$\{0, 4, 8, 12\} \quad — \quad \text{remainder } 0$$
$$\{1, 5, 9, 13\} \quad — \quad \text{remainder } 1$$
$$\{2, 6, 10, 14\} \quad — \quad \text{remainder } 2$$
$$\{3, 7, 11, 15\} \quad — \quad \text{remainder } 3$$

All the members of a class are equivalent (modulo 4) to each other, but not to the members of any other class. In general, any function f imposes an equivalence relation on its domain S, namely $x \equiv y$ if $f(x) = f(y)$. Conversely, an equivalence relation ρ defines a function that maps each element x into its equivalence class.

For any relation ρ, a further relation ρ^+ can be defined as follows:

$x \rho^+ z$ there is a sequence of elements $y_1, ... y_k$ $(k \geq 0)$ such that $x \rho y_1$, $y_1 \rho y_2$, ... $y_k \rho z$.

The result is a transitive relation known as the *transitive closure* of ρ. A simple example is provided by the integer relation $x = z - 1$, which states that x is one less than z. Its transitive closure is $x < z$. A more interesting case is relation 5 above: if a function f can call a function g_1, which can call a function g_2, ..., which can call a function h, it implies the relation 'f can activate h'. In particular, $f \rho^+ f$ means that f is recursive — a property that can affect the way in which it is implemented. A method of computing ρ^+ is described in Exercises 10 – 13.

A *partial ordering* on a set is a relation that is reflexive, antisymmetric, and transitive. The set is said to be *partially ordered* and the relation can be denoted by the symbol '$\leq$'. A convenient example is the relation '$\subseteq$' on the powerset of S (Exercise 16) and another is provided by relation 4 above. The general idea is that the elements can be sequenced in such a way that if $x \leq y$, then x precedes y in the sequence. However, there is a measure of freedom in the sequencing, since for some pairs x and y there may be no ordering defined; that is to say, neither $x \leq y$ nor $y \leq x$ is part of the relation. (For a slightly different definition of partial ordering, see Exercise 9.)

A *total ordering* on a set is a partial ordering which, for every pair of distinct elements (x, y), contains either $x \leq y$ or $y \leq x$ (but not both, since the relation is antisymmetric). A set on which a total ordering is defined is said to be *ordered*. Some familiar examples are the integers, which are ordered numerically, and the letters of the alphabet, which are ordered alphabetically. The ordering carries over to any of their subsets. The task of *sorting* is to sequence the elements of a set so that they occur in their defined order. It is an important operation in computing and will be described in Volume III.

1.5 GRAPHS

A relation on a set S has the important property that it can be modeled by a *graph*. The elements of S become *points* of the graph (or *vertexes*, or *nodes*), and a relationship $x \rho y$ is modelled by a *line* (or *edge* or *arc*) that joins point x to point y. If the relation is a symmetric one, the line can be regarded as a two-way connection and the graph is said to

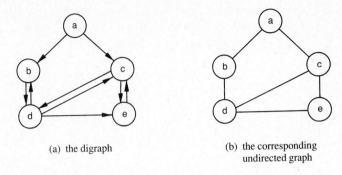

(a) the digraph

(b) the corresponding
undirected graph

Figure 1-1   A digraph

be *undirected*; but if the relation is not symmetric, the line is drawn as an *arrow*, leading from x to y, and the result is said to be a *directed* graph, otherwise known as a *digraph*. Figure 1-1(a) shows the digraph for the following relation on the set {a, b, c, d, e}:

$$\{(a,b), \ (a,c), \ (b,d), \ (c,d), \ (c,e), \ (d,b), \ (d,c), \ (d,e), \ (e,c)\}$$

It can be changed to an undirected graph by turning all the arrows into lines and removing duplicates. The result is shown in Figure 1-1(b).

In an undirected graph, a *path* is a sequence of distinct vertexes $x_1, \ldots x_k$ ($k \geq 2$) with a line joining each successive pair. If the vertexes do not have to be distinct, it is some-times called a *walk*. The *length* of the path is the number of lines involved, namely $k - 1$. A *cycle* is a path of length three or more that returns to its starting point: its vertexes are distinct, with the exception that $x_k = x_1$. (The length requirement eliminates cycles that could be formed from a single line.) A graph is *connected* if there is a path from each vertex to each other vertex. It is *acyclic* if there are no cycles.

The definitions for a directed graph are similar. A *path* is a sequence of vertexes with an arrow leading from each one to the next. A *cycle* is a path (of any length) that returns to its starting point. The graph is *strongly connected* if there is a path from each vertex to each other vertex and it is *connected* if the corresponding graph is connected (arrows being changed to lines). Two paths *converge* if they arrive at the same vertex along different arrows. The example in Figure 1-1(a) is connected but not strongly connected; it has a variety of cycles, including b–d–b and c–e–d–c; the paths a–b–d and a–c–d converge at vertex d.

In computer programming, directed graphs are much more common than undirected ones and they are nearly always (weakly) connected. As a result, the term 'graph' is sometimes used in the limited sense of a graph that is directed and connected. It is useful to classify such graphs into a simple hierarchy that places successively greater restrictions on them:

1. *digraph*   —   any connected directed graph;
2. *dag*   —   a digraph with no cycles;
3. *tree*   —   a digraph with no cycles and no convergent paths.

Examples are shown in Figure 1-2. The name 'dag' is short for 'directed acyclic graph'. It is not an established term in mathematics, but is found increasingly often in the com-puting literature. Trees are characterized by a simple branching structure and are of great

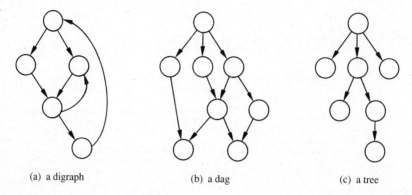

(a) a digraph   (b) a dag   (c) a tree

Figure 1-2   Three kinds of digraph

practical importance. They are described in Volume II, where several alternative but equivalent definitions are given. The mathematical definition of a tree is rather different, being framed in terms of undirected graphs (see Exercise 17).

The great attraction of graphs is that they depict relations in a way that is easily seen and understood. For example, if $x \rho y$ means that there is an arrow from point x to point y, the transitive closure $x \rho^+ y$ has the obvious interpretation that there is a path from x to y. Similarly, $x \rho^+ x$ means that there is a cycle through x. The existence of cycles and/or convergent paths is sometimes desirable and sometimes not, depending on the application. In relation 1 of the previous section, the digraph is a crude form of map and the cycles are presumably an advantage: they allow journeys to return to their starting point. On the other hand, in relation 4 the digraph is a PERT network (for Program Evaluation and Review Technique) and the existence of cycles would be somewhat embarrassing: some jobs could not be started until they had already been completed! The above classification of graphs has a variety of applications in programming and will reappear several times in later chapters.

FURTHER READING

There are several good books on discrete mathematics that have been written for computer scientists and that include an introduction to set theory. They also include material that is relevant to several other chapters of this book. Among them are Biggs (1985), Doerr and Levasseur (1985), Grimaldi (1985), Kalmanson (1986), and Skvarcius and Robinson (1986).

EXERCISES

1   Section 1.1 stated that an item cannot belong twice to the same set and that the members of a set are not ordered in any way. How are these properties embodied in the definition of a set as given in Section 1.2?

2   The problem concerning sets that can contain themselves as members is known as Russell's paradox. We define P to be the set of all sets that do *not* contain themselves as members. The question then arises: does P contain itself? The paradox is that if it does, it can't and if it doesn't, it must. To avoid the paradox, Russell proposed that sets be classified into a hierarchy — basic sets, sets of basic sets, sets of sets of basic sets, and so on. This precludes the possibility that a set can contain itself as a member and therefore evades the paradox. For a practical application of this stratagem, see Exercise 9.8.

3   The set *difference* operation, S1\S2, produces all members of S1 that are not in S2. The *symmetric difference* produces all members of S1 that are not in S2 and all members of S2 that are not in S1. Define them in terms of complement, union, and intersection.

4   If S has n members and T has m members, how many binary relations are there on the product $S \times T$?

5   Consider the relations 1 – 6 listed in Section 1.4. For each one, determine whether or not you would expect it to be (a) reflexive, (b) irreflexive, (c) symmetric, (d) antisymmetric, (e) transitive.

6   Describe, informally, the significance of the transitive closure of the relations 1 – 6 in Section 1.4. In each case, consider the significance of the expression $x \rho^+ x$ for an arbitrary element x and state whether or not such situations are desirable.

7   What is the transitive closure of the relation $|x - y| = 4$ on the set of positive integers?

8   Given an arbitrary relation ρ on a set S, we can take its transitive closure ρ^+ and then define a relation $x \sigma y$ to mean:

$$x = y \ \textit{or} \ (x \rho^+ y \ \textit{and} \ y \rho^+ x)$$

Show that σ is an equivalence relation. Now let S1, ... Sk be the corresponding equivalence classes and define a relation τ such that $Si \ \tau \ Sj$ means 'there exist elements $x \in Si$ and $y \in Sj$ such that $x \rho y$'. Show that τ is a partial ordering on the equivalence classes.

9   In Section 4, a partial ordering was required to be reflexive, antisymmetric, and transitive. An alternative approach requires it to be irreflexive instead of reflexive, thus excluding the condition $x \rho x$. To express this difference, the symbol '<' is used instead of '≤'. In fact it is sufficient to require '<' to be irreflexive and transitive: the antisymmetry is a necessary consequence. Prove this result. How would the argument of the previous exercise be affected by this alternative definition?

10   A binary relation ρ on a set $\{x_1, \ldots x_n\}$ can be represented very simply by an $n \times n$ logical matrix C. C[i,j] is set to 1 if $x_i \rho x_j$ and to 0 otherwise. In the context of graphs, C is known as the *connection* matrix and $C[i,j] = 1$ can be interpreted as the condition 'there is an arrow from x_i to x_j'. Construct the connection matrix for the graph of Figure 1-1(a). What properties will the matrix have if ρ is (a) reflexive, (b) symmetric?

11   Given a connection matrix C, as in the previous exercise, let us define a transformation $T_k(C)$ that replaces every element C[i,j] by the value of the expression:

$$C[i,j] \quad \vee \quad (C[i,k] \wedge C[k,j])$$

This sets C[i,j] to 1 either if $x_i \rho x_j$ or if $x_i \rho x_k$ and $x_k \rho x_j$. In terms of the graph, it recognizes that x_i can be connected to x_j via x_k. Write a program in some suitable language that performs this transformation. How many assignments does it require?

12   [Warshall's algorithm] If the matrix C represents the relation ρ, as in the previous exercise, then the following algorithm transforms it so that it represents the transitive closure of ρ:

$$\textbf{for } k = 1, 2, \ldots n \textbf{ do } T_k(C)$$

Informally, this allows ρ to operate transitively first via x_1, then via x_2 as well, then via x_3 as well, and so on. Prove the correctness of the algorithm by establishing an inductive assertion of the form 'after the kth iteration, C[i,j] will be 1 if ... .'

This algorithm was first presented, somewhat obscurely, in a paper by S. J. Warshall (1962). A more complicated but theoretically faster algorithm for computing transitive closures is given by Eve and Kurki-Suonio (1977).

13   Prove that the transformations T_k are commutative: that is,

$$T_p(T_q(C)) \quad = \quad T_q(T_p(C))$$

Use this fact to provide an alternative proof that the algorithm of the previous exercise is correct.

14   Prove the assertion in Section 1.4 that an equivalence relation ρ partitions a set into equivalence classes such that x and y belong to the same class if and only if $x \rho y$.

15   Prove the assertion in Section 1.4 that a partial ordering '$\leq$' on a set S allows the elements of S to be sequenced in such a way that if $x \leq y$, with $x \neq y$, then x precedes y in the sequence. (Hint: find a suitable element to come first.)

16   Prove that the relation '$\subseteq$' is a partial ordering on the powerset of a set S. Draw a digraph that depicts this ordering for the powerset of {a,b,c}.

17   In mathematics, a *tree* is usually defined to be an undirected graph that is connected and acyclic. It is a *rooted* tree if one of the vertexes is designated as the root. Prove that there is then a unique path from the root to each other vertex. Show that each line can therefore be assigned a direction 'away from' the root and that this results in a tree as defined in Section 1.5. Show that a necessary condition for a digraph to be a tree is that the corresponding undirected graph is a tree. Why is this not a sufficient condition?

2
BIT
PATTERNS

2.1   BITS, BYTES, AND WORDS

In its broad outline, this book is organized in a way that can be described as 'bottom up'.
It begins with the basic units of a computer and works its way up to the abstract structures
of high-level programming. This approach requires patience, since it takes longer to
reach the topics that are most relevant to practising programmers. But by laying the
groundwork at the outset, it provides a better context when eventually those topics are
reached. A minor bonus is that it corresponds to the way in which the subject developed
historically.

As part of the groundwork, this chapter looks at the most basic unit of all, namely the
bit. The bit is the atom — the indivisible unit whose components, if any, are not available for inspection. You cannot split the bit. The name is a contraction of 'binary digit',
indicating that a bit is a digit with two possible values, 0 and 1. The implication is that
the bit represents a number, as indeed it may. However, it can equally well represent any
other two-valued piece of information — false or true, positive or negative, female or
male, dead or alive, to be or not to be, and so on. Its significance in each case depends on
the context and on the conventions being used.

If bits are the atoms, then sequences of bits are the molecules, and to make progress it
is necessary to understand their chemistry. The most common groupings are those of six
or eight bits forming a *byte* (such as 01001101), and those of two, four, or eight bytes
forming a *word* (such as 1111100101100010). All computers have hardware operations
for handling one or other of these units, and most can handle both. Indeed, as Section 5.2
shows, their main memory is specifically designed to make this possible. By contrast,
individual bits, or arbitrary groups of bits, cannot be processed except by programming
several instructions in sequence. The techniques for doing this are described in later sections.

As noted earlier, a single bit can represent information which has two possible values.
Longer sequences can represent a much greater range of values. The following theorem
states exactly how many:

Theorem 2.1

A sequence of n bits has 2^n possible values.

For example, with n = 3, there are eight sequences — 000, 001, 010, 011, 100, 101, 110,
and 111. The observation is so elementary that it scarcely deserves to be dressed up as a

theorem. Yet the result is of fundamental importance in practice. It means that an n-bit sequence can represent 2^n distinct items of information. Thus five bits can represent the 32 points of the compass; six can represent the squares on a chess board; seven can represent the 128 members of the ASCII character set (see Section 4.5); and so on. Conversely, if k distinct items have to be represented, the following corollary states how many bits are required:

Corollary

Consider a set of k items. If $k \leq 2^n$, each item can be represented by a distinct n-bit sequence.

For example, the instruction set of a computer might have 40 different operations. Since $40 \leq 2^6$, each instruction can be represented by a sequence of six bits. Equally, it could be represented by a sequence of seven bits, or eight bits, or even more. Often it is convenient to allocate a full byte or a full word, using more bits than necessary in order to make processing faster. On the other hand, in order to save memory it may be preferable to use as few bits as possible. The minimum is the smallest integer m such that $k \leq 2^m$. Using a notation to be described later (see Section 4.3), this may be written in the form:

$$\lceil \log_2 k \rceil$$

The term $\log_2 k$ gives the power of 2 which equals k. For example, $\log_2 40$ is approximately 5.3. The operation $\lceil \ldots \rceil$ rounds it upwards to the nearest integer, in this case 6. The formula occurs in a variety of contexts and is especially important for the analysis of algorithms.

2.2 NOTATION

In order to describe the operations that computers can apply to bit patterns, this section establishes a few notational conventions. They provide the basis for a small, informal programming language. In some respects, the language will be similar to an assembly code, working close to the instruction set of a typical computer. However, the actual notation will be more like that of a higher level language, and its statements will not necessarily correspond to single instructions on any particular machine.

For our present purposes, it is sufficient to assume that all operations are applied to words. Accordingly, A, B, and C will denote words in the computer — either high-speed registers or words in main memory, as described in Chapter 5. The simplest operation is the one that copies a bit pattern from one word to another. It will be written in the form:

$$C \leftarrow A$$

This can be read as 'C is assigned the value of A', or more simply as 'C is assigned A'. It is sometimes called the *move* instruction, with A being the *source* and C the *destination*. Since A itself remains unchanged, the word 'move' is not entirely appropriate. A more accurate term would be 'copy', as commonly used in operating systems for handling files. In UNIX, for example, the *copy* command preserves the source file, whereas the *move* command (true to its name) deletes it.

A *constant* is a symbol that denotes a specific, known value. It can appear on the right-hand side of an assignment, as in:

$$C \leftarrow 1234$$

In the implementation, the value is copied either from some anonymous word or from the hardware instruction itself (see Section 5.3). In the latter case, it is called an *immediate operand* and the execution will probably be a little faster.

An integer such as 1234 is represented by a bit pattern, as described in the next chapter. To specify a particular bit pattern, such as 10011101, some extra notation is needed; otherwise the pattern could be interpreted as a decimal integer. A possible convention is to prefix the pattern with '2#':

$$C \leftarrow 2\#10011101$$

If the pattern has less than n bits, it is extended with 0s on the left. Long patterns can be shortened by using either the octal or the hexadecimal notation, as described in the next chapter. With these, the above example would appear as follows:

$$C \leftarrow 8\#235 \qquad \text{-- octal}$$
$$C \leftarrow 16\#9D \qquad \text{-- hexadecimal}$$

The details are explained in Section 3.4. Meanwhile, the binary notation is sufficient.

The arithmetic and logical operations will be embedded in instructions whose basic form is:

$$C \leftarrow A \; op \; B$$

This states that *op* is applied to (copies of) A and B, and that the result is assigned to C. If *op* requires only one operand, the form is:

$$C \leftarrow op \; B$$

The operands may also be constants, as in:

$$C \leftarrow A + 1$$

If C is the same as A, the part 'C ←' will be omitted. For example,

$$A + 1$$

means that A is increased by 1. This reflects the fact that on many machines the corresponding instruction will have only one reference to A.

Occasionally, the operands will be expressions that contain further operations. For example:

$$C \leftarrow A + (2 * B)$$

Assignments of this kind will normally correspond to two or more machine instructions. They could be broken down into simpler steps; but for describing algorithms, it is easier to use the higher-level notation.

The *word length* of a machine is the number of bits in each word and will be denoted by n. The bits will be numbered *from left to right*, as shown in Figure 2-1. Thus the first bit of A is A_0 and the last one is A_{n-1}. In a culture whose language is written from left to right, this convention is *a priori* the natural one to use. However, it is by no means

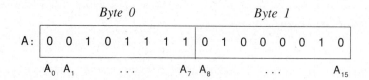

Figure 2-1   Numbering the bits of a 16-bit word

universal. The opposite, right-to-left convention has advantages in the representation of integers (see Chapter 3) and some manufacturers have accordingly adopted it. Unfortunately, this causes a certain amount of confusion, with well-known problems in the transfer of information between machines from opposite camps (see Exercise 1). But each side is committed to its position and so we have to live with both. As far as the next few chapters are concerned, the left-to-right supporters will find themselves at home. Those from the other tradition will have to make minor mental adjustments.

2.3   LOGICAL OPERATIONS

The *logical* operations are those that operate on a bit pattern treating each 0 or 1 as an independent entity. They make no assumptions about the structure of the pattern nor about its possible interpretation. Each bit is treated strictly on its individual merits. A *bitwise* operation is one that acts on each of the bit positions identically and independently. In other words, the operation

$$C \leftarrow A \ op \ B$$

is equivalent to doing

$$C_i \leftarrow A_i \ op \ B_i$$

for $i = 0, 1, \ldots n-1$ simultaneously.

There are three logical, bitwise operations that occur most commonly in practice. The simplest is the logical *not*,

$$C \leftarrow \neg A$$

which can be read as 'C is assigned *not* A'. It sets C_i to 1 if A_i is *not* 1 (and to 0 otherwise). The bits are said to be *inverted* (or 'flipped', or 'complemented'), each 0 being replaced by a 1 and each 1 by a 0.

The second is the logical *or*,

$$C \leftarrow A \vee B$$

which can be read as 'C is assigned A *or* B'. It sets C_i to 1 if A_i is 1 *or* B_i is 1 (and to 0 otherwise). It includes the case where A_i and B_i are both 1, and so it is sometimes called the *inclusive or*. This is in contrast to the *exclusive or*, which requires either B_i or C_i to be 1, but not both (see below).

The third is the logical *and*,

$$C \leftarrow A \wedge B$$

A B	0 0 1 1 0 1 0 1
¬A	1 1 0 0
¬B	1 0 1 0
A ∨ B	0 1 1 1
A ∧ B	0 0 0 1

Figure 2-2   The basic logical operations

which can be read as 'C is assigned A *and* B'. It sets C_i to 1 if A_i is 1 *and* B_i is 1 (and to 0 otherwise).

The three operations are summarized by the table in Figure 2-2, in which A and B are four-bit words with A = 0011 and B = 0101. It shows the effects of *or* and *and* on each possible combination of bits — 00, 01, 10, and 11. The effects of *or* and *and* can be described in another way. The former produces 0 only if both bits are 0, while the latter produces 1 only if both bits are 1. This reversal of the roles of 0 and 1 is reflected in De Morgan's laws:

$$A \lor B \quad \equiv \quad \neg (\neg A \land \neg B)$$
$$A \land B \quad \equiv \quad \neg (\neg A \lor \neg B)$$

It follows that one or other operation is redundant, and some machines do in fact provide only one of them.

The term 'logical' and the names *not*, *or*, and *and* remind us that these operations originated in mathematical logic. The values 0 and 1 correspond to the truth-values *false* and *true*, and the operations represent ways of combining propositions. For example, if p is the proposition 'the sun is hot' and q is the proposition 'the moon is green', the operations can be used to formulate further propositions such as:

> *not* p   —   the sun is not hot;
> p *or* q   —   the sun is hot or the moon is green (or both);
> p *and* q   —   the sun is hot and the moon is green.

If p is *true* and q is *false*, the three combinations are respectively *false*, *true*, and *false*. The formal treatment of these two-valued quantities is called *Boolean algebra*, after the English mathematician George Boole (1815–1864), and it has become firmly embedded in programming languages by means of the Boolean data type (see Section 4.4). The operations also have counterparts in set theory and are therefore known occasionally as the logical *complement*, *union*, and *intersection*. Their roles in this respect are described in Section 2.9.

Figure 2-2 shows that the effects of *not*, *or*, and *and* on A and B can be represented by the bit patterns 1100, 1010, 0111, and 0001. Since there are 16 different four-bit sequences, there are in principle 16 different bitwise operations that can be applied to A and B. The operations and their related bit patterns are shown in Figure 2-3, together with their definitions in terms of *not*, *or*, and *and*, and their descriptions. They can be

| A | 0011 | | |
B	0101		
Operator	Result	Equivalent	Comment
	0000	0	constant
∧	0001	A ∧ B	and
	0010	A ∧ ¬B	and-not
	0011	A	copy A
	0100	¬A ∧ B	
	0101	B	copy B
⊕, ≢	0110	(A ∧ ¬B) ∨ (¬A ∧ B)	exclusive or, non-equivalence
∨	0111	A ∨ B	or
	1000	¬(A ∨ B)	nor (not-or)
≡	1001	(A ∧ B) ∨ (¬A ∧ ¬B)	equivalence
	1010	¬B	not B
	1011	A ∨ ¬B	or-not
	1100	¬A	not A
⊃	1101	¬A ∨ B	implication
	1110	¬(A ∧ B)	nand (not-and)
	1111	1	constant

Figure 2-3   Logical operations

divided into three groups according to their dependence on A and B:

- the two rows 0000 and 1111, where the result is independent of A and B;

- the four rows A, ¬A, B, and ¬B, which depend either on A or on B but not on both;

- the remaining ten rows which are functions of both A and B.

Of the last group, seven operations have names and symbols that are commonly used in the literature. Besides *or* and *and*, they are the following:

$$
\begin{array}{rcl}
nor \text{ (not-or)} & — & \text{yields 1 if } A_i = 0 \text{ and } B_i = 0; \\
nand \text{ (not-and)} & — & \text{yields 1 if } A_i = 0 \text{ or } B_i = 0; \\
equivalence & — & \text{yields 1 if } A_i = B_i; \\
non\text{-}equivalence & — & \text{yields 1 if } A_i \neq B_i; \\
implication & — & \text{yields 1 if } A_i = 0 \text{ or } B_i = 1.
\end{array}
$$

These are all symmetric in A and B except for *implication* which, like the three unnamed operations, is non-symmetric.

As shown in the table, the *exclusive or* is the same as non-equivalence and can therefore be written as '$\neq$'. More usually, it is denoted by the 'hot cross buns' symbol '$\oplus$', reflecting the fact that it implements *logical addition* — that is, the addition of two bits but without generating a 'carry' bit. One other operation that is occasionally useful is the *and-not* ($A \wedge \neg B$), which yields 1 if $A_i = 1$ and $B_i = 0$. It has no recognized name, but since it is equivalent to non-implication, an obvious possibility is to call it *nimp*. The next two sections illustrate its uses.

2.4 MASKING AND SHIFTING

A *field* of a word can be defined as a group of consecutive bit positions. For example, if A is a 16-bit word, it can be divided into three fields as shown in Figure 2-4:

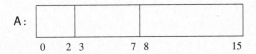

Figure 2-4   Fields of a word

The first field starts at A_0 and has three bits; the second starts at A_3 and has five bits; and the third starts at A_8 and has eight bits. The expression

$$\text{field } (A, i, k)$$

will denote the field of A starting at position i and having length k. Thus the second field shown above can be described as field $(A, 3, 5)$.

Arbitrary fields of a word can be manipulated by the operations of *masking* and *shifting*. A *mask* is a bit pattern that is used for picking out particular fields of a word, having 1s in those fields and 0s in the others. The expression

$$\text{mask } (i, k)$$

will denote the bit pattern with k 1s starting at position i and 0s elsewhere. For example, with 16-bit words, mask $(3, 5)$ is the pattern 0001111100000000. It can be used for operating on A in such a way that the mask field, namely field $(A, 3, 5)$, is treated differently from the non-mask field. In particular, a logical *and* will produce a copy of $A_3 - A_7$, as shown in Figure 2-5. As can be seen, the effect is to copy the mask field of A

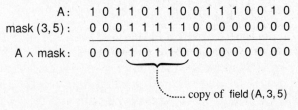

Figure 2-5   Copying a field

and to 0-fill the rest. If a logical *or* is used instead, the effect is to 1-fill the mask field and to copy the rest.

In general, the mask field and the non-mask field are each subject to one of four possible effects: they can be copied, reversed, 0-filled, or 1-filled. The 16 combinations correspond to the 16 different bitwise operations that were listed in Figure 2-3. The four most important ones are shown in Figure 2-6. Of the remaining possibilities, six produce the uninteresting results all-0s, all-1s, A, ¬A, mask, and ¬mask. The other six have a significant effect but are seldom needed in practice.

Operation	Mask field	Remainder
A ∧ mask	copied	0-filled
A ∨ mask	1-filled	copied
A ∧ ¬mask	0-filled	copied
A ⊕ mask	reversed	copied

Figure 2-6   Effects of masking operations

As its name implies, a *shift* operation shifts a bit pattern from one position to another within a word. The following four kinds are useful:

A *lshift* k   A's bit pattern is shifted k places to the left. The k leftmost bits are lost and k zeros are inserted at the right.

A *rshift* k   A's bit pattern is shifted k places to the right. The k rightmost bits are lost and k zeros are inserted at the left.

A *lcycle* k   A's bit pattern is rotated k places to the left. The k leftmost bits are wrapped around so that they reappear on the right.

A *rcycle* k   A's bit pattern is rotated k places to the right. The k rightmost bits are wrapped around so that they reappear on the left.

The first two are known as ordinary *logical* shifts and the last two as *cyclic* shifts or *rotations*. If A has eight bits denoted by 'abcdefgh', and if k=3, the effects of the shifts are as follows:

$$
\begin{array}{lll}
\text{A } \textit{lshift} \text{ 3} & - & \text{d e f g h 0 0 0} \\
\text{A } \textit{rshift} \text{ 3} & - & \text{0 0 0 a b c d e} \\
\text{A } \textit{lcycle} \text{ 3} & - & \text{d e f g h a b c} \\
\text{A } \textit{rcycle} \text{ 3} & - & \text{f g h a b c d e}
\end{array}
$$

On most machines, *rshift* is implemented by doing a negative *lshift*. That is, A *rshift* k is executed as A *lshift* −k. Similarly for *rcycle* and *lcycle*. Many machines omit either the logical shift or the cyclic shift, since the provision of both is something of a luxury. For most purposes, either form will do. If necessary, the effect of the missing one can be obtained by other means (see below).

A *double-length* shift is one that operates on a pair of words, treating them as a single unit. Thus

A, B *ldouble* k

indicates a double-length left shift with A as the first word and B as the second. The bits in A move k places to the left, the k leading ones being lost. The k leftmost bits of B move across to the right-hand end of A, and B is replaced by B *lshift* k. Interest normally centers on the resulting value of A, the change to B being regarded as a side effect. However, the side effect can occasionally be useful, as the following sequence shows:

A ← 0
A, B *ldouble* k
B ∨ A

The k leftmost bits of B are shifted into A and then returned by the *or* operation to the right-hand end of B. This provides one way of doing B *lcycle* k when the *lcycle* operation is not available.

2.5   PACKING AND UNPACKING

When a word is divided into several fields, the implication is that each field holds a separate item of data. The items are said to be *packed* into the word. This contrasts with the normal *unpacked* representation, in which each item is stored in a separate word. The advantage of the packed representation is chiefly that it saves space. It also saves effort if the items are moved around as a group. However, there is a price to be paid when the items have to be processed individually. Most machine instructions operate on single one-word items and so a packed item must first be unpacked into a separate word. Conversely, the one-word item may later have to be returned to its original field.

The operations of packing and unpacking are illustrated in Figure 2-7. The former takes a one-word item in B and stores it in field (A, i, k). It assumes that the item is held in the k rightmost bits of B, the other bits all being 0. The latter extracts a copy of field (A, i, k) and stores it in the k rightmost bits of B, with the rest of B being 0-filled. In some cases, the operations can be executed by single machine instructions. For example, if field (A, i, k) is a byte, it may be directly addressable. Generally, though, the operations have to be implemented by a judicious use of masks and shifts.

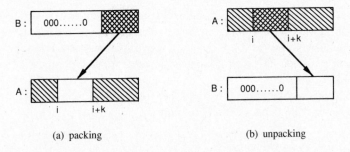

(a) packing   (b) unpacking

Figure 2-7   Accessing a field

As in real life, unpacking is considerably easier than packing and so it will be examined first. The standard technique is to extract the relevant bits of A by using a mask and a logical *and*, as described in the previous section. The bits can then be right-justified in B (that is, moved to the right-hand end):

$$\text{B} \;\leftarrow\; \text{A} \wedge \text{mask(i,k)}$$
$$\text{B } \textit{rshift } \text{(n-i-k)}$$

The *rshift* can be replaced by an *rcycle* or by *lcycle* (i+k). A different approach is to do the shifting first and then the masking:

$$\text{B} \;\leftarrow\; \text{A } \textit{rshift } \text{(n-i-k)}$$
$$\text{B } \wedge \text{ mask(n-k,k)}$$

The advantage of this is that the mask has a simpler form and it may be possible to store it as part of the *and* instruction, thereby saving a memory reference. Yet another method is to dispense with the mask and to rely entirely on shifts:

$$\text{B} \;\leftarrow\; \text{A } \textit{lshift } \text{i}$$
$$\text{B } \textit{rshift } \text{(n-k)}$$

This also saves a memory reference and for small values of i it may be quite efficient. To unpack successive k-bit fields in left-to-right sequence, a simple technique is to execute the following code inside a loop:

$$\text{A } \textit{lcycle } \text{k}$$
$$\text{B} \;\leftarrow\; \text{A } \wedge \text{ field(n-k,k)}$$

Or, better still:

$$\text{B} \;\leftarrow\; 0$$
$$\text{B, A } \textit{ldouble } \text{k}$$

As each field is extracted, the next one moves into the leading position. In all these cases, the choice of the fastest technique will depend on the details of the available machine and on the values of i and k. Often there will be little to choose between them.

The basic technique for packing is to clear field (A, i, k) to zeros, then to align the pattern in B, and then to insert it by means of a logical *or*:

$$\text{A } \wedge \neg \text{ mask(i,k)}$$
$$\text{B } \textit{lshift } \text{(n-i-k)}$$
$$\text{A } \vee \text{ B}$$

The effect of the third step is illustrated in Figure 2-8 with n = 16, i = 3, and k = 5. If the machine has an *and-not* operation, the first step involves only one instruction. The operation is sometimes known as 'bit clear', because of its role in this respect. In other cases, the *and* and *not* must be coded separately, or else ¬mask (i, k) must be supplied as an extra mask.

Several other techniques can be used, but they seldom run any faster. For example, here is a version that operates entirely by shifts:

$$\text{A } \textit{lcycle } \text{(i+k)}$$
$$\text{B, A } \textit{ldouble } \text{(n-k)}$$
$$\text{A } \textit{rcycle } \text{i}$$

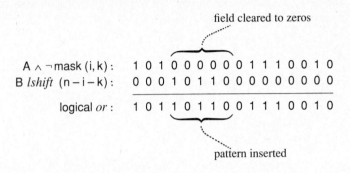

Figure 2-8   Inserting bits in a field

The only case where there is significant room for improvement is when assembling successive fields from scratch. If the items are in B1, B2, ... Br, and if they occupy fields of
length k1, k2, ... kr, the following code works well:

$$
\begin{aligned}
&A \;\leftarrow\; B1 \\
&A \;\textit{lshift}\;\; k2 \\
&A \;\vee\; B2 \\
&\qquad \cdots \\
&A \;\textit{lshift}\;\; kr \\
&A \;\vee\; Br
\end{aligned}
$$

There is no need for any masks and the progressive shifting minimizes the total amount
of shifting that is done.

2.6   BIT PICKING

Occasionally bits have to be processed individually. This can be done by treating them as
fields of length one and applying the techniques of the previous section. In some cases,
though, faster performance can be achieved by enlisting the aid of arithmetic operations.
This section looks at three examples. It assumes a knowledge of number representations,
as described in Chapter 3. It also assumes the existence of instructions for carrying out
tests of various kinds. They have the general form

$$\text{if } condition \;\text{ goto } L$$

and their effect is to transfer control to the instruction labeled *L* if the *condition* is true. A
fuller discussion of these instructions is given in Section 5.5.

It should be remarked, of course, that there are serious dangers in using arithmetic
operations in order to obtain logical effects. They can cause problems in certain cases,
especially when the sign bit is involved, and may depend on numbers being represented
in a particular way (see Section 3.6). Because of these factors, most high-level languages
prevent arithmetic operations from being applied to logical entities. However, system
implementation languages (SILs) are usually less stringent in this regard. At an even

lower level, the use of assembly code opens up a whole bagful of hazardous tricks, which bit-picking programmers occasionally like to use.

Testing a bit

As a first example, consider the problem of testing a particular bit A_i to see if it is set to 1. A simple method is to use a mask with a 1 in the required position:

```
A ∧ mask(i,1)
if A ≠ 0 goto L
```

The first step clears the remaining bits to 0; the second compares A with 0 to see if a 1 survives. This assumes that 0 is the all-0 bit pattern. To avoid the overtones of arithmetic, the test could be written as $A \neq 2\#0$, or even as $A = mask\,(i, 1)$, instead.

A second approach is to shift the bit in A_i to a position where it can be tested directly. The most common position is the leftmost one (the sign bit), which some machines can test directly:

```
A lshift i
if A₀ = 1 goto L
```

On some machines, the test is equivalent to testing whether A is negative; a SIL program could therefore write:

```
if A < 0 goto L
```

But in other cases the two tests are not equivalent and so this version is machine-dependent (see Section 3.6).

An alternative is to move the bit in A_i to the rightmost position:

```
A rshift (n−i−1)
```

Again, there may be an instruction for testing this bit directly (the parity bit). In other cases, it can be masked and tested, as in the first method:

```
A ∧ mask(n−1,1)
if A ≠ 0 goto L
```

The mask is the pattern 000...01 which, on virtually every machine, represents the integer 1. The following sequence is therefore equivalent:

```
A rshift (n−i−1)
A ∧ 1
if A ≠ 0 goto L
```

The application of '∧' to an integer would be prohibited by most high-level languages; but, as before, it may be feasible at the lower levels.

Finding the leftmost 1-bit

It is sometimes necessary to find the leftmost 1-bit of a non-zero word A (otherwise known as the *leading* 1-bit). The following code does this by testing successive bits until a 1 is found. The variable C counts the number of 0s that precede it and, on completion, gives its position:

```
       C  ←  0                -- assume A is non-zero
L1:    if A₀ = 1 goto L2
       A lshift 1
       C + 1
       goto L1
L2:    ...
```

If the number of 0s is at all great, this is rather slow and so it may be preferable to test several bits at once — for example, by looking for the first non-zero byte. The bits of the byte can then be tested individually.

A second technique is to test successive bits by means of a mask M, initialized to $1000\ldots0$. Each iteration shifts it one place further to the right:

```
       C  ←  0                -- assume A is non-zero
       M  ←  mask(0,1)        -- M = 1000...0
L1:    B  ←  A ∧ M
       if B = M goto L2
       M rshift 1
       C + 1
       goto L1
L2:    ...
```

On completion, M holds a copy of the leading 1-bit and C holds its position. As before, the method can be adapted so that it tests several bits at a time.

A third method, which is potentially the fastest, depends on the fact that floating-point arithmetic normalizes its results (see Section 3.8). In base 2, for example, this means that the fraction part of a strictly positive number must begin with a 1. Consequently, if a fixed-point fraction has its leading 1 in position i, its conversion to floating-point must involve the determination of i. If hardware operations are provided to assist the conversion process, the value of i can be found by using them. However, this will almost certainly require the use of assembly code and will be highly machine-dependent.

Finding the rightmost 1-bit

The rightmost 1-bit can be found by similar techniques. Bit-by-bit testing can shift either the pattern or a mask. A third possibility is to use an arithmetic operation, and in this case the details are considerably simpler.

The technique is to treat the bit pattern as an integer and to subtract 1 from it. The rightmost 1-bit then becomes 0 and the succeeding 0s all become 1s. The effect is shown in Figure 2-9. If the two patterns are now combined by an *and-not* operation, the only 1 that survives is the one we want. The following assignment stores it in M:

$$M \leftarrow A \wedge \neg(A - 1)$$

This works in all practical number representations, the only danger being that the subtraction might cause overflow. Some extra code may have to be added for handling this possibility.

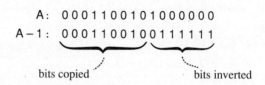

Figure 2-9   Effect of subtracting 1

Further inspection of the above example shows that if the *not* is omitted, the right-most 1 becomes 0 and all the other bits remain unchanged. The following therefore removes the rightmost 1 from A:

$$A \wedge (A - 1)$$

This is remarkably brief, though once again a check for overflow may have to be included. The next section describes one of its uses.

2.7   BIT COUNTING

The *bit-sum* operation adds together all the bits of a word A, treating each of them as an integer 0 or 1. For example, the bit sum of 01001101 is

$$0 + 1 + 0 + 0 + 1 + 1 + 0 + 1$$

which equals 4. The result is the number of 1s in A. Some machines provide an instruction for the purpose. More commonly it has to be done by software, there being several techniques to choose from.

An obvious possibility is to test each bit in turn, using a variable C to count the 1s:

```
         C  ←  0
L1 :     if A = 0 goto L3
         if A₀ = 0 goto L2
         C + 1
L2 :     A lshift 1
         goto L1
L3 :     ...
```

This is slow, though the test $A = 0$ may stop it from going through all n iterations.

A second method takes advantage of the very fast technique given in the previous section for removing the rightmost 1-bit. It simply removes 1s until there are none left, counting them in C as it proceeds:

```
         C  ←  0
L1 :     if A = 0 goto L2
         A ∧ (A − 1)              -- remove the rightmost 1
         C + 1
         goto L1
L2 :     ...
```

The method is a good one when there are only a few 1s to be counted.

In principle, the fastest method is to use table look-up. Each possible bit pattern has a separate entry in the table giving its bit sum. For example, with $n = 3$, the bit patterns 000, 001, 010, 011, 100, 101, 110, and 111 have corresponding entries 0, 1, 1, 2, 1, 2, 2, and 3. If A is the pattern 101, its numerical value 5 is used as an index for looking up the corresponding entry in the table (see Section 5.10). Thus the bit sum is obtained by a single indexed memory reference.

This is very fast, but for any practical word size the table will be far too large. With 16-bit words, for example, it will require 2^{16} entries. A compromise is to partition A into smaller fields, of size r say, and to use a table with only 2^r entries. The bit sum of each field is obtained from the table and the results are added together. The fields can be unpacked using the methods described in Section 2.5. A typical field size will be 4, requiring a table of size 16. Increasing r decreases the number of fields but at the cost of a larger table — a typical space/time trade-off.

Finally, there is a more sophisticated technique known as *sideways addition*. The basic idea is to add each pair of bits ($A_0 + A_1$, $A_2 + A_3$, etc.); then to add each pair of the results; then to add each pair of those results; and so on, until there is a single result, which is the bit sum. The advantage of this approach is that at each stage the additions can be carried out in parallel.

Problems of overflow can occur if $A_0 = 1$. We shall therefore assume that $A_0 = 0$ and shall illustrate the method for A = 01001101, whose bit sum is 4. The first stage aligns the even-numbered bits with the odd-numbered ones and adds them together. This may be depicted as follows, with dots representing mandatory 0s:

```
odd-numbered bits :    . 1 . 0 . 1 . 1
even-numbered bits :   . 0 . 0 . 1 . 0
                       ─────────────────
              add :    0 1 0 0 1 0 0 1
```

Now successive pairs of bits have the values 1, 0, 2, 1, which are the bit sums of the original pairs. Their sum is the overall bit sum, namely 4. The next stage is similar, except that it operates on the pairs:

```
odd-numbered pairs :    . . 0 0 . . 0 1
even-numbered pairs :   . . 0 1 . . 1 0
                        ─────────────────
               add :    0 0 0 1 0 0 1 1
```

Now the four-bit groups have the values 1 and 3, which are the bit sums of the original four-bit groups. Their sum is the overall bit sum, namely 4. The third stage adds them together:

```
right half :    . . . . 0 0 1 1
 left half :    . . . . 0 0 0 1
                ─────────────────
      add :     0 0 0 0 0 1 0 0
```

And this gives an eight-bit group with the value 4. Since eight bits form a complete word, this is the final bit sum.

In general, an n-bit word will require $\lceil \log_2 n \rceil$ stages (see Section 2.2). Each stage requires a mask with 0s in the dotted positions and 1s elsewhere. If stage r uses the mask M_r, it can be implemented by the assignment:

$$A \;\leftarrow\; (A \wedge M_r) + ((A \; rshift \; 2^{r-1}) \wedge M_r)$$

The shift lines up the fields, the *and* operations mask out the 'dot' positions, and the '+' carries out the parallel addition. Since the algorithm takes a time proportional to $\lceil \log_2 n \rceil$, it shows to best advantage when n is large. With n = 32, for example, it takes five iterations, and so it is probably no better than table look-up using four-bit groups. But with n = 64, it requires only six iterations, and this gives it a clear advantage. It illustrates the power of operating on several fields in parallel — a technique that is explored further in Exercises 12 and 13.

2.8   PARITY

The *parity* of a bit pattern indicates whether the number of 1s is even or odd. Thus 10001101 has four 1s and so its parity is even; 11001101 has five, so its parity is odd. This property of bit patterns is relevant in several contexts, especially as a device for detecting storage errors (see below).

Being a two-valued quantity, parity can be represented by a single bit. The natural choice is to use 0 for even parity and 1 for odd. This agrees with the normal representation of positive integers, in which even numbers end with 0 and odd ones with 1. Consequently, one way to determine the parity of a bit pattern is to compute the number of 1s — that is, the bit sum — and then to inspect the final bit.

This seems like a reasonable way to calculate the parity, but in fact it is unnecessarily heavy-handed. A much simpler approach stems from the observation that parity can be directly computed by the *exclusive or* operation (see Section 2.3). The following table verifies this for sequences of length two:

$$\text{parity ('00')} \;=\; 0 \oplus 0 \;=\; 0$$
$$\text{parity ('01')} \;=\; 0 \oplus 1 \;=\; 1$$
$$\text{parity ('10')} \;=\; 1 \oplus 0 \;=\; 1$$
$$\text{parity ('11')} \;=\; 1 \oplus 1 \;=\; 0$$

The principle can be extended to sequences of arbitrary length. For example, the parity of 10001101 is given by the expression:

$$1 \oplus 0 \oplus 0 \oplus 0 \oplus 1 \oplus 1 \oplus 0 \oplus 1$$

If the pattern is held in an 8-bit word A, the expression can be computed in three steps by 'sideways logical addition':

$$A \;\oplus\; (A \; rshift \; 1)$$
$$A \;\oplus\; (A \; rshift \; 2)$$
$$A \;\oplus\; (A \; rshift \; 4)$$

This leaves the parity in A_7. It is equivalent to 'sideways addition', as described in the previous section, but is greatly simplified by the absence of any carry bits. The technique can be generalized to words of any length, and by suitable combinations of *lshift* and *rshift* the final result can be formed in any desired bit position (Exercise 10). The technique can also be used to compute the parity of several bytes in parallel (Exercise 12).

A *parity bit* is a bit that records the parity of an associated bit pattern. A typical example occurs when a seven-bit coded character is represented as an eight-bit byte. The spare bit can be used as a parity bit, and when the byte is stored or transmitted, it provides a check that the character is correct (see Section 5.13). For larger blocks of data, an alternative is to compute the parity 'vertically' instead of 'sideways'. For example, consider the following block of five bytes:

$$1\ 0\ 0\ 0\ 1\ 0\ 1\ 1$$
$$1\ 1\ 1\ 0\ 0\ 0\ 1\ 0$$
$$1\ 0\ 0\ 0\ 0\ 0\ 0\ 1$$
$$0\ 0\ 0\ 1\ 0\ 0\ 1\ 0$$
$$0\ 1\ 1\ 0\ 1\ 0\ 1\ 0$$

The bitwise '$\oplus$' operation computes their logical sum, namely 10010000, whose individual bits are the parity bits for the *columns* — what is sometimes called the *longitudinal parity*. The two 1s indicate that the first and fourth columns have odd parity; the remainder are all even. This is much faster and easier than computing the 'sideways' parity. It is usually applied to words, rather than bytes: the result is called the *checksum* and is often included as a check on the storage or transmission of blocks of data.

2.9 IMPLEMENTING SETS

As a final excursion into bit processing, we shall return to the subject of the previous chapter, namely sets. Let T be a set with n elements x_0, x_1, ... x_{n-1}. As shown in Section 1.2, a subset of T can be constructed by either accepting or rejecting each element in turn. It follows that the subset can be represented by a sequence of bits A_0, A_1, ... A_{n-1}, with $A_i = 1$ if the i th element is accepted and $A_i = 0$ if it is rejected. For example, if T is the set of letters $\{a, b, c, d, e, f, g, h\}$, the subset $\{b, e, g\}$ can be represented by the bit pattern 01001010. The 2^n possible subsets of T correspond to the 2^n distinct sequences of n bits. T itself is the sequence 111...1 and the empty set is 000...0.

This method of representing the subsets of T is very attractive, especially as it guarantees that no element can be included more than once. It also provides an extremely simple method of implementing the basic set operations. In particular, if the subsets S, S1, and S2 are represented as the bit patterns A, A1, and A2, set complement, set union, and set intersection can be implemented by logical operations as shown in Figure 2-10. By

Set operation		*Logical operation*	
complement :	$\overline{S}$	*not* :	$\neg A$
union :	S1 $\cup$ S2	*or* :	A1 $\vee$ A2
intersection :	S1 $\cap$ S2	*and* :	A1 $\wedge$ A2

Figure 2-10   Implementation of sets

way of example, consider the sets $S1 = \{b, e, g\}$ and $S2 = \{a, c, e\}$, and the operation of forming their union. Their corresponding bit patterns are $A1 = 01001010$ and $A2 = 10101000$. Their union is computed by a logical *or*:

$$
\begin{array}{rl}
\text{A1:} & 0\ 1\ 0\ 0\ 1\ 0\ 1\ 0 \\
\text{A2:} & 1\ 0\ 1\ 0\ 1\ 0\ 0\ 0 \\
\hline
\text{A1} \lor \text{A2:} & 1\ 1\ 1\ 0\ 1\ 0\ 1\ 0
\end{array}
$$

The result corresponds to the set $\{a, b, c, e, g\}$, as required. What could be simpler? To see why the method works so well, recall the definitions that were given in Section 1.2:

$$
\begin{array}{rcl}
\overline{S} & \equiv & \{ \ x : T \ \mid \ x \notin S \ \} \\
S1 \cup S2 & \equiv & \{ \ x : T \ \mid \ x \in S1 \quad or \quad x \in S2 \ \} \\
S1 \cap S2 & \equiv & \{ \ x : T \ \mid \ x \in S1 \quad and \quad x \in S2 \ \}
\end{array}
$$

Since the bit A_i represents the condition $x_i \in S$, the *not*, *or*, and *and* of the definitions translate immediately into the *not*, *or*, and *and* of the logical operations.

The list of operations can be extended to all the other ways of combining S1 and S2, and correspondingly to all the other logical operations of Figure 2-3 (see Exercise 15). Of more interest, though, are some other possible requirements:

- testing $x_i \in S$ — this corresponds to testing the bit A_i, as described in Section 2.6;

- determining the first (or last) element — this corresponds to finding the leftmost (or rightmost) 1-bit, as described in Section 2.6 also;

- determining the cardinality $|S|$ — this corresponds to forming the bit sum, as described in Section 2.7.

The only problem that can arise is that the number of bits may exceed the word size. In that case, the bit pattern has to be extended over two or more words, with corresponding additions to the algorithms.

The technique is very powerful and yet it is not used very often in practice. There are two possible explanations for this:

1. The size of the set T is often very large and so the bit pattern would be much too long. For example, if T is the set of seven-letter names, it has 26^7 members and would therefore require a pattern of 26^7 bits.

2. Most high-level languages offer no facilities for it.

The second reason is largely a consequence of the first. However, there is a notable exception. The language Pascal allows the programmer to define a type **set of** T, and to construct and manipulate sets accordingly. It requires T to be a type with a finite number of values, and each implementation can place an upper limit on this number. For example, a popular implementation for the CDC Cyber computers restricts the number of values to 59. This allows a one-word representation without using the sign bit. Other implementations are more generous, going to 256 or even more. The facility has a wide range of uses and its absence from other languages is a matter for some regret.

FURTHER READING

The material of this chapter is usually covered in books on computer organization and assembly-code programming. Some references are given at the end of Chapter 5.

EXERCISES

[2B ∨ $\overline{\text{2B}}$ — that is the question]

1   [The NUXI problem] The confusion over the numbering of bits within a word extends to the numbering of bytes also. On some 16-bit machines, the two bytes in a word are numbered from left to right (as in Figure 2-1); on others (regrettably), they are numbered from right to left. Suppose now that two successive words contain the characters U–N–I–X and that they are written out, byte by byte, on a magnetic tape. If they are then read back into a machine of the opposite kind, how will they appear? Consult the tape-handling package on your system to see if it has any facility for coping with this problem.

2   The operation *nand* is sometimes called the *Sheffer stroke function*, written as A | B. Show that it is sufficient for defining *not* and *or*, and (consequently) all sixteen of the logical operations given in Figure 2-3. Which other operations have this property? In practice, most computers provide at least two bitwise logical operations; but it is interesting to note that, in principle, one would be sufficient.

3   Prove that $(A \oplus B) \oplus B$ is the same as A. Hence, show that if A and B are words in memory, the effect of the assignments

$$A \oplus B$$
$$B \oplus A$$
$$A \oplus B$$

is to interchange their contents. What are the advantages (if any) of this technique?

4   Suppose that field (A,i,k) contains a positive integer that has to be increased by 1. One method is to unpack the integer, add 1 to it, and then pack it back again. But could 1 be added to the field directly? What are the dangers?

5   Suppose that an n-bit word A has each bit set randomly to 0 or 1, the two values being equally probable in every case. What, on average, will be the position of the leftmost 1-bit? What will be the average number of 0s that follow the rightmost 1-bit?

6   On the computer best known to you, investigate the instructions (if any) for converting fixed-point numbers to floating-point form. How (if at all) can they be used for determining the position of the leading 1-bit in a word A?

7   Why is the rightmost 1-bit of a word A so much easier to locate than the leftmost 1-bit? For an answer, see Warren (1977).

8   What is the effect of the operation

$$A \wedge ((A \vee (A - 1)) + 1)$$

on the bit pattern A?

9   Using a suitable programming language, give a complete, precise description of the 'sideways addition' algorithm in Section 2.7. Prove that the algorithm correctly gives the bit sum. (Hint: prove a suitable inductive assertion of the form 'after the rth iteration ...'.)

10   Let A be a 16-bit word. Give algorithms for computing its parity, the result being formed in (a) A_0, and (b) A_{12}.

11   The game of Nim starts with a set of matchsticks (or coins, or other items) divided quite arbitrarily into a number of piles. Players A and B alternately take one or more matchsticks from any one pile. The player to take the last matchstick wins.

Let $p_1, p_2, \ldots p_r$ be the sizes of the piles and let them be represented as n-bit numerals $P_1, P_2, \ldots P_r$. For example, with $n = 8$:

$$\begin{aligned} p_1 &= 3 & P_1 &= 00000011 \\ p_2 &= 6 & P_2 &= 00000110 \\ p_3 &= 14 & P_3 &= 00001110 \end{aligned}$$

Either player can force a win if, by making the right selection, they can arrange for the number of 1s in each bit position to be even. In other words, they must arrange for each *column* of the set of numbers to have even parity. According to Section 8, this condition can be expressed as:

$$P_1 \oplus P_2 \oplus \ldots \oplus P_r = 0$$

Show that:

(a)   if this condition is established by player A, then it cannot be retained by player B;

(b)   when B has destroyed the condition, A can guarantee to re-establish it.

Give an algorithm by which A can determine the right move to make in (b), expressing it in terms of logical and/or arithmetic operations. For example, in the position illustrated above, A should remove 9 matchsticks from pile 3. Apart from choosing between piles of the same size, is the move necessarily unique?

Investigate the alternative game where the player to take the last matchstick *loses*.

12   [Parallel field operations] Let A be an eight-bit word. Show that the sequence of operations

$$\begin{aligned} A &\vee (A \ \textit{lshift} \ 4) \\ A &\vee (A \ \textit{lshift} \ 2) \\ A &\vee (A \ \textit{lshift} \ 1) \end{aligned}$$

sets A_0 to 1 if A was non-zero to start with and to 0 otherwise. For a single byte, this is a slow way of testing for zero. However, if A consists of four such bytes, or any number of them, the method has the advantage that it can be used for testing all of them in parallel.

Show how the method can be used for computing the parity of all the bytes in parallel. Show how it can be used for finding a byte with a specified pattern: for example, 10110000.

13   [Searching for a particular pattern] The technique of the previous exercise can be used to search for an arbitrary bit pattern within a word. As a simple example, suppose that the bits of A correspond to blocks of storage on disk, 0 indicating a free block and 1 indicating a block that is in use. Three consecutive free blocks correspond to the pattern 000. The following assignment will determine all the occurrences of this pattern:

$$B \quad \leftarrow \quad \neg \ (A \ \lor \ (A \ \textit{lshift} \ 1) \ \lor \ (A \ \textit{lshift} \ 2))$$

Except in the two rightmost positions, a 1 in B now indicates the start of a pattern 000 in A. This fact can be used for determining the first occurrence of three consecutive free blocks.

(a)   How would you look for a sequence of *exactly* three free blocks?

(b)   Extend the technique for the situation where the blocks on disk have to be represented by a bit pattern that is spread over several words.

(c)   How would you use the technique to search for the pattern 01? The pattern 1110? The pattern either 0110 or 1001?

14   How would you determine the number of sequences of 1s in a word A, successive sequences being separated by one or more 0s? For example, if A = 11010010, the result should be 3. Devise a simple way of removing the rightmost sequence.

15   Let A1 and A2 be the representation of sets S1 and S2, as described in Section 2.9. How would you compute the set inclusion operations $S1 \subseteq S2$ and $S1 \subset S2$? What about the two difference operations (see Exercise 1.3)?

NUMBER SYSTEMS

3.1 NUMBERS AND NUMERALS

According to the experts, a *number* is the cardinality of a set. For example, the number three is the cardinality of the set {a, b, c}, and of many other sets as well. In the class-rooms of today, this illuminating definition is taught to students at an impressively early age. It is accompanied by a second piece of wisdom, telling them that a *numeral* is the representation of a number. For example, 'XII' and '12' are both numerals representing the number twelve, one in the Roman system and one in the decimal. The lesson is drawn that numbers and numerals are two very different things and that all good citizens should learn to distinguish between them. The only trouble is that in our everyday language we regularly fail to do this. We use the word 'number' for both purposes, ignoring the subtleties that lie behind it. As a result, the high ideals of our early educa-tion tend to evaporate and a certain effort is required to bring them back into focus.

The method by which numbers are represented as numerals is called a *number system*. As a matter of practical convenience, it is helpful if the representation is suitable for doing arithmetic. Thus the Roman system, which was once so popular, has lost favor in recent centuries because of its drawbacks in this respect. In the meantime, the decimal system has swept the world and become the *de facto* standard. The takeover took more than a thousand years to accomplish; but its success has been so complete that today, with one notable exception, the decimal system has no serious rivals left.

This chapter is concerned with the notable exception, which (need it be said) is the binary system used by computers. It also looks at several other systems that are relevant to computer programming. It uses x to denote an arbitrary number and the sequence

$$d_0 \ d_1 \ \ldots \ d_{n-1}$$

to denote its representation as an n-digit numeral d in some particular system. The left-to-right numbering follows the convention for numbering the bits of a word, as esta-blished in the previous chapter (see Section 2.2). If the digits were to be used solely for representing positive integers, with no reference to fractions, nor to fixed-length words, nor to any other considerations, there would be a case for numbering them right-to-left instead. Each digit d_i would then have a fixed interpretation, independent of n, and the resulting formulae would be simpler. But for consistency with the wider computing con-text, we shall retain the left-to-right convention.

The characters d_i are usually drawn from the digits '0', '1', ... '9', and can therefore be regarded as having numeric values of their own, namely 0, 1, ... 9. This will be their significance when they appear in the formulae of later sections. Note that this value is usually quite different from the numeric code by which the digits are represented in a computer. Some conversion is therefore needed between the internal code for the characters '0' to '9' and their corresponding numeric values (see Section 4.5).

To describe a number system, it is necessary to address the following three questions:

1. What are the legitimate numerals? That is to say, what values can the digits d_i take and what constraints (if any) must they satisfy?

2. For each numeral d, what number x does it represent? Also, what range of values can x take? What are the minimum and the maximum?

3. Given a number x within the range, how is it represented in the system? In other words, what is its corresponding numeral d?

On the practical side, algorithms are needed for doing arithmetic within each system and for converting numbers from one representation to another.

The next four sections describe several number systems for the positive integers. The remainder look at negative integers, fractions, and (very briefly) the so-called 'real' numbers. In every case, the emphasis will be on the representation of the numbers and on the ways in which they interact with ordinary programs. The arithmetic operations will not be considered in any detail, since they are mostly implemented in hardware.

3.2 THE UNARY SYSTEM

Conceptually, the *unary* number system is the simplest. The number x is represented by a set of x objects, and its value is determined by counting the objects. For example, the objects might be the fingers on your hand, or the candles on a birthday cake, or the chimes of a clock. With ordinary digits, the numerals can be written as 1, 11, 111, 1111, ... , representing the numbers 1, 2, 3, 4, and so on. Indeed, the Roman numerals start in precisely this way. However, if every numeral has to have exactly n digits, the 1s must be 'padded out' with some other digit, the obvious choice being 0. With $n = 4$, the above numerals are written as 0001, 0011, 0111, and 1111, and zero is 0000. This is illustrated in Figure 3-1.

Number	Unary representation	4-bit unary representation
0	—	0000
1	1	0001
2	11	0011
3	111	0111
4	1111	1111
5	11111	—

Figure 3-1   Unary numerals

More formally, the n-digit unary number system can be defined as having numerals d with $d_i = 0$ or 1 subject to the constraints $d_i \leq d_{i+1}$ ($i = 0, \ldots n-2$). The value of d is the number of 1s, which must therefore lie in the range 0 to n. Conversely, an integer x in the range 0 to n is represented in the unary system as a sequence of $n-x$ 0s followed by x 1s.

The unary system is very simple — a merit that should be highly prized. However, as the Romans must have realized, it has the obvious and serious drawback that the numerals become far too long. Who wants to write 111111111111111, when XV or 15 will do instead? To put it another way, for a fixed number of bits, the range of values is far too short. Since n bits can represent 2^n different values, why use them for only $n+1$? Because of these factors, the unary system is seldom used in practice. Its applications occur mostly in theoretical work, such as the study of Turing machines, where its simplicity is a great advantage and its extravagance is of no concern.

3.3 POLYNOMIAL SYSTEMS

The decimal system is an example of a *polynomial* number system. The reason for the name is that the value of a numeral d is given by a polynomial. For example, the value of the decimal numeral 2985 is given by the expression

$$2 \times 10^3 \quad + \quad 9 \times 10^2 \quad + \quad 8 \times 10 \quad + \quad 5$$

and this is a polynomial in 10 whose coefficients are the digits of d. The number 10 is called the *base* or *radix* of the system. In general, any integer b can be used as the base and the result is a *base-b number system*. Some important cases are the following:

- base 2   —   the *binary* number system;
- base 8   —   the *octal* number system;
- base 10   —   the *decimal* number system;
- base 16   —   the *hexadecimal* number system.

The context usually makes clear which base is being used, the standard default being 10. If necessary, the base can be appended to the numeral in the form of a subscript. Thus 101_2, 101_8, 101_{10}, and 101_{16} are numerals in the four different systems listed above, their values being 5, 65, 101, and 257. If subscripts are not available, the notation of Section 2.2 can be used instead, writing 2#101, 8#101, and so on. Methods of converting numbers from one base to another are considered below.

The digits of a base-b system lie in the range 0 to $b-1$, but are not subject to any other constraints. The value of the numeral d is given by the polynomial:

$$d_0 \times b^{n-1} \quad + \quad d_1 \times b^{n-2} \quad + \quad \ldots \quad + \quad d_{n-2} \times b \quad + \quad d_{n-1}$$

For each digit d_i, the factor b^{n-i-1} is known as its *weight*. It gives the increase in the value of d that results from adding 1 to d_i. The system is an example of a *positional* number system in that the weight of a digit depends on its position in the sequence. On some computers the polynomial can be evaluated by a single instruction. In most cases, though, it has to be done by software. The standard technique is to use *nested multiplication*, treating it as the expression:

$$(\ldots(((d_0 \times b + d_1) \times b + d_2) \times b + d_3) \times b + \ldots + d_{n-1})$$

This can be evaluated by the loop:

$$x \leftarrow d_0;$$
$$\textbf{for } i = 1, 2, \ldots n-1 \textbf{ do}$$
$$x \leftarrow x \times b + d_i;$$

The method is sometimes known as *Horner's rule*. It uses $n-1$ multiplications and additions, which is the best that can be done.

With n digits, each having one of b possible values, the polynomial system provides b^n different numerals. The minimum is obtained when each d_i is 0, giving the value zero. The maximum is obtained when each d_i is $b-1$, the resulting polynomial being

$$(b-1) \times (b^{n-1} + b^{n-2} + \ldots + 1)$$

which reduces to $b^n - 1$. This looks promising, because the range 0 to $b^n - 1$ can be covered by b^n numerals. It remains to show how each integer x in the range is represented.

To obtain the representation of x, the best method is to use the inverse of the algorithm for Horner's rule. Instead of doing repeated multiplication by b, this does repeated *division* by b:

$$\textbf{for } i = n-1, n-2, \ldots 1 \textbf{ do}$$
$$x, d_i \leftarrow x \div b;$$
$$d_0 \leftarrow x;$$

The division $x \div b$ produces a quotient which replaces x and a remainder which is the digit d_i. The final value of x is the leading digit d_0. It is important to note that the digits are found in *right-to-left* sequence, and so care is needed in using the technique to output numbers from a program. Also, to avoid the production of leading zeros, it is usual to stop as soon as the quotient becomes zero. For example, the following steps convert 99 to octal using repeated division by 8:

$$99 \div 8 \;=\; \text{quotient } 12, \text{ remainder } 3$$
$$12 \div 8 \;=\; \text{quotient } 1, \text{ remainder } 4$$
$$1 \div 8 \;=\; \text{quotient } 0, \text{ remainder } 1$$

The remainders *in reverse order* give the octal numeral for 99, namely 143. Note that although the example uses decimal notation, x can equally well be represented in any other system, with all the arithmetic being done in that system. In particular, starting with x in binary, a computer can produce its decimal digits using repeated division by 10: the remainders, when converted to the corresponding characters, give the digits in right-to-left sequence.

Before moving on to the particular case of binary number systems, it is worth pointing out that polynomial systems occur from time to time in situations that are not overtly numerical. The general idea is that any object having b possible values or states can be regarded as a digit in a base-b system. A sequence of n such objects then corresponds to a base-b numeral. The observation establishes a one-to-one correspondence between the b^n different sequences and the integers 0 to $b^n - 1$. This is called a *ranking* of the sequences, with the integer for each sequence being its *rank*.

Example

A Yale lock has five pins each of which is split at one of three possible positions. The pins can therefore be regarded as digits in a base-3 number system. For example, if the pin types are numbered 0, 1, and 2, the combination 10221 represents the number

$$1 \times 3^4 \;+\; 0 \times 3^3 \;+\; 2 \times 3^2 \;+\; 2 \times 3 \;+\; 1$$

which is 106. Conversely, every number in the range 0 to 242 corresponds to one such combination (in the locksmith's sense rather than the mathematician's).

In programming, a more important instance occurs when the objects are the letters a, b, c, ... and they are interpreted as the digits 0, 1, 2, ... For example, consider the nine two-letters 'words' — aa, ab, ac, ba, bb, bc, ca, cb, and cc. Since these are formed from a three-letter alphabet, they can be regarded as numerals in a base-3 number system, with a representing '0', b representing '1', and c representing '2'. Their values are 00_3, 01_3, ... 22_3, which in decimal are simply 0, 1, ... 8. The ranking of the words is their normal alphabetical order, otherwise known as the *lexicographical* order. In general, if n-letter words are formed from a b-letter alphabet, the rank of each word in the lexicographical ordering is given by its corresponding n-digit, base-b numeral.

3.4   BINARY SYSTEMS

The binary number system is so important in computing that it deserves further consideration at this stage, along with two related systems — the octal and the hexadecimal.

The binary, or base-2, number system uses the digits 0 and 1, otherwise known as *bits* (see Section 2.1). As noted earlier, n bits can represent all the integers in the range 0 to $2^n - 1$. Figure 3-2 lists the ranges for $n \leq 10$. The case $n = 10$ gives a range of just over a thousand. It follows that $n = 20$ gives a million, $n = 30$ a thousand million, and so on.

Number of bits	Range
1	0 – 1
2	0 – 3
3	0 – 7
4	0 – 15
5	0 – 31
6	0 – 63
7	0 – 127
8	0 – 255
9	0 – 511
10	0 – 1023

Figure 3-2   The range of n-bit numerals

Number	3-bit numeral	Octal equivalent
0	000	0
1	001	1
2	010	2
3	011	3
4	100	4
5	101	5
6	110	6
7	111	7

Number	4-bit numeral	Hexadecimal equivalent
0	0000	0
1	0001	1
2	0010	2
3	0011	3
4	0100	4
5	0101	5
6	0110	6
7	0111	7
8	1000	8
9	1001	9
10	1010	A
11	1011	B
12	1100	C
13	1101	D
14	1110	E
15	1111	F

Figure 3-3   The three-bit and four-bit numerals

Figure 3-3 shows the n-bit numerals for $n = 3$ and $n = 4$, the former ranging from 0 to 7, and the latter from 0 to 15. In both cases, the number 0 is represented by a sequence of 0s, and the number $x + 1$ is derived from x by adding 1 to its least significant (rightmost) bit. If this is 0, it becomes 1; if it is 1, it becomes '0 carry 1', as in conventional decimal arithmetic. The 'carry' propagates leftwards up to the first 0, which is replaced by 1. Thus the effect of adding 1 is to invert successive bits from the right-hand end up to and including the rightmost 0. Conversely, subtracting 1 inverts each of the bits up to the rightmost 1 — a property that was used in Section 2.6 for finding the rightmost 1-bit. The maximum integer is $2^n - 1$, which is a sequence of 1s; if 1 is added to it, the carry propagates beyond the left-hand end, indicating that the result lies outside the range of representation. This condition is known as *overflow*.

Binary patterns with three or four bits are reasonably digestible, but with 30 or 40 bits they become rather daunting. Hardware can crunch them easily enough, but a human being cannot. So, if they have to be presented for human consumption (and may the occasions be few!), it is usual to print them in octal or hexadecimal instead. This means that they are divided into three-bit or four-bit groups, and each group is replaced by its corresponding octal or hexadecimal digit. The correspondence is the obvious numerical one, as shown in Figure 3-3. For example, the sequence 1011000111100010 can be divided into three-bit groups, starting from the right —

$$1 \quad 011 \quad 000 \quad 111 \quad 100 \quad 010$$

and this gives the octal form 130742. Or it can be divided into four-bit groups —

$$1011 \quad 0001 \quad 1110 \quad 0010$$

	d_0 d_1 d_2
x in octal :	1 4 3
subtract $2 \times d_0$ from $d_0 d_1$:	2
bring down d_2 :	1 2 3
subtract $2 \times d_0 d_1$ from $d_0 d_1 d_2$:	2 4
x in decimal :	9 9

Figure 3-4   Octal to decimal conversion

and this gives the hexadecimal form B1E2. Since the hexadecimal system requires 16 digits, the letters A - F are pressed into service to represent those with the values 10 - 15. The octal system may seem preferable, especially as few people know their 16-times table. In practice, the choice between octal and hexadecimal is usually determined by the byte size. Six bits favor the use of octal, eight favor 'hex'. (The author, despite his name, has no particular liking for either.)

The octal representation has advantages if we have to do decimal-binary conversion by hand. Instead of doing repeated division by 2, which is rather tedious, we do repeated division by 8 and then convert the octal digits to their binary form. With 99, for example, two divisions by 8 produce the octal representation 143_8, and the final conversion to 1100011_2 is trivial. This is easier and faster than doing six divisions by 2. Conversely, starting with 1100011_2, we can write it as 143_8 and then obtain the decimal representation by evaluating $((1 \times 8) + 4) \times 8 + 3$. If we dislike multiplying by 8, we can multiply by $10 - 2$ instead, using the scheme of Figure 3-4 with decimal arithmetic throughout. In general, the kth step involves doubling the first k digits, shifting them one place right, and subtracting them from the first k+1 digits. The algorithm and its inverse are discussed more fully in Knuth (1981), pp. 306-8.

In conclusion, it is worth noting that the octal and hexadecimal representations of a bit pattern are not simply coding conveniences. They are, in fact, base-8 and base-16 numerals in their own right, and they have the same value as the base-2 bit pattern. Thus 130742_8 and $B1E2_{16}$ have the same value as 1011000111100010_2, namely 45538_{10}. This may appear obvious, but its formal proof is not entirely trivial.

3.5 MIXED-RADIX SYSTEMS

In a base-b number system, each digit d_i has the same radix b and therefore the same range of values, namely 0 to $b-1$. In a *mixed radix* system, each digit d_i has its own radix b_i and therefore takes on its own range of values, namely 0 to $b_i - 1$. The value of d is given by the expression

$$d_0 \times w_0 + d_1 \times w_1 + \ldots + d_{n-1} \times w_{n-1}$$

which is a weighted sum of the digits, as in the base-b system. In this case, the weight w_i of digit d_i is the product of the radices to its right. Thus:

$$w_0 = b_1 b_2 b_3 \ldots b_{n-1}$$
$$w_1 = b_2 b_3 \ldots b_{n-1}$$
$$\ldots$$
$$w_{n-2} = b_{n-1}$$
$$w_{n-1} = 1$$

As previously, the weight w_i represents the amount by which the number increases when 1 is added to d_i, and it equals the number of different sequences that can occur to the right of d_i. Once again, the expression can be evaluated by nested multiplication:

$$(\ldots((d_0 \times b_1 + d_1) \times b_2 + d_2) \times b_3 + \ldots + d_{n-1})$$

It can therefore be computed by the following loop:

```
x ← d₀;
for i = 1, ... n−1 do
    x ← x × bᵢ + dᵢ;
```

When each d_i is 0, the result is the minimum value, namely zero. When each d_i is $b_i - 1$, it is the maximum value, which turns out to be:

$$b_0 b_1 b_2 \ldots b_{n-1} - 1$$

Since there are $b_0 b_1 b_2 \ldots b_{n-1}$ numerals in the system, this is what we should expect.

The inverse algorithm converts a number x to its mixed-radix representation. It does successive division by $b_{n-1}, b_{n-2}, \ldots b_0$ and, as before, the remainders provide the digits in right-to-left sequence.

Mixed-radix systems are not very common in practice. The most familiar example arises in the measurement of time, using expressions such as 12 hours 53 minutes 16 seconds. With six digits, the maximum such expression is 99 hours 59 minutes 59 seconds, which suggests that it is a system whose radices are 10, 10, 6, 10, 6, and 10. This is indeed the case. For example, the above time can be written as the numeral 125316, its value being:

$$1 \times 36000 + 2 \times 3600 + 5 \times 600 + 3 \times 60 + 1 \times 10 + 6$$

The resulting integer, namely 46396, gives the number of seconds since midnight. Conversely, successive divisions by 10, 6, 10, 6, 10, and 10 will convert the number of seconds to its hours-minutes-seconds format.

A less satisfactory system is the use of yards, feet, and inches for measuring length. The maximum five-digit expression is 99 yards 2 feet 11 inches, which suggests that it is a mixed-radix system with radices 10, 10, 3, 2, and 2. In this case, though, the inference is false! The least significant digit is not base 2, because it can in fact have any value between 0 and 9. This is more complicated than a mixed-radix system, and it may help to explain why distances are being converted to metric, whereas times are not.

As with the base-b systems, mixed-radix systems sometimes occur in situations that are not overtly numerical. Typically, a sequence of n values is drawn from n sets, one value from each set. The first set contains b_0 elements, the second contains b_1 elements, and so on. There are therefore $b_0 b_1 b_2 \ldots b_{n-1}$ possible sequences. These can be regarded as numerals in a mixed-radix system, with each value corresponding to one of the digits. The resulting numbers provide a ranking of the sequences.

Example

Consider a pack of cards. There are four suits, which can be written as S, H, D, and C; and in each suit there are thirteen values, namely A, K, Q, J, 10, 9, 8, ... 2. Each card represents a selection of one suit and one value, such as S:8, C:2, and so on. When interpreted as a numeral in a system with $b_0 = 4$ and $b_1 = 13$, it gives the card a rank between 0 and 51.

Mixed-radix systems have several applications in computing, notably in the representation of n-dimensional arrays (see Volume II) and in the ordering of blocks on a disk (see Volume III). Another example, the factorial number system, is discussed in Exercise 9.

3.6 NEGATIVE INTEGERS

The preceding sections have described a variety of systems for representing positive integers. It is now time to concentrate on the binary system and to see how it can be modified for handling negative integers, fractions, and floating-point numbers.

This section considers the representation of negative integers. As usual, it assumes that the numbers have to be represented by n-bit words, whose bits are interpreted as the digits $d_0 d_1 d_2 \ldots d_{n-1}$ of a binary numeral. In the basic binary system, the bits are either 0 or 1, and their weights are successively 2^{n-1}, 2^{n-2}, ... 4, 2, 1. The value of the numeral can therefore be found by adding the weights for which the corresponding bits are 1. For example, with $n = 4$ the weights of the digits can be depicted as follows:

$$\text{digit:} \quad d_0 \ d_1 \ d_2 \ d_3$$
$$\text{weight:} \quad 8 \ \ 4 \ \ 2 \ \ 1$$

It follows that 1001 has the value $8 + 1$, which is 9, and 1110 is 14.

As is easily verified, the bit d_0 splits the range 0 to $2^n - 1$ into two equal halves. The lower half runs from 0 to $2^{n-1} - 1$ and is characterized by having $d_0 = 0$. The upper half continues from 2^{n-1} and has $d_0 = 1$. In order to represent negative numbers, an obvious strategy is to retain the numbers in the lower half and to use the bit patterns of the upper half to represent their negatives. This has the advantage that d_0 will then act as a *sign bit*, being 0 for the positive numbers and 1 for the negative ones. The only problem is how to represent the negative values.

With this approach, there are three basic methods of representing the negative numbers:

1. *Sign and magnitude* — the negative of x is obtained simply by inverting its sign bit.

2. *One's complement* — the negative of x is obtained by inverting *all* its bits.

3   *Two's complement* — the negative of x is obtained by inverting all its bits and adding 1. In other words, two's complement is one's complement plus one (which makes it easy to remember).

n	+ n	− n in sign and magnitude	− n in one's complement	− n in two's complement
0	0 0 0 0	1 0 0 0	1 1 1 1	0 0 0 0
1	0 0 0 1	1 0 0 1	1 1 1 0	1 1 1 1
2	0 0 1 0	1 0 1 0	1 1 0 1	1 1 1 0
3	0 0 1 1	1 0 1 1	1 1 0 0	1 1 0 1
4	0 1 0 0	1 1 0 0	1 0 1 1	1 1 0 0
5	0 1 0 1	1 1 0 1	1 0 1 0	1 0 1 1
6	0 1 1 0	1 1 1 0	1 0 0 1	1 0 1 0
7	0 1 1 1	1 1 1 1	1 0 0 0	1 0 0 1
8	−	−	−	1 0 0 0

Figure 3-5 Negative integers

As we should expect, all three systems have the property that if x is negated twice, it returns to its original value. In other words, $--x = x$. This is obvious enough for the first two, and apart from one exceptional case (see below), it also holds for the third. The systems are illustrated in Figure 3-5, which shows the negative integers for the case $n = 4$. The following paragraphs review them in more detail.

The sign-and-magnitude system is the binary counterpart of ordinary decimal notation, where the negative of +48 is written as −48. This sounds simple, but in practice it causes some unfortunate complications. A factor which is particularly annoying for the programmer is that zero has two distinct representations — *positive zero* which is $000...0$, and *negative zero* which is $100...0$. Because of all the difficulties, the method is seldom used in hardware except for doing decimal arithmetic. For this purpose the numbers are held in *packed decimal* format, with the decimal digits being stored in successive half-bytes (four bits). The sign occupies a half-byte at the least significant end. The representation is slow to manipulate, but avoids the need for decimal-binary conversion. It is useful for applications with large volumes of decimal input/output and relatively little computation — typically those that are programmed in COBOL.

The one's complement system, which negates x by inverting all the bits, derives its name from the simple observation that a bit can be inverted by subtracting it from 1. The decimal equivalent is nine's complement, the negative of 48 being written as 51. The system is more attractive than the previous one in that the value of a numeral can be given as a simple sum-of-weights. Each d_i has its normal positive weight, except for d_0 whose weight is $-(2^{n-1} - 1)$. For example, the case $n = 4$ gives the following picture:

$$\text{digit:} \quad d_0 \ d_1 \ d_2 \ d_3$$
$$\text{weight:} \quad -7 \ \ 4 \ \ 2 \ \ 1$$

Thus 1001 has the value -6, and 1110 is -1. As can be seen, the weight of d_0 acts as a 'counterbalance' to the others, being the negative of all the other weights put together. This ensures that $x + -x = 0$. Unfortunately, though, it still produces two representations of zero, the positive zero being $000...0$ and the negative zero being $111...1$. Testing for $x = 0$ is therefore not the same as testing for $d = 000...0$. Similarly, neither of the conditions $x < 0$ and $x \leq 0$ is equivalent to $d_0 = 1$. So arithmetic tests and logical tests must be carefully distinguished. In spite of this, the one's complement system has been used on several machines, notably the Control Data Cyber range.

In the original, all-positive system, the weight of d_0 was 2^{n-1}. The two's complement system adopts the simple strategy of changing it to -2^{n-1}. This is one less than in the one's complement system, but *a priori* it is the more logical, consistent choice in that it maintains the basic, powers-of-two philosophy. With $n = 4$, the picture becomes:

$$\begin{array}{ll} \text{digit}: & d_0 \ d_1 \ d_2 \ d_3 \\ \text{weight}: & -8 \ \ 4 \ \ 2 \ \ 1 \end{array}$$

Thus 1001 has the value -7, and 1111 is -1. As stated earlier, x is negated by inverting all the bits and then adding 1. The inversion provides the one's complement representation, and the addition of 1 counterbalances the extra -1 in the weight of d_0. The effect is equivalent to inverting all the bits down to, but not including, the rightmost 1. For a positive integer x, it means that $-x$ has the same bit pattern as $2^n - x$ (which is no longer in the system) — hence the name 'two's complement'. The decimal equivalent would be ten's complement, the negative of 48 being written as $10^2 - 48$, namely 52 (one more than nine's complement). As might be expected, this method is the 'cleanest' of the three, partly in the logic of its arithmetic and partly because there is only one representation of zero. Negating $000...0$ simply gives $000...0$. This is attractive, but since there is no longer a negative zero, what has become of the spare bit pattern? The answer is that it appears as the number -2^{n-1} (pattern $100...0$), which was not represented in either of the other systems. Negating this number sets overflow because, as shown earlier, the maximum positive integer is $2^{n-1}-1$. It is the only instance in all three systems where negation can cause overflow. It is an anomaly, reflecting the lack of symmetry about zero; but it is seldom any trouble in practice and causes fewer headaches than the use of two different zeros.

The differences between the three systems account for the dangers that were alluded to in Section 2.6. For example, on a two's complement machine some of the arithmetic tests have logical equivalents, as shown in Figure 3-6. However, these equivalents do not hold in either of the other two systems, and so it is risky for a supposedly machine-independent program to use arithmetic operations for such purposes.

Arithmetic test	Logical equivalent
$x \geq 0$	$d_0 = 0$
$x < 0$	$d_0 = 1$
$x = 0$	$d = 000...0$
$x = -1$	$d = 111...1$

Figure 3-6   Two's complement equivalents

3.7 FRACTIONS

The invention of the decimal point was a great achievement which we tend to take for granted. It meant that the whole of the decimal system could be applied to fractions, this being very much simpler than using rationals of the form $\frac{p}{q}$. Admittedly, fractions such as $\frac{1}{3}$ had to be written as $0.33333\ldots$, which was imprecise and inconvenient. But on the whole the gains greatly outweighed the losses.

The counterpart in computing, of course, is the *binary* point. Successive bits following the binary point have weights $\frac{1}{2}$, $\frac{1}{4}$, $\frac{1}{8}$, ..., and so the numeral 0.1101, for example, has the value

$$\tfrac{1}{2} + \tfrac{1}{4} + \tfrac{1}{16}$$

which is 0.8125. This can be checked by converting 0.8125 back to binary. The technique is to do repeated multiplication by 2. The integer parts give successive bits from left to right and the fractions are retained for the next multiplication. Thus:

$$
\begin{aligned}
2 \times .8125 &= 1.625 \\
2 \times .625 &= 1.25 \\
2 \times .25 &= 0.5 \\
2 \times .5 &= 1.0
\end{aligned}
$$

Reading off the integer parts confirms that the binary fraction is 0.1101, as expected. A computer can convert a binary fraction to decimal in the same way, using repeated double-length multiplication by 10. If the fraction has to be rounded to k decimal places, the simplest strategy (at the slight risk of overflow) is to add 0.5×10^{-k} initially. An alternative is to compute k+1 digits and then to round in decimal; but this has the drawback that the effects of rounding can propagate across all the digits.

In decimal, the fraction $\frac{1}{3}$ is the non-terminating numeral $0.33333\ldots$. In binary, it is

$$0.01010101\ldots$$

and so it is still non-terminating. More importantly, the fraction 0.1 (decimal) is

$$0.00011001100110011\ldots$$

and so it is non-terminating as well, along with its multiples $0.2, 0.3, 0.4, 0.6, 0.7, 0.8$, and 0.9. In fact very few decimal fractions can be held with full precision. If limited to k binary places, they have to be either *truncated* or *rounded*. Figure 3-7 shows the two operations for the above representation of 0.1 (decimal) with k = 7. As its name implies, truncation simply abandons the extra bits. Since all their weights are positive, the resulting error is in the range 0 to 2^k. Rounding, on the other hand, converts the fraction to its

$$
\begin{array}{lll}
\textit{truncation}: & 0.0001100 & \text{abandoning } d_8, d_9, d_{10}, \ldots \\
\\
\textit{rounding}: & 0.0001100 & \text{abandoning } d_9, d_{10}, \ldots \\
& \hphantom{0.0001100}1 & \text{adding } d_8 \\
\hline
& 0.0001101 & \text{rounded result}
\end{array}
$$

Figure 3-7   Effects of rounding and truncation

closest approximation. It does this by adding d_{k+1} into position k and the resulting error is in the range 0 to $\pm 2^{-(k+1)}$. In the case of Figure 3-7, the truncated value is approximately 0.007 too low and the rounded value 0.0016 too high. Rounding has the advantage that it halves the magnitude of the errors, both in the worst case and in the average case. Moreover, it distributes them evenly about zero and so, in favorable circumstances, two or more errors will more or less cancel out. However, it would be unwise to count on such happy chances. On the contrary, with some numerical algorithms the errors are apt to snowball, in which case the method is said to be 'unstable'.

As the reader will doubtless appreciate, the binary point has no physical representation inside the computer. For integers the convention is that it follows the final digit d_{n-1}. For fractions the usual assumption is that it follows d_0:

$$d_0 \; . \; d_1 \; d_2 \; \ldots \; d_{n-1}$$

With this arrangement, d_0 is still the sign bit, d_1 has weight $\frac{1}{2}$, d_2 has weight $\frac{1}{4}$, and in general d_i has weight 2^{-i}. In the sign-and-magnitude and one's complement systems, the resulting fractions lie in the range $-1 < x < 1$. In two's complement, -1 can also be represented (see below), and so the range is $-1 \leq x < 1$. These weights and ranges are the same as for integers except that they have all been been divided by 2^{n-1}. This reflects the fact that the binary point has been moved $n-1$ places left, and so $2^{-(n-1)}$ is simply the binary scaling factor. When applied to the two's complement system, it has the effect of reducing the weight of d_0 to -1. Since the next few weights are $\frac{1}{2}$, $\frac{1}{4}$, $\frac{1}{8}$, ..., the following representations are easily verified:

$$
\begin{aligned}
-1 &= 1.000000\ldots0 \\
-\tfrac{1}{2} &= 1.100000\ldots0 \\
-\tfrac{1}{4} &= 1.110000\ldots0 \\
-\tfrac{1}{8} &= 1.111000\ldots0 \\
-\tfrac{1}{2^{n-1}} &= 1.111111\ldots1
\end{aligned}
$$

The representations can be converted to one's complement by subtracting 1 from the right-hand end; but the results are less simple, and -1 cannot be represented at all.

3.8   FLOATING-POINT NUMBERS

Integers and fractions are known as *fixed-point numbers*, because their (imaginary) binary point is fixed at a specified position — after d_{n-1} in one case, and after d_0 in the other. Notionally, the binary point can be placed at any other position, either between these limits or outside them. If placed after d_i, the effect is to scale the corresponding fraction by 2^i. This allows the programmer to work with larger numbers, or smaller ones, as the need arises. On the earliest computers this was the way in which most numerical computations were carried out. However, it raised the difficulty that if i was too low the numbers would overflow, whereas if it was too high they would lose precision. Accordingly, programmers had to predict the best value of i for each stage of their program and arrange for the (implied) binary point to 'float' from one position to another. It was a tedious and error-prone business.

To avoid all these problems, programmers introduced the concept of a *floating-point number*. This consisted of two parts, in two separate words. The first word contained the number's bit pattern and the second recorded the position of its binary point. An equivalent interpretation was that the first contained a fraction f and the second contained an integer scaling factor e. The value of the number was $f \times 2^e$, f being called the *mantissa*, 2 the *base*, and e the *exponent* (or *characteristic*). Subroutines were written for doing arithmetic on these numbers, and they ensured that overflow never took place except in the most extreme cases, such as division by zero. The resulting computations were slow, but the programming was much easier and the arithmetic much more reliable.

Despite predictions to the contrary, it was not long before floating-point representations were being handled by hardware. Instead of being stored in separate words, f and e were packed into a single word and single instructions were provided for doing the arithmetic. A simple format consists of f followed by e:

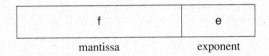

f	e
mantissa	exponent

Some machines split f into a sign bit s and an unsigned mantissa g, with e being inserted in between:

s	e	g
sign	exponent	mantissa

Both versions retain d_0 as the sign bit. On some machines, the mantissa is an integer instead of a fraction. Since e typically occupies seven or eight bits, the one-word representation loses a significant amount of precision. To offset this, the machines with a shorter word-length sometimes provide for *double-length* floating-point numbers, the mantissa being extended into a second word. Using two 32-bit words, they achieve a precision of about 15 decimal digits.

A floating-point representation can use any base, the most common choices being 2, 10, and 16. Base 10 is used for numerical output, when the range of numbers is wide or unpredictable. The decimal exponent is preceded by the letter E, as in the following examples:

```
1.5266E 03
9.6012E−02
−4.5000E 05
```

This is sometimes called *scientific notation*. The numbers are *normalized* in that the leading digit is always non-zero. This has the advantage that it retains the maximum number of significant digits. For example, it is better to print $\frac{1}{3}$ as 3.3333E−01 than as 0.0033E+02. Normalization is carried out similarly in hardware, where the floating-point operations retain as many significant digits as possible. With base 2, this means that the fraction part will always have a magnitude of at least $\frac{1}{2}$; for positive numbers it will begin 0.1..., and for negative ones it will begin 1.0... . The only exception is zero, which cannot be scaled in this way: it is therefore represented by setting all its bits to 0. With base 16, the fraction part can be as small as $\frac{1}{16}$ and so its binary pattern can begin $0.0001\ldots$. This means that it loses three bits of precision.

A further point of interest concerns the representation of the exponent e. Typically, with eight bits it has to cover the range -128 to $+127$, and so a representation for negative integers is needed. In preference to any of the systems discussed previously, many computers adopt the simple strategy of storing $e + 128$. Since this value is always positive, the problem of negative numbers disappears! The method is sometimes called the *excess-q* representation, *q* being 128 in this example. It differs from the previous systems in that zero is no longer $000\ldots0$; also the sign bit is inverted, being 1 for positive values of e and 0 for negative ones. For more general purposes, this would be inconvenient; but for the limited requirements of floating-point operations it works well.

If an operation produces a number whose exponent is greater than the available maximum, it causes *overflow*. If the exponent is less than the available minimum, it causes *underflow*. In the latter case, the result is clearly an extremely small number and we might think that it should be rounded off to zero. However, for some numerical computations this would be undesirable, and so it is better to have the underflow signaled in some way to the program. Section 8.14 describes the software mechanisms for handling these conditions.

FURTHER READING

There are many books on the history of numbers and numerals, including an extensive 'cultural history' by K. Menninger (1969), and a more recent study by G. Flegg (1983). A standard reference on computer number systems is Knuth (1981). For an excellent discussion, with greater emphasis on the hardware aspects, see Scott (1985). Some of the material in this chapter is derived from an interesting paper by D. H. Lehmer (1964).

EXERCISES

1   The decline and fall of the Roman number system provides an interesting case study on the importance of codes and representations. It shows that a long time is needed to overthrow established systems, even when the alternatives are far superior. A modern example of this is the QWERTY keyboard, which is used on almost every typewriter and terminal. It is known that alternative layouts can improve productivity by more than 30 percent, but who will make the effort to change? What other examples of this phenomenon can you think of? What about computer character codes or programming languages?

2   How many decimal digits are equivalent to n bits?

3   Horner's rule provides an efficient way of evaluating a polynomial

$$a_n x^n \quad + \quad a_{n-1} x^{n-1} \quad + \quad \ldots \quad + \quad a_1 x \quad + \quad a_0$$

at a given point x_0. Extend the algorithm so that it also evaluates the *derivative* of the polynomial at x_0. (This can be useful in algorithms for numerical integration.)

4 What is the representation of 144_{10} in (a) binary, (b) base 3, (c) octal, and (d) hexa-decimal? What is the decimal value of 011011_2, 0315_8, and $2AC_{16}$?

5 With eight-bit numerals, what is the representation of 45, 1, -1, -45 in (a) sign-and-magnitude, (b) one's complement, and (c) two's complement? What is the value of 10101110 in each of these systems?

6 Section 3.4 describes a way of converting from octal to decimal using multiplication by $10-2$. Prove that the method gives the correct result. How would you use it to convert

(a) from base 7 to decimal;
(b) from base 16 to decimal;
(c) from base x to base y?

7 The term 'weight' reminds us that number systems are implicitly present in the selection of weights for a pair of scales. The old letter-scales, for example, used weights of $\frac{1}{4}$ oz, $\frac{1}{2}$ oz, 1 oz, 2 oz, 4 oz, 8 oz, ..., which was a simple binary system. Each weight contributed one bit of information (absent or present) to the total. Metric scales use 1g, 2g, 5g, 10g, 20g, 50g, ..., which is less attractive. Indeed, the 2g and 20g weights have to be duplicated in order to weigh 4g, 40g, and so forth.

If the second 2g weight were not provided, we might have a flash of inspiration: to weigh 4g, why not put 5g on one side and 1g on the other? But this technique, of course, opens up much greater possibilities! If we can use either side of the scales, each weight can contribute a *trit* of information (left side, absent, or right side). This means that we have a special kind of base-3 system, and so the natural set of weights to adopt is 1g, 3g, 9g, 27g, ... The corresponding digits are 1, 0 and $\bar{1}$ (for -1), and the system is called the *balanced ternary system*.

(a) What range of numbers can be represented by an n-trit numeral?
(b) What is the relationship between an n-trit numeral and an n-digit base-3 numeral?
(c) If d is the n-trit numeral for x, what is the numeral for $-x$?
(d) How would you determine whether d was positive or negative?
(e) If d is the n-trit numeral for x, what is the numeral for $x+1$?

For further discussion of this system see Knuth (1981), pp. 190 – 3.

8 Convert 23 hours 15 minutes 45 seconds to seconds using nested multiplication. Convert 77777 seconds to hours, minutes, and seconds.

9 The *factorial* number system is a mixed-radix system with radices n+1, n, ... 2.

(a) What are the possible values of d_i?
(b) What is the weight of d_i?
(c) What range of values can be represented by an n-digit factorial numeral?
(d) Given x, how would you obtain its factorial digits?
(e) List all the three-digit factorial numbers in ascending order.

Given n distinct objects, there are n! ways of ordering (or *permuting*) them. Show how successive digits of an (n−1)-digit factorial numeral can specify successive objects for a permutation. Hence, establish a one-to-one correspondence between (n−1)-digit factorial numerals and n-object permutations. Note that this provides a method of generating a random permutation: we generate a random number in the range 0 to n! − 1, recover its factorial digits, and determine the corresponding permutation. On the other hand, there are much better ways of generating *all* permutations. For a full discussion, see Sedgewick (1977).

10   The *modular* (or *Chinese*) number system is of interest, partly because it is so different from anything else, and partly because it contains a number of attractive properties. Let p_1, p_2, ... p_n, be the first n prime numbers, beginning 2, 3, 5, ... The n-digit modular numeral for a number x is defined by setting:

$$d_i \;\; = \;\; x \; mod \; p_i$$

In other words, d_i is the remainder when x is divided by p_i.

(a)   What is the minimum x? What is the maximum x before an n-digit numeral is repeated?

(b)   Given two numerals d1 and d2, with values x1 and x2, what numerals represent x1 + x2, x1 − x2, x1 * x2? What advantage does this have for computer arithmetic?

(c)   Given d, how would you determine its value x? (The best method is 'an old Chinese trick which the reader may care to discover for himself' [Lehmer, 1964]. It uses no more than n additions and n multiplications, so it is comparable to more conventional systems in its efficiency.)

(d)   Discuss the use of the modular system for doing multi-length integer arithmetic. How would you represent negative numbers?

11   On your machine, what is the normalized floating-point representation of +0.25, −0.25, 0.1, and 0? What action does your machine take on underflow?

12   In base 2, a non-zero normalized floating-point number must have a fraction part that begins 0.1 ... or 1.0.... . The second bit is therefore redundant and may in principle be omitted (on the PDP-11 and VAX computers it *is* omitted). Is there any other redundancy in the system? That is to say, what proportion of the remaining 2^{n-1} patterns represent distinct numbers? What is the redundancy in base 8 or base 16?

13   [Arithmetic shift] Suppose that an n-bit word represents an integer x in two's complement. Prove that $x * 2^k$ (k≥0) can be computed by doing a left shift of k places with 0-filling at the right-hand end. Note that if $d_1...d_k$ are not all identical to the sign bit, the shifting will cause the sign bit to alter at some stage. Prove that this indicates the occurrence of overflow. Prove also that in one's complement it is necessary to use sign-filling at the right-hand end — that is, filling with copies of the sign bit. (Hint: consider the case k = 1.)

Prove similarly that $x * 2^{-k}$ (k≥0) can be computed by doing a right shift of k places with sign-filling at the left-hand end (in one's or two's complement). Ideally, for the best accuracy, round-off should be done at the right-hand end. If truncation is used instead, will the result be round $(x / 2^k)$, entier $(x / 2^k)$, floor $(x / 2^k)$, or ceiling $(x / 2^k)$?

Many computers provide an *arithmetic shift* instruction that operates in this way. It performs a shift of k places that is equivalent to multiplying by 2^k. If $k > 0$, it checks for overflow; if $k < 0$, it does round-off. It is considerably faster than ordinary multiplication by 2^k, and an optimizing compiler will take advantage of it where possible.

14 Show how to use the arithmetic shift instruction and the test for overflow to determine whether or not the first k bits of a word are all zero.

SCALAR TYPES

4.1 TYPES

Data items belong to various classes, which in programming are usually known as *types*. This chapter is concerned with the *scalar* types — that is, the types whose values are single, indivisible units. The most common examples are the integers, the real numbers, the truth values, and the characters. Their values are indivisible in the sense that no operations are provided for splitting them into smaller parts. By contrast, the *structured*, or *composite*, types are formed from other types by certain structuring techniques, and special operations are used for accessing their components. These types are the subject of Volume II.

To lay some groundwork, it is worth examining the concept of a type more closely. The above description suggests that a type is simply a set of values. But is this sufficient? In any case, what characterizes a set of values? What gives them meaning? To put it another way, what are the essential features of a type definition?

Historically, the type of an item has often been associated with its *representation*. In particular, since numbers can be represented either in fixed-point or in floating-point, an early distinction was drawn between type integer and type real. This concept was reinforced by the obvious fact that a bit pattern by itself is meaningless. Its interpretation depends on its type and on the associated method of representation.

This is all very well, and from a pragmatic point of view it is certainly very important. However, when programmers use a high-level language, they are not normally concerned about the details of representation. Indeed, if their programs are to be machine-independent, the representation should be irrelevant. What, then, is the significance of a type at this higher, more abstract level? The answer is that the type is a set of values *to which certain operations can be applied*. For example, the essential feature of type real is that it is a set of numbers which are subject to operations such as addition and subtraction. By contrast, the truth values are subject to *not*, *or*, and *and*. It would be meaningless to apply *not* to a number, or to add two truth values. High-level languages are usually designed so that such errors can be detected, either by the compiler or by the run-time system. A language with complete security in this respect is called a *strongly typed* language.

This understanding of data types is sometimes called the *abstract*, or *operational*, view. It is abstract in the sense that it is not primarily concerned with the concrete details of any particular representation. It is operational in that it defines a type in terms of the operations that can be applied to it. The following sections reflect this view by considering each type primarily in terms of its values and the related operations. The methods of implementation take second place. In most cases, the operations are easy to define. However, for ordinary arithmetic it turns out that they are surprisingly difficult, and so the definitions will not be given here. Readers with a taste for rigorous detail may care to study them in *Principia Mathematica* (Whitehead and Russell, 1910).

4.2 INTEGERS

The most familiar scalar type is integer. It is a basic type of all general-purpose, high-level languages and provides for the use of ordinary integer arithmetic. The implication is that the integers will be represented in standard fixed-point format, as described in the previous chapter (Sections 3.4 and 3.6). The range of values will be limited for each implementation by the word length of the machine. Facilities may therefore be provided that allow a program to determine the range. For example, Pascal provides a constant maxint, and Ada provides the constants system.min_int and system.max_int. Since the hardware may also handle half-word and double-word integers, some languages have types such as short integer and long integer to take advantage of them. The trouble is, though, that all these types are machine-dependent. A better approach is for the program to define its own integer types by specifying the required range. Facilities for this will be described in later sections.

The operations on integers include the usual ones of *addition*, *negation*, *subtraction*, *multiplication*, and *division*. The first four are normally implemented as single machine operations. If their results lie outside the range of the representation, they cause *overflow*. This is an example of an *exception* (see Section 8.14).

Division is more complicated because it has two results — a *quotient* and a *remainder*. Although these are produced by a single machine operation, most languages require them to be obtained separately (though COBOL is a notable exception). In Pascal, for example, they are provided by **div** and **mod**:

```
q  :=  i div j;        { the quotient }
r  :=  i mod j;        { the remainder }
```

If $j = 0$, these will cause an error. In other cases, the results are related by the equation:

$$i = q * j + r$$

Provided that i and j are both positive, the remainder r is guaranteed to lie in the range 0 to $j - 1$. However, if i or j is negative, the details have to be handled with care. As far as machine hardware is concerned, there are two main possibilities:

1.   The quotient is obtained by taking the integer part of i / j (rounding towards zero). It follows that the remainder will have the same sign as i. Thus $(-10) \div 3$ gives the quotient -3 and the remainder -1, whereas $10 \div (-3)$ gives the quotient -3 and the remainder 1.

2.   The quotient is obtained by rounding i / j towards $-\infty$. In this case, the remainder will have the same sign as j. Thus $(-10) \div 3$ gives the quotient -4 and remainder 2, whereas $10 \div (-3)$ gives the quotient -4 and remainder -2.

Typically, version 1 is found on one's complement machines and version 2 on two's complement. Whichever definition is adopted by a high-level language, there is bound to be a certain amount of mismatch.

Pascal, like most other languages, adopts version 1. In respect of **div**, this has the advantage that it retains the usual algebraic properties:

$$(-i) \textbf{ div } j \; = \; - (i \textbf{ div } j) \; = \; i \textbf{ div } (-j)$$

In respect of **mod**, though, it means that i **mod** j does not conform to the normal requirements of modulo arithmetic (see below). The term 'mod' is therefore misleading.

Ada goes for the best of both worlds by providing *three* operations:

```
q  :=  i / j;            -- the quotient
r  :=  i rem j;          -- the remainder
m  :=  i mod j;          -- the modulus
```

As in Pascal, the first two follow definition 1; so i / j does division with truncation (rounding towards zero), and **rem** gives the remainder. The third one follows definition 2, and unlike Pascal's **mod**, it therefore does genuine modulo arithmetic. In particular, if j is positive, this means that the result is guaranteed to lie in the range 0 to j − 1. Exercise 3 discusses a situation in which this can have definite practical advantages.

Another important operation is *exponentiation*, usually written as i ** j. It computes i to the power of j, and can be implemented by repeated multiplication followed by reciprocation if j is negative. (For faster techniques, see Exercise 7.) The operation has two drawbacks:

1.   If j is a variable, the type of i ** j cannot be known until run-time, being integer if j is positive and real if it is negative. This is contrary to the principle that the type of every expression must be known at compile-time.

2.   The operation is open to abuse. In particular, it should not normally be used for evaluating polynomials. For example, the expression

$$x**3 \; + \; 5*x**2 \; - \; 6*x \; + \; 1$$

is better written as

$$((x + 5) * x - 6) * x + 1$$

which, for purposes of evaluation, is clearly much simpler (see Horner's rule, Section 3.3).

Some languages cope with the first problem by restricting the exponent either to being a constant, or (as in Ada) to being positive. The latter may require a run-time check on the exponent's sign. Pascal avoids both problems by abolishing the operation entirely — a rather drastic step, especially for scientists and engineers.

The operation | i | gives the *absolute value* of i, otherwise known as its *magnitude*. In most languages it is provided by a function abs (i), which returns + i if i is positive and − i if it is negative. Thus:

$$\text{abs} \, (5) \; = \; \text{abs} \, (-5) \; = \; 5$$

In Ada, **abs** is a standard, prefixed operator.

Integers can be compared with one another using the *relational* operators, namely '=', '≠', '<', '≤', '>', and '≥'. On some machines, these are available as single operations. On others, all comparisons have to be made with zero, and so a test such as x < y has to be implemented as (x − y) < 0. This, unfortunately, carries the risk that the evaluation of x − y will cause overflow.

4.3 REAL TYPES

The type real is the traditional one for numerical computations, being found in FORTRAN IV, ALGOL 60, and most of their descendants. It provides a finite subset of the real numbers as implemented by the floating-point hardware (or in a few cases by the software). It is therefore an essential type for most scientific and engineering applications. Being related so closely to the hardware, it is machine-dependent both in the range of numbers that it offers and in their precision. So, as with type integer, a language may provide facilities that allow a program to determine these quantities. For example, ALGOL 68 has constants max real and small real, the latter being the smallest real number that can meaningfully be added to 1. Again, as with type integer, some machines can handle half-length or double-length numbers, and so types short real and long real (or double) may be provided as well.

In practice, the range and precision of type real varies widely from one machine to another. For example, the CDC Cyber computers have a word-length of 60, which allows for a sign bit, an exponent of 11 bits, and a mantissa of 48 bits. By contrast, the IBM 370-series computers have a word length of 32, the mantissa being a mere 24 bits (of which three may be wasted — see Section 3.8). As a result, a program that runs perfectly well on one sort of machine may prove hopelessly bad on another. In the latter case, it may be possible to revise the program so that it uses long real instead of real at the crucial points. But this, of course, is to admit the machine-dependency of the situation and is to that extent unsatisfactory. In any case, the conversion of FORTRAN programs in this way is not a trivial business.

In recognition of these problems, Ada has a standard type called float, whose range and precision are defined by the implementation, and optional types short_float and long_float. In general, though, the intention is that numerical computations should state the range and precision that they need to use. The following example shows how:

type real **is digits** 12 **range** −1E30 .. +1E30;

This asks for numbers with a precision of at least 12 decimal digits and a range that covers 0 to ±10^{30}. The details can be geared to the nature of the problem, independently of any particular hardware. On each machine, it is the compiler's responsibility to choose the appropriate representation — single-length, double-length, or whatever (see below). Later chapters will use the type real on the assumption that it has been defined in this way — either by the program itself, or within a library package that is provided for doing real arithmetic.

In fact, Ada allows real numbers to be represented either in floating-point or in fixed-point. The above example specifies **digits** 12, which implies the use of floating-point. Since 12 decimal digits are equivalent to approximately 40 binary digits, this could be done by single-length working on the Cyber computers, but would require double-length on the IBM computers. It should be noted that the precision is not given as an absolute quantity, but as the length d of a (decimal) mantissa. The precision of a particular number will depend on its exponent e. In principle, it will be half of the smallest change that can be made to the mantissa, namely 0.5×10^{-d}, multiplied by 10^e. In practice, of course, the implementation may make it considerably finer.

The use of fixed-point arithmetic is specified by the word **delta**. For example, the type

delta 0.1 **range** −250 .. +250

provides for numbers that cover the range 0 to ±250 at intervals of 0.1 or less. In contrast to the previous method, this gives an absolute precision — one that is independent of the size of the number. The intention is that the numbers should be implemented using a fixed-point representation, as described briefly at the start of Section 3.8. The bit pattern $d_0 d_1 d_2 \ldots d_{n-1}$ is interpreted as a number with a binary point following d_i for some fixed value i. The range determines the number of bits that must precede the point and the precision determines the number that must follow it. Thus a range of 0 to ±250 requires nine bits, including a sign bit, and the precision 0.1 requires four bits (2^{-4} being slightly less than 0.1). The numbers could therefore be handled by 16-bit words, with three bits left over as so-called 'guard' bits. The arithmetic is carried out using the same hardware operations as for fixed-point integers, though care is needed in order to keep the results properly aligned with the (imaginary) binary point. For a fixed-point argument of type T, the following cases are straightforward, and in Ada they give T-type results:

- addition to another T-type number;
- subtraction from another T-type number;
- multiplication by an integer;
- division by an integer.

Multiplication of two T-type numbers is more complicated. If they are represented with k bits after the binary point, the hardware operation produces a double-length result with 2k bits after the binary point. If the desired type is T, the result has to be shifted k places to the right (with a corresponding loss of precision) and then reduced to single length (possibly causing overflow). Division has similar problems, requiring a shift of k places to the *left*. In recognition of these problems, Ada says that the results are of type universal fixed and requires the programmer to specify the desired type by inserting an explicit transfer function. The latter is written simply as the name of the type. For example, T (x∗y) will convert x∗y to type T.

On the subject of transfer functions, it is important to note the different ways in which a real number can be converted to an integer. There are four main possibilities, as shown in Figure 4-1. In most languages the standard form of real-to-integer conversion is by rounding. If the fraction part is exactly 0.5, the number is usually rounded outwards (away from zero). The next most common form is entier (x), which gives the integer part of x. In Pascal it is called trunc, since it truncates x by removing the fraction part. In mathematics, the operation is sometimes written as [x], but this notation has not carried over to computer science since the square brackets are used for other purposes, notably subscripting. On the other hand, the variations ⌈x⌉ and ⌊x⌋ were invented especially for computing, having originated in the language APL. They have been widely used in the

Function	Notation	Rounding
round (x)	–	to the nearest integer
entier (x)	[x]	towards zero
ceiling (x)	⌈x⌉	upwards (towards $+\infty$)
floor (x)	⌊x⌋	downwards (towards $-\infty$)

Figure 4-1   Real-to-integer type conversions

analysis of algorithms. For example, Section 2.1 used the expression $\lceil \log_2 x \rceil$, which gives the smallest integer i such that $2^i \geq x$ (see also Exercise 4).

Other operations on real numbers are much the same as for integers. Division is simpler because it produces one result instead of two. On the other hand, exponentiation threatens to be more complicated. The trouble is that if the expression $x ** y$ has a fractional exponent y, it cannot be evaluated by repeated multiplication. Instead, it has to be computed as

$$b^{y * \log_b x}$$

using logarithms with some convenient base b. The most usual base is e (the 'natural' or Napierian logarithms), as provided by the Pascal functions ln and exp. Even so, if $x \leq 0$, the ln function will raise an error condition. To avoid these problems, languages such as Ada require y to be an integer (though not necessarily positive). The calculation with a real exponent has to be done explicitly; in Pascal, for example, it can be written as $\exp (y * \ln(x))$.

The functions exp and ln are examples of standard functions provided by Pascal. Other functions of the real numbers include the following:

abs (x)	—	the absolute value of x;
sqrt (x)	—	the square root;
sin (x)	—	the trigonometric sine;
cos (x)	—	the trigonometric cosine;
arctan (x)	—	the inverse tangent, $\tan^{-1}(x)$.

In Ada, **abs** is a prefixed operator (see Section 4.2). The other functions are not a standard part of the language, but will normally be provided by the library packages of an installation.

Section 3.7 discussed the limited precision that is achieved by non-integer arithmetic. Decimal fractions can seldom be represented as exact binary equivalents and so they incur a round-off error. Subsequent calculations introduce further errors. This has far-reaching consequences for all calculations involving real numbers. An immediate effect is that it is potentially dangerous to use the operators '=' and '≠'. A test such as $x = y$ may therefore have to be written as

$$\textbf{abs} \ (x - y) \ < \ eps$$

where eps is some small, positive number. (In APL, this is how the test $x = y$ is implemented anyhow, and so such stratagems are not necessary.) The same trouble can occur

under a different guise in testing for the end of a loop, as in the following **for** statement of
ALGOL 60:

for x := 0 **step** 0.1 **until** 1.0 **do** ...

If 0.1 is represented as a marginally greater number, the loop will terminate earlier than
expected. To avoid this problem, the upper limit should be set to a slightly higher value,
such as 1.01.

On a more formal note, the limited precision means that the so-called 'real' numbers
do not obey the normal laws of real arithmetic. For example, there are situations where
the following relations no longer apply:

$$
\begin{aligned}
x + (y + z) &= (x + y) + z \\
x * (y + z) &= x * y + x * z \\
-(x - y) &= y - x
\end{aligned}
$$

In order to provide some alternative axioms, W. S. Brown (1977) has proposed that the
operations be defined in terms of *model* numbers. These have the form

$$
\pm\, 0\,.\,d_1 d_2 \ldots d_t \times 2^e
$$

where $d_1 = 1$ (normalization) and the remaining digits are 0 or 1. The exponent e lies in
the range $-4t \le e \le 4t$ for some fixed integer t. Each value of t gives rise to a different set
of numbers: the larger the value, the greater the precision. A *model interval* is an interval
that is bounded by two model numbers (or, for an unbounded interval, by $\pm\infty$). A real
number is mapped into the smallest model interval containing it, and operations such as
addition are defined on the model intervals with results that are themselves model intervals — an example of *interval arithmetic* (Moore, 1966). Axioms can then be formulated
which define the accuracy of the operations in terms of the quantity $\varepsilon = \frac{1}{2^{t-1}}$.

The model is 'realistic' in the sense that every hardware floating-point system implements a set of model numbers for some value of t. Ada uses it as the theoretical basis for
its real numbers, and requires that an implementation of type real with a precision of n
decimal digits should include the model numbers for:

$$
t = \lceil 1 + n * \log_2 10 \rceil
$$

For example, **digits** 12 requires $t = 41$. The corresponding axioms can then be used for
reasoning about the arithmetic. This may be better than having no axioms at all. On the
other hand, the task of formulating good numerical algorithms remains as challenging as
ever. For further comments, see Exercises 8-10.

4.4   TRUTH VALUES

In classical logic, a proposition is either true or false. The law of the 'excluded middle'
states that there can be no values in between. The law may be challenged by politicians
and logicians; but in the computing field, with its inbuilt preference for two-valued systems, the true/false dichotomy is firmly upheld.

The two values are sometimes called *truth* values or *logical* values. In programming,
though, they are more often known as *Boolean* values, after the English mathematician

George Boole (see Section 2.3). They are implicitly present in conditional expressions, such as $i + 1 < n$, whose values must be either true or false. However, many programming languages go further by including Boolean (or possibly boolean) as a primitive type, so that programs can have Boolean variables and parameters. This provides the most natural mechanism for recording the value of a condition and for passing such values to or from a subprogram.

The type Boolean comprises the two values false and true. As Section 2.3 showed, they map very simply into the logical values 0 and 1: false corresponds to 0 and true to 1. FORTRAN emphasizes this by calling the type LOGICAL. The Boolean operations are equivalent to the logical ones and usually have the same names, the main ones being *not*, *or*, and *and*. Since the ASCII character set does not include the corresponding operators '¬', '∨', and '∧', other symbols have to be pressed into service. For example, C uses '!', '|', and '&'. Pascal and Ada use the reserved words **not**, **or**, and **and**. From Figure 2-3, it can be seen that there are eight other non-trivial diadic operations, of which the following three are the most useful:

equivalence	—	$p \equiv q$ is true if p and q are the same;
exclusive or	—	$p \oplus q$ is true if p and q are different;
implication	—	$p \supset q$ is true if p is false and/or q is true.

In Pascal and Ada, an ordering is defined such that false < true; consequently these operations can be expressed respectively as $p = q$, $p \neq q$, and $p \leq q$. In Ada, the *exclusive or* can also be written as p **xor** q.

One might expect the representation of a Boolean entity to be a trivial affair, a single bit being sufficient. In practice, though, the entity normally has to occupy a full-length word and so an extended representation must be chosen. There are several possibilities:

1.　000...0 and 000...1 — that is, the integers 0 and 1. These work well for *and* and *or*, which can be implemented by the equivalent, full-word, logical operations. The *not* operation can be implemented by subtraction from 1.

2.　000...0 and 111...1. These work well for all the operations. However, they need careful handling on a one's complement machine, since both patterns represent the number zero (see Section 3.6).

3.　0..... and 1....., where the dots represent arbitrary bits. In effect this is a one-bit representation, the word being padded out with 'don't cares'. Again, this works well for all the operations.

4.　.....0 and .....1. This is similar to method 3.

5.　000...0 for false, with all other bit patterns representing true. This works well for *not* and *or*, but not so well for *and*.

In passing, it is worth noting that in a language such as C, where the type Boolean is not provided, false and true can be introduced as named constants with values 0 and 1, as in method 1. The operations *and*, *or*, and *not* can then be implemented by multiplication, addition-and-test, and subtraction from 1. This is why they are sometimes denoted by '*', '+', and (unary) '−'.

The operations *and* and *or* involve an important point of interpretation. Consider, for example, the expression

$$C1 \quad \textbf{and} \quad C2$$

where *C1* and *C2* are two conditions. If *C1* evaluates to true, the overall result will be determined by *C2*. But if *C1* is false, the result will always be false, and so the question arises: why bother to evaluate *C2*? Why not skip over the associated section of code? A similar situation occurs with the expression:

$$C1 \quad \textbf{or} \quad C2$$

If *C1* turns out to be true, the result is again independent of *C2* and so, in principle, the code for evaluating *C2* could be skipped. However, there are two situations where skipping the code can affect the behavior of the program. The first is where the evaluation of *C2* produces side effects — a possibility that is considered in Section 9.4. The second is where it would raise an error condition. (The law of the excluded middle is not as inviolate as we might like!) A typical case of the latter arises in searching a table of values T[1], ... T[n] for a value x. A simple method is to use the following loop:

```
i := 1;
while (i ≤ n) and (T[i] ≠ x) do
    i := i + 1;
```

If x is never found, the loop will continue until i = n + 1, and at this point the second part of the **and** expression will involve a reference to T[n+1]. Since T[n+1] may not exist, it is important to know whether the second part will be evaluated or not. Unfortunately, some language definitions are silent on the matter, presumably implying that it *should* be evaluated. Even so, many implementations skip the code, and programs are sometimes written on this assumption — a highly precarious situation. In some languages, the danger can be avoided by using an expression of the form:

if *condition* **then** *expression–1* **else** *expression–2*

Skipping can be enforced by rewriting the expressions as follows:

$$C1 \text{ and } C2 \quad — \quad \textbf{if } C1 \textbf{ then } C2 \textbf{ else } \text{false}$$
$$C1 \text{ or } C2 \quad — \quad \textbf{if } C1 \textbf{ then } \text{true} \textbf{ else } C2$$

These versions were originated by J. McCarthy (1963) and are known as the *conditional and* and the *conditional or*. Various proposals have been made for including them as extra operators — for example, **cand** and **cor**. In Ada, they are called 'short circuit' conditions and are written in the form **and then** and **or else**. The above loop can therefore be written as:

while (i ≤ n) **and then** (T[i] ≠ x) **loop** ...

This notation expresses the idea in a neat and helpful way. The need for such operators has been questioned on the grounds that they generally indicate the use of a poorly structured algorithm. The above example is a case in point: as Section 8.17 shows, there are better ways of programming the search. But, like so many generalizations of this kind, it would be a pity if it led to a total ban on the facility. There are occasions when the conditional versions of *and* and *or* can come in very handy.

4.5 CHARACTERS

The type character or char comprises a finite set of characters which, like the numeric types, is to some extent dependent on the implementation. A minimal assumption is that it contains the digits '0' to '9' and the upper-case letters 'A' to 'Z'. But the sets vary greatly from one language to another and so it is difficult to generalize much further.

The characters will be represented by an internal *code*. On machines with six-bit bytes this will be a six-bit code; with eight-bit bytes it will be a seven- or eight-bit code. A seven-bit code allows for an eighth bit to be used as a parity bit, ensuring that the number of 1s is either always even or else always odd (see Section 2.8). For example, 1011100 is extended to 01011100 with even parity, and to 11011100 with odd parity. If one of the bits becomes altered during transmission between devices, the error can be detected by a parity check (see Section 5.13).

The choice of a suitable code is an important matter because it can make a significant difference to the programming, even at fairly high levels. Figure 4-2 shows the seven-bit code of the International Standards Organization (ISO), which has much to commend it. As can be seen, a few of the characters are subject to certain kinds of variation, according to national agreement. The particular version shown in the figure is the well-known seven-bit ASCII code — the American Standard Code for Information Interchange.

Last three bits

First four bits	000	001	010	011	100	101	110	111
0000	NUL	SOH	STX	ETX	EOT	ENQ	ACK	BEL
0001	BS	HT	NL	VT	NP	CR	SO	SI
0010	DLE	DC1	DC2	DC3	DC4	NAK	SYN	ETB
0011	CAN	EM	SUB	ESC	FS	GS	RS	US
0100	space	!	"	(#)	($)	%	&	'
0101	(	)	*	+	,	—	.	/
0110	0	1	2	3	4	5	6	7
0111	8	9	:	;	<	=	>	?
1000	(@)	A	B	C	D	E	F	G
1001	H	I	J	K	L	M	N	O
1010	P	Q	R	S	T	U	V	W
1011	X	Y	Z	([)	(\)	(])	(^)	_
1100	(`)	a	b	c	d	e	f	g
1101	h	i	j	k	l	m	n	o
1110	p	q	r	s	t	u	v	w
1111	x	y	z	({)	(|)	(})	(~)	DEL

Note: characters enclosed in parentheses are subject to certain kinds of variation, according to national agreement.

Figure 4-2   The ISO seven-bit character set

Another widely used code is EBCDIC — the eight-bit Extended BCD Interchange Code, which is supported by IBM. This is based on the earlier six-bit Binary Coded Decimal code which, despite some glaring inadequacies, was popular in the second generation machines of 1955–65. Unfortunately, manufacturers have invented many other codes, and so the situation is rather confused. The increasing adoption of the ASCII code is to be welcomed.

Figure 4-2 shows several features that are relevant to programming. To start with, the code 0000000 represents the *null* character, which indicates the absence of any significant information. The all-0 code is the natural one to use for the purpose, since non-significant fields are normally 0-filled anyhow. The use of 0000000 to represent an actual character would be much less convenient (in BCD it was the digit 0). At the other end of the table, the code 1111111 is very similar, since it too represents the absence of significant information. It has a special role to play in the deletion of characters that have been punched on paper tape. Overpunching a character in all its positions will convert it to 1111111, and this effectively deletes it. For this reason 1111111 is called the *delete* character.

Apart from 0000000, the codes beginning 00... all represent *control* characters. A brief explanation of their abbreviations is given in Figure 4-3. SOH to ACK are for *transmission* control, as also are DLE, SYN, ETB, and CAN. BS to CR are for *format* control; DC1 to DC4 are for *device* control; and FS to US are for *information* control. The BEL character, which produces some sort of a beep at a terminal, is presumably for *user* control. The shift and escape characters allow for a change to another code. At a terminal, some of the characters can be generated by means of the *control* key. In particular, DC1 to DC4 are commonly produced by pressing CTRL together with Q, R, S, or T. As can be seen from Figure 4-2, their codes are obtained from the corresponding characters by inverting the first bit.

NUL	=	null	DLE	=	data link escape
SOH	=	start of heading	DC1	=	device control 1
STX	=	start of text	DC2	=	device control 2
ETX	=	end of text	DC3	=	device control 3
EOT	=	end of transmission	DC4	=	device control 4
ENQ	=	enquiry	NAK	=	negative acknowledge
ACK	=	acknowledge	SYN	=	synchronous idle
BEL	=	bell	ETB	=	end transmission block
BS	=	backspace	CAN	=	cancel
HT	=	horizontal tab	EM	=	end of medium
LF	=	line feed	SUB	=	substitute
VT	=	vertical tab	ESC	=	escape
FF	=	form feed	FS	=	file seperator
CR	=	carriage return	GS	=	group seperator
SO	=	shift out	RS	=	record seperator
SI	=	shift in	US	=	unit seperator
			DEL	=	delete

Figure 4-3   Control character descriptions

The remaining twelve rows list 95 printable characters, which cover most programming requirements. (By way of comparison, the average typewriter has about 90 different characters.) Note that the digits '0' to '9' are represented by consecutive codes $x + 0$ to $x + 9$, with x in this case being 48. This makes it easy to check for digits and to convert them to their numeric values. The obvious way to convert them is by subtracting x (see below). If x is a multiple of 16, a faster method is to mask them with 0001111.

Similar considerations apply to the letters 'A' to 'Z', which are given codes $y + 1$ to $y + 26$, with y in this case being 64. Unfortunately, this convention is not so widespread. In EBCDIC, for example, the letters run from 193 to 233, there being 15 unused codes within the range. Another feature of the letters in the ISO code is that their leading bit is always 1 and the second bit defines their shift: 0 for upper-case, 1 for lower-case.

A reduced character set is obtained by omitting the first four rows and the last four rows. This leaves a set of 64 printable characters similar to the 6-bit codes found in many installations. Such codes enforce a diet of upper-case letters which would normally be associated with the ancient Romans or with telegrams. It is one of the ironies of modern technology that computer programmers seem to be so addicted to them.

In high-level languages, the details of type character are not usually spelt out fully; they are too dependent on the implementation. A minimum set is often stipulated, but other characters may be added as available. This, of course, introduces an element of machine dependency. Ada therefore breaks with tradition by equating the type with the seven-bit ASCII code, both in the set of characters provided and in their detailed ordering. However, other character types can be defined if necessary (see Section 4.6).

In a program, a character constant is denoted by enclosing the character in quotes — single quotes in some languages (such as Pascal and Ada), double quotes in others. However, the non-graphic characters, such as backspace and tab, have to be handled differently. In Ada, there is a standard package called ASCII that provides them as named constants, exactly as shown in Figure 4-2: thus backspace is ASCII.bs, tab is ASCII.ht, and so on. An alternative convention is to represent them as pairs of characters, the first member of each pair being a standard *escape* character. In the language C, for example, backspace is '\b', tab is '\t' and the backslash itself is '\\'. These can be included in strings of characters, which is a useful advantage over the Ada convention. Characters that are even more obscure can be written as '\ddd', where *ddd* is their octal representation. This, of course, is machine dependent; but a program can localize the dependency by defining such characters as named constants and then using only their names.

In principle, programmers should not need to know the code which is used for representing the characters. After all, it is a matter of implementation and may vary from one machine to another. However, there are many applications where they may need to know the *ordering* of the characters. For the letters 'A' to 'Z', this is the familiar alphabetical order; but the concept is extended to the full character set to give a *lexicographical* order, otherwise known as the *collating sequence*. In practice, the order will almost certainly be the same as that of the corresponding integer codes. For example, Figure 4-2 shows that in ASCII the following characters are in ascending order: space, dot, digits, upper-case letters, and lower-case letters. Consequently, the lexicographical order of the names Parker, P.Arker, P Arker, parker and park4 is:

P Arker
P.Arker

Parker

park4

parker

This ordering is the one specified for type character in Ada, and the usual relational operators are defined on characters accordingly, namely '=', '≠', '<', '≤', '>', and '≥'. The same operations are available in most other languages, but the detailed ordering is usually left to the implementation.

The ordering of the characters can be the basis for several tests. For example, provided that the digits '0', '1', ... '9' have consecutive integer codes, the condition

$$('0' \leq d) \text{ and } (d \leq '9')$$

tests whether d is a digit. In Pascal, it could also be written as

$$d \text{ in } ['0'..'9']$$

and in Ada as

$$d \text{ in } '0'..'9'$$

The former tests for membership of a set, and the latter for membership of a range. The assumption about the coding of the digits is a fairly safe one. Indeed, Pascal makes it a mandatory property of type char. However, a similar test for letters, such as

$$('a' \leq ch) \text{ and } (ch \leq 'z')$$

is less safe. A better approach is therefore the one taken by Simula 67, which provides Boolean functions digit and letter for the purpose. The C library has isdigit and isalpha similarly, and a variety of other functions — isupper, islower, and so on.

In spite of all this, there are still a few occasions where it is useful to be able to determine the underlying integer codes. Pascal provides the function ord (ch), which can be regarded as a char-to-integer transfer function. Since ch is normally represented by its integer code, the function does not in fact execute any run-time transformation: it is simply a high-level, type-changing device. Pascal also provides the inverse integer-to-char transformation, chr(i); this may involve a run-time check on the range of i. A simple application of ord arises in the conversion of the digits '0', '1', ... '9' to their corresponding integer values 0, 1, ... 9. As mentioned earlier, this is easily done provided that their codes are consecutive integers. In Pascal, for example, the numeric value of a digit d can be obtained from the formula:

$$\text{ord} (d) - \text{ord} ('0')$$

In Ada, the function is called pos and has to be written as character'pos. Unless the type character is redefined, its result will be the character's ASCII code.

4.6   ENUMERATED TYPES

An *enumerated* type is one whose values are explicitly spelt out. A simple example is provided by the type Boolean which, in Pascal and Ada, is defined to be the enumerated type (false, true). This implies that it has two possible values, written as false and true, and that there is an ordering relation false < true. The values are sometimes referred to as *enumerals*.

Enumerated types are useful for introducing entities that are conceptually different from any of the existing types. Suppose, for example, that a program is concerned with playing chess. There are two players, White and Black, and six kinds of piece — pawn, knight, bishop, rook, queen, king. How shall it refer to them? A Boolean type might seem appropriate for the players, since they are two-valued, and the letters P, N, B, R, Q, and K could be used for the pieces. But these are simply attempts to find a representation within existing types. It is much better to define new types specifically for the purpose. The Ada version would go as follows:

```
type player is (White, Black);
type piece is
        (pawn, knight, bishop, rook, queen, king);
```

Variables of these types can then be declared:

```
player1, player2 : player;
my_piece : piece;
```

And values from the specified lists can be assigned to them:

```
player1 := White;
my_piece := knight;
```

Thus, the enumerated types enable the programmer to operate within the domain of the problem rather than that of the representation — a very important advantage.

In Ada, the members of an enumerated type can also be characters. For example:

```
type digit is
        ('0', '1', '2', '3', '4', '5', '6', '7', '8', '9');
```

It can even have a mixture of characters and names:

```
type nursery is
        ('a', 'b', 'c', tumble, down, dee);
```

The advantage of this is that it allows character sets to be defined as enumerated types. Indeed, this is how the type character is defined. It has the form:

```
type character is
        (nul, soh, stx, ... '}', '~', del);
```

The full definition contains 128 values, exactly as listed in Figure 4-2. However, since programmers can write their own definitions in the same way, they can redefine character to be some other set if necessary.

The operations which can be applied to enumerated types are straightforward. The simplest ones are tests for equality and inequality:

```
if my_piece = pawn ...
```

As mentioned at the start, the list of values specifies an ordering and so the other relational operators can also be applied:

```
if my_piece ≤ rook ...
```

The ordering is also reflected in the following three functions, as defined in Pascal:

ord (x)   gives the ordinal number of x — that is, its position in the list, the positions being numbered from 0.

succ (x)   gives the successor of x in the list; if x is the last member, it raises an error condition.

pred (x)   gives the predecessor of x in the list; if x is the first member, it raises an error condition.

If x is represented by its ordinal number, the function ord involves no run-time transformation. As in its application to characters, it is basically a compile-time, type-changing device (but see below). The functions succ and pred provide a mechanism for stepping through successive values of the type, either forwards or backwards.

In Ada, the functions are treated as attributes of the type and are called succ, pred, and pos; the inverse of pos is val. As indicated in the previous section, these must be preceded by the name of the type. For example:

```
player' succ (White)   =   Black
piece' pos (rook)   =   3
piece' val (3)   =   rook
```

Ada also provides the attributes first and last, which give the lowest and highest values of the type. These may seem redundant, since the values are explicitly stated in the type definition. For example, piece'last is king. However, the use of first and last makes the intention clearer, and no alterations will be needed if the type is extended. The attributes are also needed for generic types (see Section 9.6).

Another facility provided by Ada is the function image, which converts an enumeral to its corresponding character string:

```
piece' image (rook)   =   "ROOK"
digit' image ('3')   =   "'3'"
```

The first example illustrates Ada's preference for upper-case letters. The second shows that the string for a character includes its enclosing quotes. The inverse of image is value, which ignores leading and trailing blanks:

```
piece' value ("rook")   =   rook
piece' value ("   Rook   ")   =   rook
piece' value ("'3'")   =   '3'
```

These two functions open the way for the input/output of enumerals. Pascal does not have anything similar, and so input/output procedures have to be tediously programmed for each enumerated type that needs them.

As already indicated, the representation of an enumerated type is basically very simple: for a type with n values, it can be the set of integers 0 to $n-1$. This requires the minimum number of bits, namely $\lceil \log_2 n \rceil$. However, other representations are sometimes needed, possibly to match a system that is already in use. The following example shows how to specify one in Ada:

```
for piece use
        (pawn => 1, knight => 2, bishop => 4,
        rook => 8, queen => 16, king => 32);
```

The only restriction is that the numerical ordering must agree with the ordering of the original definition. The functions succ, pred, ord, and val can still be used, though their implementation will be less efficient. Similar considerations apply if the type is used for indexing.

4.7 SUBRANGE TYPES

A *subrange* type is a set of consecutive values that are part of some other type. In Pascal, it is specified by giving the lower and upper limits of the range:

```
type   percentage = 0..100;
       minor_piece = knight..rook;
```

The former is a subrange of type integer; the latter is a subrange of type piece, as defined in the preceding section. The enclosing type is called the *host type*, or *supertype*. In Ada, the equivalent declarations begin with the symbol **subtype**, and they have to specify the host type explicitly:

```
subtype percentage is integer range 0..120;
subtype minor_piece is piece range knight..rook;
```

This is more verbose; but as the next section shows, it follows the general pattern that Ada uses for defining subtypes. The **range** clause is known as a *constraint*. A briefer form is allowed for defining subranges of integers:

```
type percentage is range 0..100;
```

But in this case percentage is a *new* type, rather than a *sub*type, and its usage is therefore more restricted (see Section 4.9). In either case, the operator **in** enables the program to test a variable of the host type, to see if it lies in the specified range:

```
if i in percentage ...
```

Subrange types do not introduce any new values and so their benefits may not be immediately obvious. After all, any computation that is done using percentage entities could also be done using integer ones. So why bother with a type such as percentage? Several answers can be given.

1. Subranges are already present in the handling of array subscripts, since these are restricted to discrete ranges with lower and upper bounds. So subrange types are a generalization of a familiar concept.

2. The type definitions give readers of the program a clearer picture of what is going on. For example, the above declarations suggest that percentage variables will represent percentages, and that their values will lie within the stated range.

3. The implementation can check that the values *do* lie within the range, and can signal an error if they stray outside.

4. The values can be represented by fewer bits — a factor that may have advantages when large amounts of data are being stored.

A subrange can be formed from any discrete type, including integer, character, an enumerated type, or another subrange type. In Pascal, the lower and upper limits must be constants. In Ada, though, they can be any expressions with values belonging to the host type, and if necessary they will be evaluated when the type definition is elaborated at run-time. So, for example, two values lolim and hilim can be read from input and then used (on entry to a block) for defining a range:

subtype index **is** integer **range** lolim..hilim;

This is relevant to the handling of dynamic arrays — that is, arrays whose bounds are not fixed until run-time (see Volume II).

4.8 SUBTYPES

A *subtype* is a type whose values are a subset of some other type. Subranges are an obvious example, as the above definition of percentage makes clear:

subtype percentage **is** integer **range** 0..100;

The symbol **subtype** announces the nature of the declaration. As mentioned in the previous section, the type integer is the *host type*, or *supertype*, from which the subset is taken. The **range** expression is a *constraint*, and it determines the subset of integer values which belong to percentage.

As always, a type has to be characterized not only by its set of values but also by the operations that can be applied to it. In the case of subtypes, the general rule is that the subtype *inherits* the operations of its host type. In other words, any operation applicable to the host type is also applicable to the subtype. For example, if u and v are percentage variables, operations such as '+' and '*' can be applied to them. This may seem straightforward, but in fact it leaves several questions to be answered:

1. What is the type of a number such as 10? Is it integer, or percentage, or both, or neither?

2. What is the type of an expression such as u + v? The trouble is that if u + v has type percentage, there will be a run-time error if u + v > 100.

3. If i is an integer variable, what is the status of mixed-mode expressions such as i + u?

Pascal and Ada resolve these issues by stating that for the purpose of evaluating expressions, subtype values shall be treated as though they belong to the host type. The only effect of the constraint is that it restricts the set of values that can be assumed by the subtype objects (variables, parameters, etc.). So the following assignments are all legal:

```
u := v;                  -- no problems
i := u + 10;             -- mixed modes OK
u := u + v;              -- possible range error
v := i;                  -- possible range error
```

The last two will require a run-time check to ensure that the range conditions are satisfied.
If they are exceeded, a range_error exception is raised.

Ada applies the concept of a subtype to several other situations. The basic form of a
subtype declaration is

> **subtype** *new_name* **is** *old_name constraint*;

The *old_name* is the host type and, depending on its nature, there are five kinds of constraint that can be applied to it.

1. A *range* constraint — the host can be any discrete or numeric type, and the constraint limits its range of values. It is introduced by the symbol **range**, as
   described in the previous section.

2. A *floating-point* constraint — the host is a floating-point type, and the constraint
   is a relative precision and/or a range constraint. The relative precision is introduced by the symbol **digits**, as described in Section 3.8.

3. A *fixed-point* constraint — the host is a fixed-point type, and the constraint is an
   absolute precision and/or a range constraint. The absolute precision is introduced
   by the symbol **delta**, as described in Section 3.8.

4. An *index* constraint — the host is an array type with unspecified bounds, and the
   constraint supplies the bounds (see Volume II).

5. A *discriminant* constraint — the host is a record type with an unspecified
   discriminant, and the constraint supplies the discriminant (see Volume II).

In every case the ground rules are the same. When appearing in expressions, the subtype
entities are treated as part of the host type; they therefore inherit the host type's operations and can be assigned to host type objects. But if an assignment is made in the other
direction — from the host type to the subtype — a check is needed to ensure that the
relevant constraint is satisfied.

4.9 DERIVED TYPES

As remarked in Section 1, a high-level language can use type information to ensure that
operations are applied in a meaningful fashion. For example, addition can be used for
types integer and real, but not for Boolean or character. Most high-level languages
enforce type security of this kind.

The policy is a good one as far as it goes. Unfortunately, though, it still allows us to
do meaningless things. To take a popular example, suppose that we are processing data

concerning people's heights and weights. Using Ada's subtype facility, we can limit their values to appropriate ranges:

```
subtype height is integer range 50 .. 250;     -- in cm
subtype weight is integer range 1 .. 150;      -- in kg
```

We can then declare variables of these types:

```
my_height : height;
my_weight : weight;
```

The trouble is that, having done all this, we can now write an assignment such as

```
my_height := my_height + my_weight;
```

As explained in the previous section, this is a perfectly legitimate statement. Nevertheless, in terms of the real-world situation it is rather odd. Who would ever add a weight to a height? It would be just as peculiar as adding a truth value to a character. Perhaps high-level languages should extend their treatment of types so that they can enforce this more sophisticated form of security.

In response to these considerations, Ada introduces the concept of a *derived* type. It is designated by the symbol **new**, followed by the name of a previously declared type, known as the *parent* type, followed optionally by a constraint. For example:

```
type height is new integer range 50..250;
type weight is new integer range 1..150;
```

The effect is that height and weight are new types, distinct from all other types. They inherit the standard operations of the parent type integer, but in expressions and assignments they cannot be mixed with integer entities, nor with one another. The above addition of a weight to a height is therefore illegal, exactly as intended.

To take this a step further, consider the assignment:

```
my_height := my_height + 2;
```

This is legal, because the constant 2 is taken to be of type height. By contrast, if i is an integer variable, the assignment

```
my_height := my_height + i;
```

is not legal, because of the mixed modes. To make it legal, the name height can be used as a function to force a type conversion:

```
my_height := my_height + height (i);
```

It can even be used to force a conversion from type weight:

```
my_height := my_height + height (my_weight);
```

So we can still do meaningless things if we really insist!

This is all very well, and it meets the basic objective that was outlined at the start. However, there are some conceptual problems lurking in the background. The expression my_height + 2 makes the assumption that two heights can meaningfully be added to form a third one, which all seems very reasonable. On the other hand, an expression such as

2 * my_height is more questionable. It produces a result of type height, which is probably the one intended, but in doing so it makes three dubious assumptions:

- that the expression 2 is a height, instead of a plain integer;

- that two heights can meaningfully be multiplied together;

- that the product of two heights is a height, instead of something more like an area.

In this case, the false assumptions lead to the right conclusion. But three wrongs do not usually make a right, and so the security is not as good as it might have seemed.

To override the default treatment of a derived type, it is possible to redefine the operators, using the notation for defining functions as described in Section 9.4. For example, consider the declaration of two types length and area:

```
type length is new integer range 0..100;
type area is new integer range 0..10000;
```

As indicated earlier, these can be abbreviated to the form:

```
type length is range 0..100;
type area is range 0..10000;
```

If side is a variable of type length, the default states that 2 * side will be a length, and so will side * side. To make the latter an area, the operator '*' can be redefined for the case when its arguments are both lengths:

```
function "*" (a, b : length) return area is
begin
    return area (a * b);
end "*";
```

Now side * side is an area, as required. Unfortunately, though, 2 * side is also an area, which is less desirable. This suggests that it might be better to interpret 2 as a plain integer, rather than a length. However, derived types were not designed for emulating the laws of physics, and so this is pushing them further than they were intended to go. A more comprehensive system, based on the physicists' notion of 'dimension', is described in Manner (1986).

FURTHER READING

An excellent introduction to data types is given in the book by J. C. Cleaveland (1986). For some of the more technical concepts, see Cardelli and Wegner (1986).

Chang (1985) discusses the *mod* operator for integers. A draft standard for floating-point numbers was published by the IEEE (1981), and its implications for programming were discussed by Fateman (1982). The final standard, ANSI/IEEE 754-1985, is reproduced in *SIGPLAN Notices* (IEEE, 1985). The Ada approach is based on the 'realistic' model of W. S. Brown (1979). For an 'idealist's' view, see Brent (1982).

The practical implications of floating-point arithmetic are discussed in textbooks on numerical analysis. A good example is Forsythe, Malcolm, and Moler (1977), whose introductory material is based on an earlier paper on the 'pitfalls of computation' (Forsythe, 1970). The classical work on round-off errors is Wilkinson (1963).

The conditional *and* and *or* were introduced by J. McCarthy (1960, 1963). For some recent comments on the subject, see Salvadori and Dumont (1979).

EXERCISES

Note   The phrase 'your language' refers to any high-level programming language with which you are familiar. Similarly, 'your machine' refers to any computer whose instruction set is known to you.

1   According to Section 4.2, there are two common ways of defining integer division. Method 1 defines the quotient to be entier (i/j); method 2 defines it to be floor (i/j) — hence the term 'floored division'.

Which definition is used in (a) your language and (b) your machine? Prove that with method 1 the remainder will have the same sign as i, and that with method 2 it will have the same sign as j.

2   Most languages define i **mod** j according to method 2 of Section 4.2. As remarked at the time, this has the drawback that the remainder may be negative even though j is positive. Given this version of **mod** and a positive value j, how would you compute the remainder as stipulated by method 2?

3   In your language, check the definition of i **mod** j, or MOD (I, J), or whatever, including the cases where i and/or j are negative (see Section 4.2).

The *mod* operation is useful for moving a variable i cyclically round the integers 0, 1, 2, ... n−1, with 0 being regarded as the successor of n−1. The assignment

$$i := (i + 1) \textbf{ mod } n$$

does precisely this: when i + 1 reaches the value n, the **mod** operation reduces it to 0. To move i in steps of size k, for some integer k > 1, the increment 1 is simply replaced by k. The **mod** ensures that the value remains within the range 0..n−1, as required. However, if k is negative, greater care is needed. Why?

What assignment gives a similar effect for cycling through the integers b, b+1, b+2, ... b+n−1? Compare this with other methods of producing the same effect.

4   If an integer n is repeatedly divided by k, how many steps will be needed to reduce it to 1? For example, if n = 32 and k = 2, successive results are 16, 8, 4, 2, and 1, and so the answer is 5. In general, with real arithmetic, the answer is $\log_k n$. However, suppose that integer division is used instead, taking the quotient and ignoring the remainder. In other words, suppose that each result is rounded downwards, computing x / k as $\lfloor x/k \rfloor$. Prove that the answer is then $\lfloor \log_k n \rfloor$. Now suppose that it is rounded upwards, computing x / k as $\lceil x/k \rceil$. Prove that the answer is $\lceil \log_k n \rceil$.

5   Suppose that the only available function for doing real-to-integer conversion is round (x). How would you use it to compute entier (x), floor (x), and ceiling (x)?

6   If your language allows integer exponentiation, as in the expression i ∗∗ j, what restrictions (if any) does it place on i and j? How is the operation defined and what is the type of its result?

7   Write a loop for evaluating the expression x ∗∗ i, where i is a non-negative integer. The simplest method is to use i multiplications. A faster method takes advantage of the fact that $x ** 2j = (x^2) ** j$. Use this, together with Pascal's function odd (i), or some equivalent function, to develop a fast exponentiation algorithm. How many iterations does it require? How many multiplications?

The formal derivation of the algorithm is covered in Exercise 8.18. For a detailed analysis and further improvements, see Knuth (1981), pp.441–466. For a discussion of some published Pascal algorithms and a list of references, see Hamilton (1986).

8   Just because a floating-point number system offers a precision of n decimal digits, it should not be assumed that in the course of a calculation every particular number has that precision. For one thing, the data may have less precision; for another, in a poorly designed algorithm the precision can be whittled away.

With n = 6, for example, suppose that 1.26514 is subtracted from 1.26589. How many significant digits will the result have?

The subtraction of almost equal values is a well-known hazard and should be avoided where possible. For example, the two roots of the equation

$$a x^2 + b x + c = 0$$

are $(-b \pm \sqrt{(b^2 - 4ac)}) / 2a$. If 4ac is very small compared with b^2, one of the roots runs into this difficulty. Which one? Can you find a better way of computing it? For a thorough discussion of this problem, see Forsythe (1969, 1970).

9   In *The Matador of the Five Towns*, Arnold Bennett describes the hero as having to wrestle with 'the incurable naughtiness of figures'. Show sympathy for his troubles by finding numbers which, on your computer or calculator, do not obey the following laws of arithmetic:

$$x + (y + z) = (x + y) + z$$
$$x * (y + z) = x * y + x * z$$
$$-(x - y) = y - x$$

10   Chapter 4 of Knuth (1981) opens with a quotation from Mrs La Touche (nineteenth century):

> I do hate sums. There is no greater mistake than to call arithmetic an exact science. There are ... hidden laws of number which it requires a mind like mine to perceive. For instance, if you add a sum from the bottom up, and then again from the top down, the result is always different.

Investigate the truth of this remark by writing a program to evaluate

$$1 - \frac{1}{2} + \frac{1}{3} - \frac{1}{4} + \frac{1}{5} - \cdots - \frac{1}{100}$$

first from left to right and then from right to left. Alternatively, try the first ten terms on your pocket calculator. Explain the reason for any differences that arise.

Similar difficulties occur in the evaluation of e^x using the formula:

$$e^x = 1 + \frac{x}{1!} + \frac{x^2}{2!} + \frac{x^3}{3!} + \cdots$$

Try evaluating it for $x = -5.5$ to an accuracy of five decimal places. (The correct answer is $0.00408677\ldots$.) Can you find a better way? For a discussion of the problem, see Forsythe (1970) and Forsythe, Malcolm, and Moler (1977).

11 A common problem in statistics is to compute the *average*, or *mean*, of a set of numbers $x_1, x_2, \ldots x_n$, defined by:

$$\mu = (x_1 + x_2 + \cdots x_n) / n$$

For large values of n, what are the dangers in simply accumulating the sum and then dividing by n? Can you suggest a better algorithm?

The *standard deviation* of the series is the quantity σ given by:

$$\sigma^2 = ((x_1 - \mu)^2 + (x_2 - \mu)^2 + \cdots + (x_n - \mu)^2) / n$$

What are the dangers here? Can you find a better algorithm? — preferably one that calculates μ and σ in parallel. For a discussion and some earlier references on the problem, see Cloutier and Matthew (1983).

12 Section 4.4 discussed the problem of evaluating expressions of the form *C1* **and** *C2*. In particular, it observed that if *C1* turns out to be false, the code for *C2* can be skipped. This has the implied advantage that the code will be more efficient, and if *C2* is sufficiently complicated this will certainly be the case. But what if *C2* is simply a Boolean variable? In any case, if *C1* turns out to be true, the code may well be *less* efficient. Investigate the detailed timing of these factors on your machine. What is the *real* advantage of using the conditional *and* and *or*?

13 Describe informally the significance of the following two Boolean expressions:

(p **and** q) **or** (q **and** r) **or** (r **and** p)
(**not** p **and** q **and** r) **or** (**not** q **and** r **and** p)
or (**not** r **and** p **and** q)

Can you transform them into equivalent expressions that might be computed more efficiently? Consider the influence of (a) the use or non-use of the conditional *and* and *or*, and (b) the probabilities of p, q and r being true.

The simplification of Boolean expressions has been extensively studied in the design of digital hardware. In that context, the above expressions would be written much more compactly:

PQ + QR + RP
$\overline{P}$QR + $\overline{Q}$RP + $\overline{R}$PQ

In programming, though, Boolean expressions are seldom very complicated and so brevity is less important.

14 In your language, how (if at all) is the *newline* character represented? Note that in the ASCII set it is treated as two separate characters — *carriage return* and *line feed*. This provides greater flexibility but can occasionally be inconvenient.

15 In your language, if ch is a character, how would you determine whether or not it is (a) a digit, (b) a letter, (c) an upper-case letter, (d) a space, tab, or newline?

16 Investigate the collating sequence of the characters in your language and/or implementation. What order does it give to the names P Arker, P.Arker, Parker, parker, and park4?

17 In processing data about people, it is often necessary to record their sex. Discuss the advantages and drawbacks of doing this by means of the following types:

   (a) a Boolean type — false for female, true for male;
   (b) a character type — 'F' for female, 'M' for male;
   (c) an enumerated type — (female, male).

Note that the use of a Boolean type introduces the operations *and*, *or*, and *not*. Might there be any advantages in this?

18 Section 4.7 remarked that the use of a subrange type such as 0 .. 100 enables the compiler to represent the values using fewer bits than it would for type integer. How many bits would be needed for the range 1900 .. 2000? (There are two possible answers, depending on the representation: what are their relative merits?) How many bits would be needed for the range 0 .. n if n is not known until run-time?

19 Section 4.7 considered types that are subranges of other types. Investigate the possibility of generalizing this to types which are *subsets* of other types. For example, here is a type for vowels:

> **type** vowel **is** character **subset** 'a', 'e', 'i', 'o', 'u';

A variable of this type would be restricted to these five specified characters. An operator could be provided for testing set membership:

> **if** ch **in** vowel ...

This would determine whether or not the character ch is a vowel. Compare this with the **set** facility of Pascal (see Section 2.7). Why (if at all) should sets be handled differently from ranges?

MACHINE ARCHITECTURE

5.1 THE VON NEUMANN COMPUTER

Programming a computer is a bit like driving a car: to obtain the best performance, the practitioner should know how it works. This is especially true for the systems engineer, who checks the parts and 'tunes' the system, much like a motor mechanic. But it is also true in some measure for anyone whose program consumes major resources — whether of processing, or memory, or input/output, or anything else. To explain its behavior, to improve its performance, or even to track down obscure bugs, the programmer needs to understand what is going on behind the scenes. Accordingly, this chapter makes a brief excursion into the realms of machine architecture, looking at the features that are most relevant to ordinary programming. Later chapters will use the material to describe the implementation of various high-level programming structures.

The machine to be considered is the so-called 'von Neumann computer'. The term is a generic one, referring to any computer that adopts the basic architecture described in a classic paper by Arthur Burks, Herman Goldstine, and John von Neumann (1946). The ideas expressed in that paper were embodied in the 'first generation' computers and the remarkable fact is that so far, with few exceptions, later generations have retained the family likeness. They have elaborated the basic features, and added to them, and produced endless variations on them; but at heart they are still von Neumann machines.

As a matter of historical justice, it should be remarked that these basic features were not all invented by von Neumann. On the contrary, some of them had been developed by Charles Babbage for his analytical engine a hundred years earlier. Others may be attributed to J. Presper Eckert and John Mauchly, whose Electronic Numerical Integrator and Computer (ENIAC) was working in 1946, and historians can point to other pockets of activity that anticipated various aspects of von Neumann's proposals. The origins of the key feature, namely the stored program concept (see Section 5.4), have been the subject of claims, counter-claims, and considerable debate. As with many other revolutionary ideas, there may well have been several sources and contributors. But just as Darwin's name is associated with evolution, so is von Neumann's with the digital computer. In each case the name comes from the person who enunciated the germinating idea with particular force and clarity.

The next few sections outline the principal features of von Neumann's proposals — the structure of the main memory, the use of high-speed registers, the stored program concept, and the sequencing of instructions. The remaining sections follow their historical development through a number of important variations and additions.

5.2 MAIN MEMORY

The first key to a von Neumann machine is its *main memory*. This is a set of *cells*, numbered 0, 1, ... N−1, each capable of holding some unit of information (see Figure 5-1). The numbers 0, 1, ... N−1 are used by the hardware to refer to the cells and are known as their *absolute addresses*. Overall, the memory can be described as a *linear address space*. The low-numbered cells constitute the *low* end of the memory and the high-numbered cells are the *high* end. Note that in the figure the low end is at the top and the high end is at the bottom. This may seem unnecessarily confusing. Would it be better, perhaps, to number them like the floors of a building, with the high numbers at the top? The answer is, definitely not! The cells are more like the lines of a program or the rows of a matrix, both of which are always numbered downwards. It is therefore more consistent, and in the wider context less confusing, to treat them in the same way.

On the earliest machines a cell was a full n-bit word, as described in Chapter 2. The word was capable of holding a number and was therefore the basic storage unit for numerical computations. However, with the rise of business data processing, the handling of characters became increasingly important and so machines were designed on which the unit of addressing was the byte. These are the machines most commonly used today. A few machines go even further and use bit-addressing. This offers the maximum flexibility, but the advantages have to be weighed against the complexity of the hardware and the need to use three extra bits for addresses.

The cell is not necessarily the only unit on which the hardware operates. For example, most byte-addressing machines also retain the concept of a word. Typically, on smaller machines the word-length is two bytes, and on larger machines it is four, six, eight, or even ten bytes. Instructions are provided for accessing words as on a conventional word-addressing machine. In some cases the words are restricted to starting at specific 'boundaries'. For example, with four-byte words the effective word addresses might be 0, 4, 8, 12, and so on. In others they can start at an arbitrary byte position. Some machines also provide instructions for accessing double-words, half-words, and (believe it or not) third-words.

The hardware provides *direct* access to these units in the sense that, given any address, it can retrieve or update the information in the related cell without reference to any of the other cells (see Section 5.8). In its raw form, it also provides *random* access,

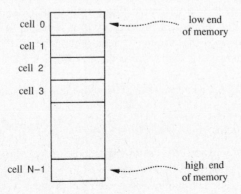

Figure 5-1   Main memory

in the sense that all cells can be accessed equally quickly. On some machines, though, the raw form is overlaid with a *virtual memory*, in which case this desirable property is sacrificed in favor of size. The term 'random' must therefore be interpreted with discretion. In principle, all cells are equal; in practice, it turns out that at any particular moment some may be more equal than others. The reasons for this are discussed in Section 5.12.

The size of the main memory is usually measured in bytes. A convenient unit used to be the kilobyte ($= 2^{10}$ bytes), sizes being given as 256K, 640K, and so on. More recently, tumbling costs have allowed sizes to move into the megabyte range ($= 2^{20}$ bytes), with memories being anything from 1M to 256M. The next step is the gigabyte ($= 2^{30}$). This trend has had beneficial effects on programming practices, and it seems set to continue for several years to come. Gone are the days when it was necessary to squeeze the last literal bit out of the paltry few that were available. Instead, the programmer is increasingly free to forget the limitations of storage and to program in ways that match the problem rather than the machine.

5.3   REGISTERS

Section 2.2 introduced assignment statements of the form

$$A \leftarrow B \ op \ C$$

where A, B, and C denoted arbitrary words in the main memory of the computer. If this were a single machine instruction, it would be known as a *three-address* instruction. It involves three addresses, namely those of A, B and C, and accordingly it makes three memory accesses — two 'fetches' and a 'store'. Similarly,

$$A \leftarrow B$$
$$A \leftarrow op \ B$$
$$A \ op \ B$$

are all *two-address* instructions, though the last one (being equivalent to A $\leftarrow$ A *op* B) still requires three memory accesses.

In practice, the memory accesses tend to be slower than the operations themselves. So, in order to reduce the need for them, most machines are equipped with high-speed *registers*. The earlier computers were designed with one such register. It was called the *accumulator*, since it was used for accumulating results (much like the display register of a pocket calculator.) But the use of eight or sixteen registers is now fairly standard. Their size is the word-size of the machine, typical figures being 16, 24, 32, and 36 bits. Following common practice, we shall refer to them as R0, R1, R2, ... and, in general, as Ri and Rj.

In considering their use it is easiest to start with the *move* instruction. As stated in Section 2.2, its basic form is:

$$destination \leftarrow source$$

With the introduction of registers, the destination can be of two kinds — either a memory location or a register. Similarly, the source can be of three kinds — a memory location, a register, or a constant. The six combinations lead to six versions of the instruction, as tabulated in Figure 5-2. The last column of the table gives the number of memory

Instruction type	Notation	Memory accesses
memory-to-memory	A ← B	2
memory-to-register	Ri ← B	1
register-to-memory	A ← Ri	1
register-to-register	Ri ← Rj	0
constant-to-memory	A ← *const*	1 or 2
constant-to-register	Ri ← *const*	0 or 1

Figure 5-2   The move instruction

accesses that each requires, ranging from two for the memory-to-memory version down to none for the register-to-register. If the source is a constant, the number of accesses depends on where the constant comes from. The lower figure assumes that it is stored as part of the instruction itself, in which case it is called an *immediate operand*. If it is too large to be included in the instruction, it has to be stored in a separate location and so an extra memory reference is involved.

As already mentioned, the number of memory references is usually the most important factor in determining the speed of an operation. The time for accessing a register is negligible in comparison. For example, the memory-to-memory move

> A ← B

is not significantly faster than the sequence

> Ri ← B
> A ← Ri

which achieves the same effect. For this reason many machines do not provide the memory-to-memory move. Similar arguments apply to the size of the code. The addresses of A and B are usually the dominant factors, and so the second code sequence may be only a byte or two longer than the first.

To illustrate the benefits of using registers, consider the task of interchanging the values in A and B. In most high-level languages, it is necessary to introduce a third variable, temp say, and to write something like this:

> temp := A;
> A := B;
> B := temp;

If temp is a word in main memory, this involves six memory accesses. By contrast, an assembly code program can use a register instead:

> Ri ← A
> A ← B
> B ← Ri

This requires only four memory accesses and so it runs faster. Of course, a good compiler might optimize the high-level version by allocating a register to temp, in which case the two versions would be equivalent. However, this is not as simple as it may sound, and so it is not always done.

Similar considerations apply to most other operations. Take, for example, the addition:

$$A \leftarrow B + C$$

As implied earlier, some machines would implement this as a single, three-address instruction. More commonly, though, it has to be implemented as three one-address instructions, using a register Ri to accumulate the sum of B and C:

$$Ri \leftarrow B$$
$$Ri + C$$
$$A \leftarrow Ri$$

This looks as though it would be slower than the single instruction; but since both versions require three memory accesses, the difference between them is unlikely to be significant. For more elaborate expressions, the registers offer greater flexibility and a definite advantage in the speed of execution (see Exercise 3).

With high-level languages, the need for machine-independence means that programmers are seldom given any control over the registers, and so the choice of optimal code is left to the compiler. However, some languages allow the program to give 'hints' to the compiler, possibly in the form of special comments. In Ada they can be provided by *pragmas* (see Section 7.9). An implementation can define pragmas of its own, and it is easy to imagine one such as:

$$\textbf{pragma} \text{ register (temp);}$$

If the compiler accepted the hint, temp would be allocated a register rather than a word in memory.

5.4   THE STORED PROGRAM CONCEPT

What was the most significant innovation of the von Neumann machine? Some people might argue that it was the use of binary arithmetic instead of decimal. Others, though, would point unhesitatingly to the *stored program concept* — that is, the idea that the instructions of a program could be stored in the computer's memory. Since the days of the Jacquard loom (1804), mechanical machines had stored their programs on punched cards or paper tape, each instruction being executed directly from input. However, this made it hard to execute loops, and in any case it was far too slow for an electronic machine.

To overcome these difficulties, instructions for the ENIAC were supplied manually by setting a large number of connections and switches — the original hand-wired programs! But this in turn was not very satisfactory, being a very slow and tedious business for the programmers. Von Neumann's team therefore proposed the crucial concept of reading the instructions from cards or tape and storing them in the computer's own memory. Once the program was in the memory, it could be executed from there. This combined the best of both worlds — ease of programming and speed of execution — and it paved the way for a wide range of other important developments. Several groups immediately took up the proposals and their stored-program machines were in operation by the late 1940s. The computing world has never looked back.

In order to implement the stored program concept, a convention must first be established for representing instructions as bit patterns within the computer's memory. The hardware is then designed so that it responds to the bit patterns by executing the intended operations. A program is *encoded* when its instructions are converted to a suitable set of bit patterns. It is *decoded* when the hardware reads the bit patterns and reacts in the appropriate way. In the earliest days the encoding was done by hand: the programmers converted the instructions to binary (or octal or hexadecimal) and supplied them to the computer in that form. They did coding in its most literal, basic sense. In due course, though, they invented assemblers and 'autocode' programs to save themselves this trouble, and so the detailed representation of their programs gradually slipped from view. With the advent of high-level languages, it disappeared entirely.

The basic principle of encoding instructions is quite simple. A typical instruction consists of an *operation* and a number of *operands*. For example, the instruction

R5 + A

denotes the operation of memory-to-register addition with register 5 as one operand and word A as the other. Each part is coded separately. Thus the addition is represented by an integer 'opcode', register 5 can be represented simply as 5, and word A is represented by its address. So if the opcode were 27 and the address 1688, the instruction would be the triple $(27, 5, 1688)$. The three integers are packed into a group of bytes according to some standard format. For example, the designers might allocate eight bits for the opcode, three for the register, and 21 for the address. The instruction would then fit neatly into a 32-bit word:

opcode	*reg*	*address*
27	5	1688

0   8 11   31

The hardware is constructed so that it will unpack the three fields and initiate the required operation. As another example, consider the instruction:

R3 ← 255

If the constant-to-register move has the opcode 38, this could have the form:

opcode	*reg*	*immediate operand*
38	3	255

0   8 11   31

As mentioned in the previous section, the constant 255 is stored as an 'immediate operand' and so it does not have to be retrieved from a separate location. But if the constant required more than 21 bits, it would have to be stored elsewhere and a memory-to-register move would be needed instead.

These examples show that operands can be of several kinds — registers, addresses, and constants (immediate operands). In practice, the situation is further complicated by the provision of several different addressing modes, as described in later sections. An operand may therefore consist of several parts — a mode, a register number, and possibly a constant or an address. To cope with all the different combinations, the instructions have a variety of lengths and formats. On a VAX computer, for example, the first byte of an instruction contains its opcode and extra bytes are added according to the number and nature of the operands.

The stored program concept introduces a serious problem. The trouble is that since programs and data are both stored as ordinary bit patterns, their roles can become confused. A program can start operating on itself as if it were data; conversely, a section of data can be 'executed' as if it were ordinary code. Either way, the program is liable to crash in an abrupt and puzzling fashion. In the early days, programmers took advantage of the flexibility by arranging for programs to alter their own address fields, or even their own operation fields, at run-time. This enabled them to work around some of the limitations of the instruction sets and to produce 'clever' effects. Nowadays such practices are frowned on: for reasons both of logic and of practical necessity, it is preferable that programs should be fixed, unalterable entities. Accordingly, some machines impose a rigid division between programs and data. The hardware prevents the former from being overwritten and the latter from being executed. This retains the advantages of the stored program concept, but avoids its potential hazards.

5.5   INSTRUCTION SEQUENCING

In the normal mode of operation, the instructions of a program are executed *sequentially*: that is, each one is completed before the next one is begun. This is very much simpler than allowing two or more to execute in parallel (see Chapter 11).

In order to control the execution sequence, there must be a mechanism for determining each instruction's successor. On some of the early computers each instruction had to designate its successor explicitly (see Section 8.6). However, von Neumann's proposals included a much better mechanism in which control passes by default to the next instruction in memory. It is only the occasional *branch* instruction that can cause this sequence to be broken (see below). The scheme has several advantages:

- The representation of the program reflects the flow of control more directly.

- Since there is no need for each instruction to store the address of its successor, the instructions are shorter.

- The hardware can fetch the next instruction from memory before the current one has been completed, and this makes the execution faster.

The last of these is known as *instruction lookahead*. It is interesting to note that the lookahead would be much harder to implement if the next instruction could be overwritten by the current one. This illustrates a point that was made at the end of the previous section — that there are benefits in not allowing programs to modify their own code.

To implement this strategy, the machine has a register that holds the address of the next instruction to be executed. It is known by a variety of names, including *instruction pointer*, *program counter*, and *sequence control register*. The first of these is reasonably descriptive and will be abbreviated here to IP. Using IP, the machine executes each instruction in two phases:

1.   The *fetch cycle* — the hardware fetches the instruction at the address given by IP, extracting first the opcode and then the associated operands. Having done that, it sets IP to the address of the instruction that comes next.

2.   The *execute cycle* — the hardware then executes the specified operation. On completion, it returns to phase 1.

As indicated in phase 1, the basic idea is that as each instruction is executed the hardware automatically advances IP to the address of the next one. However, if the instruction specifies a branch to address α, phase 2 sets IP to α and so control will pass to α instead.

On some machines IP is a special register provided for the purpose and it can only be altered by these sequencing mechanisms. On others, though, it is one of the standard registers Ri and in principle it can be treated in the same way as any other register. This increases the flexibility and also the attendant hazards. For example, if IP were used for floating-point arithmetic, the effects on the sequencing would be rather drastic.

As mentioned above, a *branch* instruction can change the flow of a program so that the static sequence is broken and control moves to a specified point elsewhere. The simplest form is the *unconditional* branch which does this unconditionally, transferring control to the instruction in some other location, L say. If the expression @L denotes the address of L (as opposed to its contents), the instruction can be written as:

$$IP \leftarrow @L$$

However, it is more usual and more helpful to have a special notation for it, a familiar one being:

goto L

The **goto** symbol reminds us that whatever programmers may think of **goto** statements in high-level languages, the corresponding operation is certainly there in the hardware. Indeed, the computer would be paralysed without it.

In most programs, L will be a symbolic address known as a *label*. It is written in front of the instruction to which it refers, as in the following sequence:

```
L :    R4 + 1
       A + B
       goto L
```

When the program is compiled the corresponding address is calculated, and this is the value used by the branch instruction. If L denotes a point earlier in the sequence, the branch is known as a *backward* jump; otherwise it is a *forward* jump. The backward jump is the more radical of the two since it enables instruction sequences to be repeated many times over.

A *conditional* branch allows the program to choose between different courses of action at run-time. The basic form is

if *condition* **goto** L

where the *condition* is some simple test. Since the result of an operation is usually found in a register, one form of test is to compare the contents of a register with zero. For example:

if Ri = 0 **goto** L

Similar tests can be provided for '≠', '<', '≤', '>', and '≥'. A more flexible approach is to test *status bits*, or *condition codes*. These are set by any instruction that operates on data (as opposed to merely moving it), and they record information about the result. For example, on the IBM 370-series computers, two bits record the following four conditions:

    00   —   result is zero;
    01   —   result is less than zero;
    10   —   result is greater than zero;
    11   —   result is out of range (overflow).

Arithmetic operations automatically set these bits to indicate the condition of the result. A *test* operation sets them to indicate the condition of a single operand, and a *compare* operation sets them by comparing two operands. For example, the test

if A = B **goto** L

can be implemented by comparing A with B and testing for result-is-zero. This is safer than evaluating A − B and comparing the result with zero, since A − B could be out of range. The approach has several other advantages:

  •   it includes overflow as a special case;
  •   it tests two bits rather than a full-length word;
  •   it can be used for memory-to-memory arithmetic;
  •   it does not depend on the representation of the result.

The last factor means that the same branch instructions can be used for the results of all comparisons, whether fixed-point, floating-point, single-length, double-length, or anything else. In particular, they can be used for the results of lexicographical comparisons as needed in the handling of non-numeric data.

5.6 SUBROUTINES

The preceding sections have described the basic features of a von Neumann computer. The remaining ones consider various ways in which they have been elaborated. Continuing with the theme of instruction sequencing, they look first at subroutines and then at interrupts. They then examine various mechanisms for accessing the main memory and for handling input/output.

As originally conceived, a *subroutine* is a group of instructions that can be executed as a single unit. It performs some specific function — for example, calculating a square root — and can be used at several different points within a program. If it meets a widespread need, it can be placed in a subroutine *library* and made available for general use.

There are two ways in which the code of a subroutine can be incorporated in a program. If it is an *inline* subroutine, a complete copy of its code is inserted at every point where it is needed. More usually, though, a single copy is stored elsewhere and control is transferred to it by means of special branch instruction (see below). This is known as *calling* the subroutine. On completion, the main program is resumed just as if the subroutine had been a single hardware instruction.

The sequence of events is depicted in Figure 5-3. Control leaves the main program at the *point of call* and the subroutine is then *entered* at its *entry point*. On completion, control leaves at an *exit point* and moves back to the *return address* following the point of call. The effect is achieved by two special instructions — the *subroutine branch* and the *return*. The former records the return address in some agreed location and then transfers control to the entry point of the subroutine. The latter recovers the return address from the agreed location (on the assumption that it has not been overwritten) and assigns it to IP. The agreed location is usually one of the following:

- a standard register;

- a word that is associated with the subroutine;

- a word at the top of a stack.

The possibilities are related to the extent to which subroutines can activate each other. The first method has the drawback that if subroutine X calls subroutine Y it will overwrite its own return address. The second avoids this danger, except in the case where X calls itself; so it cannot support recursion. The third is the most general and, as we shall see in Section 5.11, it has had a significant influence on machine architecture.

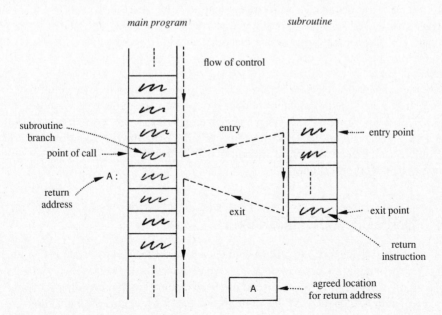

Figure 5-3   Executing a subroutine

5.7   INTERRUPTS

An *interrupt* is an event that suspends the normal execution of a program and transfers control to some other sequence of instructions. It is triggered by an interrupt *condition*. Some familiar conditions are arithmetic overflow and address-out-of-range, both of which arise from unorthodox actions within the program. Other conditions arise from external causes, such as the 'tick' of a clock or the completion of an input/output operation. In such cases they usually have to be transparent to the executing program.

When the interrupt occurs, control is transferred to an address that is associated with the interrupt in some standard way. For example, it can be stored in a location that is known to the hardware or that is specified by the interrupt itself. The resulting instruction sequence constitutes the *interrupt handler* and its execution is known as *servicing* the interrupt. Since the interrupted program may have to be resumed later on, the interrupt mechanism must preserve its resumption address. This is similar to the way in which a subroutine branch instruction saves the return address. However, there is an important difference: if the interrupt is to be transparent to the executing program, the program's registers and status bits have to be saved as well. The handler resumes the program by executing a 'return from interrupt' instruction, which re-instates this information and returns control to the resumption address. Thus the interrupt handler can be regarded as a special sort of subroutine — one that is initiated by an unscheduled event and not by an explicit instruction.

Problems arise if an interrupt occurs while another one is being serviced. For example, there is the danger (as with subroutines) that the resumption information will be overwritten. Facilities are therefore provided for disabling the interrupts while the critical part of the handler is being executed. During the non-critical part, it may be best for the program to accept urgent interrupts but to defer any others. (Clocks keep ticking but line printers can wait.) The interrupt conditions may therefore have various *priorities*, with the consequence that a handler can only be interrupted by a condition of higher priority. Alternatively, and more flexibly, some machines provide a *mask* register with a bit for each interrupt condition. Each interrupt can then be enabled or disabled by setting or unsetting its bit.

Interrupts are tricky things to handle and so they are usually concealed behind several layers of software. The programmer seldom has to know about them, even though they are used for input/output and other mundane activities (see Section 5.14). Some languages allow handlers to be written for special cases, such as overflow (see Section 8.14). A high-level version of interrupts will be described in Section 11.13, in the context of parallel programming.

5.8   DIRECT ADDRESSING

Most computers have several *addressing modes* for referring to locations in main memory. The simplest is *direct addressing*, which refers to the location with address α by specifying α itself. It is the mode that has been assumed in the preceding sections for the references to A, B, and C. As shown in Section 5.4, for example, the instruction

R5 + A

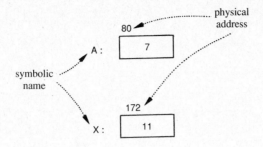

Figure 5-4   Pictorial notation

is implemented by storing the address of A as an operand of the opcode for '+'. When the instruction is executed, the machine uses the address to access that location.

Figure 5-4 introduces some pictorial notation for describing the situation. It shows two locations, one named A at address 80 containing the integer 7, and one named X at address 172 containing 11. As can be seen, the locations are represented by boxes with their contents written inside. Each box is labeled by its name, the labeling being indicated by a colon, and a superscript gives its address. In most cases the particular address is of no interest and so it can be omitted.

As a further example of direct addressing, consider the memory-to-memory move instruction:

$$A \leftarrow X$$

This says 'take the content of location X and assign it to location A'. The occurrence of X on the right-hand side refers to the *content* of X, namely the integer 11, and therefore involves an implied *content-taking* operation. By contrast, the occurrence of A on the left-hand side refers only to the *address* of A: the original content of A, namely the integer 7, is never used.

Suppose now that A has to be assigned the *address* of X (as opposed to its content) so that it takes the value 172. Using the '@' symbol from Section 5.5, this can be written as

$$A \leftarrow @X$$

which says, 'take the *address* of location X and assign it to A'. In effect, the '@' symbol suppresses the content-taking operation that would otherwise be implied. The instruction looks more complicated than the previous one, but in fact it is simpler. It is exactly equivalent to

$$A \leftarrow 172$$

and is therefore an ordinary constant-to-memory move.

5.9   INDIRECT ADDRESSING

Figure 5-5(a) shows the effect of the preceding assignment: location A contains 172, which is the address of location X. As usual, though, the detailed addresses are of no particular concern, and so it is more helpful to display the relationship between A and X as in Figure 5-5(b). The arrow denotes a *pointer* and we say that A *points to* X.

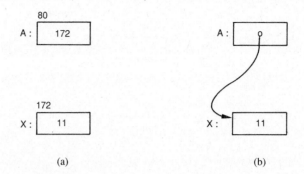

(a)   (b)

Figure 5-5   Indirect addressing

Suppose now that a program needs to access the location that A points to (which happens to be X). This can be done by a mechanism known as *indirect addressing*. Given the address of A, the mechanism retrieves the pointer (which is the address of X); using the pointer it then accesses the required location (namely X). Thus X is accessed indirectly via A. In Pascal's notation, the address is written as A↑, meaning 'the location that A points to'. For example, in the situation of Figure 5-5(b), the instruction

$$A\uparrow \leftarrow 22$$

assigns 22 to location X. Similarly,

$$R5 \leftarrow A\uparrow$$

copies the content of X into R5. More formally, the indirect address A↑ can be defined by the relation:

$$@ (A\uparrow) \quad \equiv \quad A$$

This states that the address denoted by the expression A↑ is simply the content of A.

It is interesting to note that whereas the '@' symbol calls for one *less* content-taking operation, the '↑' symbol calls for one *more*. Thus A↑ on the left of an assignment requires one content-taking operation instead of none, and on the right it requires two instead of one. As the definition implies, the '@' and '↑' symbols are, in some sense, inverses of each other. However, since '@' does not represent an actual operation, this should not be pressed too closely. As remarked earlier, its role is simply to suppress an operation that would otherwise be implied.

Indirect addressing can be extended over several 'levels'. Figure 5-6 shows three-level indirection, in which A points to a location, which points to a location, which points to a location, which contains 33. The assignment

$$A\uparrow\uparrow\uparrow \leftarrow 44$$

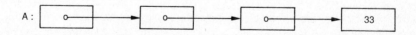

Figure 5-6   Multiple-level indirect addressing

would replace the 33 by 44. On most machines this would have to be implemented by at least three instructions — one for each level of indirection (though see below).

On the earliest machines indirect addressing was achieved by altering the address field of an instruction at run-time. For example,

$$A\uparrow \leftarrow 22$$

was executed by copying the content of A into the address field of a constant-to-memory move instruction. However, as noted earlier, tampering with code at run-time is generally undesirable, and in this context it is also very inefficient. So most machines provide for indirect addressing by other means, using special operations in the hardware. Some allow it only through registers, in which case the above assignment has to be carried out in two steps:

$$Ri \leftarrow A$$
$$Ri\uparrow \leftarrow 22$$

Others allow indirect addressing through A itself and so a single step is sufficient. A more radical approach is to allow *any* address to be tagged as indirect. Consequently, if the address in A is itself tagged, a second level of indirection will automatically take place. This can go on for an arbitrary number of levels, and if the addresses go round in a circle, the indirection will continue *ad infinitum*.

Indirect addressing is needed for several important purposes, such as parameter handling (see Section 12.5) and the construction of linked data structures (see Volume II). Because of the extra content-taking that is involved, it is liable to take twice the time of normal, direct addressing. But this is usually a small price to pay for the benefits that it brings.

5.10   INDEXED ADDRESSING

Another important mode of addressing is *indexed addressing*. This is used when the location to be accessed is displaced by a certain amount from a known address. For example, it might be 12 cells beyond location A. More generally, it might be i cells beyond A, where i is an integer held in some other location I. In such cases, A is said to be *indexed* by I. The great advantage of this arrangement is that a simple loop can access a series of different locations simply by varying I. It provides the basis for handling tables, arrays, and other such data structures.

The indexed address will be denoted by the expression A.I, where A is known as the *base address* and I is the *index*, or *offset*, or *displacement*. Its meaning is given by the relation

$$@(A.I) \equiv @A + I$$

which states that the address A.I is the address of A plus the value of I. For example, if A is location 80 and I contains 12, A.I is location 92.

The accessing of A.I is depicted in Figure 5-7. Since I can be either positive or negative, the displacement may be made either forwards or backwards in memory. The displacement is measured in cells, and so care is needed when handling larger units. For

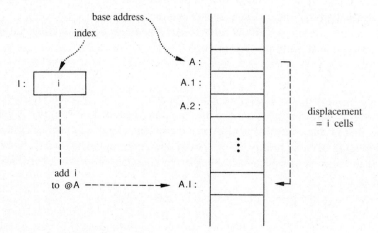

Figure 5-7   Indexed addressing

example, on a byte-addressing machine with four bytes per word, a displacement of n words requires the address A.4n rather than A.n.

It is worth noting that indexed addressing includes indirect addressing as a special case. Thus, let Z be the location with address zero and consider the address Z.A, which uses A as the index. By definition:

$$
\begin{aligned}
@\,(\text{Z.A}) \ &= \ @\,\text{Z} + \text{A} && \text{(definition of `.')} \\
&= \ 0 + \text{A} && \text{(definition of Z)} \\
&= \ \text{A} \\
&= \ @\,(\text{A}{\uparrow}) && \text{(definition of `}{\uparrow}\text{')}
\end{aligned}
$$

So Z.A is simply the indirect address A↑. Of course, there is no need to introduce a special name for zero. With suitable conventions, Z.A could be written as 0.A instead. More generally, if n is any integer, the expression n.A can denote the address n modified by the contents of A — in other words, the address n + A. This is equivalent to the indexed indirect address (A↑).n, for which it provides a more efficient alternative (see below).

Indexed addressing is a standard feature of nearly all computers. In its simplest form it requires that A be a direct address and that the index be held in an *index register*. The overheads of the indexing are then very slight, since the addition is considerably faster than the memory access. In the earlier machines the index registers were distinct from the accumulator and were reserved especially for indexing. Since they handled addresses rather than full-length numbers, they were also somewhat shorter. However, many of the more recent machines allow the main registers to serve both as accumulators and as index registers. The basic idea is that any direct address can be modified by a register, as in the following examples:

$$
\begin{aligned}
\text{R1} \ &\leftarrow \ \text{A.R2} \\
\text{B.R3} \ &\leftarrow \ \text{B.R3} + \text{C.R3}
\end{aligned}
$$

In fact *every* address has a field for indexing, and the only way to avoid indexing is to set the field to zero. On some machines, R0 is permanently zero, and so its use implies a zero index. On others, R0 is simply ignored.

Some machines also allow *double indexing*, with addresses of the form A.Ri.Rj. The IBM 370-series computers are a case in point, though Ri is normally tied down as the base register of a memory segment. An obvious application is for processing two-dimensional arrays, with Ri varying over one dimension and Rj over the other. If double indexing is not available, Ri + Rj has to be formed as a single index. Thus

$$X \leftarrow A.Ri.Rj$$

is implemented as:

$$Rk \leftarrow Ri + Rj$$
$$X \leftarrow A.Rk$$

Variations can then be made to Rk directly.

Relative addressing

A *relative* address is a particular kind of indexed address. It is measured by its displacement from some known location B; the relative address x therefore has an effective address of @B + x. This, of course, is the same as the indexed address B.x; so in what way is a relative address any different? The answer is that B is implied by context. This means that the address can be represented simply by x itself, and it is only when x is used that @B is brought into play.

If B is a fixed location, its address is called the *base address* and x can be described more precisely as a *base-relative* address. The point is that there is another version of relative addressing in which B is *the location that contains x itself*. In that case, x can be described as a *self-relative* address. The two different versions are illustrated in Figure 5-8. Both have a block of eight cells starting at address 80, with cell 82 containing the relative address 5. In the base-relative case the base is assumed to be cell 80 and so the effective address is 85. In the self-relative case B is the cell containing 5 itself, namely cell 82, and so the effective address is 87.

The advantages of relative addressing are two-fold. First, a relative address is often much smaller than its equivalent absolute address. This has been used to good effect in

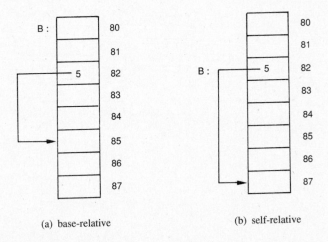

(a) base-relative   (b) self-relative

Figure 5-8   Relative addressing

computer hardware. For example, the IBM 370-series computers use 12-bit base-relative addressing as their standard mode, and the VAX computers provide eight-bit self-relative addresses as a special mode for instructions. The latter is called 'PC-relative' because, when the instruction is executed, its address will be in the program counter PC (= the instruction pointer). Second, the consistent use of relative addressing helps to make a code segment or data segment *relocatable*. The addresses will be independent of the position of the segment in the main memory and so will not need to be altered if the segment is moved around.

Indexed indirect addressing

Indexed addressing and indirect addressing can be combined in two ways:

- the indexed indirect-address A↑.I
- the indirect indexed-address (A.I)↑

As the notation shows, A↑.I does indexing based on A↑, whereas (A.I)↑ does indirection via A.I. The terminology needs watching, since 'indexed indirect' (or sometimes 'indexed deferred') is frequently taken to mean (A.I)↑, presumably on the grounds that the indexing is done first. It takes us into the debate about 'light house keepers': are they light housekeepers or lighthouse keepers? The contention here is that they are light housekeepers. Adjectives, like unary operators, should associate to the right.

Roughly speaking, A↑.I treats A as a pointer to a table, whereas (A.I)↑ treats it as a table of pointers. For ordinary programming the former is more important, since it is needed for implementing arrays and linked data structures. Its meaning can be deduced from the previous definitions as follows:

$$
\begin{aligned}
@\,(A↑.I) \;=\;& @\,(A↑) + I \qquad \text{(definition of `.')} \\
=\;& A + I \qquad\quad \text{(definition of `↑')}
\end{aligned}
$$

Thus the effective address is A + I. To reflect the symmetry between A and I, the expression A↑.I can be written in the form A!I, as used in the language BCPL. It is usual to

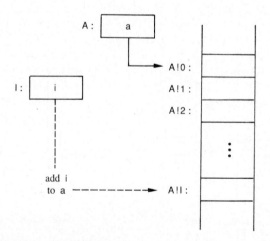

Figure 5-9   Indexed indirect addressing

think of A as pointing to the base address and I as providing the offset. The situation is depicted from this point of view in Figure 5-9, where A is shown as a pointer to a sequence of cells A!0, A!1, A!2, and so on. As can be seen, the special case A!0 is the same as A↑.

Unfortunately, although machines such as the VAX provide for (A.I)↑ in their hardware, hardly any of them provide for A!I. The code for A!I therefore has to compute A + I in a register and then use indirect addressing. However, in the case where I is a constant n, the situation is simpler. As noted above, (A↑).n is equivalent to n.A and so it can be implemented by ordinary indexing. This is particularly useful for handling linked data structures, as described in Volume II.

5.11   STACKS

At the end of Section 5.6 it was remarked that the most general method of handling the return addresses of subroutine calls is to store them on a stack. It is now time to consider how a stack operates and to look at the hardware support that may be provided for implementing it. In Volume II, stacks will be described from a more abstract point of view and their basic properties will be defined more formally.

In earlier days, stacks used to be illustrated by that familiar, homely object — the magazine of a rifle. Nowadays, however, the popular example is the pile of plates in a cafeteria. The basic operations on the pile are the following:

1.   to see whether or not it is empty;

2.   to put a plate on the top (assuming that there is room for it);

3.   to take a plate off the top (assuming that the pile is not empty).

In some cafeterias, the pile is supported on a spring in order to keep the top plate at a fixed level. When a new plate is put on top, the other plates have to be pushed down to make way for it. Conversely, when it is removed, they all pop up again. For this reason, operations 2 and 3 are usually called *push* and *pop*, and the stack itself is called a *push-down store*. These names are less appropriate in computing, since the stack elements are not moved up and down the memory. The terms *load* and *unload* are sometimes used instead, but they lack the drama of pushing and popping. Whatever their names, the operations have the essential feature that they only access the stack at its top. The objects further down are left in limbo until the ones above them have been removed. It follows that the elements are always removed in the reverse order from that in which they are loaded. This is known as a *last-in, first-out* discipline, or LIFO for short; so a stack has yet another name — a LIFO store.

Stacks are relevant to subroutine calls for the simple reason that subroutines follow a LIFO discipline. If A calls B, which calls C, which calls D, then A, B and C all have to wait until D has finished. In other words, the last subroutine to be entered is the first one to be left. Because of this, a stack is the natural structure for handling the return addresses. When A calls B, its return address α is loaded on the stack; during the execution of B various other return addresses may be loaded and unloaded; finally, when B has finished, α is unloaded and the execution of A is resumed.

Stacks have been given hardware support in many different ways. One of the first machines to take them seriously was the English Electric KDF9, which called them 'nesting stores' (the subroutine calls being 'nested' inside each other). One nesting store was used for handling return addresses in the way described above. The addresses were automatically loaded by the subroutine branch operation, and automatically unloaded by an *exit* operation. A second nesting store was provided for a completely different purpose, namely the evaluation of expressions. Its rationale can be illustrated by the execution of an assignment such as

$$w := (x + y) * z;$$

This was implemented by the following sequence of instructions:

> load x
> load y
> add
> load z
> multiply
> store in w

The sequence of operations is obtained by converting the expression $(x + y) * z$ to the form $x\,y + z\,*$, which is known as *Reverse Polish* notation. Figure 5-10 shows its effect on a stack that is initially empty. The first two *load* instructions put x and y on the stack; the *add* replaces them by their sum; the next *load* brings in z; the *multiply* forms the required product; and the final *store* leaves the stack empty again. *Load* and *store* are one-address instructions, but *add* and *multiply* do not refer to memory at all and so they are known as *zero-address* instructions.

The KDF9 stacks were implemented by high-speed memory devices, which made them very efficient. However, they were each restricted to a maximum of 16 elements, and for general-purpose programming this proved to be a severe handicap. In particular, if subroutines called themselves recursively, the limit of 16 was very quickly exceeded

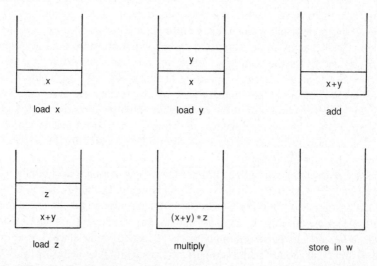

Figure 5-10   Evaluating an expression on a stack

and so the program had to offload the return addresses into main memory. As for the evaluation of expressions, it was argued that the stack offered no worthwhile advantage over the use of 16 independent registers. On the contrary, it had the drawback of being less flexible. For these reasons most subsequent architectures have abandoned the use of limited, special-purpose stacks. They have instead provided support for general-purpose stacks of arbitrary size in main memory.

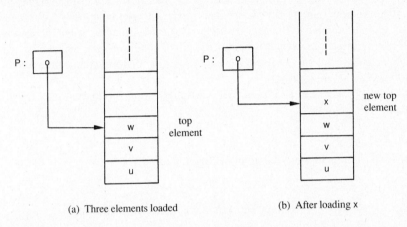

(a) Three elements loaded (b) After loading x

Figure 5-11 Stacks

In order to implement a stack of this kind, the basic strategy is to set aside an area of memory and to use a register P as either a pointer or an index to the top element. If it is a pointer the top element is P↑; if it is an index the top element is B.P, where B is the base address. Figure 5-11(a) shows the situation after the elements u, v, and w have been loaded. The top of the stack is the entry containing w, and P gives its address. According to the conventions established in Figure 5-1, the bottom of the stack has the highest address and so the stack is growing downwards in main memory. But it could equally well grow upwards if preferred. If each element occupies c cells, the *load* operation has to decrease P by c. Taking P to be a pointer, the following instructions will therefore copy X to the top of the stack:

$$P \leftarrow P - c$$
$$P\uparrow \leftarrow X$$

This produces the situation shown in Figure 5-11(b). Conversely, *unload* copies P↑ back to X and restores P to its previous value:

$$X \leftarrow P\uparrow$$
$$P \leftarrow P + c$$

Note that the decrementing is done *before* the move and the incrementing *after*.

One way of supporting these operations in hardware is to provide an addressing mechanism that automatically adjusts P upwards or downwards as required. The language C has a notation that expresses this concept, using "++" to denote an increment of one element and "−−" to denote a corresponding decrement. They enable the *load* and *unload* operations to be written as follows:

$$(--P)\uparrow \ \leftarrow \ X \qquad\qquad \text{-- load } X$$
$$X \ \leftarrow \ (P++)\uparrow \qquad\qquad \text{-- unload } X$$

The former decrements P *before* using its value; the latter increments it *after* using its value. The VAX computers provide operations of precisely this form and so, to that extent, they support the use of stacks that grow downwards in main memory, as in Figure 5-11. The addressing modes are described as 'autodecrement' and 'autoincrement'. The operations do not include any checks that P remains within the stack's allocated area, and so they are vulnerable to the dangers of stack *overflow* (loading when the area is full) and *underflow* (unloading when it is empty). If either condition goes undetected, the program may behave in an extremely puzzling way. A more helpful architecture would provide these checks automatically.

With this approach it is easy to execute many operations other than the official *load* and *unload*. For example,

$$X \ \leftarrow \ P\uparrow$$

copies the top element into X without unloading it, and

$$P!c \ \leftarrow \ Y$$

overwrites the element immediately beneath the top one. More drastically,

$$P \ \leftarrow \ P - 100c$$

creates 100 new entries on the stack but without loading any elements into them. All this is contrary to the pure principles of handling stacks, and if used carelessly it could cause a few headaches. Nevertheless, the resulting flexibility can be very useful.

With more sophisticated architectures this sort of freedom is taken away. The general idea is to prevent a program from damaging the stack structure by doing unprincipled things. So the pointer P is consigned to a non-addressable register, and the program has to work at or near the top of the stack using the special operations provided. For example, it may be allowed to interchange the top two elements, or to add them, and so on. The details depend on the role which the stack is intended to play — handling subroutine calls, evaluating expressions, or whatever. At the top of the scale are machines like the Burroughs B6700, whose architecture supports the block-structured facilities of high-level languages. The relevant mechanisms will be described in Chapter 12.

5.12   VIRTUAL MEMORY

As mentioned at the outset, the proposals of von Neumann have been elaborated in many ways. A case in point is the architecture of the main memory, which has undergone several important developments. The general aim is to provide greater efficiency, greater flexibility, and greater (apparent) size. In every case the hardware has been designed so that the complications are transparent to the users. Even when programming in assembly code they are presented with a memory that behaves in conventional von Neumann style. However, behind the facade of this *virtual* memory lies a much more complex *actual* memory. And although the details are hidden from view, it is sometimes advisable for the programmer to understand their basic principles.

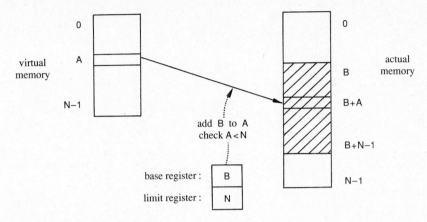

Figure 5-12   Memory relocation

A preliminary example is provided by the device called a *cache memory*. This is faster (and more expensive) than the main memory and helps to speed up execution, especially when short instruction sequences are repeated many times in succession. In its simplest form, it keeps a copy of the last few instructions executed by the program. If these instructions are then repeated, as in a small loop, they are read directly from the cache memory rather than the slower main memory. The idea can be extended to all memory accessing, covering data as well as instructions. Problems arise if the data are overwritten, because the new values in the cache must sooner or later be copied back to the main memory. However, with enough hardware and ingenuity, these problems can be overcome without degrading performance.

An important requirement is that a program's code should be *relocatable*. This means that it should be able to execute at any position in the main memory. It is written on the basis that it starts at word 0; in practice, it may start at some other address B. Figure 5-12 depicts the situation, with the actual memory having addresses 0 to $M-1$ and the virtual memory being allocated N of them, starting at B. Thus an address A in virtual memory (as seen by the program) is mapped onto address A+B in the actual memory (as seen by the hardware). The conversion of A to A + B may be carried out by special software — a 'relocating loader' — which adds B to all the addresses when the program is loaded into memory. More flexibly, the conversion is left to the hardware, which adds B to each address whenever the address is used. The hardware uses a *base register* to hold B and a *limit register* to hold N. Every reference to memory then checks the condition $0 \leq A \leq N-1$ and forms the actual address A + B. These operations take negligible time compared with the accessing of memory itself.

A more complicated method of relocation is to use *paging*. This means that the virtual memory is divided into a number of pages, a typical page size being 1K, 2K, or 4K bytes. The advantage is that the pages no longer have to form a contiguous block in the actual memory. Instead, they can be mapped onto any set of actual pages, as shown in Figure 5-13. The mapping is performed by hardware using a *page table* and, as with the cache mechanism, it takes negligible time. The table is maintained by the operating system and can also include protection information, so that some pages can be marked as 'read only' or 'execute only'.

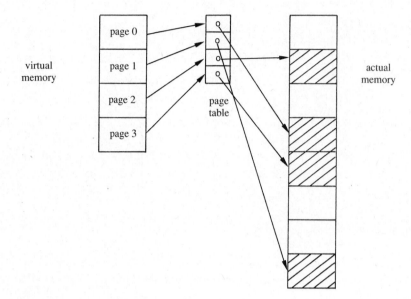

Figure 5-13   Paged memory

The technique of paging gives rise to the full-blooded *virtual memory* of many modern machines. Here each page of virtual memory is held either in main memory or on disk. The page table lists the ones that are currently in main memory, while the operating system keeps track of the rest. The situation is depicted in Figure 5-14. Whenever a virtual address A is used, the hardware separates out the page number (usually the top few bits) and looks for it in the page table. If the page is in main memory, the table will give its base address B, as with ordinary relocation. But if the page is not present a so-called 'fault' is signaled. The program is then interrupted while the operating system brings the required page into memory and removes another one (if necessary) to make way for it. In effect, the main memory acts as a large-scale cache for the disk. Despite its name, the 'fault' is perfectly harmless. The only trouble is that accessing the disk is a comparatively slow process. The operating system may therefore turn its attention to other programs until the process is complete.

The great advantage of this scheme is that the program's virtual memory can be considerably larger than the space allotted to it in real memory. In fact, it can use a larger memory than actually exists! That is why the term 'virtual' memory normally refers to this particular situation. The main drawback is that frequent page faults can be a serious drag on performance.

For programmers, there are two main conclusions to be drawn from all this.

1.   They can continue to write their programs exactly as if they were using a conventional von Neumann machine.

2.   Performance can be improved by taking advantage of a cache memory, and can be degraded by poor use of a virtual memory.

Broadly speaking, programs will run better if memory references are concentrated in

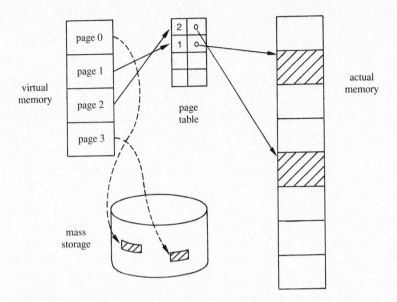

Figure 5-14 Virtual memory

small areas over long intervals, whereas they may run slower if the references skip frequently across the entire range. These remarks apply not only to the reading of instructions but also to the accessing of data. In fact, the reading of instructions tends to be concentrated in a few small areas anyhow. The greater danger lies in the extravagant use of large data structures when access to the memory is not truly random.

5.13 INPUT/OUTPUT OPERATIONS

Input/output operations enable a computer to communicate with its peripherals and with the outside world. Without them, it would be totally useless. The earliest machines had one operation for reading a character and another for writing a character, and they used punched cards or punched paper tape as the communication medium. Since then, the mechanisms have been elaborated in a number of ways, and they now have to handle a large variety of increasingly sophisticated devices.

Punched paper tape is seldom used these days, but it illustrates some important principles in a way that is easily visualized. A typical tape is one inch wide with a series of sprocket holes running along its length. Across its width there is room for eight larger holes to be punched, three on one side of the sprocket hole and five on the other (Figure 5-15). Each position along the tape can therefore record one eight-bit byte. When characters are being handled, the usual convention is to have a seven-bit code and to use the eighth position for a parity bit (see Section 2.8). Most systems work with even parity, setting the bit so that the number of 1s (that is, the number of holes) is always even. Figure 5-16 shows the result for the letters A – E of the seven-bit ISO code of Figure 4-2. When characters are written out, the hardware sets their parity bits appropriately. Conversely, when they are read back, it checks that they have the required parity and sets an

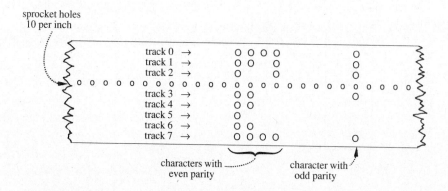

Figure 5-15   Punched paper tape

error indication if they do not. It then removes the parity bits, by setting them to zero, and hands the characters over. For handling binary (non-character) information, there are operations that transmit all eight bits without regard to their parity. To check the accuracy of the recording, it is therefore necessary to take special precautions in the software. The usual strategy is to augment each block of data with a *checksum*, which gives the sum of all its words. It is normally computed by means of the *exclusive or* operation, and is therefore the logical sum rather than the arithmetic one. This avoids any problems caused by overflow and produces the 'longitudinal parity' as its result (see Section 2.8). The sum is re-computed when the block is read back in, and emergency action is taken if it does not agree with the recorded value.

As mentioned earlier, the simplest operations are to read or write a single character, transferring it to or from some location in the computer — either a register or some agreed position in main memory. On almost all devices, the transfer is very slow when compared with internal operations, such as an addition or a memory access. With a paper tape reader, it takes about one millisecond; with an interactive terminal it may be even slower, depending on the speed of the line. The implications of this are discussed below.

It would be very tedious and inefficient if all input/output had to be done by transmitting characters one at a time. Most operations therefore read or write a *block* of characters all at once. The instructions designate an area of memory, known as a *buffer*, and the characters are transferred to or from the buffer. A typical example occurs in the reading of a standard 80-column punched card. The instruction specifies an address A, and on a

Character	Seven-bit code	Parity bit	Holes
A	1000001	0	2
B	1000010	0	2
C	1000011	1	4
D	1000100	0	2
E	1000101	1	4

Figure 5-16   Representation of A – E

byte-addressing machine successive characters from the card are stored in the cells A.0, A.1, ... A.79. From there they can be handled one at a time, in whatever way is required. In the case of the card reader, the number of characters is determined by the nature of the device and so the instruction uses *fixed-length* blocks. On most other devices, though, it is possible to use *variable-length* blocks — that is, blocks of arbitrary size. In some cases, the instruction specifies the number of characters that are to be read or written. In others, a special terminating character is used to mark the end.

Since a computer can be connected to many different devices, an input/output instruction has to include some indication of the one that is to be used. It is not as though there is one instruction for reading from a terminal, another for reading from cards, and so on. Instead, there is normally a single input instruction that says 'read data into area A from device X', and a single output instruction that says 'write data from area A to device Y'. As far as the instructions are concerned, all devices are logically equivalent: they transfer data to or from the buffer in apparently identical fashion. In reality, of course, the devices have widely differing characteristics and the transfer of the data can be quite a complicated process. The hardware that handles the overall communication is called a *channel*. In the simplest cases, the channel behaves much like any other hardware operation, carrying out the required task and then allowing the CPU to continue to the next instruction. However, as noted above, communicating with peripherals is a comparatively slow business, since their operations usually require several milliseconds to complete. So this simple approach has the serious drawback that it ties up the CPU for long periods of time, when in principle it could be doing useful work. On the more advanced machines the channels are therefore designed so that they operate *autonomously* — that is, independently of the CPU and of each other. This means that several processes can be executing in parallel. On encountering an input/output instruction, the CPU merely passes it to the relevant channel and then resumes its work. There is a problem, of course, if its work is dependent on the completion of the transfer. This requires additional mechanisms, as described in the next section.

On larger computers the trend is to make channels increasingly sophisticated. In effect, they operate as computers in their own right. On the main IBM computers, for example, they execute special instructions known as Channel Command Words. The number of input/output instructions provided to the CPU is reduced to four — start I/O, halt I/O, test channel status, and test device status. On the CDC Cyber computers this is taken to its logical conclusion: all input/output is handled by separate Peripheral Processor Units, each with 4K words of programmable memory. By such means the CPU can be shielded from the complexity of specific input/output requirements.

5.14 AUTONOMOUS INPUT/OUTPUT

The hazards of autonomous input/output can be illustrated by the basic requirement of reading a block of characters into a buffer A and then processing it:

```
read the block into A
process A
```

If implemented as a *read* instruction followed by the processing instructions, this will almost certainly be wrong. The CPU will initiate the *read* and then try to process A without waiting for the characters to arrive. So unless the hardware applies a lock-out mechanism to A, the program must include code for checking that the transfer has been completed

To assist in this, each channel is equipped with a status bit that indicates whether or not it is busy. It is sometimes called the *busy flag*. An instruction enables the program to inspect the flag and to branch if it is set. The above code can therefore be revised as follows:

```
        read the block into A
L:      if the channel is busy goto L
        process A
```

The second line is known as a *busy loop*, since it keeps repeating itself as long as the channel is busy. When the transfer is complete, the channel unsets the flag and so the processing can begin. A similar precaution is needed for doing output:

```
        write a block from A
L:      if the channel is busy goto L
        refill A
```

In this case the busy loop protects the buffer from being refilled before its contents have been written out.

Testing the busy flag in this way is very crude and inefficient, since it dissipates the resources of the CPU inside the loop. In fact it defeats the whole purpose of allowing the CPU and the channels to operate in parallel. To take advantage of their autonomy, the program has to be written so that the CPU can perform some other task while the transfer is in progress. There are several strategies for doing this, ranging from simple buffering techniques (see Volume III) to the activation of other programs by sophisticated operating systems. Whatever the strategy, there must be a mechanism for recognizing when the transfer is complete. There are three main possibilities:

1.   The CPU completes the other task and then executes a busy loop, if necessary, to fill in the rest of the time.

2.   If the task is a very long one, the CPU can inspect the busy flag at regular intervals — a technique known as *polling*.

3.   The CPU can carry on with the task until the completion of the transfer automatically interrupts it.

Of these, the third method is potentially the most efficient. Since it is also the most common one in practice, we shall explore it a little further.

The basic principle is simple enough. When a channel completes an input/output operation it issues an *end-of-transfer interrupt*. This suspends the currently executing process and activates an associated interrupt handler, as described in Section 5.7. When the handler has taken the necessary action the original process is resumed. A simple application is to copy a file from one device to another — for example, from a disk to a tape. Since the copying requires very little work from the CPU, it can be done as a background job to an entirely separate program P. It uses a buffer that is alternately filled from the disk and then written to tape. Each device has an end-of-transfer interrupt handler whose main responsibility is to activate the other one. The handler for the disk initiates the writing to tape, and the handler for the tape initiates the reading from disk. The code for the disk handler might therefore go as follows:

> *disk end-of-transfer interrupt:*
> save register(s)
> read block from disk to buffer
> restore register(s)
> return from interrupt

Note that, since the interrupt can occur at any point in the execution of P, it is essential to save and restore any registers that are used by the handler. The program P can then be resumed as if nothing had happened. The handler for the tape is similar:

> *tape end-of-transfer interrupt:*
> save register(s)
> write block from buffer to tape
> restore register(s)
> return from interrupt

The overall process is called *interrupt-driven I/O*. It is initiated when P or some other routine executes the first read operation. It terminates when the end-of-file condition is detected (see Exercise 8).

This example is particularly simple because the two processes do not have to cooperate in any way. By contrast, if they have to access common variables, the situation is very hazardous. For example, a variable i may be a counter that is incremented by the main program and decremented by the interrupt handler. Now watch what can happen:

main program	*interrupt handler*
...	...
R1 ← i	R2 ← i
R1 ← R1 + 1	R2 ← R2 − 1
i ← R1	i ← R2
...	...

Suppose that i has the value 3 and that the main program begins to increment it by copying it into a register R1. Suddenly, without any warning, the interrupt routine may intervene and decrement i to 2. The main program then continues by incrementing R1 to 4 and copying it back to i. The effect is that i ends up with the value 4 *even though the interrupt had decremented it*. This sort of hazard can lead to very obscure bugs, especially as the precise moment of the interrupt can vary from one run to the next.

One way to avoid the hazard is for the main program to disable the interrupts during the critical phase. This can be done either by disabling all of them at once, or by a more selective facility that allows them to be disabled individually (see Section 5.7). Even so, the writing of such routines is a very difficult business and should only be done for special purposes. Chapter 11 explores the topic in more detail.

Operating systems, of course, are a whole story in themselves and the reader is referred to the literature for a proper account of them. The miniature system described above is typical of the techniques that were being developed in the early 1960s. Since then the software has become more and more elaborate, enabling simple, single-user machines to be developed into complex, multi-user systems. By contrast, the underlying hardware has not altered in any radically significant ways. When the layers of software are stripped away we find that the basic instructions still do the same sorts of thing. But this, as we have observed all along, is true of computers as a whole. After several genera-tions of development, they still reflect their von Neumann pedigree.

FURTHER READING

An account of the earliest computers is given by one of the participants in Goldstine (1972). The classic paper by Burks, Goldstine, and von Neumann (1946) is reprinted in Traub (1963), and also in Bell and Newell (1971). For further comments on the role of von Neumann, see Stern (1980). The contributions made by A.M. Turing are docu-mented in Carpenter and Doran (1986). Metropolis *et al.* (1980) is a collection of articles on the history of modern computing, and Shurkin (1984) is a book on the same subject. The journal *The Annals of the History of Computing* is a rich source of additional material, and it documents the origins of most of the ideas in this chapter.

Good introductions to computer architecture are Tanenbaum (1984) and Hamacher, Vranesic, and Zaky (1984). Bell and Newell (1971) describes many of the early com-puter designs; its successor is Siewiorek, Bell, and Newell (1982). For stack-based machines, see the special issue of *IEEE Computer* **10:5** (May 1977). A survey on cache memories is given by Smith (1982), and on virtual memory by Denning (1970) and Doran (1976). Much of this material is also covered by textbooks on operating systems — for example, Lister (1984) or Peterson and Silberschatz (1985).

EXERCISES

1   What is the unit of addressing on your computer (that is, the computer best known to you)? How many bits are used for an address in the instructions? If n is the number of bits and 2^n is less than the memory size (real or virtual), what techniques are used so that the whole of the main memory can be addressed? If 2^n is very much larger than the memory size, what is the use (if any) of the extra bits?

2   How many registers does your computer have? What instructions does it provide for doing the following:

- copying word A to word B

- copying k consecutive bytes starting at address A to an area starting at address B

- the conditional branch, **if** Ri = 0 **goto** L

- the conditional branch, **if** A > 0 **goto** L

- the conditional branch, **if** A > B **goto** L

- comparing two sequences of k bytes for their lexicographic order
- entering and leaving subroutines.

3 Let A, B, C, and D be locations in main memory, each containing an integer. Describe the implementation of the assignment

$$A \leftarrow A * B + C * D$$

on machines of the following kinds:

- with one-address instructions and a single accumulator R0;
- with one-address instructions and registers R0 – R7;
- with two-address instructions and registers R0 – R7;
- with zero-address instructions operating on a stack.

Give the number of memory accesses required for each, and discuss the advantages and drawbacks of each design.

4 As stated in Section 5, the IBM 370-series computers use two status bits p and q for providing information about the result of an operation. Thus:

$p = 0, q = 0$ —	result is zero;
$p = 0, q = 1$ —	result is less than zero;
$p = 1, q = 0$ —	result is greater than zero;
$p = 1, q = 1$ —	result is out of range (overflow).

Express the following conditions in terms of p and/or q:

(a) result $\neq 0$;
(b) result ≤ 0;
(c) result ≥ 0.

5 Consider a Pascal statement of the form:

if $(i > 0)$ **and** $(j > 0)$ **then** ... ;

What code might be generated by a compiler if (a) it implements the conditional **and** and (b) it evaluates both parts of the condition and combines the results? Show that with conventional *test* and *compare* instructions, the conditional version works better.

6 Suppose that subroutines are executed by storing their return addresses on a stack. Suppose further that the main program calls subroutine A, which ends with the instructions:

```
call subroutine B
exit
```

Show that under certain reasonable conditions these two instructions can be replaced by

goto B

without significantly affecting the computation. How many memory accesses would this save? Would the same technique work if the return addresses were stored in any other way?

7   What addressing mechanisms are provided in the machine that is best known to you? What facilities are provided for (a) double indexing, (b) relative addressing, and (c) stack addressing?

8   Revise the interrupt routines of Section 14 so that they handle the end-of-file condition. Assume that the end is signaled by a card that contains '$' in column 1 and consider (a) the case where the last card is copied to disk and (b) the case where it is not.

9   In Section 4, it was stated that the stored program concept 'paved the way for a wide range of other important developments'. What were some of these developments?

SEQUENCES, LANGUAGES, AND GRAMMARS

6.1 SEQUENCES

In one form or another, sequences pervade every aspect of programming. They are inherent in the sequential nature of the von Neumann computer, and from there they spread to everything else. In fact, it is hard to get away from them! For example, they are present in this very paragraph: each sentence is a sequence of words; each word is a sequence of characters; each character has other sequences lurking within it.

In order to manage sequences in all their variety, it is important to understand their common features and to develop concepts that give them structure and coherence. The detailed theory can then be developed according to the needs of each situation. The following are some of the applications to which it has special relevance:

1.   At a purely syntactic level every program is a sequence of symbols. Grammars are needed for distinguishing the legal sequences from the illegal ones.

2.   On a von Neumann computer every program determines a sequence of operations for the hardware to execute. Methods are needed for formulating sequences that will achieve the program's goal.

3.   In the design of data structures sequences again play a major part. They appear in the guise of arrays, lists, files, and so on, with different techniques being needed for their different forms.

This chapter pays special attention to the area of languages and grammars. However, the basic principles are applicable to sequences of any kind and will occur repeatedly in later material.

In order to set the scene, it is appropriate to begin with a definition:

Definition

A *sequence* is a set of items on which an ordering relation has been imposed.

A special case is the *empty* sequence, or *null* sequence, which contains no items at all. It is denoted by ε. In the remaining cases, an ordering is 'imposed' on the items in the sense that it is not inherent in the items themselves; instead, it is defined by some sort of physical or logical arrangement. Thus the ordering of the list (3, 5, 2) is not the numerical one, but the textual one — first 3, then 5, then 2.

Operationally, two other definitions can be formulated. These help to clarify the intention of the earlier version, but at the expense of splitting it into two alternatives. The first says that a sequence is a set of n items (for some $n \geq 0$), which are in effect numbered 1, 2, ... n. Thus there is a first item, a second item, and so on. The other says that it is a set of n items, one being designated as the first and the remainder being a sequence of n−1 items. The former is basically an iterative definition, whereas the latter is a recursive one (defining a sequence in terms of itself). The difference has far-reaching consequences and will be a matter of detailed consideration in later sections.

6.2   CATENATION

There are three basic operations for describing and/or constructing sets of sequences. The first is *catenation*, which combines shorter sequences into longer ones. The second is *alternation*, which forms sequences into sets of alternatives. The third is *repetition*, which applies catenation repeatedly to members of a set. Together they form a powerful and very important trio. They appear under various names and guises in virtually every context where sequences are used.

This section examines the first member of the trio, namely catenation. The name is a shorter version of *concatenation*, which means 'string together'. This is exactly what catenation does: it takes the basic units and strings them together to form a sequence. The following are some typical examples:

1.   If the basic units are characters, catenation forms them into a string. Thus a, b, and c can be catenated to form the string abc. The operation is denoted by physical juxtaposition of the characters.

2.   If the units are words or other symbols, the resulting sequence is some sort of grammatical unit, such as a sentence or an algebraic expression. Once again, physical juxtaposition is used, but this time the items may have to be separated by spaces, as in the sentence 'mice like cheese'.

3.   If the units are program statements, catenation forms them into a statement sequence:

$$S1 \; ; \; S2 \; ; \; S3$$

The semicolon can be regarded as the sequencing operator. It catenates not only the grammatical units but also the machine operations that they specify.

4.   If the units are data items, catenation is often denoted by commas, as in the expression (x, y, z). Depending on the context, this could be an array, or a list, or some other sort of sequence.

For the time being, it is convenient to focus on the first of these, working with sequences that are character strings. This is the context in which the ideas are normally developed. However, it should be emphasized that the theory is equally applicable to sequences of any other kind. In fact, we can transfer it to sequences of another kind simply by assuming that the characters denote items of that kind. For example, we could interpret them as machine instructions: a string such as abc would then represent a short program.

Catenation can be used not only for constructing strings in the first place, but also for joining two existing strings. When applied to the strings foot and ball, for example, it produces the string football. In mathematics, the operation is sometimes written as foot ˆ ball. In programming languages, it is denoted by various other operators, including '+' and '&'. It can be defined more formally by starting with one of the operational definitions of a sequence as given in the previous section. Since the intention is clear enough, the details are left as an exercise (see Exercise 1).

Not surprisingly, catenating the null string with any other string σ leaves σ unchanged. Thus $\varepsilon\,\hat{}\,\sigma = \sigma\,\hat{}\,\varepsilon = \sigma$. (In mathematical jargon, ε is the *identity* element of the operation.) By itself, this is a rather pointless thing to do. However, the next section shows that it can be combined with alternation to give some useful effects.

6.3 ALTERNATION

The second operation of the trio is one that takes two or more strings and forms them into a set. It is called *alternation*, suggesting that the result is to be regarded as a set of alternatives. For example, the alternation of alpha, beta, and gamma is denoted by the expression

$$\text{alpha} \cup \text{beta} \cup \text{gamma}$$

which may be read as 'alpha *or* beta *or* gamma'. Its value is the set {alpha, beta, gamma}, with the implication that in due course some person or process will have to make a choice between the three elements. There are several other notations, depending on the nature of the items that are being handled. Sometimes the alternation is denoted by '+' or '|' instead of '$\cup$'. If the items are program statements, it may involve a more elaborate construction, with symbols such as **if**, **case**, or **select**.

The above example applied '$\cup$' to individual sequences and the result was a set of alternatives. More generally, it can be applied to existing sets of alternatives, S1 and S2, in order to produce a larger one, namely S1 $\cup$ S2. The result is the union of the two sets, exactly as defined for '$\cup$' in Section 1.2. Choosing an element from S1 $\cup$ S2 is the same as choosing one from S1 *or* from S2; so the term '*or*' retains a useful connotation in this context.

Alternation and catenation can be combined by allowing catenation to operate on sets. If S1 and S2 are two sets, their catenation S1.S2 is defined to be the set of all strings formed by catenating one from S1 with one from S2. More formally:

$$S1 . S2 \;\equiv\; \{\,\sigma1\,\hat{}\,\sigma2 \;\mid\; \sigma1 \in S1,\; \sigma2 \in S2\,\}$$

For example, if S1 is {in, out} and S2 is {put, law}, their catenation is the set

$$\{\text{input, inlaw, output, outlaw}\}$$

There is an obvious parallel with the Cartesian product S1 $\times$ S2, as described in Section 1.3. However, as the reader may care to verify, the two are by no means equivalent. In particular, the cardinality of S1 . S2 is not necessarily |S1| $\times$ |S2| (see Exercise 2).

An interesting case arises when one of the alternatives is the null string ε. In effect, this makes the other alternatives optional. For example, the expression

$$(\varepsilon \cup \text{con}) \; . \; \text{catenation}$$

provides a choice between catenation and concatenation, indicating that con is optional. Of course, the same effect can be achieved by writing

$$\text{catenation} \cup \text{concatenation}$$

and so to that extent the use of ε is not essential. Nevertheless, the device is a useful one. Its counterpart in program sequencing is an **if** statement without an **else** clause.

6.4 REPETITION

The third operation of this important trio is the one that applies catenation repeatedly to the members of a set. In the simplest case there is a single string σ, and if it has to be repeated exactly n times the repetition is denoted by σ^n. For example, $(\text{abc})^3$ is equivalent to abcabcabc. (The parentheses distinguish this from abc^3, which is equivalent to abccc.) As a special case, σ^0 is defined to be the null string, and the following 'multiplication' rule can then be stated:

$$\sigma^m . \sigma^n \;=\; \sigma^{m+n} \qquad (m, n \geq 0)$$

More generally, repetition can be combined with alternation. For example, $(0 \cup 1)^2$ is equivalent to $(0 \cup 1).(0 \cup 1)$, which produces the alternatives 00, 01, 10, and 11. Furthermore, if S is a set of alternatives, an expression of the form

$$S^0 \cup S^1 \cup S^2 \cup \;...\; \cup S^n$$

means that S is to be repeated no times, or once, or twice, ... or n times. In other words, it specifies repetition for an arbitrary number of times up to some limit n.

As long as the limit n remains finite, repetition can be defined in terms of catenation and alternation. However, repetition in its fullest sense breaks new ground by allowing S to be repeated an *unbounded* number of times. It is denoted by S^* and can be defined informally as follows:

$$S^* \;\equiv\; S^0 \cup S^1 \cup S^2 \cup S^3 \cup \;...$$

Alternatively, and more formally:

$$S^* \;\equiv\; \{ \sigma_1\sigma_2...\sigma_n \;\mid\; n \geq 0 \; and \; \text{for } i = 1..n, \; \sigma_i \in S \}$$

An important consequence is that, unlike any of the previous sets, S^* is infinite. For example, $(\text{ab})^*$ is the infinite set:

$$\{ \varepsilon \;,\; \text{ab, abab, ababab, } ... \}$$

Similarly, $(0 \cup 1)^*$ is the set of all possible binary strings. As usual, the notation varies with the context. Sometimes braces are used, as in the expression $x\{ + x\}$, which produces the strings x, x + x, x + x + x, and so on. In program sequencing, the relevant symbols are usually reserved words, such as **while, do,** and **loop.**

As a matter of terminology, it is worth noting that the above form of repetition is sometimes called *closure*, or *Kleene closure* (after the logician S.C. Kleene). The underlying idea is that there is a set S together with an operation that can be applied to its elements in order to produce more elements. In the case of $(0 \cup 1)^*$, S is $\{0, 1\}$ and the operation is catenation. When applied to 0 and 1, catenation produces the new elements 00, 01, 10, and 11, which are added to S. When applied to the enlarged set, it produces elements such as 000, 0011, and 1101, which are also added to S. The *closure* of the set (under catenation) is the set of all elements that can be produced by repeatedly applying catenation in this way. The Kleene closure also includes the identity element, which in this case is ε. It is called 'closure' because the resulting set is said to be 'closed under catenation'. This means that when catenation is applied to any of its elements the result will always belong to the set.

An alternative form of closure, and hence an alternative form of repetition, is the one that does not include ε. It is denoted by S^+, which specifies repetition over S for an arbitrary *but non-zero* number of times. Informally:

$$S^+ \equiv S^1 \cup S^2 \cup S^3 \cup \dots$$

It is equivalent to $S . S^*$ and so it does not introduce anything essentially new. Its value lies in situations where the null case has to be excluded. In program sequencing it corresponds to the **repeat** statement of Pascal, whose body has to be executed at least once.

6.5   REGULAR EXPRESSIONS

The preceding sections have introduced expressions such as ε, a, abc, $a \cup b \cup c$, abc^*, and $(a \cup b)^*$, each representing a set of one or more strings. Expressions of this kind are known as *regular expressions* and play an important role in the theory of languages and grammars. Their values — the sets of strings — are called *regular sets*. The following definition shows how they are built up from a set of basic symbols by means of catenation, alternation, and repetition:

1. The empty sequence ε is a regular expression, representing the one-element set $\{\varepsilon\}$.

2. A basic symbol a is a regular expression, representing the one-element set $\{a\}$.

3. If R1 and R2 are regular expressions, then so is R1 . R2, representing their catenation.

4. If R1 and R2 are regular expressions, then so is R1 ∪ R2, representing their alternation.

5. If R is a regular expression, then so is R^*, representing its closure (under catenation).

In practice, the '.' is usually omitted, and so (as previously) catenation is represented by direct juxtaposition. Furthermore, '*' has precedence over catenation, and catenation has precedence over '∪'. This means that ab*c∪d, for example, is interpreted as (a (b*) c) ∪ d. Parentheses can be used to improve clarity and to override these conventions when necessary.

The set of basic symbols is called the *alphabet* and can be described as a regular expression A. For example, if it is the set of lower-case letters:

$$A = a \cup b \cup c \cup \ldots \cup z$$

Its closure A* is the set of all strings over the alphabet — in this case, any sequence of letters. A regular expression defines a subset of these strings and this constitutes a *language*. The members of the set are the 'legal' strings of the language, otherwise known as *sentences* (or in some contexts as *words*). For example, Section 6.3 used the regular expression (in ∪ out) . (put ∪ law) to define the set:

$$\{ \text{input, inlaw, output, outlaw} \}$$

This can be regarded as a language with four 'sentences'. More realistically, let A be the set of ASCII characters and consider the following definitions:

$$
\begin{aligned}
L &= a \cup b \cup c \cup \ldots &&\text{-- the letters}\\
D &= 0 \cup 1 \cup 2 \cup \ldots &&\text{-- the digits}\\
I &= L \, (L \cup D)^*
\end{aligned}
$$

This defines I to be the set of strings consisting of a letter followed by an arbitrary sequence of letters and/or digits. They could be the legal identifiers in a programming language such as Pascal.

In general, any language that can be defined by a regular expression is said to be a *regular language*. As the following sections show, this is a very important class of languages.

6.6 FINITE AUTOMATA

A *finite automaton* is another mechanism for generating sequences of symbols (or of anything else). Figure 6-1 shows a simple example. As can be seen, its basic structure is that of a finite directed graph, the nodes being called *states* and the branches *transitions*. Each transition is labeled with a symbol drawn from an associated alphabet A. There is a *start* state S and a *final* state F, and it is usual (though not essential) to require that no transitions enter S or leave F. The machine operates by starting in state S and following a path along the transitions until it arrives at F. As it moves along a transition it 'emits' the corresponding label. On its journey from S to F, it therefore generates a sequence of symbols. In Figure 6-1, for example, the machine could follow the path S–D–E–E–D–D–F and the resulting string would be aababb.

In generating a string the finite automaton can follow any path that it chooses, and in that respect its operation is nondeterministic. By following all the different paths from S to F, it can generate many different strings. As with regular expressions, the strings are a subset of A* and can be regarded as the sentences of a language. In the case of Figure 6-1 the language is a subset of (a ∪ b)*. In fact, it consists of all the strings of two or more symbols that have an odd number of a's (see Section 8.2).

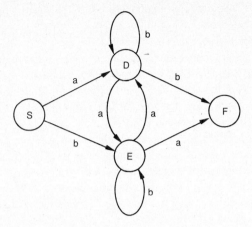

Figure 6-1   A finite automaton

There are several variations on this basic theme. As already implied, transitions may be allowed to enter S and to leave F. Moreover, if they can leave F there are advantages in allowing more than one state to be designated as final. If S itself can be designated as final the machine will be able to generate the null sentence ε. Another possibility is to allow *unlabeled* transitions. These have no labels, and so when the machine follows them it does not emit any symbol. In particular, an unlabeled transition from S to F provides another mechanism for generating ε. These variations simplify the design of some machines. However, apart from allowing ε to be generated, they do not add to the essential power of the mechanism. The range of definable languages remains the same (see Exercises 5 and 6).

As Figure 6-1 shows, a finite automaton provides its own version of the three basic sequencing operations:

catenation	transitions can be joined together to form a path;
alternation	when two or more transitions leave a given state, the machine can choose between them;
repetition	a path can return to an earlier state, thus forming a cycle.

The observation strongly suggests that finite automata can 'imitate' regular expressions and that they can therefore define the regular languages. This is indeed the case. The only point to watch is that since regular expressions can generate ε, the finite automata must be given this capability too (see above). Less obviously, it turns out that finite automata can generate *only* the regular languages. The situation is summarized in the following theorem, first formulated and proved by S.C. Kleene (1956):

Theorem 6.1

The languages definable by finite automata are the regular languages.

This means that for every regular expression there is an equivalent finite automaton (one that defines the same language). Conversely, for every finite automaton there is an equivalent regular expression.

The first part of the theorem can be proved quite simply by designing machines for the five forms of regular expression that were given in the previous section. The machines for ε and the basic symbols are trivial. The machines for R1 . R2 and R1 $\cup$ R2 are constructed by linking the ones for R1 and R2 in appropriate ways (using unlabeled transitions makes this easy). The machine for R^* is an extension of the one for R. The details are left as an exercise (see Exercise 9).

The converse is more difficult. Given a finite automaton, the task is to construct a regular expression that defines the same language. The trouble is that finite automata are much less 'structured' than regular expressions — their transitions can go from anywhere to anywhere. However, for a machine with n states there is a 'brute force' method that constructs regular expressions for approximately n^3 different languages, including the one required. It begins by numbering the states $A_1, A_2, \ldots A_n$, with $S = A_1$ and $F = S_n$. It then defines $L_k(i,j)$ to be the language whose strings are generated by all the possible paths from A_i to A_j going optionally via some or all of $A_1, \ldots A_k$ (with multiple visits if desired). For each $k = 0, 1, 2, \ldots n$, there are n^2 such languages — one for each pair of states A_i, A_j. For $k = 0$, the paths from A_i to A_j are restricted to single transitions and so a regular expression for $L_0(i,j)$ is easily found. For the remaining values of k, the method proceeds by induction. On the basis that the L_{k-1} languages are all regular, it shows that $L_k(i,j)$ can be defined as the regular expression:

$$L_{k-1}(i,j) \quad \cup \quad L_{k-1}(i,k) . L_{k-1}(k,k)^* . L_{k-1}(k,j)$$

The term $L_{k-1}(i,j)$ provides for paths from A_i to A_j that do not include A_k. The other term describes the paths that include A_k one or more times. This proves that $L_k(i,j)$ is regular and hence (by induction) that all the languages are regular. In particular, $L_n(1,n)$ is regular; and since this is the language defined by paths from S to F, the result follows.

It is important to note that a finite automaton can be viewed from a rather different angle. Instead of *generating* the sentences of a language L, it can be used for *recognizing*, or *accepting*, them. This means that if it is given a string $\sigma = x_1 x_2 \ldots x_k$, it determines whether or not σ belongs to L. It does this by looking for a path from S to F with the required labels $x_1, x_2, \ldots x_k$. If it finds one, it knows that σ is in L and therefore *accepts* it; otherwise it concludes that σ is not a sentence and *rejects* it. Its basic strategy is clear enough. Starting at S, it looks for a transition that is labeled x_1; having followed that, it looks for one labeled x_2; and so on. The only trouble is that it may sometimes be confronted by two or more transitions with the required label. Which one should it choose? In general, there is no simple way of making the right choice. The best way to tackle the problem is therefore to convert the machine into an equivalent one in which such dilemmas can never occur. The new machine will be characterized by the property that, for each state, the outgoing transitions will all have different labels. Such a machine is called a *deterministic* finite automaton (DFA). Fortunately, the conversion to deterministic form is always possible (the algorithm is given in Volume II). Figure 6-2 shows the result for the machine of Figure 6-1. As can be seen, every state has one outgoing transition labeled a and one labeled b. The example is unusual in that it has the same number of states as the original. In most cases, the DFA will require more states, including several that are designated as final.

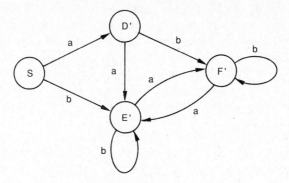

Figure 6-2   A deterministic finite automaton

As its name implies, a DFA responds to a string $x_1x_2\ldots x_k$ deterministically. Starting in state S, it looks for a path with the labels x_1, x_2, ... x_k. Being deterministic, it will have at most one matching transition at each stage, and so the path (if it exists) will be unique. If it completes the path and arrives at a final state, it accepts the string; but if its progress is blocked at any stage, with no transition to match the next symbol, or if the path takes it to a non-final state, it rejects the string. The determinism is useful in establishing various properties of regular languages. For example, it provides a neat way of proving that if R is a regular language, then so is its complement $\overline{R}$ (the strings over the alphabet that are *not* in R). It also provides a method of determining whether two regular expresssions are equivalent (see Exercises 10 - 13).

6.7   GRAMMARS

A *grammar* is the specification of a language. As usual, the language is based on an alphabet A, and the grammar specifies the strings over A that are to be accepted as legal sentences. In computing, the most familiar examples are the grammars for programming languages, with A being the set of basic symbols and the sentences being programs. However, Section 6.1 reminds us that grammars can be interpreted more widely as defining sequences of *anything* — basic symbols, data items, machine operations, or whatever.

If the language is finite the grammar might simply be an enumeration of the sentences, one by one. For example, here is a two-sentence truth language:

$$\text{truth\_language}\;=\;\{\text{false, true}\}$$

In practice, most languages are infinite and so a different kind of specification is needed. One method is to define the language as the set of sentences satisfying some property P:

$$L\;=\;\{\sigma\;\mid\;P(\sigma)\}$$

This states that the language L is the set of strings σ for which $P(\sigma)$ is true. For example, if σ^R denotes σ written in reverse, the language

$$L\;=\;\{\sigma\;\mid\;\sigma=\sigma^R\}$$

is the set of palindromes over the given alphabet.

In practice, it is more usual to specify a language by means of a *generative* grammar — one that states how the sentences can be generated. In this respect, a regular expression can be regarded as a generative grammar and so can a finite automaton: they provide two different mechanisms for generating sets of sentences. But many other mechanisms have been devised, with varying degrees of power and complexity, each hoping to provide acceptable definitions for a particular range of languages. We shall be concerned with only one of them — the ever-popular *context-free* grammars, which will be described in the next section.

The *parsing* problem is to determine, of any string σ, how (if at all) it can be generated by the grammar. If there are two or more essentially different ways, σ is *ambiguous*, and the grammar is said to be ambiguous also. The English language offers many examples, ranging from 'They are eating apples' to others that are more entertaining. This one was quoted in the 'Country Life' column of *Punch*:

> Police officers last month bugged a courtroom where seven inmates were to be tried for killing a fellow convict without first obtaining the trial judge's consent.

For Delphic oracles and politicians occasional ambiguities have a certain value. In programming, though, they are a hazard, and so it would be reassuring to know that the grammars are free of them. Unfortunately, there is no algorithm that can determine, of any context-free grammar G, whether or not it is ambiguous. In other words, the ambiguity problem for context-free grammars is *undecidable*. However, there are algorithms that can pick out all the potential trouble-spots: if none are found, the grammar is free of ambiguity. So the situation is better than the theory suggests.

Two grammars are *equivalent* if they define the same language. This term has been used several times already. For example, the previous section stated that for every regular expression there is an equivalent finite automaton (and vice-versa). The *equivalence problem* is to determine, of two grammars G and G', whether or not they are equivalent. For regular expressions and (equivalently) for finite automata, the problem can always be solved (see Exercise 13). For most other kinds of grammar, though, it is another undecidable problem: there is no algorithm for determining whether or not G and G' are equivalent. In practice, this seldom causes any hardship. The more usual need is to transform G into an equivalent grammar G', where G' has some desirable property (such as being deterministic). Methods for doing this can often be found and are frequently used in the design of compilers.

6.8   PHRASE STRUCTURE GRAMMARS

As noted above, a generative grammar is one that states how the sentences of a language can be generated. Typically, the method is to start with a symbol S, representing a sentence, and to use a series of *rewriting rules*. For example, to generate sentences in the English language, the rule

$$S \rightarrow NP\ VP$$

states that a sentence S can be rewritten as a Noun Phrase followed by a Verb Phrase.

The additional rules

$$NP \rightarrow the N$$
$$N \rightarrow boy$$

enable the Noun Phrase to be rewritten as 'the N', which in turn can be rewritten as 'the boy'. The situation can be expressed by writing

$$NP \rightarrow the N \rightarrow the boy$$

which is called a *derivation sequence*. Similarly, the rules

$$VP \rightarrow V NP$$
$$V \rightarrow saw$$
$$N \rightarrow ball$$

support the derivation:

$$VP \rightarrow V NP \rightarrow saw NP \rightarrow saw the N \rightarrow saw the ball$$

Together they can generate the sentence 'the boy saw the ball'.

For programming languages, the rewriting rules are usually called *productions*, or *production rules*, or *derivation rules*. The symbols on the left-hand side of the rules are *non-terminal symbols*, or *categories*. In the above example, they are represented by upper-case letters. The others constitute the alphabet mentioned above and are called *terminal symbols*, or *basic symbols*, or *tokens*. In some contexts, the symbols are called *characters*, even though in the normal sense of the word they may be several characters long. In programming, for example, the tokens can include names and numbers consisting of several letters or digits. The combined set of symbols is sometimes called the *vocabulary*, with the alphabet being the *terminal vocabulary*.

With a grammar of this kind, a sentence is any string of basic symbols that can be derived from S by repeated application of the rewriting rules. The grammar breaks the sentence into a number of *phrases*, such as 'the boy' and 'saw the ball', and gives them a certain structure. It is therefore known as a *phrase structure grammar*. The structure can be depicted by a *derivation tree*. For example, the tree in Figure 6-3 shows the derivation of 'the boy saw the ball'. As is usual in computing, the tree grows downwards. The positions in the tree are called *nodes*. Those at the bottom are *terminal nodes*, the others being *non-terminal* — a description that agrees with the two kinds of symbol they contain.

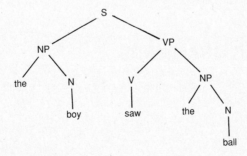

Figure 6-3 A derivation tree

The above discussion shows that a phrase structure grammar has four components:

- a set of terminal symbols (the alphabet);
- a set of non-terminal symbols (the categories);
- a set of rewriting rules (or productions);
- a special category S (the *start* symbol).

The grammars can be classified according to the form of their rules. Four classes are defined in an important paper by N. Chomsky (1959), where they are called *type 0*, *type 1*, *type 2*, and *type 3*. The following notation is used:

χ, ω arbitrary strings of one or more symbols;
α, β arbitrary strings of symbols, possibly null;
A, B   single categories;
a, b   single basic symbols.

The different types of grammar allow rewriting rules with the following forms:

type 0 $\chi \rightarrow \omega$
type 1 $\alpha A \beta \rightarrow \alpha \omega \beta$
type 2 $A \rightarrow \omega$
type 3 $A \rightarrow aB, \quad A \rightarrow a$

Type 0 is completely general: any occurrence of the string χ can be rewritten as the string ω. Type 1 allows a category A to be rewritten as ω. The rewriting can be restricted to a context $\alpha \ldots \beta$, such rules being called *context-sensitive*. Type 2 is the kind illustrated above. It allows A to be rewritten as ω, but not with any restrictions on the context; its rules are therefore called *context-free*. Type 3 limits the context-free rules to two particularly simple forms; for reasons that will appear, it is sometimes called a *regular* grammar.

These four types of grammar place increasing restrictions on the kinds of rule that can be used. One might therefore expect them to define a progressively limited range of languages. This is indeed the case, being established by Chomsky in the paper referred to. If a language can be generated by a grammar of type *i*, but not by one of type *i+1*, it is called a *type i language*. The type 0 grammars are so powerful that they can generate any language for which an effective generating procedure exists. However, they do not correspond to any simple structuring process, nor do they throw much light on programming techniques. In practice, only the type 2 and type 3 grammars have much relevance. The next few sections examine them more closely, with particular concern for the essential factor that distinguishes them.

6.9   REGULAR GRAMMARS

According to the classification given above, a type 3 (regular) grammar allows productions of two kinds:

$$A \rightarrow aB$$
$$A \rightarrow a$$

The following is a simple example, based on the alphabet {a, b} and having three categories S, D, and E. The start symbol is S:

S	→	a D	S →	b E
D	→	a E	E →	a D
D	→	b D	E →	b E
D	→	b	E →	a

It generates strings such as ab, ba, aaa, bba, baaba, and so on. The string baaba, for example, has the derivation:

$$S \rightarrow bE \rightarrow baD \rightarrow baaE \rightarrow baabE \rightarrow baaba$$

As can be seen, each step adds one more symbol to the string that is being generated. The final step produces a 'terminal' string — that is, a string with no categories — and this terminates the rewriting process.

The importance of the type 3 grammars is that they generate the regular languages and are therefore equivalent in their expressive power to regular expressions and finite automata. This is why they are called the *regular* grammars. The property can be established by showing that they are an exact model of finite automata. The correspondence between the two mechanisms is summarized in Figure 6-4. If it is applied to the above grammar it produces the automaton of Figure 6-1. For example, the production S → aD becomes the transition from S to D labeled a. Similarly, D → b becomes the one from D to F labeled b. The grammar generates a sentence by starting with category S and applying a series of rewriting rules. The finite automaton generates the same sentence by starting in state S and following the corresponding series of transitions. This shows that the two mechanisms are logically identical and that they generate the same language. It follows that the type 3 languages are the regular languages.

Type 3 grammars can be varied in a number of minor ways. One possibility is to allow productions of two further kinds:

$$A \rightarrow B$$
$$A \rightarrow \varepsilon$$

In terms of finite automata, these correspond to the use of unlabeled transitions. The former models an unlabeled transition from state A to state B; the latter models one from state A to the final state F. As shown in Section 6.6, these extensions allow languages to include the null sentence ε, but they do not affect the essential power of the grammars in any other way.

Type 3 grammar	*Finite automaton*
basic symbol a	basic symbol a
category A	non-final state A
start symbol S	start state S
production A → a B	transition A $\xrightarrow{a}$ B
production A → a	transition A $\xrightarrow{a}$ F
production sequence	path

Figure 6-4 Two equivalent mechanisms

Another extension is to allow productions of the form:

$$A \;\rightarrow\; a_1 \; a_2 \; \ldots \; a_k \; B \qquad\qquad (k \geq 1)$$
$$A \;\rightarrow\; a_1 \; a_2 \; \ldots \; a_k \qquad\qquad (k \geq 1)$$

These maintain the restriction that a category can appear only as the rightmost symbol of a production, and so the grammars are called *right-linear*. They can be converted to standard type 3 form by the introduction of intermediate categories. For example, a production of the first kind is replaced by k simpler productions:

$$A \;\rightarrow\; a_1 \; Q_1$$
$$Q_1 \;\rightarrow\; a_2 \; Q_2$$
$$\ldots$$
$$Q_{k-1} \;\rightarrow\; a_k \; B$$

The right-linear grammars therefore generate the same (regular) languages as the standard type 3 grammars. Their only advantage is brevity.

A final variation changes the role of B so that it has to be the *leftmost* symbol. The allowable forms are therefore:

$$A \;\rightarrow\; B \; a_1 \; a_2 \; \ldots \; a_k \qquad\qquad (k \geq 1)$$
$$A \;\rightarrow\; a_1 \; a_2 \; \ldots \; a_k \qquad\qquad (k \geq 1)$$

These are the *left-linear* grammars and they too are equivalent to the regular grammars. The proof of this is left as an exercise (see Exercise 18).

6.10 RECURSION

Type 3 grammars define the regular languages, but unlike regular expressions they do not have a repetition operator. What has taken its place?

The answer is that they use a new structuring mechanism, namely *recursion*. In its most general sense, a definition is *recursive* if the defining part refers to the thing that is being defined. We noted an example of this in Section 6.1:

> A sequence is a set of n items, one being distinguished as the first and the remainder being a sequence of n − 1 items.

Thus a sequence is defined in terms of a smaller sequence. This sounds quite plausible; but as it stands it is insufficient. In fact it is about as helpful as saying 'a rose is a rose is a rose'. The trouble is that the definition is circular. In order to evade the circularity, there has to be an *escape clause* — that is, an alternative to the main definition which is *not* recursive. For sequences, this can be provided by the special case of the null sequence, which corresponds to the empty set:

> A sequence is
>   *either* the null sequence ε
>   *or* a set of n items (n ≥ 1)
>   one being distinguished as the first and
>   the remainder being a sequence of n−1 items.

This illustrates one of the basic rules of recursion: *always make sure that there is an escape clause*.

Now consider a simple type 3 grammar:

$$S \rightarrow a\,S$$
$$S \rightarrow b$$

This states that an S is either the letter a followed by an S, or else the letter b. The first part is recursive and the second part provides the escape clause. As is easily verified, the grammar is equivalent to the regular expression $a^* b$. It shows how recursion can be used as an alternative to repetition.

The above grammar is an example of *direct* recursion — S is defined directly in terms of itself. The following example is a bit more complicated:

$$S \rightarrow a\,A$$
$$A \rightarrow b\,B$$
$$B \rightarrow c\,S$$
$$S \rightarrow d$$

Here S is defined in terms of A, A is defined in terms of B, and B is defined in terms of S. Thus S is defined in terms of itself, but in this case the recursion is *indirect*. In fact, A, B, and S are all defined in terms of each other, so they can be described as *mutually recursive*. The grammar may seem more complicated than the previous one. However, it can be converted to the right-linear form

$$S \rightarrow a\,b\,c\,S$$
$$S \rightarrow d$$

and this shows that it is equivalent to the regular expression $(abc)^* d$. Once again, the recursion has provided an alternative to repetition.

The examples could be made more and more complicated; but as long as they are restricted to type 3 grammars, the conclusion will always be the same. Each grammar will be equivalent to a regular expression, and so the recursion will be nothing more than a disguised form of repetition.

Dropping the type 3 restriction opens up some wider possibilities. In general, a category A is recursive if it can generate a string containing itself; that is to say, there is a derivation sequence of the form:

$$A \rightarrow \omega_1 \rightarrow \omega_2 \rightarrow \ldots \rightarrow \alpha\,A\,\beta$$

This can be abbreviated to

$$A \xrightarrow{+} \alpha\,A\,\beta$$

which states that A is defined, either directly or indirectly, in terms of itself. Since α and/or β may be null, there are four possibilities that need to be distinguished:

$A \xrightarrow{+} A$	—	A is *circular*	
$A \xrightarrow{+} A\,\omega$	—	A is *left-recursive*	
$A \xrightarrow{+} \chi\,A$	—	A is *right-recursive*	
$A \xrightarrow{+} \chi\,A\,\omega$	—	A is *self-embedding*	

The first possibility is usually eliminated from a grammar since it does not contribute anything useful. The remaining three are all significant and a grammar is said to be left-recursive and/or right-recursive and/or self-embedding if it contains categories of the corresponding kinds. It can be shown that a type 2 grammar generates an infinite number of sentences if and only if it contains recursion in at least one of these three forms (Exercise 21).

Against this background it is important to note that type 3 grammars can only be right-recursive. This is because their derivation sequences always have the form

$$A \rightarrow a_1 B_1 \rightarrow a_1 a_2 B_2 \rightarrow a_1 a_2 a_3 B_3 \rightarrow \dots$$

and so the only possibility for recursion is

$$A \xrightarrow{+} \chi A$$

More generally, with right-linear grammars the categories are restricted to being right-recursive, and with left-linear grammars they are restricted to being left-recursive. There is no way in which their categories can be self-embedding.

The above observations can be summarized as follows:

1. Right-linear grammars can only be right-recursive.

2. Left-linear grammars can only be left-recursive.

3. For any right- or left-linear grammar there is an equivalent regular expression.

4. Regular expressions use repetition, but not recursion.

Putting these together, we arrive at the following important conclusion. *Right-recursion by itself, or similarly left-recursion by itself, is basically a disguised form of repetition.* To provide a structuring mechanism that is more powerful than repetition, recursion has to be used in its self-embedding form.

6.11   CONTEXT-FREE GRAMMARS

A type 2 (context-free) grammar allows the right-hand side of a production to be any sequence of terminal and/or non-terminal symbols. In Section 6.8, it was asserted that such grammars can define a greater range of languages than the type 3 grammars; in other words, they can generate languages that are non-regular. This can be proved by considering the grammar

$$S \rightarrow a\ S\ b$$
$$S \rightarrow x$$

which defines the language consisting of the sentences $a^n x b^n$ ($n \geq 0$). No finite automaton can generate these sentences without generating other ones as well (see Exercise 19), and so the language is not a regular one. Of course, sentences of the form $a^n x b^n$ may not seem very exciting. But if a and b are replaced by opening and closing parentheses, their relevance becomes more apparent. The sentences are x, (x), ((x)), (((x))), ... , and the grammar ensures that the parentheses are properly matched. A regular grammar could not do this. Similarly, in the context of program execution, a and b might represent the actions of entering and leaving a procedure. Under normal conditions each entry will have to be matched by a corresponding exit. So once again the ability to pair the a's and b's has great practical significance.

What is it that gives the type 2 grammars their extra power? What is the essential characteristic that distinguishes them from type 3 grammars? The answer to these questions was anticipated in the previous section and is simply this: they allow categories to be self-embedding. The following theorem states the situation more precisely:

Theorem 6.2

In order to generate a non-regular language a context-free grammar must be self-embedding.

For example, the above two-line grammar generates a non-regular language. The theorem states that S must therefore be self-embedding; and, sure enough, it is. The theorem can also be stated the other way round:

Corollary

If a context-free grammar G is *not* self-embedding the language L(G) is regular.

The considerations of the preceding section make this look very plausible. Nevertheless, the formal proof requires some non-trivial spadework and will therefore be deferred until the end of the next section. (For a third way of stating the theorem, see Exercise 24.)

The converse of the theorem is false. Given that a grammar G is self-embedding, it does *not* follow that L(G) is non-regular. A sufficient counter-example is the grammar

$$S \rightarrow a\,S\,a$$
$$S \rightarrow a$$

which is self-embedding in exactly the same way as the previous one. Yet it is equivalent to the regular expression a (aa)*, which shows that the language is regular.

In programming, a frequent use for type 2 grammars is in defining the syntax of expressions. The following example involves the variable x and the operators '+' and '*'. Typical expressions are x, x + x, x * (x + x), (((x))), and so on. The start symbol is E, with T denoting a term and P a primary:

$$E \rightarrow T$$
$$E \rightarrow E + T$$
$$T \rightarrow P$$
$$T \rightarrow T * P$$
$$P \rightarrow x$$
$$P \rightarrow (E)$$

From the second and fourth productions, it is clear that E and T are left-recursive. This provides for the repetition that is inherent in expressions such as T + T + T or P * P * P * P. More importantly, the derivation sequence

$$E \rightarrow T \rightarrow P \rightarrow (E)$$

shows that E is also self-embedding. One expression can be embedded or 'nested' inside another. (Beds and nests serve similar purposes.) As is readily verified, T and P are self-embedding too, and in fact the three categories can all embed each other.

The upshot of all this is that recursion is a more powerful structuring mechanism than repetition. However, if its full power is to be realized it has to be recursion of the self-embedding kind — *real* recursion, as opposed to the 'pseudo' varieties that are repetition in disguise. This real, self-embedding recursion is inherent in structures that can have substructures of the same kind. In program execution, for example, routines can execute subroutines (see Section 6.13). In data structures, lists can have sublists, trees can have subtrees, and so on. These are recursive structures and they stand in contrast to the merely repetitive ones, such as loops, files, and arrays. Theorem 6.2 shows that there is a fundamental difference between the two groups. In later chapters, this difference will be reflected in the structures of the programs that handle them.

6.12   TESTING FOR RECURSION

This section outlines algorithms for testing whether or not an arbitrary context-free grammar is (a) left-recursive, (b) right-recursive, and (c) self-embedding. Following on from (c), it proves Theorem 6.2 of the previous section. The earlier parts use techniques that are important in the theory and practice of writing compilers. The later parts are more mathematical in nature, drawing on material from Chapter 1. Their details are mostly relegated to the exercises.

The test for left recursion is based on a relation $A \, h \, B$ meaning 'the category A has a definition that starts with B'. The relation can be represented by a square matrix H, with a row and column for each category. $H[A, B]$ is set to 1 if there is a production

$$A \;\to\; B \, \beta$$

where β is an arbitrary string of symbols, possibly empty; otherwise it is set to 0. Now consider its transitive closure $A \, h^+ \, B$ (see Section 1.4). This means that there is a chain of one or more productions of the form

$$
\begin{aligned}
A &\;\to\; B_1 \, \beta_1 \\
B_1 &\;\to\; B_2 \, \beta_2 \\
&\;\cdots \\
B_{k-1} &\;\to\; B \, \beta_k
\end{aligned}
$$

and hence that there is a derivation sequence:

$$A \;\xrightarrow{+}\; B \, \beta_k \; \cdots \; \beta_1$$

We say that B is a *head* symbol of A. The relevance of this is that if A is left-recursive, it must be a head symbol of itself. So the test proceeds by computing the transitive closure of H (see Warshall's algorithm, Exercise 1.12) and then examining its diagonal elements. If A is left-recursive, $H[A, A]$ will be 1.

Not surprisingly, the test for right recursion is very similar. It defines a relation $A \, t \, B$, meaning that there is a production of the form

$$A \;\to\; \alpha \, B$$

The transitive closure $A t^+ B$ states that B is a *tail* symbol of A, and $A t^+ A$ means that A is right-recursive.

In order to test for self-embedding categories it is natural to define a relation $A g B$ meaning that there is a production of the form:

$$A \;\to\; \alpha \; B \; \beta$$

Its transitive closure $A g^+ B$ states that A can *generate* a B (that is, a string containing a B), and the case $A g^+ A$ states that A can generate itself — it is recursive. This is a necessary condition for A to be self-embedding, but unfortunately it is not sufficient. Since α and β can be empty, A could equally well be left-recursive, or right-recursive, or any combination of all three.

In order to proceed further it is helpful to start with the case of a grammar in which every category can generate every other category. The grammar for expressions, as given in the previous section, provides a simple example. Its categories are E, T, and P, and the derivation sequence

$$E \;\to\; T \;\to\; P \;\to\; (\,E\,) \;\to\; (\,T\,) \;\to\; (\,P\,)$$

shows that each of them can generate the others. We shall describe them as a *mutually generating set*. In such cases, the required test is very simple: the grammar is self-embedding if and only if it is neither left-linear nor right-linear (see Exercise 25).

The strategy for testing an arbitrary context-free grammar is to partition its categories into mutually generating sets and then to test each set separately. The sets are based on the 'mutuality' relation:

$$A = B \quad \textbf{or} \quad (A \; g^+ \; B \;\; \textbf{and} \;\; B \; g^+ \; A)$$

It is easily shown that this is an equivalence relation and that it therefore partitions the categories into equivalence classes (see Section 1.4). These are the required sets and they have the property that two categories A and B can generate each other if and only if they belong to the same set. In searching for self-embedding categories it is therefore sufficient to test each set separately. Its productions are treated as an independent subgrammar in which categories from other sets have the status of basic symbols, and the above test is applied to it. If any set is self-embedding, the grammar is also; otherwise it is not (see Exercise 27).

The test is the key to proving Theorem 6.2, to the effect that a non-self-embedding grammar defines a regular language. It is sufficient to show that if every subgrammar in the above construction is either left-linear or right-linear, then every category can be replaced by an equivalent regular expression. Within each subgrammar this is straightforward (see Section 6.9). A partial ordering on the sets enables the regular expressions to be combined across the entire grammar, resulting in a single expression for the start symbol. The details are left as an exercise for readers with a mathematical bent (Exercises 28 – 30).

6.13 PUSHDOWN AUTOMATA

Section 6.9 showed that type 3 grammars can be modeled by a very simple device, namely the finite automaton (FA). This has a finite number of states and is therefore an example of a more general sort of machine — the *finite state automaton* (FSA). However, apart from its states and transitions, it has no other means of recording or handling information and so the single term *finite* describes it more accurately. In fact, its finiteness is what prevents it from handling the self-embedding languages, such as $\{a^n x b^n \mid n \geq 0\}$. To cope with an arbitrary value of n, a machine has to be infinite.

The best way of achieving this is not to create an infinite number of states but to augment a conventional FA with a suitable storage device. For example, to handle the sentences $a^n x b^n$ it is sufficient to add a *counter* with the following set of operations:

- initialize the counter to zero;
- increment it by one;
- decrement it by one;
- test it for zero.

The machine could then check that the number of a's and b's were equal (Exercise 32). Since the capacity of the counter would have to be unbounded, the machine would no longer be finite; but it would still be an FSA.

To handle arbitrary type 2 languages, a single counter is not sufficient. In principle (and with a lot of ingenuity), two counters can do the trick. In practice, a preferable strategy is to use a more powerful storage device — the *stack* or *pushdown store*. The resulting machine is called a *pushdown automaton* (or PDA for short — abbreviations run riot in this field). Stacks were introduced earlier, in Section 5.11, where they were used for controlling the execution of subroutines; so there is no need to define their 'push' and 'pop' operations here. However, it is instructive to note the reason for their re-appearance in this context. The point is that the categories of a type 2 grammar are very similar to subroutines. Consider, for example, a typical type 2 production:

$$A \;\rightarrow\; b\,C\,d$$

This states that a string of category A can be constructed from a b, followed by a string of category C, followed by a d. So it is, in effect, equivalent to the following routine:

> to generate a string of category A:
> > emit b;
> > generate a string of category C;
> > emit d;

This is the routine for A and, as can be seen, it treats the rule for C as though it were a subroutine. In its turn, C can call on other categories as though they were sub-subroutines; and so on. This being the case, the re-appearance of the stack is hardly surprising. It is needed for handling the return addresses of all these subroutine calls.

To formalize this, we shall define a PDA of a particularly simple kind. The basic idea is that to generate a string of category A it starts in a state named A and follows a transition sequence to a final state F. If the rule is $A \rightarrow b\,C\,d$, the transition sequence will be the one shown in Figure 6-5, which uses Q_1 and Q_2 as intermediate states. The chief

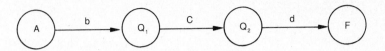

Figure 6-5   A simple transition sequence

novelty lies in the transition from Q_1 to Q_2, which is labeled not by a basic symbol, but by the category C. To handle it, the PDA loads Q_2 on its stack, moves to state C, and then starts following one of the rules for C. On completing the rule (by reaching F), it unloads Q_2 from the stack and this tells it where to resume the rule for A. Thus Q_2 is, in effect, the return address for the call of C.

The complete PDA for a type 2 grammar G, with start symbol S, is constructed as follows. For each category A there is a corresponding state A, and for each production A → ... there is a series of transitions leading from A to F, as illustrated in Figure 6-5. The machine starts in state S, with an empty stack, and then operates according to the following rules:

1. If it is in state X and there is a transition X $\xrightarrow{a}$ Y, it may follow the transition by emitting the symbol a and moving to state Y.

2. If it is in state X and there is a transition X $\xrightarrow{A}$ Y, it may follow the transition by putting Y on the stack and moving to state A (a subroutine entry).

3. If it reaches the final state F and there is a state Q on the top of the stack, it pops the stack and moves to Q (a return jump).

4. If it reaches the final state F and the stack is empty, it stops.

A category with several rules will give rise to a state in which the machine has several transitions to choose from. So, as with the finite automaton, the machine is non-deterministic. By choosing different paths, it can generate different sentences and the set of possible sentences is the language L(G).

This device demonstrates that a simple form of pushdown automaton can be used for modeling type 2 grammars and, equivalently, for executing a set of routines. It shows that stacks, or some equivalent mechanism, are essential for handling recursive structures. This fact has important implications for programming: whenever recursion is involved, a stack in some guise or other will always be present. Examples of this will be given in Chapter 9 (see also Exercise 33).

For completeness it should be mentioned that pushdown automata are usually defined with a rather more sophisticated mechanism. The items held on the stack are not simply states (return addresses) but are symbols with additional significance. Their purpose is to give greater power to pushdown automata that are deterministic, and hence to machines for *accepting* type 2 languages. Their ability to *generate* type 2 languages is no greater and it turns out, in fact, that they still cannot accept all of the type 2 languages. This contrasts with the type 3 languages, for which deterministic acceptors can always be found (see Section 6.6). For a study of these topics, the reader should consult the literature on automata theory and on top-down parsing techniques.

6.14   GRAMMARS FOR PROGRAMMING LANGUAGES

Ever since the publication of the ALGOL 60 report (Naur, 1960), grammars have been widely used in the definition of programming languages. This section reviews some of the formalisms that have been devised for the purpose, relating them to the types of grammar discussed previously.

The grammar for COBOL provides a good starting point. The following definition is a simplified version of its MOVE statement:

$$\text{MOVE} \left\{ \begin{array}{l} \text{data-name-1} \\ \text{literal} \end{array} \right\} \text{TO} \quad \text{data-name-2} \quad [\,\text{data-name-3}\,] \quad ...$$

This uses curly brackets to enclose alternatives, square brackets to enclose options, and the three-dot notation to indicate repetition. Such definitions embody catenation, alternation, and repetition, and are therefore equivalent to regular expressions. In the notation of Section 6.5, for example, the above definition would be written as the regular expression:

$$\text{MOVE} \;(\text{data–name} \cup \text{literal}) \quad \text{TO} \quad \text{data–name} \quad \text{data–name}^{*}$$

COBOL's notation is an attractive alternative for the same thing. However, since regular expressions cannot define self-embedding categories, it is not sufficient by itself for defining nested expressions, nested statements, and so on. Some sort of type 2 facility is needed as well. COBOL provides this by including a few recursive categories and allowing them to occur in the regular expressions (though see Exercise 33).

ALGOL 60 was developed at the same time as COBOL, but the form of its grammar made a much greater impact. It used the notation that has become widely known as BNF. Originally the initials stood for Backus Normal Form; but the term 'normal form' was later deemed inappropriate and so the name was changed to Backus Naur Form, in honour of the notation's two main originators — John Backus and Peter Naur. The following is a typical piece of BNF syntax, describing expressions that involve the variable x and the operators '+' and '∗':

```
<expression>    ::=    <term>  |  <expression> + <term>
     <term>     ::=    <primary>  |  <term> ∗ <primary>
   <primary>    ::=    x  |  ( <expression> )
```

This grammar is essentially the same as the one given in Section 6.11. It is simply a type 2 grammar expressed in a different notation. The categories are enclosed in angle brackets; '→' is written as "::="; and alternative definitions of a category are separated by '|'. Strictly speaking, there is a difference in that a BNF grammar can use the null string ε; but as with type 3 grammars, this does not make them significantly more powerful.

Since a type 2 grammar is context-free, it follows that ALGOL 60 is a context-free language. This may provoke some misgivings. For example, a production such as

```
<identifier>    ::=    x
```

implies that x can be used as an identifier in any context. Yet it is a rule of ALGOL 60 that x can only be used as an identifier in the context of a block in which it has been declared. Similar restrictions apply in most other programming languages. So it appears that BNF grammars have a serious drawback: they generate large numbers of programs that are not in fact legal. This is indeed the case. Worse still, the situation is not easily remedied. We might think that the type 1 grammars would help at this point, since they are called 'context-sensitive'. Unfortunately, though, their interpretation of 'context' is not nearly sophisticated enough to handle languages such as ALGOL 60. The only way to overcome the problem is to devise a notation that somehow accumulates tables of declared identifiers and restricts the use of <identifier> to the current set. Unfortunately, this requires some complicated apparatus and destroys the attractive simplicity of BNF.

Some other deficiencies of BNF are more easily remedied. The main problem is that there is no simple way of specifying repetition. For example, given a category <subscript>, suppose that a definition is needed for a list of subscripts separated by commas. With regular expressions, this is very easy:

$$\text{<subscript>} (, \text{<subscript>})^{*}$$

By contrast, BNF has to use recursion, introducing an extra category <subscript list> for the purpose:

<subscript list>   ::=   <subscript> |
                          <subscript> , <subscript list>

This is rather clumsy. It makes the grammar unnecessarily long and results in derivation trees that are overstructured. More recent languages have therefore extended BNF in a variety of ways. Two common extension are the following (Wirth, 1977b):

[x]   denotes an optional occurrence of the sequence x;
{ x }   denotes nought or more occurrences of x (repetition).

If these conventions are applied to the syntax of the ALGOL 60 report, the number of categories can be reduced by more than half.

Another way of defining a language is to use *syntax diagrams*. Figure 6-6 illustrates the diagram that defines the category constant in Pascal. An equivalent definition in extended BNF is the following:

constant   ::=   [sign] constant_identifier |
                   [sign] unsigned_number |
                   ' character { character } '

sign   ::=   + | −

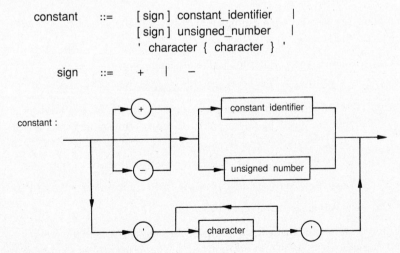

Figure 6-6   A syntax diagram

The diagram is harder for a machine to follow but easier for most human beings. It is, in effect, a finite automaton to which recursion has been added. As Exercise 40 shows, such diagrams are easily converted to equivalent type 2 productions. It follows that their power is the same as that of BNF, or extended BNF, or any other type 2 notation.

Many other kinds of grammar have been devised — transformational grammars, indexed grammars, two-level grammars, and so on. They aim to overcome the deficiencies of the type 2 grammars, and in many respects they succeed. However, their advantages are won at the cost of much greater complexity and so far none of them has gained widespread acceptance in the programming field. Since they do not throw light on any other aspects of programming structures, there is no need to examine them here.

FURTHER READING

Some standard references on the material of this chapter are the books by Minsky (1967), Hopcroft and Ullman (1969, 1979), and Salomaa (1973). These contain references to the earlier literature on the subject. The proof of Theorem 6.1 was first published by McNaughton and Yamada (1960); an alternative proof, which results in simpler regular expressions, is given in Denning, Dennis, and Qualitz (1978). An interestingly different approach is provided by Conway (1971). The proof of Theorem 6.2 is adapted from Kurki-Suonio (1971): it is chosen because it reflects the structural principles that are involved. Grammars for programming languages are discussed in books on compilers, including Backhouse (1979) and Aho, Sethi, and Ullman (1986).

EXERCISES

1   Section 1 gave two operational definitions of a sequence — one iterative and one recursive. Using each of these in turn, give a formal definition of the catenation of two sequences.

2   Give the simplest possible example of two sets of sequences, S1 and S2, for which: $|S1.S2| \neq |S1| \times |S2|$.

3   Write regular expressions for the following languages:

   (a)   The strings over $(0 \cup 1)^*$ with a length divisible by three.

   (b)   The numerals that consist of a sequence of digits, followed by a decimal point, followed by a sequence of digits: one or other sequence may be empty, but not both.

   (c)   The strings over $(a \cup b)^*$ that have exactly one a or exactly one b.

   (d)   The strings over $(a \cup b \cup c)^*$ in which no c may be adjacent to an a.

   (e)   The Roman numerals I, II, III, ... C.

4   Construct finite automata that define the same languages as in the previous exercise. For which of the languages are finite automata easier to use than regular expressions? What sort of features distinguish such languages?

5   Suppose that finite automata are allowed to have transitions into S and out of F. Show that this does not extend the range of languages that they can define. (Show how they can be converted to equivalent machines in which such transitions have been removed.)

6   Suppose that finite automata are allowed to have multiple final states. This means that S itself can be designated as final and so the machine can generate the null string ε. Show that apart from this factor the range of definable languages remains the same. (Hint: start by applying the construction of the previous exercise.)

7   Suppose that finite automata are allowed to have unlabeled transitions. Show that apart from allowing the inclusion of ε, this does not extend the range of definable languages. (Hint: the general strategy is to add extra transitions that allow the unlabeled ones to be 'bypassed'. For example, a transition sequence A → B $\overset{x}{\rightarrow}$ C can be bypassed by adding A $\overset{x}{\rightarrow}$ C. Care is needed in handling S and F.)

8   Construct finite automata that are equivalent to the following regular expressions:

   (a) $a\,(b \cup c)\,d^*e$

   (b) $((a \cup b)\,(a \cup b))^*$

   (c) $(a^* \cup b^*)\,(c^* \cup d^*)$

   If it is helpful, begin by using unlabeled transitions and then remove them.

9   Given finite automata that are equivalent to the regular expressions R1, R2, and R, show how to construct ones that are equivalent to $R1 \cup R2$, $R1\,.\,R2$, and R^*. Note that since R^* includes the sentence ε, the equivalent automaton must be allowed one of the extensions described in Exercises 6.6 and 6.7. Choose whichever is more convenient. (Hint: restrict the automata to having a single start state with no transitions entering it, and a single final state with no transitions leaving it.)

10   Given a finite automaton that is equivalent to the regular expression R, show how to construct one that is equivalent to its complement $\overline{R}$ (the strings over the alphabet that are not in R). Assume that the finite automaton can be converted to an equivalent one that is deterministic, as described in Section 6.

   This proves that if R is a regular language then so is $\overline{R}$. Deduce that if R1 and R2 are regular languages, then so is their intersection $R1 \cap R2$ (the sentences common to both).

11   Section 6.6 described a 'brute force' method of converting a finite automaton into an equivalent regular expression. Using this, or any other method, find a regular expression that is equivalent to the automaton of Figure 6-1.

12   Are the following pairs of regular expressions equivalent or not?

   (a) a^*b^* and $(ab)^*$;

   (b) $(x^* \cup y^*)\,(y^* \cup x^*)$ and $(x^*\,y^* \cup y^*\,x^*)$;

   (c) $00\,(01)^*11$ and $000\,(10)^*111$;

   (d) $0001\,(01)^*11$ and $000\,(10)^*111$.

13   Outline an algorithm that will determine, of two arbitrary finite automata, whether or not they are equivalent. Assume that each of them can be converted into an equivalent one that is deterministic, as described in Section 6.6.

14   Consider the fragment of English grammar given in Section 6.8 and add the following productions:

$$V \rightarrow \text{hit}$$
$$V \rightarrow \text{ran}$$

What sentences can the grammar now generate? Which of them would you regard as legitimate English sentences?

The problem of defining a grammar for the entire English language is an exceedingly difficult one. Yet we can all recognize sentences, so presumably there is a mechanism for it somewhere. The mechanism has obvious importance for programs that handle natural languages, but its precise nature is a matter of considerable debate.

15   Show that the following grammar is ambiguous:

$$S \rightarrow E$$
$$E \rightarrow E + E$$
$$E \rightarrow x$$

Devise an equivalent grammar that is not ambiguous.

16   Show that the following grammar is ambiguous:

$$S \rightarrow P\ P$$
$$P \rightarrow a\ P\ a$$
$$P \rightarrow b\ P\ b$$
$$P \rightarrow a$$
$$P \rightarrow b$$

Characterize the strings generated by P and hence the sentences of the language. Can you find a non-ambiguous grammar for the language? Or is it *inherently* ambiguous?

17   The derivation of a sentence for a type 2 grammar can be represented by a derivation tree. What sort of derivation structure would be needed for a type 3 grammar? A type 1 grammar? A type 0 grammar?

18   Prove that the left-linear grammars define the regular languages. (A possible approach is to prove that if a language L is regular, the language obtained by reversing its sentences is also regular.)

19   Prove that a type 3 grammar cannot define the language $\{a^n x b^n \mid n \geq 0\}$. (Hint: using finite automata, show that if a regular language includes the sentences $a^n x b^n$ for arbitrarily large n, it must include other sentences as well.)

20   A category is said to be *useless* if it cannot appear in the derivation of a sentence. Such categories can be removed from a grammar without affecting the language generated. Indeed, it is generally assumed that this has been done, since the presence of useless categories complicates some of the theory. In the case of type 2 grammars, a category A is useless unless it can appear in a derivation sequence

$$S \;\rightarrow\; \ldots \;\rightarrow\; \alpha\,A\,\beta \;\rightarrow\; \ldots \;\rightarrow\; \sigma$$

for some terminal string σ. This implies

(a) $S \overset{+}{\Rightarrow} \alpha\,A\,\beta$;

(b) $A \overset{+}{\Rightarrow} \tau$ for some terminal string τ.

These conditions are necessary for non-uselessness, but are they sufficient?

21   In Section 6.10 it was stated that a type 2 grammar generates an infinite language if, and only if, it is recursive. In fact, this requires a qualification: the grammar must not contain any useless categories (as defined in the previous exercise). Why is this qualification necessary? To prove the 'if' part, assume that there is a category A with a recursive derivation sequence,

$$A \overset{+}{\Rightarrow} \chi\,A\,\omega$$

where either χ or ω may be empty, but not both. Using conditions (a) and (b) of the previous exercise, show that there is an infinite set of derivation sequences

$$S \overset{+}{\Rightarrow} \alpha\,\chi^r\,A\,\omega^r\,\beta \qquad (r \geq 0)$$

and deduce that the language is infinite.

To prove the 'only if' part, show that if there are no recursive categories the language must be finite. (Hint: a path through a derivation tree could not contain the same category twice, and so there would be certain bounds on the size of the tree.)

22   Use the previous exercise to show that if a grammar is recursive it can generate a series of sentences whose lengths form an arithmetic progression. Use this observation to prove that the language

$$\{a^i \mid i \text{ is a perfect square}\}$$

is not a type 2 language. Give a grammar for the language

$$\{a^i \mid i \text{ is divisible by 2 and/or 3}\}$$

23   Consider the following grammar:

S	→	A a	B	→	A
A	→	b B	C	→	S
A	→	c C	A	→	a
A	→	C	B	→	b

Which categories are (a) circular, (b) left-recursive, (c) right-recursive, and (d) self-embedding?

24   A language is *inherently* X if its defining grammars must necessarily have property X. For example, it is inherently ambiguous if all its possible grammars are ambiguous. Show that the following statement is equivalent to Theorem 6.2: 'A language is inherently type 2 if and only if it is inherently self-embedding'.

Note   The next few exercises fill in the details concerning the test for 'real' (self-embedding) recursion, as given in Section 6.12, and they complete the associated proof of Theorem 6.2.

25   Given a grammar in which every category can generate every other category, prove the assertion that it is self-embedding if, and only if, it is neither left-linear nor right-linear.

26   Next, let A and B be two categories and consider the relation:

$$A = B \quad \textbf{or} \quad (A\ g^+\ B \quad \textbf{and} \quad B\ g^+\ A)$$

Prove that it is an equivalence relation on the categories of a grammar and that the corresponding equivalence classes are mutually generating sets. Since each category in a class can generate all the others, does it follow that each category can generate itself? Prove that if one category in a class is self-embedding, then so are all the others.

27   Suppose that the categories of a grammar G have been partitioned into mutually generating sets, as described in the previous exercise. Prove that G is self-embedding if and only if at least one of the sets, treated as an independent grammar, is self-embedding.

28   Let G be a grammar that is *not* self-embedding. The preceding exercises have shown that its categories can be partitioned into mutually generating sets, none of which is self-embedding. Defining the relation S > S' to mean that the categories of set S can generate those of set S' (if one can, they all can), prove that '>' is a partial ordering on the sets. (Note: this is a special case of Exercise 1.8.)

29   A *regular definition* is a sequence of productions

$$\begin{aligned}
A_1 &\rightarrow re_1 \\
A_2 &\rightarrow re_2 \\
&\cdots \\
A_n &\rightarrow re_n
\end{aligned}$$

where, for each i, A_i is a category and re_i is a regular expression over the set of basic symbols and the preceding categories $A_1, \dots A_{i-1}$. Prove that each A_i can be defined as a regular expression over the basic symbols alone.

30   Use the results of the previous two exercises to show that if a type 2 grammar G is not self-embedding, it can be formulated as a regular definition. Deduce that it defines a regular language. (This completes the proof of Theorem 6.2.)

31   Construct a grammar that is left-recursive and right-recursive but not self-embedding. Do not include any useless categories (see Exercise 20).

32   Construct a finite-state automaton, with a counter C, that generates the language $\{a^n x b^n \mid n \geq 0\}$. The transitions may be either labeled or unlabeled, and they may also be marked by symbols indicating that additional actions are to be taken:

0	—	set C to zero;
+	—	increment C by one;
−	—	decrement C by one;
=	—	test $C = 0$.

A transition marked by '=' may be followed only when $C = 0$.

33 In Section 6.13 it was asserted that wherever real, self-embedding recursion is present there must be some sort of stack for handling it. Yet the previous exercise shows that the self-embedding language $\{a^n x b^n \mid n \geq 0\}$ can be handled simply by using a counter. So where is the stack?

34 Consider the simplified form of pushdown automaton that was described in Section 6.13. According to Rule 2, a transition of the form $X \xrightarrow{A} Y$ is executed by loading Y on the stack and moving to state A. Show that if Y is the final state F, there is no need to load it on the stack. What implications does this have for right-linear grammars? What is the corresponding trick in machine code programming? (See Exercise 5.5.)

35 In Section 6.13, the description of pushdown automata stated that a transition $X \xrightarrow{A} Y$ is handled by putting Y on the stack and moving to state A. It then assumed that when the transitions for A were completed, Y would be available at the top of the stack. Prove that this assumption is valid. (Note: the basic approach is to prove that each transition leaves the stack unaltered. The difficulty is to keep the argument from being circular.)

36 Using the grammar for expressions that was given in Section 6.11, draw the derivation tree for $x + x * x$ and show that it implies the interpretation $x + (x * x)$. Prove that the grammar does not allow the alternative interpretation $(x + x) * x$. The obvious conclusion is that, in effect, the grammar gives '$*$' a higher precedence than '$+$'.

The concept can be carried much further. For example, by using more categories a grammar can embody the six levels of operator precedence that are listed in Section 7.7. However, the grammar becomes more complex and the derivation trees become correspondingly larger. For example, the expression x produces a derivation tree that is six levels deep! Perhaps it is better to use a simpler grammar and to specify the precedence levels separately. For a theoretical analysis of this topic, see Floyd (1963).

37 Section 6.14 illustrated the syntactic notation used for defining COBOL. Unfortunately the standard syntactic definitions of COBOL do not cover the entire language. As an example of the difficulties that this can cause, try reading any book that describes and/or defines COBOL. (If you are feeling really ambitious, choose the official definition put out by the Standards Association.) Try to deduce a BNF syntax for the categories <paragraph>, <sentence>, <statement>, and <imperative statement>.

38 The original Report on the Algorithmic Language ALGOL 60 (Naur, 1960) was a historic document. Among other things, it introduced BNF to an unsuspecting world. As an exercise in reading BNF, use the report to track down the answers to the following questions:

(a)   Which of the following expressions are legal?

$$- - 2$$
$$x \uparrow - 2$$
$$p \wedge \neg q$$

(b)   Show that the expression

if x = y **then** p **else** q < r

is ambiguous. How does the Revised Report (Naur, 1963) resolve this ambiguity?

(c)   Are there any situations in which a statement may not be preceded by a label?

39   The syntax of ALGOL 60 appears to exercise some control over the use of identifiers. For example, a subscripted variable is defined by

<subscripted variable>   ::=
            <array identifier> [<subscript list>]

The use of <array identifier> ostensibly prohibits other sorts of identifier from being used at that point. Yet the control is purely illusory. Why? Do you think that the device is helpful in any other respect? What parallels are there in the syntax of Ada?

40   As remarked in Section 6.14, syntax diagrams are like finite automata with the addition of recursive categories. With this observation in mind, show how any syntax diagram can be converted to an equivalent set of type 2 productions of the following forms:

$$A \rightarrow a$$
$$A \rightarrow a B$$
$$A \rightarrow B C$$

Show how further manipulation can eliminate productions of the form A → a B. The resulting grammar is said to be in Chomsky Normal Form (Chomsky, 1959).

7

STRAIGHTLINE PROGRAMS

7.1 PROGRAMS

In the world at large, a *program* is the schedule of events at a concert, or a conference, or some other such occasion. It is frequently set out in a document called a 'program', or possibly a 'programme', which lists all the events in the order of their occurrence. At a concert, for example, it may state that a particular overture comes first, then a symphony, then a 20-minute interval, and so on. At a conference, it sets out all the meetings that are to be held.

When computers first began to operate, the word 'program' was adopted for describing a sequence of instructions that the computer was expected to execute, usually for the purpose of solving some problem or performing some task. The scheduled events were machine operations: fetch A, add B, store in C, and so on. Compared with the items at a concert or a conference, they took place at an unprecedented rate — thousands of them, or even millions, per second. Nevertheless, the underlying idea remained the same. A program set out the precise schedule of events for solving the problem or performing the task. To use another term, it gave a step-by-step *procedure* for achieving the desired goal. The computer carried out the procedure by performing the operations in the order specified.

With the development of *problem-oriented* languages, this concept began to be replaced by another one. Programs no longer had to be written as sequences of machine instructions; instead, they were expressed in terms of the problem or task at hand. They became less concerned with the nitty-gritty of how to do something, and more concerned with making a clear formulation of what that 'something' should be. For example, they could use an expression such as $(x + y) * z$, indicating that a certain value was to be computed. But they did not state *how* it was to be computed. On any particular machine, several sequences of instructions could be used, and it was left to the compiler to choose a suitable one. In similar fashion, the languages introduced control structures and data structures, all of which reinforced the trend towards specifying 'what' rather than 'how'.

The shift across the 'what–how spectrum' led to the development of so-called *non-procedural* languages. In these, a program does not set out an algorithm in a conventional, step-by-step way. Instead, it lists a series of definitions, constraints, and rules, together with a desired goal. The implementation then tries to attain the goal within the given framework. As the name 'non-procedural' implies, the intention is that the program should be a pure statement of 'what', with no element of 'how'. In practice, the

135

underlying mechanism often induces a definite sequence of actions over which the programmer has close control, and so the programs are more procedural than might appear at first sight. To that extent, they still retain the original notion of a program as a sequence of operations.

The logical conclusion of the trend is the *specification* language, in which a program is solely concerned with 'what' and has no control over 'how'. The task is stated and the rest is left to the machine. Within some specialized fields of application, this ideal has already been reached — for example, packages for doing symbolic integration. In such cases, though, the statement of the problem is not usually called a 'program'. The feeling persists that, by definition, a program must contain some element of 'how'. If this disappears completely, then so does the act of programming.

This book takes a bottom-up approach to the subject of programming, starting with its smallest components and working up towards the higher-level structures. In terms of the 'what–how spectrum', this corresponds to starting at 'how' and moving towards 'what'. The earlier chapters looked at the most basic elements of 'how' — the actual operations of the computer. This one begins the journey across the spectrum, away from the machine and towards the problem. Along the way, we shall encounter programs and languages at many different points in the spectrum. We may even have occasional glimpses of the far end — that world where programs are irrelevant and programmers no longer needed. There, at the rainbow's end, a pot of gold doubtless awaits the traveler. But it is an elusive destination and, until we reach it, there will still be cause to study programs in their original, step-by-step, procedural sense.

7.2   PROGRAM STRUCTURE

The simplest kind of procedural program is one whose execution proceeds in a (notionally) straight line through the program text, obeying each instruction or statement exactly once. There are no loops, conditions, subroutines, or anything like that. It might be called a *linear* program, except that the term 'linear programming' has an entirely different meaning as a technique for mathematical optimization. So it is usually called a *straightline* program instead.

An example of a straightline program is provided by the following 'mind-reading' exercise:

> Think of a two-digit number.
> Multiply it by 100.
> Add the original number but with its digits reversed.
> Divide by 11.
> Subtract the sum of the original two digits.
> Divide by the number you first thought of.

The answer (as announced by the alleged mind-reader) is 9. As a program, this may seem unexciting. Nevertheless, its formulation in a high-level language introduces a variety of important topics, including types, constants, variables, expressions, assignments, and assertions. It also provides an elementary case study in formal specification and in techniques for proving that programs are correct.

To place these in context, it is worth taking a brief look at the overall structure of a program. In a conventional, procedural, high-level language, this usually consists of three parts:

- a *program heading* — to interface the program with the environment;

- a *declarative part* — to introduce the entities required by the statements;

- a *statement part* — to specify the computations that are to be performed.

In some languages the program heading can be omitted, in which case a standard interface is assumed. If there are no entities to be declared, the second part can also be omitted. The simplest programs can therefore be very short. In FORTRAN 77, for example, the following program produces the message 'Hello World':

```
print *, 'Hello World'
stop
end
```

In C, the equivalent program is:

```
main ()
{
    printf ("Hello World\n");
}
```

The example is a popular one for introducing a new language. After all, if you cannot do this, what *can* you do? The length of the minimum program says something about the philosophy of the language towards the use of unnecessary verbiage. The time taken to compile and link the program is also of interest.

In Pascal and Ada, the program heading is compulsory and the statement part is enclosed between the symbols **begin** and **end**. A program therefore has the following syntactic structure:

```
program heading
    declarations
begin
    statements
end.
```

Pascal requires a terminating period, as shown. Ada requires a semicolon instead. The structure is illustrated in Figure 7-1, which lists an Ada program for performing the 'mind-reader' exercise. Syntactically, the code is a procedure; but it can be used as a main program if required (see below).

The program heading provides an interface with the environment. In Pascal, it has the form:

```
program P (F1, ... Fn);
```

P is the name of the program and F1, ... Fn are the *program parameters*. The name P has no further use or significance in the program text, but it helps in identifying the program

```
        procedure exercise (x : integer) is
                -- a program to simulate a mind reading
                -- exercise, as described in the text
            subtype digit is integer range 0..9;
            digit1, digit2 : digit;
            think : integer := x;
            answer : constant integer := 9;
        begin
                -- assert 1 ≤ think ≤ 99
            digit1 := think / 10;
            digit2 := think mod 10;
                -- start the calculations
            think := 100 * think;
            think := think + (10 * digit2 + digit1);
            think := think / 11;
            think := think − (digit1 + digit2);
            think := think / x;
                -- assert think = answer
        end exercise;
```

Figure 7-1   A simple Ada program

when compile-time or run-time messages are produced. The parameters F1,.... Fn are the means by which the program can refer to external files. For example, the heading

```
        program crunch (data, results);
```

states that the program crunch will operate on two files which, inside the program, are referred to as data and results. When the program is run, the actual files may have different names and so system commands are needed to link them to the program in the required way.

In Ada there is no specific unit called a 'program'. Instead, a program consists of one or more *compilation units*. As indicated by Figure 7-2, a compilation unit may be either a *subprogram* or a *module*. The former may be a *procedure* or a *function*; the latter may be a *package* or a *task*. According to the reference manual (Section 10.1), a subprogram that is a library unit 'can be used as a main program in the usual sense'. As with most languages, the means by which its execution is initiated 'are not prescribed by the language definition'. An obvious possibility is that the system commands should be able to call the main program in the same way as any ordinary procedure or function. In that case the program parameters would not be restricted to files but could be integers or truth values or any other kind of value. To execute the sample program with x = 25, for example, the appropriate command might be:

```
        exercise (25)
```

If output parameters were allowed as well, the operating system could receive results back from the program — a feature that has great practical value. However, implementations are not required to do all this, and they may in fact restrict the program parameters

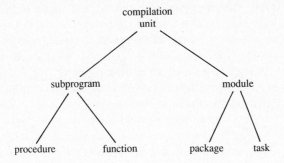

Figure 7-2   Ada compilation units

in whatever ways they like. The minimum requirement is that they be able to execute procedures with no parameters at all. This is so minimal that if it were any less, there would be nothing left. In practice, most implementations offer more than the minimum. Nevertheless, if portability is important, program parameters have to be excluded, and this is a matter for some regret.

7.3   DECLARATIONS

Declarations are like the list of *dramatis personae* in a play. They introduce the participants and give a brief description of their roles. Here, for example, are the leading characters from *Hamlet*:

Claudius:	*King of Denmark*
Hamlet:	*Son to the late and nephew to the present king*
Fortinbras:	*Prince of Norway*
Horatio:	*Friend of Hamlet*
Polonius:	*Lord Chamberlain*

In programming, the names have to be distinct and there are certain conventions about the ways in which they are written. The *scope* of a declaration is the region of text in which its names have their stated significance. For straightline programs, it begins at the declaration itself and continues to the end of the program. For programs with a general block structure, the scope has to be defined more carefully (see Section 10.3).

There are several kinds of declaration, depending on the nature of the items that are being declared. Languages usually place restrictions on the order in which they can be written. In Pascal, for example, the declarations have to be grouped into separate parts, each of which is optional:

- *label declarations*;
- *constant definitions*;
- *type definitions*;
- *variable declarations*;
- *procedures and functions*.

The label declarations do not serve any essential purpose and so they will not be considered further. The other four groups form a logical sequence, each being able to build on the ones that precede it. However, the sequence has one or two drawbacks. For example, it does not allow the definition of a new type to be followed by constants of that type. Ada is more flexible. In the program of Figure 7-1, for example, the variable val is declared before the constant answer. Even so, the constants, types, and variables must precede the bodies of any subprograms or modules. The reasons for this are purely pragmatic: it is supposed to make the programs more readable.

In some languages declarations may involve expressions that have to be evaluated. The expressions can be used for defining constants, initializing variables, specifying array bounds, and so on. An example is provided by the declaration of a subrange type in Ada, as described in Section 4.7:

> **subtype** index **is** integer **range** 1..2*n+1;

If n is a variable, the expression 2*n+1 has to be evaluated when it is encountered at run-time. The declaration is said to be *elaborated* — a term taken from ALGOL 68. In principle, the expressions can be completely general and they may even require the evaluation of one or more function calls. This leads to various problems of definition and implementation. For example, what happens if evaluation raises an error condition such as overflow? This is the sort of problem that has to be dealt with in the reference manuals and that can be a big hassle to the implementors. The average user will do well to steer clear of it.

7.4   CONSTANT DEFINITIONS

A *constant* is a symbol that denotes a particular value. Some familiar examples are numerals such as 99 and strings such as "abc". These are known as *literals* and their meaning is usually fixed over all programs. Thus 99 always denotes the number ninety-nine and "abc" always denotes the string abc. In COBOL terminology 99 is a *numeric literal* (which, strictly speaking, is a contradiction in terms), and "abc" is a *non-numeric literal*. The members of an enumerated type can also be described as literals. For example, the declaration

> **type** salad_dressing **is**
>   (French, Italian, Thousand_Island);

introduces the symbols French, Italian, and Thousand_Island as the literals (or 'enumerals') for that type. Throughout the scope of the declaration, they denote the salad_dressing entities.

In order to supplement the literals, most languages allow a programmer to introduce *constant definitions*. In Pascal, they are introduced by the symbol **const**:

> **const**
>   nbuffs = 8;
>   terminator = '.';

Following this, nbuffs denotes the integer 8 and terminator denotes the character '.'. They are sometimes called *named* constants, to distinguish them from the literals.

(Alternatively, if literals are *not* classified as constants, nbuffs and terminator can simply be called constants.)

The use of named constants is to be encouraged for at least two reasons:

1. A well-chosen name makes the meaning of the program much clearer. For example, if a program is manipulating eight buffers, it is more helpful to write the number as nbuffs than as the numeral 8.

2. The constant can be changed simply by altering the definition. For example, the number of buffers can be doubled by redefining nbuffs to be 16. This is much simpler and safer than changing numerous occurrences of '8' to '16' throughout the program.

These advantages underlie the general rule that a program should not contain 'magic' numbers — that is, numbers that have apparently been conjured out of a hat. If a number of any special significance is to be used, it should be specified in a constant definition and then referred to only by its name.

The above definitions are examples of *static* constants (also known as *manifest* constants); that is, their values can be determined by direct inspection of the program text. Pascal restricts the defining expressions to being literals or previously named constants. In C, they can be any expression composed of literals, named constants, and operators. They are called *static expressions*, since they can be evaluated by the compiler. When the values have been determined, they are said to be *bound* to the corresponding identifiers. Their *binding time* is the time when this takes place. For manifest constants it is the time of compilation. One advantage of this early binding time is that the compiler may be able to incorporate the constant in the compiled code. For example, to implement the test

> **if** i < nbuffs ...

a good compiler might represent nbuffs — that is, the integer 8 — as an immediate operand of the comparison instruction. This would not be possible if nbuffs had to be determined at run-time.

In Ada, constant declarations take a rather more elaborate form:

> nbuffs : **constant** integer := 8;
> terminator : **constant** character := '.';

The inclusion of the type is necessary because a literal such as 8 may have several possible types. Similarly '.' could belong to several possible character sets. The use of the assignment operator ':=' is more questionable. It implies that a constant is a variable of a particular kind — namely, one whose value cannot be altered. However, this is a rather dubious line to take. As we shall see in Section 7.6, a variable is conceptually very different. The use of '=', as in C, ALGOL 68, Pascal, and FORTRAN 77 (in its **parameter** statement), would therefore be more appropriate.

Ada allows the defining expression to be any expression whose components are valid at that point. In particular, it may include variables and parameters. This means that the constants are not necessarily static. For example, consider the declaration:

> midpoint : **constant** integer := n / 2;

If the value of n is not known until run-time, midpoint will not be static. Its binding time will therefore be delayed until the declaration is elaborated, at which point there will be no way of representing it as an immediate operand. In this respect, it could equally well be a variable. The advantage of specifying it to be **constant** is that it is protected from accidental alteration. Its declaration indicates that its value can never be changed.

The above constants are all scalars — that is, they denote single data items. It is natural to extend the concept so that they can denote multiple data items — for instance, a table of integers for code conversion. Unfortunately, most languages are rather poor in this respect. FORTRAN and PL/I offer rudimentary facilities in their **data** statements and **initial** attributes, but Pascal has nothing at all. Ada provides *aggregates*, as in the following example of a simple code conversion table:

```
code : constant table(1..8) := (0, 2, 4, 6, 1, 3, 5, 7);
```

These will be considered further in Volume II, in the chapters on arrays and records.

7.5   TYPE DEFINITIONS

Variables and parameters are usually given a specific type, which defines the set of values they can assume and the operations that can be applied to them. The types may involve structures of various kinds and may be built up into quite complicated expressions. Here are two relatively simple examples in Pascal:

```
w : (loss, draw, win);
V : array [1..100] of (loss, draw, win);
```

These state that w is a variable whose possible values are the enumerals loss, draw, and win, while V is an array of 100 elements whose possible values are also loss, draw, and win. It would be reasonable to infer that the elements of V have the same type as w, with the implication that assignments can be made between them. In the old days this would have been the case; but times have changed, and for reasons discussed below the types are now treated as different.

Since the same type expression was liable to occur at several different points in a program, Pascal introduced *named* types. These are specified by a *type definition* in much the same way as a named constant:

```
type
    result = (loss, draw, win);
    result_vec = array [1..100] of result;
```

Following this, w and V can be declared with types result and result_vec, and so can other variables and parameters later on. The strategy has the same advantages as the use of named constants in that it improves the clarity and flexibility of the program. It also provides a simple solution to an important problem — the problem of *type equivalence*.

The problem was illustrated by the declarations of w and V given at the start. The basic question is this: are the two occurrences of the type expression (loss, draw, win) equivalent, or do they denote two distinct types? To say that they are equivalent seems innocuous enough. In fact, though, it leads to a series of problems in more awkward cases. For example, if n is a named constant with the value 100, are the types 1..100 and 1..n equivalent? If so, redefining n to be some other value may have unintended consequences. The problem becomes even harder with more elaborate structures. It can be solved by defining the notion of *structural equivalence*. This states the conditions under which two basic types are equivalent. It then says that two structured types are equivalent if they have the same overall structure and their corresponding component types are equivalent. ALGOL 68 demonstrates that this approach is feasible. However, the rules require careful formulation and they allow two types to be equivalent even though they appear to be different. At the end of the day, the feeling persists that if two types are meant to be the same, the program should make this clear. The simplest way of doing this is to give the type a name and then to use only the name.

This philosophy can be enforced by the policy of *name equivalence*, which states that two types are equivalent only if they are the same named type. This means that, in the original declaration of w and V, the two occurrences of (loss, draw, win) are *not* equivalent. They are *anonymous* types, and under the policy of name equivalence an anonymous type cannot be equivalent to anything else — not even to another anonymous type which is lexically identical. The only way to make w compatible with the elements of V is to introduce a named type, as in the above definitions of result and result_vec.

In languages without named types, structural equivalence is the only policy that can be adopted. The early implementations of Pascal followed a similar line, though the details were not fully spelt out in the language definition. In Standard Pascal, this policy was rejected and name equivalence was adopted instead. The definition states that a *new-type* is any type expression other than a type identifier and 'every occurrence of a *new-type* shall denote a distinct type'.

Ada goes one step further by requiring all types to be named: with one exception, anonymous types cannot be used. For example, the declaration

w : (loss, draw, win);

is illegal, even though w may be the only entity of that type. Instead, it has to be split into two parts:

type result **is** (loss, draw, win);
w : result;

The one exception is that array variables can have anonymous types, as in:

V : **array** (1..100) **of** result;

It is not clear why this exception was made, when others were rejected. It would have been cleaner to have none at all. Overall, the policy has the merit of simplicity, even though it entails some inconvenience. It has the important consequence that the parameters of a subprogram can never have anonymous types, otherwise there is no way in which the actual parameters can match them. More seriously, it implies that the rows and columns of multi-dimensional arrays cannot be handled as single units. Since their types would be anonymous the program would be unable to use them. This is not just an inconvenience, but rather a fundamental limitation of the language.

7.6 VARIABLES

Variables are one of the most distinctive features of the programming scene. Unlike the so-called variables of conventional mathematics, they really do vary. One moment x will have the value 3; the next it will have changed to 4. Such slippery behavior gives rise to many problems, both in theory and in practice. Consequently, some people argue that variables should be abolished and that programmers should learn to live without them (Backus, 1978). Indeed, their abolition is a major feature of the non-procedural languages (see Section 7.1). The move has theoretical backing in that languages without variables can still compute anything that is known to be computable. Nevertheless, practical experience suggests that in most areas of application, programming can be done more easily when variables are available.

One of the most basic problems is to define what a variable actually *is*. This is not as easy as it might seem. In fact, it runs into an ancient paradox that was discussed by the Greek philosopher Heraclitus. If the definition states that a variable is such-and-such a thing, it implies that it is something fixed; and yet the essence of a variable is that it can in some sense vary! How do you get round the difficulty? Exercise 4 explores this philosophical nicety in more detail. For practical purposes, it is easier to take an operational view and to ask how a variable *behaves*. The answer is that a variable x can be subjected to two basic operations:

assign (x, e) :   assign to x the value of the expression e;

value (x) :   obtain the value of x.

The relationship between the two is simply that value (x) yields the value which was assigned to x most recently — what is commonly called the *current* value of x. The term 'value' is not a particularly good one in this context, since there is no evaluation involved. (It is expressions that are evaluated, not variables.) A better term is the *content* of x, in which case the second operation is called the *content-taking* operation (see Section 5.8). The two operations can be illustrated by the assignment

x := x + 1

which is equivalent to:

assign (x, value(x) + 1)

The term value(x) shows that there is an implied content-taking operation for x on the right-hand side (see Section 7.8).

The debate over terminology may seem rather inconsequential, but it touches on an issue of some importance. Even though the meaning of a variable has been defined, there are still two different ways of interpreting the occurrences of x in the above assignment statement:

1.   The name x is similar to a constant in that it denotes a value. It differs from a constant in that the name-value association can be changed by an assignment.

2.   The name x denotes some sort of value-holder. This association is permanent, although the content of the value-holder can be changed by an assignment.

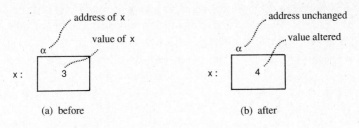

Figure 7-3 The assignment x := x + 1

In the simplest languages, the difference hardly matters. However, in most major languages a name such as x can be used for different variables at different points in the program. The crunch comes when one of these variables is passed as a parameter to a procedure P. If the name x is passed, how is P to know which one is intended? With the first interpretation, the only thing to do is to pass the extended name 'x of such-and-such a part of the program'. With the second one, the value-holder, or a reference to the value-holder, can be passed instead. Logically there is no ultimate difference between the concept of the extended name and the concept of a reference to a value-holder. But the latter is simpler to define and also easier to visualize. It is reflected in Figure 7-3, which shows the effect of the assignment:

$$x := x + 1;$$

The box denotes the value-holder and it is labeled by the name x of the variable that it represents. It has an *address*, denoted by α, which gives it a unique identification and to which the name x is bound throughout its lifetime. It also has a *content*, which is the variable's value and which can be altered by an assignment. In practice, of course, the box will be implemented as an area of memory and the address is its physical or virtual address. The variable is bound to this address in the same way as a constant is bound to its value (see Section 7.3). The binding time may be at compile time, or at declaration time, or when specifically requested. The detailed mechanisms will be described in Chapter 12.

It is interesting to see how various languages deal with these issues. ALGOL 68 sets the pace with an approach that is precise and carefully unified. It can be illustrated by the declaration of a constant c with the value 100, and a variable x initialized to 3:

> **real** c = 100;
> **real** x := 3;

According to the jargon of the language, the identifier c possesses (an instance of) the number 100. By contrast, the identifier x possesses a name which refers to an object which contains (an instance of) the number 3. In more familiar terms this means that c denotes the number 100 and x denotes the address of a location. This follows the second interpretation, but with one minor snag: the declarations appear to say that c and x are both **real**. In answer to this, ALGOL 68 says that in reality x is not **real** but **ref real** ('reference-to-real'), the second declaration being shorthand for:

> **ref real** x = **loc real** := 3;

Thus, x is bound to a name that refers to a local, real object (initialized to 3) in exactly the

same way as c is bound to 100. The concept of a name (or address) and the associated
type **ref real** carries over to pointers and to a unified mechanism for passing parameters.

In Pascal the notation is rather different:

> **const**
> > c = 100;
>
> **var**
> > v : real;

The language definition states that c 'denotes' the number 100, and v 'denotes' a real
variable. Furthermore, a variable is 'an entity to which a (current) value may be attributed'. As in ALGOL 68, this follows the second interpretation, though it avoids the
suggestion that c and v have the same type. On the other hand, there is no concept of v
having an address and this leads to a less unified treatment of pointers and parameters.

Ada treats c and v as though they were basically the same sort of thing:

> c   :   **constant** real := 100;
> v   :   real := 3;

They both denote 'objects', an object being 'an entity that contains (has) a value of a
given type'. The only difference between them is that the value in c's object cannot be
changed. This creates a unity between constants and variables which may seem artificial.
A potential advantage is that it could be applied to fields of a record: all the fields are
objects, but some of them could be designated **constant**. In the preliminary version of
Ada, this facility was allowed. However, it ran into practical difficulties, notably when
records were assigned as single units, and so it was eventually dropped.

The above declarations illustrate the usual requirement that every variable should
have a type which determines the set of values that can be assigned to it. An attempt to
assign it any other value should result in an error message, either at compile-time or (in
the case of subtypes) at run-time. This, of course, is essential in any language which
enforces strong typing (see Section 4.1).

A more neglected topic is that of initial values. In most languages it is possible (or
even compulsory) to declare variables without giving them initial values. Their initial
values are therefore 'undefined' and any attempt to use them should cause a report. A
good compiler will detect such attempts and will issue appropriate warning messages
before the program is ever run. For example, if the first statement of the program is

> x := x + 0.1;

the compiler could report 'variable x used before it has been assigned'. However, there
are other situations where detection is not so easy. They might involve array elements, or
dynamic data structures, or procedure calls, or unorthodox loops. In such cases, some of
the checking would have to be done at run-time. Unfortunately, on most machines there
is no simple, inexpensive way of making the checks and so they are usually omitted. If
an unassigned value is used, the language definition states that 'the meaning of the program is undefined' — a soothing phrase which really means 'you are heading for trouble'.

Because of these dangers, some language designers have sought to eliminate the problem entirely. An obvious strategy is to insist that all variables be initialized when they
are declared. In SIMULA 67, for example, they are all given default values — 0 for

numbers, **false** for truth values, and so on. In effect, the initialization is done by guess-work. A better approach is taken by BCPL, in which every variable has to be initialized explicitly. This has the advantage of forcing the programmer to think about the matter. The drawback is that the initialization may be premature and so the chosen values will be meaningless. A third approach is to design the language so that compile-time checking *is* always possible. For a discussion of one such design, see the essay on these issues by E. W. Dijkstra (1976, Chapter 10). Unfortunately, the language restrictions can become rather severe, and so the net result is that none of the approaches is entirely satisfactory. A good hardware solution would be very welcome. One is provided by the Burroughs B6700 computer, where a value can be flagged as 'undefined'; an attempt to use it will then cause an interrupt. It would be helpful if more machines were to follow its example.

7.7 EXPRESSIONS

Expressions are the main vehicle for performing calculations. Whereas assignments merely move data from one place to another, expressions allow them to be compared, combined, and transformed. Like machine instructions, they consist basically of *operations* and *operands* (or *arguments*). The operations are represented in the program text either as special symbols, known as *operators*, or as the names of functions (sometimes known as *functors* — a functor denotes a function in the same way that an operator denotes an operation). When combined with their arguments, they constitute an *expression*. The following are some simple examples:

$$-i$$
$$p\uparrow$$
$$x + 1$$
$$\max(k, 10)$$

In the first two, '−' and '↑' are examples of *monadic* or *unary* operators (having one argument), the former being written in *prefix* form and the latter in *postfix* form. In the third one, '+' is *dyadic* or *binary* (having two arguments) and is written in *infix* form. In the last one, max is a function with its arguments enclosed in parentheses.

When expressions are extended to include two or more operators, care is needed in determining the order of evaluation. For example, $2 * 3 + 4$ will have the value 10 if the '∗' is applied first, and 14 if the '+' is applied first. The ambiguity is usually resolved by stating that some operators have higher *precedence* or *priority* than others. Thus '∗' is generally taken to have higher precedence than '+', and so the expression has the value 10. However, if there is any doubt about the matter, parentheses can be used to enforce a specific interpretation, as in $(2 * 3) + 4$. Parentheses can also be used to override the precedence rules, as in $2 * (3 + 4)$.

The general rules for interpreting expressions can be summarized as follows:

1. Operators inside parentheses or brackets are applied first.

2. Operators of high precedence are applied before those of lower precedence.

3. Operators of equal precedence are applied from left to right (or in some cases from right to left).

Ada has six precedence levels, which is about average for a general-purpose language:

- first, highest precedence   **** abs not**
- second, multiplying operators   *** / mod rem**
- third, unary adding operators   **+ −**
- fourth, binary adding operators   **+ − &**
- fifth, relational operators   **= ≠ < ≤ > ≥**
- sixth, logical operators   **and or xor**

On the face of it, **and**, **or**, and **xor** have equal priority, which is rather unusual. In fact, competition between them is banned (p **and** q **and** r is legal, but p **and** q **or** r is not). The placing of **not** is also unusual, since it interprets **not** x = y as (**not** x) = y. This is acceptable because, if the intended interpretation is **not** (x = y), most people would write x ≠ y instead. In general, the rules interpret an expression such as

$$x ** 2 / y + 3 * z < 0 \text{ and } i \neq j + 1$$

in the way that we would expect. However, the details vary from one language to the next, with the result that life is full of surprises. In Pascal, for example, the expression

$$x = 0 \text{ and } y = 0$$

does not compare x and y with zero. Instead, **and** has precedence over '=', which makes the expression illegal. Furthermore, as mentioned in rule 3, some languages apply operators of equal priority from right to left. PL/I specifies this for the top level of its hierarchy, and so e ** x ** 2 means e ** (x ** 2). APL adopts the extreme policy of abolishing all precedences and using right-to-left evaluation throughout. Thus 2 * 3 + 4 has the value 14 — another of life's surprises. The practical implications of this are clear: *for clarity and safety, use parentheses.*

The precedence of the operators is important for interpreting an expression, but it is not the whole story. A further question arises: in what order are the operands evaluated? For example, in an expression of the form *E1* + *E2*, which subexpression is evaluated first — *E1* or *E2*? For most purposes, the order of evaluation does not affect the final value and so the answer is irrelevant. However, it becomes important if the evaluation of *E1* or *E2* has a *side effect* — that is, an effect that changes the environment in some way (see Section 9.4). A simple example arises in an expression such as nextnum − nextnum, where nextnum is a function that produces the next number from an input file. If the next two numbers are 4 and 5, the value will be −1 if evaluation is from left to right, and +1 if it is from right to left. It would be simple and natural to specify that evaluation is always from left to right. However, there are many situations where this is not the most efficient. For example, to evaluate x + y * z, the most efficient code might start with y * z:

```
R1 ← y
R1 * z
R1 + x
```

Compilers can be very good at optimizing code in this sort of way and most languages prefer to give them a free hand in doing so. If side effects can influence the value of an expression, the value is officially undefined. In practice, of course, it is unlikely that the compiler will detect such a situation and so the expression will be given one of its two possible values. Since this is a hazardous state of affairs, language designers have occasionally tried to restrict functions in ways that will make side effects impossible. The preliminary version of Ada embodied one such attempt. However, if the restrictions are to be enforceable, they have to be very severe and so (as in Ada) the proposals are usually abandoned.

Most high-level languages allow operators to be used in several different senses. For example, '+' can be used for integer addition, real addition, complex addition, set union, and even for logical *or*. Similarly '<' can compare numbers, characters, or strings. Such operators are sometimes described as *polymorphic* (having many forms) or, in Ada's terminology, as *overloaded*. When one is used, its particular form has to be determined from the types of its arguments. Most languages are designed so that this can be done by the compiler, thereby avoiding the overheads of dynamic type-checking. In a typeless language, the operations cannot be differentiated in this way and so there has to be a separate symbol for each.

A *mixed mode* expression is one in which the two arguments of an operator are of different types. The most usual case is an expression such as x ∗ i, which combines a real argument with an integer one. In general, the surreptitious mixing of types is undesirable and so such expressions are mostly illegal. However, some languages allow for implicit integer-to-real type conversions, and PL/I is notorious for allowing many others. In Ada, the standard operators are not defined for mixed modes except in the case of x ∗∗ i. So either the type conversions must be inserted explicitly, or mixed-mode versions of the operators must be defined by the programmer.

Some languages allow various forms of 'structured' expressions, such as the **if-then-else** expression. These are related to the control structures that are described in the next chapter, and so they will not be considered here.

7.8 ASSIGNMENTS

In most ALGOL-related languages, the assignment statement has the form

$$variable \quad := \quad expression$$

and it causes the value of the expression to be assigned to the variable. For example, the statement

$$x \quad := \quad 44$$

assigns the number 44 to the variable x. It should be read as 'x becomes 44', or 'x is assigned 44'. The symbol ':=' was introduced by ALGOL 60 and may be regarded as an approximation to the arrow '←'. It is a great improvement on '=' as used in FORTRAN, COBOL, PL/I, C, and other languages (see below).

A fuller account of the assignment statement depends on the interpretation given to a variable, as discussed in Section 7.4. If x denotes its value directly, the effect of the assignment is to change the denotation. If x denotes a value-holder, the effect is to change the content of that value-holder. This second interpretation is slightly more complicated; as remarked earlier, though, it has advantages if x is to be passed as a parameter to a procedure. It also corresponds closely to what happens in practice. The expression x is evaluated as a reference to a location and the assignment is then carried out.

The view of x as an expression needs to be emphasized further. The fact is that the left-hand side of the assignment may need evaluating just as much as the right-hand side. In the case of simple variables such as x, this is not so evident. But with an assignment such as

$$A[i*n+j] := 0$$

a multiplication and an addition are visibly involved, and there is also an operation of subscripting that needs to be carried out.

These observations help to explain the paradox presented by FORTRAN's statement:

$$X = X + 1$$

If this is read as 'X equals X plus 1', it is patently false. Not much better is 'the new value of X equals the old value of X plus 1'. This avoids the paradox, but it interprets the statement as an assertion rather than a command. On that basis, the statement could equally well be written as:

$$X - 1 = X$$

To say that 'the new value of X is *assigned* the old value of X plus 1' is still inaccurate. The assignment is made not to the value of X, but to X itself. The correct interpretation is made only by recognizing that the two occurrences of X represent two different things. On the left-hand side of the assignment it denotes a location; on the right-hand side it denotes the content of that location. The phrase 'the value of X' normally means the second of these. However, it is useful to have terms for both meanings, and so *L-value* and *R-value* are sometimes used for the purpose (Strachey, 1966). The two sides of the assignment are then said to be evaluated in *L-mode* and *R-mode*. Alternatively, the terms *reference value* and *data value* may be preferred, since they reflect the underlying ideas rather more directly.

For every context in which an expression can occur, the intended mode should be stated. Is the expression to be evaluated in reference mode, data mode, or what? Not all expressions are legal in reference mode. For example, X + 1 is not a variable and so it can be used only in data mode. On the other hand, any expression that is legal in reference mode is also legal in data mode: its reference value is a reference to a location, and its data value is the data item that is stored there. The conversion of a reference value to a data value is known as *dereferencing*. In less abstract terms, it is simply the content-taking operation which was mentioned in Section 7.6. It can be regarded as a special form of type conversion (or *coercion*, or *cast*), and is automatically inserted when the context calls for data mode evaluation. In the expression X + 1, for example, the term X is dereferenced (from **ref real** to **real**) in order to produce its numerical value.

Some languages allow *parallel assignments*. These have the form

$$V1, V2, ... Vn := E1, E2, ... En$$

where the *Vi* are variables and the *Ei* are expressions. In BCPL, this is simply shorthand for *n* successive assignments — *V1 := E1, V2 := E2, ... Vn := En*. In most other cases it implies that the assignments are to be carried out in parallel. The *Vi* are evaluated in reference mode, the *Ei* in data mode, and then the assignments are made. The popular example is

$$x, y := y, x;$$

which interchanges the values of x and y. If parallel assignments are not allowed, an extra variable has to be introduced and three single assignments are needed:

```
temp := x;
x := y;
y := temp;
```

This is less concise and potentially less efficient (see Section 5.3). If two or more of the Vi have the same reference value, there is a potential ambiguity. For example, the effect of

```
x, x  :=  1, 2;
```

depends on the order in which the two assignments are made. Because of this, some versions require the assignments to be carried out in left to right sequence. This is similar to requiring that the operands of an expression be evaluated from left to right (see Section 7.5), and is open to the same objections. The unambiguous cases become over-specified and the efficiency of the code may be reduced. Other languages prefer to leave the order unspecified, with the caveat that ambiguous cases are 'undefined'.

7.9 COMMENTS

Since comments do not affect the meaning of a program, they tend to be neglected. Language manuals dismiss them in a few lines. Textbooks urge their use but say little else about them. Programmers tend to regard them as a bore — things to be added to the program once it is working (if there is time). They do not belong to the real business of programming and their intrinsic interest is nil. Of course, everyone will agree that this attitude is to be regretted. Nevertheless, it may be asked: apart from agreeing that comments should be used, what is there of any significance that can be said about them?

A point of obvious practical interest is the way in which comments are written. As Figure 7-4 shows, there are almost as many notations as languages. They can be divided into two main classes, according to the nature of the delimiters:

1. In languages such as FORTRAN, BCPL, and Ada, the comments begin with a special start-of-comment symbol and continue to the end of the line. A multi-line comment therefore has to include the start-of-comment symbol on every line.

2. In languages such as ALGOL 60, ALGOL 68, PL/I, and C, they begin with a start-of-comment symbol and continue to an end-of-comment symbol. The two symbols are usually distinct, and there are advantages in treating them as a pair of parentheses that have to be properly matched (see below).

Method 1 is simple and has the further advantage that the status of each line is immediately apparent from the line itself. Method 2 is slightly more flexible: short comments can be included in the middle of a line and long ones do not require a delimiter on every line. On the debit side, method 2 has the potential drawback that if the terminator is accidentally omitted, the comment will quietly swallow up a series of statements and other significant items, only stopping when it comes to a matching terminator. A good

```
C      This is FORTRAN (the 'C' is in column 1)
*      So is this.

       comment this one is ALGOL 60 and it can be
              continued over several lines;

           Note that a comment in COBOL is a sentence or
           paragraph starting with 'Note'.
*      It may also be a line with '*' in column 1.

       /* This convention is used
          in PL/I and also in C  */

           .....                       // This is BCPL

       ¢ This is ALGOL 68 ¢

       { This is Pascal }

           .....                       -- this is Ada
```

Figure 7-4   Notations for writing comments

compiler will usually detect that this is happening and issue a warning message (Exercise 9). Even so, method 1 is preferable in this respect.

Comments may appear to have no significant structure. In fact, though, there are advantages in allowing them to be nested. This works best with method 2, where the delimiters are treated as brackets that have to be properly paired. In PL/I or C, for example, a section of program can be 'commented out' by enclosing it in the brackets /* ... */. This provides a convenient way of removing the code from the effective part of the program, while retaining it in the program text. Later on, it can be reinstated simply by removing the brackets. With method 1, the process has to be carried out for each line individually. Text editors enable this to be done quite easily and, as mentioned above, there is the advantage that the status of each line is always clearly evident.

Comments normally have no effect on the behavior of a program. The ALGOL 68 Report refers to them as 'a source of innocent merriment' (quoting W. S. Gilbert's *The Mikado*), and goes on to say:

> It is the intention that comments should be entirely ignored by the implementation, their sole purpose being the enlightenment of the human interpreter of the program.

In practice, implementations occasionally allow them to be used for other purposes. For example, a convention may be adopted that if the first non-blank symbol is '$', the comment is a directive to the compiler. Some possible directives are:

- begin a new page in the program listing;

- suppress certain kinds of checking until further notice;

- omit the following code if certain compile-time conditions are satisfied.

In ALGOL 68, directives of this kind are provided by a special facility called a *pragmat*. In Ada, they are called *pragmas*. For example,

> **pragma** list (off);

turns off the program listing, and

> **pragma** optimize (time);

asks the compiler to optimize the time efficiency rather than the space efficiency of the compiled code. The program of Figure 7-1 includes comments that begin with the word **assert** (in boldface simply for emphasis — it is not a reserved word), and these too can be treated in a formal manner. Comments of this kind are so important that they will be considered separately in the next section.

Returning to the notion that the sole purpose of comments is 'the enlightenment of the human interpreter', it is worth concluding with a general observation concerning the extent to which they achieve this. The simple fact is that most programs are written with the computer as their principal target: the human reader comes a poor second. D. E. Knuth (1984a) has shown how it is possible to turn the whole concept upside down, treating the human reader as primary and the computer as secondary. In the approach that he describes, a program is written as a piece of literature to be read and appreciated by humans. The comments are the pieces of code and are provided, presumably, for the enlightenment of the machine interpreter. This reversal of roles should appeal to anyone who supports a 'people first' philosophy.

7.10 ASSERTIONS

As noted above, the program in Figure 7-1 contains several comments of the form:

> -- **assert** *condition*

They express the confidence of the programmer that when execution reaches that point in the program, the stated condition will be true. The condition is sometimes called a *predicate* — that is, a function of the program variables whose value is either true or false. Comments of this kind are known as *assertions*. They play a fundamental role not only in documenting a program but also, and more significantly, in designing the program and proving that it is correct. The basic idea is that the program starts with an assertion describing the initial conditions. In the mind-reading program, for example, the assertion

> -- **assert** $1 \leq$ think ≤ 99

corresponds to the requirement 'think of a number between 1 and 99'. At the end, it concludes with an assertion describing the desired goal. In between, it contains a sequence of statements that transform the truth of the initial assertion into the truth of the final one. If the gulf between them is too great, the programmer formulates some intermediate assertions and develops statements that move in smaller stages from one to the next.

The next two sections look at the basic philosophy in more detail. At this stage, we shall simply note that the concept has led to proposals for an **assert** statement. For example, in the preliminary version of Ada it had the form:

> **assert** *condition*;

As far as the human reader is concerned, the assertion serves the purpose just described. However, unless there is a pragma to the contrary, it has the further effect that whenever it is encountered during execution, the run-time system checks the condition and raises an assert_error exception if it turns out to be false.

The facility was dropped from the final version of Ada, and that is why the assertions have been 'commented out' in Figure 7-1. It is interesting to speculate on the reasons for its omission. The following factors may have played a part:

1.   Run-time checks can be provided by ordinary procedures and so a special facility is not necessary.

2.   The primary role of assertions is to assist in the development of bug-free programs. Their use for run-time checks is tantamount to an admission of failure.

3.   In any case, the proposed form was too restrictive. The asserted condition had to be an ordinary Boolean expression and for most programs this was not sufficient for proving their correctness.

To overcome this last deficiency, the statement would have to allow more powerful conditions, such as:

$$\textbf{assert} \ \textit{for some} \ \text{i} \ \textbf{in} \ 1..n, \ V(i) = x$$
$$\textbf{assert} \ \textit{for all} \ \text{i} \ \textbf{in} \ 1..n-1, \ V(i) < V(i+1)$$

The first states that the vector V contains at least one element equal to x; the second states that the elements of V are in ascending sequence. They are examples of *quantified* conditions ('for some ... ', 'for all ... '), and they take the associated correctness proofs into the domain of first-order logic (the predicate calculus).

By writing assertions as comments, the programmer can avoid the restrictions of the language and can express them in whatever way is suitable. Informally, such comments provide valuable insight concerning the way in which the program works. When expressed in a formal notation, they can also be used by mechanical correctness-proving procedures.

7.11   SPECIFICATIONS

As indicated in Section 7.1, a specification is intended to be a bald statement of what a program is required to do, with no indication of how it should actually do it. It presents a 'black box' view of the program — an input and an output, but no account of the internal workings. Its only role is to say how the input and the output are related.

In the simplest form of specification, the input is a set of values and the output is defined as a function of those values. In the more general case, the input can include a set of *variables*, and the specification states how their final values should be related to their initial values. The standard way of doing this is by means of two assertions. The first one, known as the program's *precondition*, states any constraints that the initial values are required to satisfy. The second one, known as its *postcondition*, states the properties that the final values must satisfy — in other words, the program's goal. For example, if the program is to calculate the square root of a number x and assign it to a variable y, a simple specification might look like this:

$$\text{variables}: \quad \text{x, y}$$
$$\text{precondition}: \quad \text{x} \geq 0$$
$$\text{postcondition}: \quad \text{y} \geq 0 \ \textbf{and} \ \text{y}^2 = \text{x}$$

A fuller version would specify that x and y are real, and a more pragmatic one would not insist on exact equality (see Section 4.3). But the general idea is clear enough.

In the postcondition $\text{y}^2 = \text{x}$, it is presumably intended that x should have its initial value (otherwise a sufficient program is to set $\text{x} = \text{y} = 0$). However, if x is a variable, there is no guarantee that it will remain unchanged and so the specification, as it stands, is wrong. A correct version must either indicate that x is to remain constant, or else replace x in the postcondition by a symbol such as x_0, denoting its initial value. The former follows a path that is well established for the specification of procedure parameters (see Section 9.3). With the latter, the specification can dispense with y, stating that x is to be replaced by its square root:

$$\text{variables}: \quad \text{x}$$
$$\text{precondition}: \quad \text{x} \geq 0$$
$$\text{postcondition}: \quad \text{x} \geq 0 \ \textbf{and} \ \text{x}^2 = \text{x}_0$$

An alternative technique is to 'capture' the initial value of x in a constant init_x (say):

$$\text{variables}: \quad \text{x}$$
$$\text{precondition}: \quad \text{x} \geq 0 \ \textbf{and} \ \text{x} = \text{init\_x}$$
$$\text{postcondition}: \quad \text{x} \geq 0 \ \textbf{and} \ \text{x}^2 = \text{init\_x}$$

This device does not involve any special notation and is therefore better suited for use with ordinary programs.

A second example is provided by the 'mind-reading' exercise of Section 7.2. In this case, the input is an integer x in the range 1 to 99, and the output is a function of x as prescribed by the exercise. The only trouble is that the exercise uses phrases such as 'the original number with its digits reversed'. How are these to be expressed within the specification language? Given the Pascal operators **div** and **mod**, an obvious way is to compute the two digits from the expressions x **div** 10 and x **mod** 10. The specification could therefore be written as follows:

$$\text{variables}: \quad \text{x}$$
$$\text{precondition}: \quad 1 \leq \text{x} \leq 99$$
$$\text{postcondition}: \quad \text{x} = ((100 * \text{x}_0 + \text{y}) \ \textbf{div} \ 11 - \text{z}) \ \textbf{div} \ \text{x}_0$$
$$\textbf{where} \ \text{y} = 10 * \text{digit2} + \text{digit1},$$
$$\text{z} = \text{digit1} + \text{digit2}$$
$$\textbf{where} \ \text{digit1} = \text{x}_0 \ \textbf{div} \ 10,$$
$$\text{digit2} = \text{x}_0 \ \textbf{mod} \ 10$$

This is all very well, but it should be noted that the specification is no longer a bald statement of what is required. By translating the original phrases into precise mathematics, it has provided a strong indication of how the computation is to be performed. Given other operators, it might have used other methods. This bears out the contention made in

Section 7.1 that a truly 'pure' specification — all 'what' and no 'how' — will only be found at the rainbow's end.

The two examples illustrate some of the basic issues that arise in writing formal program specifications. As indicated in Section 7.1, the ideal is that the specification should be implemented automatically, either by conversion to a program or by some sort of problem-solving process. Indeed, it is possible to formulate a *specification statement* as part of a conventional programming language (Morgan, 1988). On encountering such a statement, a compiler would attempt to generate code for it, just as if it were any other kind of statement. In the case of the square-root specification, the compiler would require unusual intelligence to devise a suitable algorithm from scratch. However, if it were equipped with special facilities for solving numerical equations, its task would be simple. By contrast, the specifications for the 'mind-reading' exercise are at a level where automatic conversion to a conventional program would be relatively easy. Indeed, an intelligent, optimizing compiler might even implement them by the program:

$$x \quad := \quad 9;$$

This is contrary to the spirit of the exercise; but from a purely functional point of view, it would be eminently satisfactory!

7.12   PROOF RULES

Let *prog* be a program for which a precondition and a postcondition have been specified. With Pascal's notation for comments, it can be written in the form:

> { *precondition* }
> *prog*
> { *postcondition* }

To prove that *prog* is correct, it must be demonstrated that if the precondition is true prior to execution, the postcondition will be true on completion. A proof of *total* correctness must include a proof that *prog* will always terminate. A proof of *partial* correctness is weaker: it states that if *prog* terminates, the postcondition will be satisfied, but termination is not guaranteed.

In a straightline program, *prog* is a sequence of statements

$$S1; \; S2; \; ... \; Sn;$$

where each *Si* is a basic, non-conditional, non-iterative statement. In fact, within the framework of the preceding sections, each *Si* is restricted to being an assignment. The strategy for proving its correctness is to insert intermediate assertions *A1, A2, ... A(n-1)* between each pair of successive statements. If the initial condition is named *A0* and the final one *An*, this creates a program of the form:

$$\{A0\} \; S1; \; \{A1\} \; S2; \; \{A2\} \; ... \; \{A(n-1)\} \; Sn; \; \{An\}$$

Thus each statement *Si* becomes a mini-program, with its own precondition and postcondition:

$$\{A(i-1)\} \; Si \; \{Ai\}$$

The task is to prove that if its precondition holds beforehand, its postcondition will hold afterwards. For total correctness, the proof must also show that Si is sure to terminate.

The standard technique is to use a set of *proof rules*. These are commonly written in the form

$$\{P\} \ S \ \{Q\}$$

where S is a particular kind of statement (such as an assignment) and where P and Q are generalized predicates. The rule describes the relationship between P and Q that must be satisfied to ensure a valid proof. It asserts that if P is satisfied prior to the execution of S, then execution will terminate in a state that satisfies Q.

In the case of the assignment statement, the appropriate rule is the following:

$$\{ Q[V\backslash E] \} \ V := E \ \{Q\}$$

Here $Q[V\backslash E]$ denotes the condition obtained from Q by replacing every occurrence of the variable V by the expression E. The rule states that if the value of V satisfies some predicate after the assignment, then the value of E must satisfy the same predicate beforehand. Since V's value afterwards is the same as E's beforehand, this is eminently reasonable. For example, consider the following Pascal code:

```
{ y < 1 }
x := y + 3;
{ x < 4 }
```

The proof rule states that $x < 4$ will be true afterwards provided that $y + 3 < 4$ is true beforehand. Since $y + 3 < 4$ is equivalent to the assertion $y < 1$, the required conclusion follows.

Rules of this kind were invented by R. W. Floyd (1967) in the context of flowchart programs. They were developed for higher-level structures by C. A. R. Hoare (1969), who described them as *axioms* for defining the semantics of a language. For example, the above rule for $V := E$ defined the meaning of the assignment statement. It is possible to debate the adequacy of the definition (see Exercise 18). More importantly, we can ask: does it really describe what the assignment *means*? Surely it states far more than necessary. The simple meaning of the assignment is that the value of E beforehand becomes the value of V afterwards. The rest follows as a matter of logic. The term 'proof rule' is therefore more appropriate than 'axiom'.

The next chapter develops this discussion further. It gives proof rules for a wide variety of statements, and uses them for proving the correctness of some more interesting programs. Meanwhile, Exercises 19 – 21 provide some simple examples for the assignment rule, and Exercise 22 takes a final look at the mind-reading program.

FURTHER READING

Books on programming languages include material on most of the topics in Sections 7.1 – 7.9. See, for example, Sammet (1969), Tennent (1981), Pratt (1984), Marcotty and Ledgard (1986), and Horowitz (1987). The Appendix gives details of specific languages.

Welsh *et al.* (1977) discusses the problem of type equivalence in Pascal. For a thorough treatment of the topic, see Fleck (1984). Strachey (1964) considers the formal definition of variables, assignments, and other basic language features. Winner (1984) considers the problem of variables that have not been initialized. Floyd (1963) is the standard theoretical treatment of operator precedence and its relation to syntactic definition.

Assertions for establishing the meaning and/or correctness of programs were advocated first by Floyd (1967) and later, in a different form, by Hoare (1969). Good introductions to specifications and correctness are given in Gries (1981) and Backhouse (1986). Chapter 8 gives further references on the subject. Hayes (1986) gives some case studies in specification. Jones (1986) describes a methodology for converting specifications to programs. Research is very active in this field and so more literature on the subject can be expected over the next few years.

EXERCISES

1   In your implementation(s) of Ada, what restrictions does the operating system impose on the nature and use of program parameters? Are there similar facilities for any other language?

2   When a constant is defined in Pascal, its type is not mentioned. In Ada, however, its type has to be explicitly stated. Why do the two languages differ in this respect?

3   The principle of name equivalence causes a problem when program units are independently compiled. What is the problem? How is it handled in Ada? If you know of any Pascal implementations that allow separate compilations, how is it handled there?

4   The Greek philosopher Heraclitus (c.500 B. C.) had trouble defining variables. For example, he wrestled at length with the problem of defining a river. The problem was that if he identified it with the water flowing in a certain channel at a certain time, the water would soon be somewhere else. On the other hand, if he identified it with the channel itself, he missed out the most essential element, namely the flowing water. One of the proposed solutions was to say that the river had two parts — a fixed part that was the channel and a variable part that was the water. The fixed part enabled it to retain its identity while the variable part allowed it to change. However, Heraclitus objected (a) that this did not solve the problem because there was still a variable part to be defined, and (b) that in any case all things, including channels, were in a state of flux, so nothing was constant at all. Karl Popper gives an interesting discussion of the problem stating the difficulty as follows:

> For all change is the change of something: change presupposes something that changes. And it presupposes that, while changing, this something must remain the same.

Later he makes a comment that is of obvious interest to the computer scientist:

> With his uncanny intuition Heraclitus saw that things are processes, that our bodies are flames.

Would you agree with Heraclitus? See Popper K., *Conjectures and Refutations*, 4th edition (1972), Routledge and Kegan Paul, pp.136-146.

5   Investigate any formal or semi-formal definition of a programming language and determine how it defines variables and the assignment statement. To which of the interpretations in Section 7.6 does it correspond most closely?

6   Consider any language that you have available. Does it require that variables be initialized? If not, investigate what happens if an attempt is made to use an undefined value.

7   In the 'mind-reading' program of Figure 7-1, the assertions include the Ada expression:

$$x \ \textbf{in} \ 1..99$$

In BCPL the condition can be written using ordinary mathematical notation:

$$1 \le x \le 99$$

In what other languages would this expression be legal and what would it mean? How would you express it in Pascal? COBOL allows expressions such as

$$X = 6 \ \textbf{or} \ 7$$

which have an obvious meaning. However, it sets a trap for the unwary with:

$$X \ \textbf{not} = 6 \ \textbf{or} \ 7$$

What is the value of this expression? (Clue: its value is independent of X!)

8   Section 7.7 distinguished two different ways of evaluating expressions — in reference mode and data mode. The former is used on the left-hand side of an assignment and the latter on the right. Consider other contexts in which expressions can occur (constant definitions, loop parameters, procedure parameters, ... in various languages). Which mode of evaluation (if either) do they require?

9   As remarked in Section 7.9, there is a potential problem with comments that require an explicit terminator: if the programmer omits it, or mistypes it, the comment can swallow up large slabs of significant code. A good compiler will usually be able to spot when this is happening and will issue a warning message. Investigate your compiler's reactions for any available language that has comments of this kind.

10   Ada's comments begin with two minus signs. It is unlikely that anyone would write an expression such as $x - - y$, meaning $x - (-y)$; but would such an expression be legal?

11   In the languages with which you are familiar, what pragmas (or other equivalent facilities) are available?

12   Write formal specifications for programs to do the following. Using any appropriate notation, give a precondition and a postcondition for each case:

   (a)   Interchange the values of two variables, x and y.

   (b)   Set a variable x to the largest value in the array of numbers $V(1..n)$, where $n \ge 1$.

(c)   Set x to the sum of the numbers in V(1..n), where n≥0.

(d)   Sort the numbers in V(1..n) into ascending order.

(e)   Set i to the position of the first occurrence of the number x in V(1..n).

In the last case the specification must either assert that x occurs in V or specify the outcome if it is missing. Give versions for both.

13   Section 7.10 noted that assertions often involve quantification over the elements of an array. Unfortunately, conventional programming languages provide no means of expressing this within a single expression. However, the array-processing language APL is excellent for the purpose. Show how it can be used for the specifications in the previous exercise.

14   The game 'Mastermind' (*alias* 'Cows and Bulls') is played between two players, using a set of colored pegs. The first player selects four pegs and places them in a row (hidden from the second player), where they constitute the *code*. The second player has to determine the code by means of successive tries coupled with logical deduction. A *try* is a row of four pegs that attempts to match the code. A *bull* is scored for each peg in the try that matches a code peg both in color and in position. A *cow* is scored for each peg that matches in color but not in position. For example, consider the configuration:

code :	red	green	blue	red
try :	blue	green	red	black

This scores one bull and two cows. The information is supplied by the first player and is used by the second player in formulating the next try.

A program is required which, given the code and the try, will compute the number of bulls and the number of cows. Using whatever notation you consider appropriate, write a formal specification for the program. To what extent is it a 'pure' (non-procedural) specification?

(Note: the above informal specification is based on one that is supplied with the game. As is often the case with the rules of games, it leaves certain situations undefined. The first task is therefore to fill in the gaps with plausible guesswork concerning the author's intentions.)

15   [Josephus' problem] Some condemned criminals are made to stand in a circle, awaiting their execution. They are numbered 1, 2, ... n around the circle, and a number k (1 ≤ k ≤ n) is then announced. Starting with criminal k, the executioner shoots every kth criminal, working round the circle and ignoring the gaps that are created, until only one remains. As a display of mercy, this last one is spared.

A program is required which, given n and k, will determine the number of the survivor. (If n = 5 and k = 3, the result should be 4.) Using whatever notation you consider appropriate, write a formal specification for the program. To what extent is it a 'pure' (non-procedural) specification?

This problem is cited by D. E. Knuth (1973, p.158), who credits it to W. Ahrens (1918). It is discussed in Rouse Ball (1892).

16 The rationale behind the proof rule for the assignment statement $V := E$ is very simple: the value of V afterwards equals the value of E beforehand, so what was true of V afterwards must have been true of E beforehand. Why cannot this argument be reversed, with the proof rule being written the other way round? Thus:

$$\{ P \} \ V := E \ \{ P[V \backslash E] \}$$

Give an example of a situation where this rule would lead to a false inference.

17 Section 7.6 described two interpretations of the concept of a variable. Which of these is reflected in the proof rule for assignments? What troubles might it lead to in more complicated situations?

18 Let $A(1..n)$ be a vector of integers. Apply the proof rule for assignments to the third assignment in the following sequence:

```
A(1) := 1;
A(2) := 0;
    -- assert 2 = 2;
A(A(1)) := 2;
    -- assert A(A(1)) = 2;
```

The precondition is certainly true and can be derived from the postcondition by substituting 2 for $A(A(1))$. Yet the postcondition is false! What has gone wrong? How might the rule be revised so that it handles this situation correctly? To what extent is your proposed revision *ad hoc*?

Discuss the claim that this difficulty is evidence of a fundamental weakness in the rule's concept of a variable.

19 Use the definition of integer division, as given in Section 4.2, to prove the correctness of the following:

```
{ 0 < i < j }
m := (i + j) div 2;
{ 0 < i ≤ m < j }
```

20 If gcd (m, n) denotes the greatest common divisor of m and n, prove the correctness of the following:

```
{ 0 < m < n and x = gcd(m,n) }
n := n - m;
{ 0 < m and 0 < n and x = gcd(m,n) }
```

21 Let $V(1..n)$ be a vector of numbers. Prove the correctness of the following:

```
{ i ≥ 0 and x = V(1) + V(2) + ... + V(i) }
i := i + 1;
x := x + V(i);
{ i ≥ 0 and x = V(1) + V(2) + ... + V(i) }
```

The interesting point is that the postcondition is the same as the precondition. When included inside a loop, it is known as an *invariant* of the loop (see Section 8.11). Note also the use of the 'three dots trick' for quantification.

22   Section 7.11 gives a specification of the program for implementing the 'mind-reading' exercise of Section 7.2. Prove that the program

```
x := answer;
```

is a correct implementation.

If 'correctness' means that the program has to go through the steps as originally specified in Section 7.2, it is (in effect) requiring the program to perform a simulation. This raises the interesting question: what does it mean for a simulation to be correct? Furthermore, how can its correctness be formally established? Consider these questions in the context of straightline programs. For some possible clues, see Naur (1969).

SEQUENTIAL CONTROL STRUCTURES

8.1 STRUCTURED PROGRAMMING

This chapter examines mechanisms for controlling the flow of execution in a procedural program. It restricts its attention to the *sequential* control structures, leaving the parallel ones until later (see Chapter 11). They are sequential in the sense that they require the statements of the program to be executed one at a time in a well-defined sequence. However, unlike straightline programs, they do not restrict the order of execution to the static sequence of the program text, with each statement being executed exactly once. Instead, they allow it to follow an entirely different, dynamic sequence, with some statements being executed many times over and others not at all. They liberate programs from the straightline straitjacket, enabling them to handle choices, loops, exceptions, and other such beneficial things.

The most primitive mechanism for the purpose is the **goto** statement, which is derived from machine-level programming (see Section 5.5). If a program uses this as its only method of control, it is called a *goto program*. At a higher level, there are statements for implementing the more structured mechanisms of sequencing, selection, and iteration. In their simplest forms, they can be expressed as follows, with B representing a Boolean expression and S, $S1$, and $S2$ representing arbitrary statements:

$S1$; $S2$	-- sequencing
if B **then** $S1$ **else** $S2$	-- selection
while B **do** S	-- iteration

These three control structures correspond to the three structuring operations of catenation, alternation, and repetition, as described in Chapter 6, and like them they constitute a powerful trio. In fact, they are sufficient for computing anything that is known to be computable. Many other versions have been proposed, varying widely both in syntax and in semantics. Later sections examine the more important ones, defining their properties and exploring their roles in practical programming.

The three basic control structures are commonly associated with the term 'structured programming'. This was a catchcry of the 1970s, when many people rallied to its call. The general notion was that good programs must be structured programs. (After all, who wants them to be *un*structured?) To achieve this desirable goal, it was asserted that structured programs must restrict their control mechanisms to the above three. In particular, some people argued that no self-respecting programmer would ever, under any circumstances, use a **goto** statement. This was the most unstructured thing that anyone could do and was definitely a sign of bad programming. Indeed, it would be better if modern programming languages abolished the **goto** statement entirely.

These propositions gave rise to a controversy that has had a major impact on the programming community. Its origins can be traced to a growing awareness in the 1960s that programs were being written in a casual, slapdash fashion and that, as a result, they were difficult to understand, expensive to maintain, and plagued with bugs. The indictment of the **goto** statement as a prime contributor to the problem was heard in some early rumblings of discontent, and then surfaced in a note by E. W. Dijkstra (1968) with the famous heading *'Go to statement considered harmful'*. There followed a long and spirited debate about the merits or otherwise of using **goto**s, and on the broader issues of what constitutes good programming. One outcome was a bewildering variety of proposals for making **goto**s redundant. Most of them amounted to saying 'OK, you can use **goto**s for such-and-such a purpose, but to make your intentions clearer you must give them a special name (such as **exit** or **break** or **loop**).' So disguised **goto**s sprang up like drugs for a new disease, and there was even a proposal for a **come from** statement (Clark, 1973). When the dust finally settled, it was a relief to find agreement on several useful points:

1. All high-level languages should include constructs similar to the above three.

2. When these have been provided, the use of **goto**s should be limited to very special circumstances.

3. Structured programming is not simply a matter of abolishing **goto**s.

As already indicated, there was less agreement on the details. Even so, the debate was a very healthy one and it brought about valuable improvements in the general practice of programming.

Point 3 emphasizes that in the final analysis the presence or absence of **goto**s is not the most basic issue. In fact, it can be shown that any program, however badly written, can be converted to **goto**-less form in a purely mechanical way; but the result is not necessarily a better program (see Exercise 28). Conversely, when a beautifully structured program is compiled into machine code, it suddenly acquires a plethora of **goto**s; but this does not destroy its underlying quality. What really matters is the abstract structure to which the code gives concrete expression. Does it match the structure of the problem? Does it match the structure of the data? Above all, can it be clearly shown that the program is correct? These are the issues that need to be addressed in any evaluation of control structures.

8.2 STATES

Before looking at particular mechanisms, it is useful to review the concept of a *state*. This was introduced in the discussion of finite automata (see Section 6.6), and it carries over to ordinary programs in an obvious way. Thus a program starts in an initial state; it moves from one state to another by executing its statements; and on reaching a final state, it stops. In the graphical representation of a finite automaton, the states are clearly visible, being depicted as circles. In ordinary programs, though, they are not so evident: the only indications of their presence are statement separators and the occasional label. The best way of highlighting them is to include assertions, as described in the previous chapter. The assertions for the initial and final states constitute the program's specification (see Section 7.11). An assertion at an intermediate state describes the significance of that state and the conditions that should be true when it is encountered during execution.

Transitions between states are notionally instantaneous, and so at any moment during execution a program has a *current* state. In the narrow sense of 'state', as used above, this means its current point of execution. However, in discussions about assertions, the term 'state' is often used in a different sense, meaning the values of the variables. After all, these are the only things that assertions can refer to. In its widest sense, 'state' means *both* of these factors — the point of execution and the values of the variables. It may even include the input/output files, these being regarded as variables of a special kind. This information constitutes a 'snapshot' of the computation, describing the program's execution at a moment in time.

In summary, the term 'state' is used in three different senses, depending on which components of a computation it embraces:

1. It may mean simply the point of execution, as in a finite automaton.

2. It may mean the values of the variables, as used by assertions in a program.

3. It may mean both, as required by an execution snapshot.

In ordinary programming it is usually taken in the second or third sense. To avoid any confusion, the point of execution is sometimes called a *program point* instead.

It is worth exploring the relationship between these three definitions a bit more closely, since it has some interesting practical consequences. Thus, suppose that a program has k program points and n variables, $V_1, V_2, \ldots V_n$. If each variable V_i can take p_i different values, the n variables in combination can take N different values, where N is the product $p_1 p_2 \ldots p_n$. The number of different states, in each of the three senses, is therefore as follows:

1. There are k states in the sense of program points.

2. There are N states in the sense of the values of the variables.

3. Taking 1 and 2 together, there are kN states in the sense of execution snapshots.

Whenever the program executes a statement, it moves from one state (in the third sense) to another. In this respect it is therefore similar to a finite automaton with kN states (in the first sense). In fact, it would be possible — though excessively tedious — to reformulate it in exactly this way, increasing the number of program points by a factor of N and dispensing with all the variables. States in the sense of snapshots would then have been replaced by states in the sense of program points.

For each variable V_i that is eliminated in this way, the number of program points increases by a factor of at most p_i. Generally speaking, the trade-off favors the retention of the variable. However, on a suitably modest scale, the replacement of variables by program points can sometimes prove quite effective. For example, consider the following code for reading a sequence of m digits:

```
            i  :=  0;
next :   if i = m then goto done;
            read_digit;
            i  :=  i + 1;
            goto next;
done :    ...
```

This has five program points and a variable i that takes m+1 values, namely 0, 1, ... m. The following version dispenses with the variable by using m+1 program points instead:

```
            read_digit;
            read_digit;

              ...

            read_digit;
done :    ...
```

For large values of m the loop has obvious advantages. But for small values, such as m = 3, the m calls of read_digit are shorter, simpler, and more efficient. Exercise 1 discusses some other situations in which this technique can occasionally prove useful.

8.3 MORE ON PROOF RULES

In order to deal with issues of correctness it is necessary to take a closer look at proof rules. These were introduced at the end of the previous chapter in the context of a statement S, with a precondition P and postcondition Q:

$$\{P\} \ S \ \{Q\} \tag{1}$$

A rule of this form sets out a relationship between P, S, and Q, which ensures that if P is true before the execution of S, then Q will be true afterwards. If it guarantees that S will terminate, it can be used for proving the total correctness of a program. If it does not guarantee termination, it can only prove partial correctness.

Section 7.12 showed how such rules can be used for proving the correctness of a straightline program. The same principles can be applied to any program that is based on transitions between states. For example, consider the finite automaton of Section 6.6, which is reproduced here as Figure 8-1. It was claimed earlier that this generates all sequences of two or more a's and b's that contain an odd number of a's. To prove that the number of a's will be odd, the technique is to supply each state with an assertion:

S :   the number of a's so far is zero;
D :   the number of a's so far is odd;
E :   the number of a's so far is even;
F :   the number of a's so far is odd.

It then has to be shown (a) that the assertion for S is true when the machine starts, and (b) that every transition from a state X to a state Y transforms the truth of X's assertion

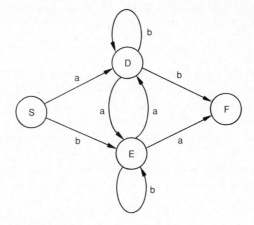

Figure 8-1 A finite automaton

into that of Y's. For example, it must be shown that if D's assertion is true when the machine is in state D, then the transition

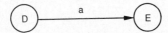

will make E's assertion true when it moves to E. Together, (a) and (b) guarantee that as the machine moves from state to state, the assertion for its current state will always be true. In particular, when it terminates at F, the number of a's will be odd.

A similar technique can be applied to any sequential program, including the flowchart programs and **goto** programs described later (see Section 8.6). However, it has the serious drawback that it does not guarantee termination. This is evident in two respects. First, rules of the form $\{P\}\,S\,\{Q\}$ say nothing about the termination of S. Second, even if each individual transition terminates, a circular sequence may continue indefinitely.

To handle termination, it is helpful to isolate the phrase $S\{Q\}$ and to treat it as a predicate meaning that if S is executed in the current state, it will terminate in a state that satisfies Q. In particular, since every state satisfies true, the predicate $S\{\text{true}\}$ means that the execution of S will terminate. Like all predicates, it may be either true or false, depending on the current state. It does *not* means that S always terminates: there may be some states for which it does and others for which it does not.

The advantage of this formulation is that $S\{Q\}$ can be treated in the same way as any other predicate, being subject to the ordinary laws and operations of the predicate calculus. For example, the formula

$$P \Rightarrow S\{Q\} \tag{2}$$

means that the initial condition P ensures that the execution of S will terminate in a state that satisfies Q. A rule of this form is stronger than (1) in that it guarantees termination. In particular, since every state satisfies true,

$$\text{true} \Rightarrow S\{\text{true}\}$$

means that S always terminates.

The notation can be taken one step further. If P describes *all* the initial states for which $S\{Q\}$ is true, the relation is one of equivalence:

$$P \equiv S\{Q\} \qquad\qquad (3)$$

In such cases, P is called the *weakest precondition* of S and Q. The concept was introduced by E. W. Dijkstra (1975, 1976), who denoted it by the expression $wp(S, Q)$. It is 'weaker' in the sense that it covers the widest set of conditions and is therefore the most easily satisfied. Paradoxically, though, a rule of this kind is a very strong one: it asserts that P is both *necessary and sufficient* for ensuring that S will terminate in a state that satisfies Q.

The assignment statement provides a simple example of these ideas. Its proof rule, as given in Section 7.12, is

$$\{Q[V\backslash E]\} \ \ V := E \ \{Q\}$$

where $Q[V\backslash E]$ denotes Q with every occurrence of V replaced by E. With the interpretation given above, this means that if the precondition $Q[V\backslash E]$ is true, and if $V := E$ terminates, then the postcondition Q will also be true. However, on the assumption that an assignment always terminates, the rule can be expressed much more strongly in the form of (3):

$$Q[V\backslash E] \ \equiv \ V := E \{Q\}$$

This adds a guarantee of termination and also states that $Q[V\backslash E]$ is the *weakest* precondition for ensuring Q. For example, let S be the assignment

$$x := y*y$$

and let Q be the postcondition $x = 9$. The predicate $S\{Q\}$ asserts that the assignment will terminate with $x = 9$. A sufficient precondition is $y = 3$, and this can be expressed formally by writing:

$$y = 3 \ \Rightarrow \ x := y*y \ \{x = 9\}$$

However, according to the above rule, the weakest precondition that guarantees $x = 9$ is $(x = 9) [x \backslash (y*y)]$, which is the condition $y*y = 9$. Hence the weakest precondition is not $y = 3$, but $y = \pm 3$.

For convenience in subsequent discussion, it is helpful to describe the meaning of $S\{Q\}$ by saying that S *guarantees* Q. This is an abbreviation for: 'starting in the current state, the execution of S is guaranteed to terminate in a state that satisfies Q'. If S is deterministic, the word 'guarantee' may seem unnecessarily strong. After all, given the current state the execution of S can have only one outcome. However, if S is nondeterministic the word is more significant: there may be several possible outcomes and the guarantee covers them all. Examples of nondeterministic statements will be given in later sections.

The following properties of $S\{Q\}$ are useful for reasoning about programs:

1. $S\{\text{false}\} \ \equiv \ \text{false}$

S cannot terminate in a state that satisfies false, for the simple reason that *no* state can satisfy false. Hence the predicate 'S guarantees false' must always be false. This has been described as 'the law of the excluded miracle' (Dijkstra, 1976). A statement that *does* perform miracles is described in the next section.

2. $(S\{Q\} \wedge Q \Rightarrow Q1) \Rightarrow S\{Q1\}$

If *S* guarantees *Q*, and *Q* implies *Q1*, then *S* guarantees *Q1*. This is the *rule of inference*. A similar rule can be formulated using (1) or (3). A more elaborate version introduces a precondition *P1* as a counterpart to the postcondition *Q1*. Using (3), it has the form:

$$\frac{P1 \Rightarrow P, \ P \equiv S\{Q\}, \ Q \Rightarrow Q1}{P1 \Rightarrow S\{Q1\}}$$

In this notation, the clauses above the line are *hypotheses* and the one below the line is the *conclusion*. The rule states that if the three hypotheses are true, then so is the conclusion. It says, in effect, that when applying rules of the form $P \equiv S\{Q\}$, it is legitimate to start with a stronger precondition than *P* and to end with a weaker postcondition than *Q*.

3. $S\{Q1\} \wedge S\{Q2\} \equiv S\{Q1 \wedge Q2\}$

If *S* guarantees *Q1* and it also guarantees *Q2*, then it must guarantee $Q1 \wedge Q2$. Conversely, if *S* guarantees $Q1 \wedge Q2$, it must guarantee *Q1* and it must also guarantee *Q2*.

4. $S\{Q1\} \vee S\{Q2\} \Rightarrow S\{Q1 \vee Q2\}$

If *S* guarantees *Q1* or it guarantees *Q2* (or both), then it must guarantee $Q1 \vee Q2$. If *S* is deterministic, the converse is also true: if it guarantees $Q1 \vee Q2$, then it must guarantee *Q1* or else guarantee *Q2* (or both). On the other hand, if it is nondeterministic, either outcome may be possible and so the converse is false. A familiar example is the spinning of a coin (Gries, 1981). This guarantees the outcome *heads* $\vee$ *tails*; but for normal coins it does not guarantee *heads*, nor does it guarantee *tails*.

The following summary of the notation may be helpful:

$\{P\} S \{Q\}$ A statement asserting that if *P* is true before the execution of *S*, and if the execution of *S* terminates, then the concluding state will satisfy *Q*.

$S\{Q\}$ The predicate '*S* guarantees *Q*', meaning that if *S* is executed, starting in the current state, then it is guaranteed to terminate in a state that satisfies *Q*.

$P \Rightarrow S\{Q\}$ A statement asserting that *P* is a sufficient precondition for *S* to guarantee *Q*.

$P \equiv S\{Q\}$ A statement asserting that *P* is the weakest precondition for *S* to guarantee *Q*.

It should be mentioned that some authors use $\{P\} S \{Q\}$ in the stronger sense of $P \Rightarrow S\{Q\}$; for example, Gries (1981). The notation $S\{Q\}$ has been introduced here as a convenient way of expressing and distinguishing the concepts. As remarked earlier, it is basically equivalent to $wp(S, Q)$, which was introduced by E. W. Dijkstra (1975) and has been widely followed. However, it is worth remarking that the term 'weakest precondition' is largely redundant and that it diverts attention from the essential idea. Why take a predicate such as $x = y$ and express it as 'the weakest condition such that $x = y$', or 'the set of all states for which $x = y$'? It makes life considerably harder for the unfortunate reader! In this case, the predicate is 'S guarantees Q', and a notation such as $S\{Q\}$, or $S(Q)$, or even SQ, expresses it perfectly well.

8.4   NULL, HALT, ABORT, AND MAGIC

The above concepts can be illustrated by considering four statements of a particularly simple kind, namely **null**, **halt**, **abort**, and **magic**. These play a fundamental role in the theory of control structures.

The *null* statement is the statement that does nothing. In several languages of the ALGOL family it is implied by the occurrence of the null string in a context where a statement is expected. For example, the sequence

$$\textbf{begin}\ x := 0;\ \textbf{end}$$

has an implied null statement after the semicolon. As a syntactic device this has the advantage that it allows semicolons to appear in some contexts where otherwise they would be illegal. For semantic purposes, though, it is preferable to make the null statement more visible. Some languages use **continue** for the purpose, others use **skip** (Dijkstra, 1975). Since neither of these terms is particularly appropriate, we shall follow Ada by using **null**. Its proof rule is:

$$\{P\}\ \equiv\ \textbf{null}\ \{P\}$$

This states that the precondition P is both necessary and sufficient for **null** to terminate with the postcondition P. Since this is true for all predicates P, it implies that the final state of **null** is always the same as its initial state. In other words, **null** never changes anything. It is conceivable that it meanders through a series of intermediate states, eventually arriving back at the one from which it started. More probably it does nothing at all.

The *halt* statement terminates execution. It seems simple enough, and yet any attempt to give it a proof rule runs into problems. For example, if its precondition is P, its postcondition must surely be P also. Furthermore, it certainly terminates. The rule

$$P\ \equiv\ \textbf{halt}\ \{P\}$$

might therefore seem appropriate. However, this makes it equivalent to **null**! Another approach is to take the view that it never reaches a concluding state. This can be expressed by removing the guarantee of termination and imposing the postcondition false:

$$\{P\}\ \textbf{halt}\ \{\,\text{false}\,\}$$

Unfortunately, this makes **halt** equivalent to an infinite loop and so it is not much better. The trouble is that **halt** is not really an executable statement. It is a *state*, rather than a statement. In the terminology of finite automata, it is a *final* state. Alternatively, if the only legitimate final state is defined to be the end of the main program, then **halt** is a null transition to that point — an extreme form of **goto**. Either way, it is an anomaly that is best avoided, and in practice most languages do not provide it.

The *abort* statement terminates execution with overtones of failure; it is therefore to be distinguished from **halt**, for which the connotations are not so bad. (It is also to be distinguished from the **abort** statement in Ada, which terminates tasks.) If the goal is Q, one thing is certain: **abort** will not achieve it. This can be expressed very simply by a rule stating that **abort** $\{Q\}$ is always false:

$$\text{false} \equiv \textbf{abort} \; \{Q\}$$

Since no state can satisfy false, the rule can also be interpreted as saying that, whatever postcondition Q is specified, there is no precondition that allows **abort** to achieve it. In other words, **abort** is incapable of doing anything. Unlike **null**, it cannot even do nothing!

The *magic* statement is not found in any practical programming languages, for the simple reason that there is no way of implementing it — hence its name. However, it has some interesting properties. Its proof rule is:

$$\text{true} \equiv \textbf{magic} \; \{\,\text{false}\,\}$$

This means that whatever the initial state, **magic** will arrive at a state for which false is true. Remarkable, powerful, and highly dangerous! In fact, since every predicate $P1$ satisfies $P1 \Rightarrow \text{true}$ and every predicate $Q1$ satisfies $\text{false} \Rightarrow Q1$, the rule of inference shows that for any $P1$ and $Q1$:

$$P1 \; \Rightarrow \; \textbf{magic} \; \{Q1\}$$

In other words, **magic** can do anything at all! You rub the lamp and the genie appears to do your bidding. Perhaps it is just as well that it cannot be implemented.

Clearly, **abort** and **magic** are at opposite ends of some sort of spectrum. One is incapable of doing anything; the other can do everything. A suitable 'spectrum' can be obtained by defining a partial ordering on statements (or programs), with $S1 \le S2$ meaning that for all Q:

$$S1 \{Q\} \; \Rightarrow \; S2 \{Q\}$$

In other words, $S1 \le S2$ means that if $S1$ can do something, then $S2$ can do it also. For a fuller, more precise discussion of this concept, see Morgan (1988).

8.5 FLOWCHARTS

Flowcharts provide a graphical notation for describing control structures. From an early stage in the history of computing they have been used for this purpose, and they are still found in many introductory courses on programming. They depict the flow of a program in a way that some people find helpful, especially when they first learn a programming language. The boxes and arrows look more dynamic than a prosaic series of statements, and so they help to bridge the conceptual gap between the static program text and the dynamic sequence of run-time operations.

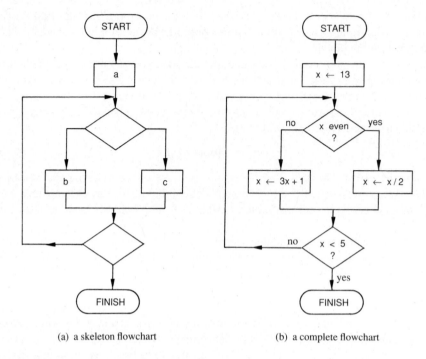

(a) a skeleton flowchart   (b) a complete flowchart

Figure 8-2   Flowcharts

Figure 8-2(a) shows the skeleton of a simple flowchart. As is usual, the rectangles represent various *actions* that the program can perform, and the diamonds represent *decisions* about which way it should go. In this case, the decisions are binary ones, being based on conditions that are either true or false, and the actions are denoted by the letters a, b, and c. They may be assignments, as described in the previous chapter, or input/output operations, or any other action that can be expressed by basic program statements. *A priori*, it is clear that many different action sequences might be executed. Some examples are ac, abb, and abcccb, but there are infinitely many other possibilities. In fact, the entire set of possibilities can be neatly described by the regular expression a (b∪c) (b∪c)*. An obvious inference is that flowcharts can express the three basic control structures — sequencing, selection, and iteration. A more tentative one is that they must be similar in some respects to finite automata.

The relationship between flowcharts and finite automata is worth exploring a little further. Each has a starting point and a finishing point; each can trace paths that generate sequences; and each can perform sequencing, selection and iteration. Indeed, some simple rules can be formulated for converting a flowchart, such as the one in Figure 8-2(a), into an equivalent finite automaton. The diamonds become states; the symbols inside rectangles become labels on transitions; and extra nodes are inserted between adjacent labels where necessary. Conversely, given a finite automaton, it is easy to derive a corresponding flowchart.

These arguments show that there is an equivalence between flowcharts and finite automata. However, it is important to appreciate that the equivalence applies only to *skeleton* flowcharts. It does not apply to *flowchart programs* — that is, to flowcharts in which the actions and conditions have all been fully specified. If the term 'flowchart' is taken in this more usual sense, the parallel with finite automata breaks down. This can be illustrated by filling in Figure 8-2(a) to give the flowchart program of Figure 8-2(b). In contrast to finite automata, the flowchart is now deterministic, its only action sequence being abcccbcc. Some nondeterminism can be introduced by reading the initial value of x from input; but the range of sequences would still be smaller than that of the original skeleton (Exercise 5).

In spite of its initial appeal, the flowchart should not be rated too highly. Its graphical layout may look impressive, and occasionally it is helpful in depicting the flow of a program. But as the next section shows, its control mechanisms are no better than those of machine code, and as a tool for structured programming it has little to commend it. Indeed, some people prefer to call it a 'flawchart' (Gries, 1981). Several other notations have been devised for depicting the control structures of a program in a graphical way, of which the best known are the Nassi–Shneiderman diagrams (Nassi and Shneiderman, 1973). These do not show the flow of execution so clearly, but emphasize the program's logical structure instead. For most purposes this is more helpful.

8.6   GOTO PROGRAMS

A *goto program* is one whose only control mechanism is the **goto** statement. In its purest form it does not even allow sequential control as a default. Instead, every statement must explicitly nominate its successors. So if S is a basic statement, it has to be expanded to some more elaborate form, such as

do S **then goto** L

where L is a statement label. To handle selection, a conditional **goto** is also needed:

if B **then goto** $L1$ **else goto** $L2$

It is useful to let the label S denote the start of execution, and F the finish (a **halt** statement). With these conventions, the flowchart of Figure 8-2(b) can be expressed as the following 'pure' **goto** program:

```
S  :   do x := 13 then goto L1
L1 :   if x is even then goto L2 else goto L3
L2 :   do x := 3x + 1 then goto L4
L3 :   do x := x/2 then goto L4
L4 :   if x < 5 then goto L1 else goto F
F  :   halt
```

One feature of this style of programming is that the statements can be written in any order. This provides considerable scope for confusing the unfortunate reader.

A simple property of 'pure' **goto** programs is that they are directly equivalent to flowchart programs. The **do** statement corresponds to a rectangle and the **if** statement to a diamond; the phrase **goto** L becomes an arrow to the appropriate point. Again, it is possible to confuse the reader by distributing the components of the flowchart to random positions on the page, allowing the arrows to criss-cross in arbitrary fashion. The result is spaghetti-like code in its finest form.

The pure **goto** program reflects the control mechanisms of some of the early computers (for example, the Elliott 402E of the 1950s). However, most machines adopted the much better method described in Section 5.5, whereby control passes by default to the next instruction in memory. To override the default, there are two kinds of branch instruction — one unconditional, the other conditional. In ALGOL-like notation, they can be written as follows:

$$\textbf{goto } L$$
$$\textbf{if } B \textbf{ then goto } L$$

When added to the straightline programs of the previous chapter, they create the class of *sequential goto* programs. Here is a version for the flowchart of Figure 8-2(b):

```
        x := 13;
L1 :    if x is even then goto L2;
        x := 3x + 1;
        goto L3;
L2 :    x := x/2;
L3 :    if x < 5 then goto L1;
        halt
```

This sort of code was typical of early FORTRAN programs and is found in many BASIC programs even today.

A sequential **goto** program can be converted to the 'pure' form by labeling every statement and then making the sequencing explicit. The first statement is labeled S and the **halt** statement is labeled F. Each statement is then rewritten according to the following rules, with σ denoting the label of its successor:

Sequential form	*Pure form*
S	**do** S **then goto** σ
goto L	**do null then goto** L
if B **then goto** L	**if** B **then goto** L **else goto** σ

Other rules can be added in order to 'optimize' the code. For example, the sequence

$$S;$$
$$\textbf{goto } L1;$$

can be transformed to:

$$\textbf{do } S \textbf{ then goto } L1$$

Similarly

$$\textbf{if } B \textbf{ then goto } L1;$$
$$\textbf{goto } L2;$$

can be transformed to:

$$\textbf{if } B \textbf{ then goto } L1 \textbf{ else goto } L2$$

The reverse transformations can convert any pure **goto** program into an equivalent sequential **goto** program.

These observations show that the two forms of **goto** program are equivalent to each other, and that both are equivalent to flowchart programs. Since the sequential form is much the most common, the term '**goto** program' is normally interpreted in that sense; but it may be taken in the pure sense or the flowchart sense equally well.

It might be thought that sequential **goto** programs are more 'structured' than the pure ones. However, the above transformations show that a pure **goto** program can be mechanically converted to a sequential one whose basic structure is exactly the same. It follows that a sequential **goto** program is not necessarily any more structured than an equivalent pure one. The conversion eliminates some of the **goto** statements; but, as remarked in Section 8.1, the underlying structure is neither better nor worse.

Since **goto** programs are based on transitions between states, the strategy for proving their correctness is the one that was outlined at the start of Section 8.3. It can be described most simply for the 'pure' form. Each label L represents a state that has a corresponding assertion $\alpha(L)$. Each statement executes a transition from one state to another that must preserve the truth of the current assertion. In the case of the statement

$$L : \textbf{do } S \textbf{ then goto } L1$$

this requires:

$$\alpha(L) \Rightarrow S\{\alpha(L1)\}$$

In the case of the conditional statement

$$L : \textbf{if } B \textbf{ then goto } L1 \textbf{ else goto } L2$$

it requires

$$\alpha(L) \wedge B \Rightarrow \alpha(L1)$$

and:

$$\alpha(L) \wedge \neg B \Rightarrow \alpha(L2)$$

If these requirements are all met, a program that starts at S in a state that satisfies $\alpha(S)$ will, on reaching F, satisfy $\alpha(F)$.

A similar strategy can be used for sequential **goto** programs. However, it must be emphasized that in both cases the strategy can only prove *partial* correctness. It offers no guarantee that F will ever be reached and that the program will therefore terminate. This is not just an oversight. On the contrary, a well-known theorem states that it is impossible to find a completely reliable procedure for determining whether or not an arbitrary **goto** program will terminate. This is known as 'the undecidability of the Halting Problem', and it shows that there can never be a universal strategy for proving the total correctness of **goto** programs. The only way to handle termination is to impose restrictions on the way in which programs are written, and even then the problem is far from easy. Later sections will consider it in some detail.

8.7   THE GOTO STATEMENT

This section considers the **goto** statement in the more general context of a high-level programming language. Its basic form is

goto *L*

where *L* is a statement label or possibly a label expression (see below). When executed, its effect is that control moves to the program point designated by *L*. The conditional version,

if *B* **then goto** *L*

can be regarded as a special case of the **if** statement, and so there is no need to consider it separately. Its semantics are obtained by combining those of the unconditional version with those of the **if** statement.

In most languages, the label *L* is an ordinary identifier and is prefixed to its statement by means of a colon:

L :   *statement*

It is implicitly declared at this point and is visible throughout the smallest enclosing block (see Section 10.3). This makes it impossible to transfer control to *L* from outside the block. Pascal's reluctant inclusion of **goto**s is reflected in the fact that *L* has to be an integer (as in FORTRAN and BASIC) and that it has to be declared separately. Ada allows ordinary identifiers but uses a less conventional notation:

<< L >>   *statement*

The reasons for choosing << ... >> are not clear, but at least it lightens the load on the overworked colon.

According to the definition of the proof rules, as given in Section 8.3, the rule for the **goto** statement is simply:

$$P \equiv \textbf{goto } L \ \{ P \}$$

This says that if **goto** *L* is executed in a state that satisfies *P*, it will terminate in a state that still satisfies *P*. Since 'state' in this context refers only to the values of the variables, this is clearly correct. Equally, it makes **goto** *L* equivalent to **null**, which is clearly incorrect. The trouble is that the proof rules say nothing about the effect of a statement on the current program point. They are therefore inadequate for handling **goto** statements.

To obviate this difficulty, it is necessary to use a proof *strategy*, rather than a proof *rule*. The strategy is the one that was described for **goto** programs in the previous section. It can be extended to the more general context of a high-level language by requiring (a) that *P* be true at the point labeled *L*, and (b) that the program point following the **goto** statement have the assertion false, implying that it cannot be reached. This captures the basic logic of what is happening. However, as later sections show, its interaction with other proof techniques causes serious complications. The difficulties can be reduced by imposing various restrictions — for example, forbidding **goto**s into loops or to the branches of a conditional statement. Even so, the presence of **goto**s has two major drawbacks:

1. The first and most obvious point is that the strategy does not concern itself with termination. As mentioned at the end of the previous section, this is not just a minor oversight. On the contrary, it relates to the undecidability of the Halting Problem. The unrestricted use of **goto**s cannot be allowed in any methodology that seeks to guarantee termination.

2. The other major problem is that **goto**s militate against the decomposition of programs into smaller, independent, more manageable units. If assertions carry across from one part of a program to another, those two parts cannot be considered separately. The unrestricted use of **goto**s means that the composition of units can be arbitrarily complicated.

Other arguments can be adduced, including those of the original note '*Go to statement considered harmful*' by E. W. Dijkstra (1968). But these two are arguably the most important.

In both cases it is the *unrestricted* use of **goto**s that causes the trouble. The question therefore arises: for what purposes (if any) are **goto**s acceptable? The answer should surely be that they are acceptable for implementing good control structures when these are not provided by other, higher-level means. For example, if a **while** statement is not provided, it may be necessary to use **goto**s to implement a loop. In that case, no-one would call them a sign of bad programming. The issue then becomes one of deciding which control structures are 'good'. By providing a rich enough range of statements, the language designer may claim that the remaining uses for **goto**s are all 'harmful' and that the **goto** statement should therefore be abolished. However, even if everyone agreed with the choice of statements (which seems improbable), there is a further reason for retaining the **goto** statement. This concerns program generators — that is, programs for generating other programs. If the target language excluded **goto**s, their task would be very much harder. Writing **goto**-less programs is one thing; writing programs to *generate* **goto**-less programs is something else!

By way of conclusion, it should be mentioned that some languages allow the destination of a **goto** to be determined at run-time. In other words, the 'argument' of **goto** can be an expression that has to be evaluated dynamically. ALGOL 60 offers the following two instances:

> **goto if** B **then** $L1$ **else** $L2$
> **goto** $S[i]$

The first can be expanded into an ordinary **if** statement with a **goto** in each branch (as in the previous section). The second is known as a *switch* (or in FORTRAN as a 'computed **goto**'). The switch S has to be declared as a list of labels or label expressions:

> **switch** S := London, Bombay, Sydney;

The statement **goto** S[i] transfers control to the ith label in the list; so if i = 3, control goes to Sydney. If i is outside the range 1 .. 3, the effect is undefined. Figure 8-3 shows the structure of some code that uses this switch, together with its corresponding flowchart. As can be seen, in the absence of any further **goto**s, execution 'falls through' from the London section to the Bombay section, and then from Bombay to Sydney. If i = 3, control goes only to Sydney; but if i = 2, it goes to Bombay first, and if i = 1 it goes to

switch S := London, Bombay, Sydney;

goto S[i];

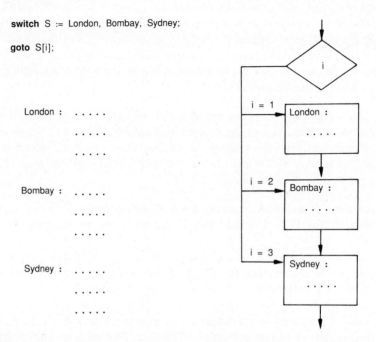

London :   . . . . .

. . . . .

. . . . .

Bombay :   . . . . .

. . . . .

. . . . .

Sydney :   . . . . .

. . . . .

. . . . .

Figure 8-3   A switch

all three. Exercise 7 presents a program that puts this accumulative behavior to good effect. However, it must be admitted that such applications are not very common.

The implementation of a switch is very simple and efficient. The labels are stored as addresses in consecutive locations and the value of i is used as an index. After checking that i lies in the required range, the code fetches the relevant address and assigns it to the instruction pointer, thus effecting the desired transfer of control (see Section 5.5).

The switch is a powerful mechanism for implementing a multiway branch. Nevertheless, since it is basically a glorified **goto** statement, it is open to all the criticisms that are leveled at **goto**s. Modern languages generally prefer a more disciplined facility, namely the **case** statement, in which the **goto** disappears from view. This will be described in Section 8.10.

8.8   SEQUENCING

Sequencing is the first of the three basic control mechanisms that were mentioned in Section 8.1 — the counterpart of catenation in regular expressions. It was used for the straightline programs of the previous chapter and also for the sequential **goto** programs of Section 8.6. This section examines it more closely.

The sequencing of two statements *S1* and *S2* is illustrated in the flowchart of Figure 8-4. The intention is clear enough: *S1* is executed first, and then *S2*. Of course, if *S1* includes a **goto**, control may never reach *S2*; consequently, remarks about the execution of *S2* have to be hedged about with ifs and buts. This illustrates the problems caused by **goto**s that were mentioned in the previous section.

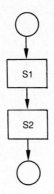

Figure 8-4   Sequential statements

Sequencing is usually expressed by writing *S1* and *S2* on separate lines (as in FOR-
TRAN, BASIC, etc.), or by using the semicolon or some similar symbol as a separator:

$$S1 \; ; \; S2$$

The semicolon makes the sequencing operation more explicit, but it has the practical
drawback that it is a common source of trivial, syntactic errors. In Ada, it is treated as a
terminator rather than a separator, and so the sequence is written as:

$$S1 \; ; \; S2 \; ;$$

Or, more usually, as:

$$S1 \; ;$$
$$S2 \; ;$$

Conceptually this is less attractive. In practice, though, it has the advantage that existing
programs are easier to alter. In particular, if a third statement *S3* has to be added, there is
no need to insert a semicolon following *S2* (because it is already there), and so the editing
is a simple one-line insertion.

The proof rule for *S1* ; *S2* is very brief:

$$S1 \, \{S2 \, \{Q\}\} \equiv (S1 ; S2) \, \{Q\}$$

This states that if *S1* guarantees that *S2* will guarantee *Q*, then *S1* ; *S2* guarantees *Q*. A
more elaborate version introduces a precondition *P* and an intermediate assertion *A*:

$$\frac{P \Rightarrow S1 \, \{A\}, \;\; A \Rightarrow S2 \, \{Q\}}{P \Rightarrow (S1 ; S2) \, \{Q\}}$$

This states that if *P* is sufficient for *S1* to guarantee *A*, and if *A* is sufficient for *S2* to
guarantee *Q*, then *P* is sufficient for *S1* ; *S2* to guarantee *Q*. When combined with the
rule for **null** it shows that:

$$\textbf{null} \; ; \; S1 \quad \equiv \quad S1 \; ; \; \textbf{null} \quad \equiv \quad S1$$

In other words, **null** is the identity element of the sequencing operation.

In the context of program design the rule asserts that to move from the precondition P to the postcondition Q a possible strategy is to use a sequence $S1 ; S2$ that proceeds via an intermediate condition A. It does not say what A should be; so programmers have to draw on a combination of experience, insight, and heuristics in choosing it. A simple heuristic is that if Q has the form $Q1 \wedge Q2$ (or if it can be put in that form), A should be $Q1$. This gives $S1$ the task of establishing $Q1$, after which $S2$ can attend to $Q2$. It is a heuristic in the sense that it does not necessarily lead to a good solution. After all, $S2$ has to establish $Q2$ while also preserving $Q1$, and this may not be particularly easy. In other cases, A is chosen so that it is in some sense 'nearer' to satisfying Q; but quite what 'nearer' means will depend on the nature of the application.

Repeated use of sequencing gives rise to the more general *statement sequence*:

$$S1 ; S2 ; \quad \ldots \quad Sn$$

In ALGOL 60 and several related languages, the statements can be enclosed between the brackets **begin** and **end** (or other equivalent symbols) to form a *compound statement*. This enables an **if** clause or **while** clause to control a group of statements — rather like the parentheses in $a * (b + c)$. The corresponding proof rule can be derived from the earlier one by treating the sequence as a recursive structure of the form $S1 ; S$, where S is itself a statement sequence, namely $S2 ; \ldots Sn$. For $S1 ; S$, the rule introduces an intermediate state $A1$; when applied recursively to S, it introduces states $A2, \ldots A(n-1)$ similarly. This leads to the situation that was described in Section 7.12.

8.9 SELECTION

Selection is the mechanism for choosing between several statements on the basis of one or more conditions. The general case is illustrated by the diagram of Figure 8-5, where the choice between $S1, S2, \ldots Sn$ is made on the basis of the conditions $B1, B2, \ldots Bn$. The usual implication is that exactly one Bi must be true and that the corresponding Si is then executed. But, as shown later, certain other interpretations are possible.

In high-level languages the choice is usually provided by means of an **if** statement and possibly by a **case** statement as well. The simplest version, as found in Pascal, is the form

$$\textbf{if } B \textbf{ then } S1 \tag{1}$$

where (as usual) B denotes a Boolean expression and $S1$ denotes a statement. If B evaluates to true, $S1$ is executed; otherwise it is skipped. To provide for the case when B is false, an **else** clause is added:

$$\textbf{if } B \textbf{ then } S1 \textbf{ else } S2 \tag{2}$$

If B evaluates to true, $S1$ is executed; otherwise $S2$ is executed.

In all these constructions, the implication is that $S1$ and $S2$ represent arbitrary statements. For example, they could be compound statements, as described in the previous section. They could also be **if** statements, so that we can write things such as:

$$\textbf{if } B1 \textbf{ then if } B2 \textbf{ then } S$$

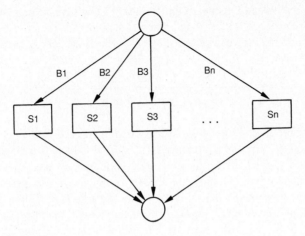

Figure 8-5   Selection

This is equivalent to the use of the conditional *and*, as described in Section 4.4:

if *B1* **and then** *B2* **then** ...

The former version provides a good alternative if the 'short circuit' condition is not available.

Substituting (2) for the occurrence of *S1* in (1) produces the form:

if *B1* **then if** *B2* **then** *S1* **else** *S2*

However, the same form is obtained by substituting (1) for *S1* in (2). This creates a potential ambiguity: to which **if-then** does the **else** belong? When the problem surfaced in ALGOL 60 it became known as 'the case of the dangling **else**' and several Perry Masons rose up to solve it (Abraham, 1966). In Pascal, the rule is that the **else** belongs to the second **if-then**. This is usually the programmer's intention; even so, there is scope for confusion and some unfortunate bugs. Ada's solution to the problem (following ALGOL 68, etc.) is to terminate every **if** statement with a special symbol:

> **if** *condition* **then**
>   *statement_sequence_1*
> **else**   (3)
>   *statement_sequence_2*
> **end if**;

The **else** part is optional but the terminating **end if** is mandatory. It solves the dangling **else** problem by not allowing the ambiguity to occur — a safer policy than Pascal's. The **end if** makes the simplest cases slightly more verbose, but this is offset by the fact that the statement sequences do not need **begin-end** brackets. The result is a neat, safe construction. The intention is that it should be spaced out and indented in the way suggested by (3).

The proof rules for these constructions are straightforward. Here is the one for the **if-then-else** statement:

$$(B \Rightarrow S1\,\{\,Q\,\}) \wedge (\neg B \Rightarrow S2\,\{\,Q\,\}) \;\equiv\; (\textbf{if } B \textbf{ then } S1 \textbf{ else } S2)\,\{\,Q\,\}$$

This says that the weakest precondition for the **if** statement to guarantee Q is that B should be sufficient for $S1$ to do so and that $\neg B$ should be sufficient for $S2$ to do so. As with the rule for $S1 \, ; S2$, this can be recast in a form that introduces a precondition P:

$$\frac{P \wedge B \Rightarrow S1 \{Q\}, \;\; P \wedge \neg B \Rightarrow S2 \{Q\}}{P \Rightarrow (\textbf{if } B \textbf{ then } S1 \textbf{ else } S2) \{Q\}}$$

In the context of program design the rule states that to proceed from the precondition P to the postcondition Q, a possible strategy is to split P into two stronger conditions — $P \wedge B$ and $P \wedge \neg B$ — and to treat them separately. It does not say what B should be; so, as in the previous section, the choice requires a combination of experience, insight, and heuristics. An obvious possibility is that if P has the form $P1 \vee P2$ (or if it can be put in that form), B should be either $P1$ or $P2$. The statement will then treat the two conditions separately. If B is $P1$, for example, it follows formally that $P \wedge B \equiv P1$ and $P \wedge \neg B \equiv P2$.

As a simple example, suppose that i^n has to be computed in a language that requires exponents to be positive. If n might in fact be negative, the precondition is written as $n \geq 0 \vee n < 0$ and the two cases are treated separately:

```
if n ≥ 0 then
    x := i ** n;
else    -- n < 0
    x := 1/(i ** (-n));
end if;
```

On the understanding that i and n remain constant, the required postcondition Q is $x = i^n$. The above rule therefore states that the two assignments must satisfy the following:

$$n \geq 0 \;\;\Rightarrow\;\; x := i{**}n \; \{x = i^n\}$$
$$n < 0 \;\;\Rightarrow\;\; x := 1/(i{**}(-n)) \; \{x = i^n\}$$

The first is verified by observing that $n \geq 0$ implies $i{**}n = i^n$ (by definition of '**' for positive exponents), and then applying the proof rule for assignments. The second is similar, but the initial reasoning is a bit more complicated:

$$
\begin{aligned}
n < 0 \Rightarrow\;\; &{-}n \geq 0 && \text{-- rules of arithmetic} \\
\Rightarrow\;\; &i{**}(-n) = i^{-n} && \text{-- definition of '**'} \\
\Rightarrow\;\; &1 / i{**}(-n) = 1/i^{-n} && \text{-- rules of arithmetic} \\
\Rightarrow\;\; &1 / i{**}(-n) = i^n && \text{-- rules of arithmetic}
\end{aligned}
$$

The complete proof may seem rather long-winded, but the basic reasoning must be there, whether it is formally expressed or not.

8.10   MULTIPLE SELECTION

Figure 8-5 shows a choice that is based on several conditions — $B1$, $B2$, ... Bn — the implication being that if Bi is true then Si is executed. A choice of this kind can be expressed by repeated use of the **if-then-else** construction. In Pascal it produces:

if $B1$ **then** $S1$
else if $B2$ **then** $S2$
else if $B3$ **then** $S3$

$\qquad \cdots$ (4)

else if Bn **then** Sn
else S

The final **else** S is optional. It provides a default if the conditions Bi are all false. In Ada, each **if** has to have a matching **end if** and so the equivalent statement would end with n occurrences of **end if**. An alternative version is therefore provided:

if $B1$ **then**
　　　statement_sequence_1
elsif $B2$ **then**
　　　statement_sequence_2
elsif $B3$ **then**

$\qquad \cdots$ (5)

elsif Bn **then**
　　　statement_sequence_n
else
　　　statement_sequence
end if;

As before, the **else** part is optional. The construction is easy to understand and has obvious parallels with the diagram of Figure 8-5. Even so, (4) and (5) are not quite as simple as they might appear, and they differ from the diagram in a significant way. The point is that if Si is to be executed, the conditions prior to Bi must all be false. So the full condition for the execution of Si is:

$$\neg B1 \,\wedge\, \neg B2 \,\wedge\, \cdots \,\wedge\, \neg B(i{-}1) \,\wedge\, Bi$$

This is a more complicated expression to deal with. Only when the B's are mutually exclusive does it reduce to the condition Bi. In practice, if the number of clauses is more than one or two, the B's usually *are* mutually exclusive; and in other cases, the full condition may well be the one that is needed anyhow. Nevertheless, the extended conditions clutter up the theory (as in the proof rules, for example), and the lack of symmetry between them is unattractive.

To remedy these defects, a more elegant construction was formulated by E. W. Dijkstra (1975):

if　　$B1$　$\rightarrow$　$S1$
　▯　　$B2$　$\rightarrow$　$S2$

$\qquad \cdots$ (6)

　▯　　Bn　$\rightarrow$　Sn
fi

Each phrase $Bi \rightarrow Si$ is a *guarded command*, Bi being the *guard* that controls its execution and Si being any statement sequence. Unlike (4) and (5), the commands have no implied priority and so the correspondence with Figure 8-5 is much closer. The only question is how to interpret them. The rules are as follows:

1.   The guards *Bi* may be evaluated in any order.

2.   If exactly one *Bi* is true, execute the corresponding *Si*.

3.   If several *Bi*'s are true, execute any one of the corresponding *Si*'s.

4.   If no *Bi* is true, there is an error condition.

The rules do not specify that all the guards have to be evaluated. On finding one that is true, the implementation is free to stop searching and to execute the corresponding statement sequence. On the other hand, it may continue evaluating the guards if it chooses to.

The most radical feature of the construction is that it is *nondeterministic*. This is seen partly in rule 1, but more especially in rule 3, where the choice between executable statements is arbitrary. In some cases, this reflects the true nature of the algorithm. In others, though, it may simply express some redundancy. Consider, for example, the following statement that sets the variable m to the maximum of x and y:

$$
\begin{array}{lll}
\textbf{if} & x \geq y & \rightarrow \quad m := x \\
\textbf{[]} & y \geq x & \rightarrow \quad m := y \\
\textbf{fi} & &
\end{array}
$$

When x = y, the guards are both true and so either statement may be executed. Equally, when x = y the two statements do the same thing. So the nondeterminism, in this case, is of no significance.

The fact that the guarded commands all have equal status is obviously attractive and it results in a proof rule for (6) which is cleaner and simpler than the one for (4) or (5). Even so, it raises some interesting questions. For example, in the simple case where one guard is *B* and the other is ¬*B*, it is unnecessary to evaluate them both; so there is a need for a good optimizing compiler. The lack of a catch-all clause, such as an **else** statement, also calls for comment. On the one hand, catch-all clauses are an inducement to lazy thinking. On the other hand, there are situations where they can save a lot of tedious writing. Language designers have to weigh up these two considerations. As it turns out, none of the mainstream languages have adopted this form of **if** statement. The nearest equivalent is Ada's **select** statement, which is used for real-time applications. In this context, the nondeterminism finds a natural home (see Section 11.10).

A simpler form of multiway selection is provided by the more popular **case** statement, first advocated by C. A. R. Hoare (1964). The following is Ada's version:

```
case expression is
    when choice_1 =>
            statement_sequence_1
    when choice_2 =>
            statement_sequence_2
        . . .
    when choice_n =>
            statement_sequence_n
end case;
```

The *expression* must have a value, *x* say, of some discrete type *T*. In its simplest form each *choice* is a manifest constant of that type, and when *x* equals that constant the corresponding statement sequence is executed. It works particularly well for an enumerated type, such as the type result that was defined in Section 7.5. This has the values (loss, draw, win); so if x is of that type, a corresponding **case** statement might go as follows:

```
case x is
    when loss =>
            their_score := their_score + 2;
    when draw =>
            their_score := their_score + 1;
            our_score := our_score + 1;
    when win =>
            our_score := our_score + 2;
end case;
```

The general form is quite flexible. Several choices can be grouped together, separated by the symbol "|"; a choice can be a static expression (see Section 7.4), a discrete range, or the symbol **others**. If a choice requires no action at all, the corresponding statement is **null**. For example, if you live in the northern hemisphere, the following might be your idea of a good keep-fit program:

```
case month is
    when March | November =>
            play (bowls);
    when April..June | August..October =>
            play (golf);
    when July =>
            sunbathe;
            swim;
            sunbathe;
    when others =>
            null;
end case;
```

Ada requires that every *T*-type value should appear exactly once in the choices — either explicitly, or in a range, or (by implication) in **others**. Thus the construction is (a) deterministic and (b) protected against run-time failure. It also allows **goto**s that lead from one branch to another:

```
    when ... =>
            S1;
            goto share;
    when ... =>
            S2;
        <<share>>
            S3;
```

This has the advantage that separate branches can link up and share some common code. On the other hand, the **goto** cuts across the basic structure of the **case** statement and raises all the standard issues of the **goto** controversy. In particular, it invalidates the standard proof rule.

Provided that the range of T-type values is small, the start of a **case** statement can be implemented by a switch, as described in Section 8.7, with x being the index. The remaining code differs from the switch in that each statement sequence is then terminated by a branch that joins them all up again (see Figure 8-5). A simple switch uses a table with an entry for each possible value; so if the range of values were very large some other method might be needed. For example, the compiler might handle the choices as though they were the branches of an extended **if-then-else** statement. This would save space but at the cost of slower code.

8.11   DECISION TABLES

An alternative approach to handling multiple choices is to use some sort of table. As a rather trivial example, consider the problem of putting two array elements, A_i and A_j, into ascending order without knowing anything about i or j in advance. The table in Figure 8-6 summarizes the conditions that need to be considered and the corresponding actions that must be taken. It provides a non-procedural statement of the requirements and therefore operates at a higher level of abstraction than conventional **if** statements or **case** statements. It allows the programmer to define and assess the situation without being committed to any particular method of implementation. Incidentally, it will be noticed that two of the entries are marked error. They indicate situations that are logically impossible; so, if the program is logically watertight, there is no need to test for them. Other error conditions may be more like undesirable exceptions, in which case the code should be included.

When satisfied that the requirements are correctly stated, the programmer can consider ways of implementing the table in a program. One possibility is to convert it into a standard control structure. For example, if the table is a one-dimensional array, it translates very neatly into a **case** statement; if it is a binary tree, it can be implemented as a nested set of **if-then-else** statements. The other possibility is to have a *table-driven* program — that is, one in which the table is represented as a data structure. The program locates the relevant entry, extracts the data, and acts accordingly. A simple method is to define an enumerated type with a value for each possible action — such as (swap, leave, error). Each entry in the table contains one such value and a **case** statement can then be

	$A_i < A_j$	$A_i = A_j$	$A_i > A_j$
$i < j$	leave	leave	swap
$i = j$	error	leave	error
$i > j$	swap	leave	leave

Figure 8-6   Actions for sorting

used to define the appropriate actions. With a two-dimensional table, for example, the look-up and the selection can be combined in a single clause:

```
case table (x,y) is
    when swap  =>  ...
    when leave =>  ...
    when error =>  ...
end case;
```

A certain amount of work is needed in setting up the data structure; but, once established, it provides a powerful, efficient, and flexible technique.

Systems have been written that convert tables into programs automatically. The tables are usually restricted to a particular kind, known as *decision tables*. Figure 8-7 shows a simple example that relates to serving a customer in a store. As can be seen, there are two main parts — the *conditions* and the *actions*. In this case there are three conditions:

- Is the customer a regular one?
- Is the payment by cash?
- Is the purchase worth at least $100?

Conditions can be entered as Y for 'yes', N for 'no', or blank for 'don't care'. Then there are three actions that can be taken:

- Sell the goods.
- Give a 10% discount.
- Include a free bonus gift.

Each column represents a *rule*: if the conditions marked Y are true and those marked N are false, then the actions marked X are to be taken. For example, column 2 shows that a regular customer, who pays cash for a small purchase, is to be given a discount but no free gift. In essence, it is a simple form of rule-based programming.

Given a table of this kind, there are various things that an automatic system can do with it. For a start, it can check for several properties:

	rule	R1	R2	R3	R4	R5	R6	R7
	frequency	.05	.35	.20	.15	.02	.20	.03
	regular?	Y	Y	Y	Y	N	N	N
conditions :	cash?	Y	Y	N	N	Y		N
	≥ $100?	Y	N	Y	N	Y	N	Y
	sell	X	X	X	X	X	X	
actions :	discount	X	X	X				
	bonus	X				X		

Figure 8-7   A decision table

> *Incompleteness* — are any sets of conditions not covered?
>
> *Ambiguity* — are any sets of conditions covered twice?
>
> *Redundancy* — can two rules be merged (by combining a 'yes' and a 'no' into a 'don't care')?

These properties are not necessarily undesirable. For instance, incompleteness may simply reflect the fact that some sets of conditions can never occur (as in Figure 8-6). When the checks have been made, the system can convert the table into an equivalent program. A simple-minded translation could test the conditions for each rule in turn. For large tables, though, this is too inefficient and so a variety of other techniques are sometimes used instead:

1.   The Yes-No pattern of the actual conditions is coded as a bit string, which is then treated as an integer and used as the index of a switch or **case** statement.

2.   The bit string is compared with the equivalent bit strings for each of the rules (though the 'don't care' entries require special handling).

3.   Each condition is tested in turn, using **if-then-else** statements that are nested sufficiently deep:

```
if  condition–1  then
    if  condition–2  then
        if  condition–3  then
            apply rule 1
        else
            apply rule 2
        end  if
    else
        if  condition–3  then
            apply rule 3
        else
            apply rule 4
        end  if
    end  if
else
    if  condition–2  then
        etc.
```

There may be scope for considerable optimization, taking advantage of the fact that some rules are applied much more frequently than others. As shown in Figure 8-7, a decision table may therefore include an estimate of these frequencies. The costs of evaluating the conditions can be taken into account similarly.

The example shown in Figure 8-7 is a *limited entry* decision table: the conditions are restricted to the values 'yes', 'no', or 'don't care'. A more general form of table allows the conditions to be replaced by expressions with many possible values. In COBOL, it can be implemented by means of the **evaluate** statement:

evaluate *expr–1 expr–2 ... expr–n*
    when *choice–1 choice–2 ... choice–n   statement–list*
    when *choice–1 choice–2 ... choice–n   statement–list*

    ...

    when *choice–1 choice–2 ... choice–n   statement–list*
end evaluate

This is similar to Ada's **case** statement except that it can test several expressions at once. Each *choice* is a constant, a range, or **any**. If the values of the expressions are matched by one of the lists, the corresponding *statement-list* is executed. This form of table gives greater flexibility, but efficient implementation is more difficult.

Decision tables are usually implemented within the framework of some existing language, such as FORTRAN or COBOL. Despite their support by a band of enthusiasts, they have never been provided as a major feature of any mainstream language. There are several reasons for this. One is that their two-dimensional format does not fit very well into the linear structure of ordinary programs. Another is that their usefulness seems to be limited to rather special sorts of situation, mostly in the commercial field. Elsewhere they tend to be unnecessarily complicated. In theory, they are very appealing and many people have sung their praises. In practice, they have not received the recognition and status that was predicted for them.

8.12 ITERATION

Iteration is the mechanism for executing code segments more than once. It is implemented by statements known as *loops* and these, like most other things, come in several varieties. A particularly simple form is Ada's *basic loop*:

    loop
        statement_sequence
    end loop;

This threatens to repeat the statement sequence indefinitely. (The nearest equivalent in other languages is usually something like **while** true **do** ... .) There are situations, particularly in real-time applications, where an infinite loop is appropriate. More usually, though, a device is needed for bringing the repetition to an end. The most primitive is the **goto** statement, which can transfer control to an arbitrary point outside the loop. A more restrained version is Ada's **exit** statement, which transfers control to the statement following the **end loop** symbol. A conditional exit is provided by the version:

    exit when *condition*;

A typical example is a loop that reads a sequence of values, processing each one up to, but not including, a special terminating value:

    loop
        get (x);
        exit when x = terminator;
        process (x);
    end loop;

If one loop is nested inside another, the situation is slightly more complicated:

```
<< L >>
    loop                                    -- start of outer loop
        ...
        loop                                -- start of inner loop
            ...
            exit when ... ;                 -- exits inner loop
            exit L when ... ;               -- exits outer loop
            ...
        end loop;                           -- end of inner loop
        ...
    end loop L;                             -- end of outer loop
```

As indicated by the comments, the first **exit** applies (by default) to the inner loop. The second leaves the outer loop by prefixing it with a label and then referring to the label. The name of the label must also be included after the matching **end loop**.

In general, there are three kinds of loop, depending on whether the exit is made from the beginning, the end, or the middle:

```
loop                    loop                    loop
    exit when B;            S;                      S1;
    S;                      exit when B;            exit when B;
end loop;               end loop;                  S2;
                                                end loop;
```

The corresponding flowcharts are shown in Figure 8-8. We shall consider each version in turn.

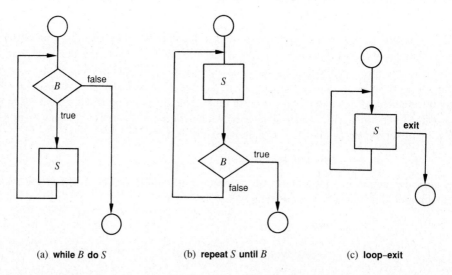

   (a) **while** B **do** S (b) **repeat** S **until** B (c) **loop–exit**

Figure 8-8   Loops

The first version, with the exit at the start, is more commonly written in the form of a **while** statement. In this case, the exit condition B becomes the continuation condition $\neg B$:

> **while** $\neg B$ **do** S;

If S is a sequence of statements, it has to be bracketed by **begin-end**. As with the **if** statement, Ada avoids the need for brackets by requiring an explicit terminator:

> **while** B **loop**
> *statement_sequence*
> **end loop**;

This kind of loop has the important property that if B is initially false, the statement sequence will never be executed at all. It should therefore be used in situations that have a *null* case — that is, a case where there is nothing to do. If the null case cannot occur, the **while** statement makes a redundant test when it is first entered; but apart from this rather trivial drawback, it still works perfectly well. It is therefore the most common and important form of the iterative statement.

The second version, with the **exit** at the end, has no special form in Ada but corresponds to the **repeat** statement of Pascal:

> **repeat** S **until** B

It has the property that S must be executed at least once — a slightly risky state of affairs. There are some situations where this is a predictable requirement; more often, though, it is advisable to allow for the null case, and so the **while** statement is to be preferred.

The third version, with the exit in the middle, is sometimes known as the 'n-and-½ times' loop. It was illustrated in the example above. If this form of loop is considered undesirable, it can be 'unwound' so that the first execution of $S1$ is made prior to entry:

> $S1$;
> **while not** B **loop**
> $S2$;
> $S1$;
> **end loop**;

This uses the more familiar **while** statement, though at the cost of some extra code. It also places $S2$ before $S1$ inside the loop, which is sometimes rather confusing.

A more general form of loop has been advocated by E. W. Dijkstra (1975) as a counterpart to the **if-fi** statement described in Section 8.10. It allows the repetition to depend on one of several conditions, with each condition leading to the execution of a different statement sequence:

> **do** $B1$ $\rightarrow$ $S1$
> ▯ $B2$ $\rightarrow$ $S2$
> $\cdots$
> ▯ Bn $\rightarrow$ Sn
> **od**

As previously, each phrase $Bi \rightarrow Si$ is a guarded command and if more than one guard Bi is true, a nondeterministic choice is made between the corresponding statement sequences

Si. The loop is repeated until all the guards are false and then it terminates normally. If only one guarded command is specified, it is equivalent to an ordinary **while** statement, and in practice this is the most common case.

The proof rules for loops will be illustrated for the case of Pascal's **while** statement:

$$\textbf{while } B \textbf{ do } S$$

The question is: what precondition will guarantee that this terminates in a state that satisfies Q? The undecidability of the halting problem warns us that the weakest precondition will sometimes be uncomputable. It follows that, in general, the question can only be answered either by giving a precondition that may not be computable or by giving one that may not be the weakest. We shall explore both possibilities.

A simple approach is to formulate conditions that guarantee Q after exactly n iterations, taking n to be successively $0, 1, 2, \ldots$. The conditions are as follows:

$H0$:	$\neg B \wedge Q$	—	termination in 0 steps
$H1$:	$B \wedge S \{H0\}$	—	termination in 1 step
$H2$:	$B \wedge S \{H1\}$	—	termination in 2 steps

and so on.

For $i \geq 1$, Hi states that the loop will terminate after exactly i iterations if B is true and if one execution of S leads to a state that guarantees Q after a further $i\text{-}1$ iterations. The following rule guarantees termination of the loop by requiring that at least one of the H's is true:

$$H0 \vee H1 \vee H2 \vee \ldots \equiv (\textbf{while } B \textbf{ do } S) \{Q\}$$

Its drawback is that if the loop does not terminate, then neither does the evaluation of the hypotheses.

A more workable rule is obtained by dropping the guarantee of termination. The simplest version merely asserts that on completion B will be false. To establish Q, it is therefore sufficient that $\neg B \Rightarrow Q$:

$$\frac{\neg B \Rightarrow Q}{\{\text{true}\}\ \textbf{while } B \textbf{ do } S\ \{Q\}}$$

The rule holds for any initial state; but, as the notation indicates, it does not guarantee termination. In practice, the required conclusion is usually stronger than $\neg B$ and has to be attained by introducing a predicate P such that $P \wedge \neg B \Rightarrow Q$. If P is satisfied initially, and if its truth is preserved by the execution of S, then Q will be satisfied on completion. The following rule expresses this principle:

$$\frac{P \wedge \neg B \Rightarrow Q, \quad P \wedge B \Rightarrow S\{P\}}{\{P\}\ \textbf{while } B \textbf{ do } S\ \{Q\}}$$

P is known as the *invariant* of the loop, since it remains true at the start of each iteration. Once again there is no guarantee of termination. In fact, the rule remains valid even if S itself is not guaranteed to terminate.

As an example of this proof rule, consider the simple task of calculating n!. The following loop accumulates the required product in the variable fac:

```
i := 0;
fac := 1;
         -- assert fac = i!
while i ≠ n loop
    i := i + 1;
    fac := i * fac;
         -- assert fac = i!
end loop;
```

The invariant P is fac = i!, which is established for the case i = 0 prior to entry. The proof rule for assignments shows that after each iteration of the loop:

$$fac = i * (i - 1)!$$

From the definition of factorial it follows that P is maintained. The condition B is i≠n. On completion of the loop, the postcondition is therefore:

$$fac = i! \ \land \ i = n$$

This entails the required conclusion, namely fac = n!. As already mentioned, the proof says nothing about termination. In fact, if n is negative the loop will continue indefinitely.

Of all the proof rules so far considered, this one is the most instructive. It shows that the key factor in designing a loop is to find the appropriate invariant. If the desired postcondition is Q, the basic technique is to express it in the form $P \land \neg B$ and then to use P as the invariant. P is 'weaker' than Q in that it is more easily satisfied than $P \land \neg B$. The strategy is therefore to find some way of weakening Q, opening it up to a wider range of conditions. There are several ways of doing this, the two most common being the following:

1. Replace a constant by a variable. For example, if n is a constant that occurs in Q, replace it by a variable i and make $\neg B$ the condition i = n.

2. Delete a conjunct. If Q has the form (or can be put in the form) $Q1 \land Q2$, take $Q1$ (say) as the invariant P, leaving $Q2$ to play the role of $\neg B$.

The above loop for computing n! used the first of these. As an example of the second, we shall write a loop to compute $\lceil \log_2 n \rceil$ — that is, the smallest integer k such that $2^k \geq n$. The properties of 2^k allow the postcondition to be written in the form

$$2^{k-1} < n \leq 2^k$$

which is the conjunction:

$$2^{k-1} < n \ \land \ 2^k \geq n$$

Taking the first term to be the invariant P and the second to be $\neg B$, we design a loop of the following form:

...

-- **assert** $2^{k-1} < n$

while $2^k < n$ **loop**

...

-- **assert** $2^{k-1} < n$;

end loop;

To establish $2^{k-1} < n$ initially, we must impose the precondition $n \geq 1$, reflecting the fact that $n \leq 0$ would leave $\log n$ undefined. Setting $k = 0$ will then do the trick. Turning to the body of the loop, we see that its precondition $P \wedge B$ is

$$2^{k-1} < n \quad \wedge \quad 2^k < n$$

which *a fortiori* is equivalent to $2^k < n$. The '...' must therefore satisfy:

$$\{ 2^k < n \} \quad ... \quad \{ 2^{k-1} < n \}$$

This can be achieved trivially by the statement **null**. However, to ensure that the loop terminates it is essential that each iteration should increase k. The change from k to $k-1$ in the two assertions suggests that it be increased by 1. This leads to the following algorithm:

-- **assert**: $n \geq 1$

$k := 0$;

while $2^k < n$ **loop**

$k := k + 1$;

end loop;

-- **assert**: $2^{k-1} < n \leq 2^k$

The proof rules for assignments and loops confirm that this works correctly.

As previously, the details of the proof are rather tedious, and for loops of any complexity we might wonder if the effort is worthwhile. As always, though, any effort is worth making if it leads to a better understanding of the program. It is fuzzy thinking that so easily allows errors to pass undetected. A complete, formal proof of correctness is seldom necessary; but if we cannot see the lines along which it would develop, how can we be confident that the algorithm is correct?

8.13 BOUNDED ITERATION

The above proof rule for loops is very instructive, but it leaves a crucial question unanswered: *is the loop guaranteed to terminate?* With the **if** statement and the **case** statement, there is no problem in this respect. As indicated in the proof rules, they will terminate provided that their branches terminate. With loops, though, we face the problem head on. Even though the proof rule for **while** B **do** S assumes that S always terminates, it does not follow that the loop itself will terminate. Evidence for this is seen in the fact that many programs — even structured programs — continue to execute indefinitely.

The simplest way to ensure termination is to allow a control variable to step through a finite range of values, stopping when it reaches the upper or lower bound. This is called *bounded iteration*. It can be illustrated by the loop for computing n!, as given in the previous section, where i steps through the values 1, 2, ... n. The requirement is so common that most languages provide a special statement for it. In Pascal, it has the form

for $V := E1$ **to** $E2$ **do** S

where V is a control variable of some ordinal type T, and $E1$ and $E2$ are expressions of type T. Successive values from the range $E1..E2$ are assigned to V, and for each one the statement S is executed. A simple example is provided by rewriting the algorithm of the previous section for computing n!:

```
fac := 1;
for i := 1 to n do
    fac := i * fac;
```

The usual precondition is $E1 \leq E2$, in which case the number of iterations will be $ord(E2) - ord(E1) + 1$. If $E1 > E2$, there are no iterations and so the statement is equivalent to **null**. (Early versions of FORTRAN were regrettably different in this respect, always requiring at least one iteration.) If the symbol **downto** is used instead of **to**, the usual precondition is $E1 \geq E2$ and the values in the range $E2..E1$ are assigned to V in reverse order, starting at $E1$ and working down to $E2$. On completion, the value of V is undefined: it could be $E2$, or succ $(E2)$, or any other value that happens to suit the compiler. It is therefore necessary to treat V in the same way as an uninitialized variable at this point (see Section 6.4).

Since the number of iterations is $ord(E2) - ord(E1) + 1$, the termination of the **for** statement should be guaranteed. However, this depends on two factors that call for some comment. First, it is important that $E2$ should not be re-evaluated each time round the loop (as happens in ALGOL 60), otherwise it could become an ever-receding target. Second, V must not be changed during the execution of S. Pascal avoids the first danger by requiring that $E1$ and $E2$ be evaluated only when the loop is first entered. It attempts to avoid the second one by stating that V behaves like a constant inside S. A compiler can easily enforce this as long as V does not have an *alias* — that is, an alternative name, W say (see Section 9.3). An assignment to W would then surreptitiously change V. To check for this contingency is very difficult; so, with enough determination, a Pascal programmer could probably produce a non-terminating **for** statement. Meanwhile, in the more conventional cases, all will be well.

In Ada, the syntax is another variation on the **loop** theme:

for V **in** *range* **loop**
    statement_sequence
end loop;

As in the **case** statement, the *range* can have the form $E1..E2$, or it can be a discrete type, or it can be the subscript range of an array. For example, the following loop sums the elements of an array A:

```
sum := 0;
for i in A'range loop
    sum := sum + A(i);
end loop;
```

If the symbol **reverse** is inserted after **in**, the values are assigned in descending order. The most significant difference from the Pascal version is that the **for** clause acts as a declaration of V and so V is local to the loop. Also, within the body of the loop it is treated as a constant. These rules ensure that the number of iterations will be bounded by the length of the range. They also sidestep any controversy about the value of V on completion (since it then no longer exists). V is known as the 'loop parameter' rather than the more traditional 'control variable'.

With termination guaranteed, it is now possible to formulate the appropriate proof rule. The basic idea is usually expressed by considering the special case of a loop variable i that takes the values $1, \ldots n$:

$$\textbf{for } i := 1 \textbf{ to } n \textbf{ do } S$$

The corresponding rule is based on the principle of mathematical induction, for which it requires a condition $P(i)$, involving the value of i, with the following properties:

1. $P(0)$ is true on entry to the loop (the precondition).

2. If $P(i-1)$ is true prior to the ith iteration, then $P(i)$ will be true after it.

3. $P(n)$ is the required postcondition.

The proof rule uses induction to assert that the precondition $P(0)$ will then produce the postcondition $P(n)$:

$$\frac{1 \leq i \leq n \wedge P(i\text{-}1) \implies S\{P(i)\}}{P(0) \implies (\textbf{for } i := 1 \textbf{ to } n \textbf{ do } S)\{P(n)\}}$$

In the case of the loop for calculating n!, $P(i)$ is the condition $\text{fac} = i!$. Property 1 is satisfied because $0! = 1$. Property 2 becomes:

$$\text{fac} = (i{-}1)! \implies \text{fac} := i*\text{fac} \{\text{fac} = i!\}$$

— which is a consequence of $i! = i*(i{-}1)!$. And property 3 is satisfied because $P(n)$ is $\text{fac} = n!$. As previously, $P(i)$ is known as the *invariant* and it is the key to the design of the loop.

For completeness, it is worth mentioning two features of **for** statements that Pascal and Ada omit. The first is the use of a step length greater than 1. This is available in FORTRAN, COBOL, PL/I, ALGOL 60, ALGOL 68, BCPL, and several other languages, and there are many situations where it is the simplest and most natural construction to use. It is particularly important for processing arrays (see Volume II), and its omission by Pascal and Ada is a matter for some regret. The second is the use of a 'jump-to-the-next-iteration' command, sometimes written as **loop** or **cycle** or **continue**. This terminates the current iteration, but not the entire loop. It is, of course, another 'disguised **goto**' and the case for it is not particularly strong. Nevertheless, it can occasionally prove useful.

8.14   TERMINATION

A well-designed **for** statement enforces bounded iteration and can be used for loops where the number of iterations is known at the outset. In cases where the number of iterations is not known, some other form of loop has to be used, such as a **while** statement or a **do** statement. This section looks at ways of ensuring that these will also terminate, with particular reference to loops of the following form:

$$
\begin{aligned}
&\text{-- \textbf{assert} } P \\
&\textbf{while } B \textbf{ loop} \\
&\quad\text{-- \textbf{assert} } P \wedge B \\
&\qquad S; \\
&\quad\text{-- \textbf{assert} } P \\
&\textbf{end loop;} \\
&\quad\text{-- \textbf{assert} } P \wedge \neg B
\end{aligned}
$$

Here P is the invariant and termination depends on a condition B becoming false. How can we guarantee that this will eventually happen?

The basic strategy is to ensure that each execution of S makes progress towards the goal of satisfying $\neg B$. The notion of progress has to be quantified in terms of one or more variables, x say, and a function $t(x)$ with the following two properties:

1.   Each iteration of S decreases $t(x)$.

2. $t(x) \leq 0 \Rightarrow \neg(P \wedge B)$.

Provided that the decrements cannot be arbitrarily small, property 1 implies that repeated execution of S must eventually make $t(x)$ negative. On the other hand, property 2 implies that if $t(x)$ becomes negative the loop cannot continue. If both properties are satisfied, it follows that the loop must terminate.

In practice, property 2 can usually be established by expressing $\neg(P \wedge B)$ as $\neg P \vee \neg B$ and proving one of the alternatives:

2(a). $t(x) \leq 0 \Rightarrow \neg B$

2(b). $t(x) \leq 0 \Rightarrow \neg P$

The reasoning behind 2(a) is simple enough: if $t(x)$ reaches 0, B becomes false and so the loop terminates. (Of course, it might terminate earlier anyway.) With 2(b), P cannot become false and so the loop must terminate while $t(x)$ is still strictly positive. The mechanism requires a connection between P, $t(x)$, and B that causes B to become false. The details will depend on the application and can be quite complicated. In most cases 2(a) is therefore the easier property to satisfy.

For each particular loop, the problem is to find a suitable function $t(x)$. It has to provide some measure of the distance to the goal, with each iteration reducing the distance until finally the goal is reached. A possible technique is to establish an upper bound on the number of iterations and to define $t(x)$ to be that bound. If x_i is the value of x after the ith iteration, $t(x_i)$ will be an upper bound on the number of iterations that are still needed. Property 1 requires each iteration to reduce the bound by at least 1. Property 2 states that this cannot continue indefinitely.

A function of this kind is called a *bound function*, or sometimes a *terminating function*. As a simple example, consider the loop for computing $\lceil \log_2 n \rceil$ that was developed in Section 8.12:

```
k := 0;
while 2ᵏ < n loop
    k := k + 1;
end loop;
```

Provided $n > 0$, the number of iterations will be exactly $\lceil \log_2 n \rceil$ and so a suitable bound function is $\lceil \log_2 n \rceil - k$. This satisfies property 1 because of the assignment $k := k + 1$; and it satisfies 2(b) because $\lceil \log_2 n \rceil - k \leq 0$ implies $2^k \geq n$. Either way, termination is guaranteed. It will be noted that the bound function does not have to be evaluated by the loop. On the contrary, this one uses the value $\lceil \log_2 n \rceil$ which the loop is in the process of computing. It is a 'ghost' function, whose role is similar to that of an assertion. It is used for establishing correctness, but the algorithm itself can ignore it.

The function $\lceil \log_2 n \rceil - k$ uses an upper bound that is the exact number of iterations still required. The next example shows that there is no need for such precision: on the contrary, the bounds can be as pessimistic as we please. It also illustrates a condition B, and hence a bound function t, that involves more than one variable. This complicates the search for the right measure of 'progress'. The algorithm is the well-known method of Euclid for finding the greatest common divisor, or *gcd*, of two positive integers, m and n:

```
while m ≠ n loop
    if m > n then
        m := m − n;
    else
        n := n − m;
    end if;
end loop;
```

If the required value is x, the invariant P is:

$$m > 0 \quad \wedge \quad n > 0 \quad \wedge \quad x = gcd\,(m,n)$$

On conclusion, $m = n$ and so:

$$
\begin{aligned}
x \quad &= \quad gcd\,(m,\,n) & &\text{-- by } P \\
&= \quad gcd\,(m,\,m) & &\text{-- since } m = n \\
&= \quad m & &\text{-- rules of arithmetic}
\end{aligned}
$$

The terminating condition $m = n$ suggests that $abs(m - n)$ would be a suitable bound function since it clearly satisfies property 2(a). However, further investigation shows that it does not always decrease and so it fails to satisfy property 1. Looking for alternatives, we note that each iteration decreases either m or n — whichever is the larger. A simple bound function is therefore $m + n$; a tighter but trickier one is $\max\,(m, n)$. As is easily verified, these satisfy 1, 2(a), and 2(b). From 2(b) it follows that the loop will terminate before $\max\,(m, n) = 0$ and so the *gcd* (as expected) will be at least 1.

Proving termination sounds easy in principle, but it runs into a variety of difficulties in practice. Numerical algorithms, with floating-point arithmetic, offer special hazards. To take a trivial example, the following loop will almost certainly fail to terminate:

```
x := 0.0;
while x ≠ 1.0 loop
    . . .
    x := x + 0.1;
end loop;
```

The reason is that 0.1 is seldom held with complete precision and so the terminating condition, namely x = 1.0, may never be exactly satisfied (see Section 4.3). Like a rocket that misses the moon, x will continue for ever on a voyage to infinity. Replacing x ≠ 1.0 by x ≤ 1.0 would prevent this from happening, but it runs the risk that ten increments of 0.1 will leave x marginally less than 1.0, so executing the loop once too often. A better condition would therefore be x < 0.95. On the grander scale, such algorithms involve all the difficulties and technicalities of numerical analysis.

Integers are easier to work with, but in a modest way they can have their problems too. For example:

```
i := 1;
while i ≠ n loop
    . . .
    i := i + 2;
end loop;
```

This will terminate only if n is positive and odd. If it is even, i will miss its target in the same way as x did. More interestingly, consider the loop from the flowchart of Figure 8-2(b):

```
while x > 5 loop
    if x is even then
        x := x / 2;
    else
        x := 3*x + 1;
    end if;
end loop;
```

Extensive experiments suggest that it always terminates; but finding a bound function has baffled the best brains (and lesser ones too) for many years.

In spite of such difficulties, the search for a bound function should not be abandoned lightly. As with invariants, the formal proof of termination may involve a tedious amount of detail; but if we have no feel for it at all, our understanding of the problem must surely be deficient and the certainty of termination must be correspondingly weaker.

8.15 EXCEPTIONS

An *exception* is an event that suspends the normal execution of a program. Some familiar examples are:

- attempting to divide by zero;
- using an array subscript that is out of bounds;
- reading invalid data.

These all indicate that something has gone wrong, making it undesirable for the program to continue on its expected path. Traditionally, such events have suspended execution by the simple expedient of bringing the program to an abrupt and permanent halt. But this is rather defeatist and for some applications, notably those doing continuous, real-time control, it is unacceptable. In any case, exceptions are not necessarily a sign of trouble. On the contrary, they can be triggered by something that is exceptionally *good* — like Archimedes jumping out of his bath. When these happier events occur, we certainly do not want everything to be halted. As with the real-time applications, we would much prefer control to be transferred to some other part of the program, where execution can continue.

Of course, a simple way of implementing this behavior is to use a **goto** statement:

if *exception_condition* **then goto** *L*;

This suspends 'normal execution' and transfers control to some other part of the program, exactly as required. However, it puts no restrictions on the placement of *L* or on the way in which execution should then continue. It is therefore open to all the abuses of unstructured programming that were discussed earlier.

In order to support a more disciplined approach to the problem, some languages have provided a higher-level construct, in which the **goto** disappears from view. The basic features typically include:

- a set of predefined exceptions;
- the ability to define new exceptions;
- a statement for triggering an exception;
- a facility for responding to an exception.

Predefined exceptions will normally be triggered by the system; but those defined by the programmer have to be triggered explicitly. This is known as *signaling* or *raising* the exception (see below). In either case, the effect is to transfer control to a special piece of code called the *exception handler*. Each handler is associated with one of the program units, P say, in which the exception can occur. It responds to the exception by taking whatever action is specified — issuing messages, setting flags, and so on. Following that, the course of action will depend on the 'model' that is being used. There are two main possibilities:

1. In the *resumption model* control returns to the point at which the exception was triggered and normal execution of P is then resumed.

2. In the *termination model* the execution of P is terminated and control passes to the program unit from which P was entered.

These two models lead to radically different ways of dealing with exceptions. We shall illustrate the first from PL/I and the second from Ada, after which we shall compare their basic philosophies.

In PL/I, exceptions are called **on** conditions. Eight such conditions are predefined, including zerodivide, overflow, subscriptrange, and endfile. Their default handlers execute some 'standard system action' that usually halts the program. They can be suppressed by prefixing a program unit with 'no zerodivide', or 'no overflow', or whatever. But this is risky — after all, writing no overflow does not mean that no overflow will occur! So a better way of overriding the default is to write a new handler in the form of an **on** statement:

```
on overflow
   begin
      put list ('overflow in ... ');
      ovflag = 1;
   end;
```

The **begin-end** block will then be automatically activated whenever floating-point overflow occurs. If the exception is a new one (not predefined), the handler begins slightly differently:

```
on condition (inputerror) ...
```

This introduces an exception called inputerror and gives it a handler. In this case, there is no automatic mechanism for triggering the exception in response to some condition. Instead, a **signal** statement has to be executed:

```
signal condition (inputerror)
```

This 'signals' the exception and activates its associated handler.

In keeping with the resumption model, PL/I states that, on completion of the handler, control returns to the point where the exception occurred and the program unit then resumes its normal execution. Accordingly, the predefined exceptions are regarded as interrupts and the program-defined ones are regarded as procedure calls. However, the handler can divert control elsewhere by executing a **go to** statement, in which case the resumption model no longer applies.

Ada has five predefined exceptions, namely constraint_error, numeric_error, program_error, storage_error, and tasking_error. Each exception can be triggered by one or more *checks*: for example the numeric_error exception can be triggered by division_check or overflow_check. Checks can be suppressed by pragmas:

```
pragma suppress (overflow_check);
pragma suppress (index_check, on => reg_table);
```

In the second example, the 'on' parameter allows the check to be suppressed selectively. Presumably reg_table is an array, in which case it will be accessed without any checking of the subscript bounds; but it could also be a type or subtype, or even an entire program unit.

A program unit P can introduce new exceptions by means of a declaration:

```
input_error : exception;
```

The exception can then be 'raised' by the statement:

```
raise input_error;
```

This transfers control to the corresponding handler, which will normally be provided at the end of P. If P is a simple block (see Section 10.2), its outline might therefore go as follows:

```
declare
    input_error : exception;              -- declare the exception
begin
    . . .
    if ... then
        raise input_error;                -- raise the exception
    end if;
    . . .
exception
    when input_error =>
        . . .                             -- handle the exception
end;
```

The handlers are listed following the symbol **exception**, using a syntax that is similar to that of the **case** statement. The following example illustrates the notation more fully:

```
exception
    when input_error =>
        put_line ("bad data");
        put_line ("try again");
    when numeric_error | constraint_error =>
        put_line ("you bombed it!");
    when others =>
        put_line ("that's impossible!!!");
end;
```

If a **raise** statement fails to find a handler with the specified name, and if there is no **others** clause, control passes to the handlers of the surrounding unit, where the search is repeated. If it eventually passes out of the main program, with a suitable handler still not found, the run-time system takes some appropriate but undefined action.

Ada's choice of the termination model is reflected in the placement of the handlers at the end of the unit, P say, to which they belong. The implication is clear: when an exception occurs, the handler is executed and then control passes through the end of P as though it had finished in the normal way. The handler may *not* include a **goto** statement that takes control back into P. The only way to repeat P is to re-enter it on a new activation.

In both of these languages, it will be observed that a handler is not told anything about (a) the place or (b) the cause of the exception. For example, if overflow occurs, it does not know where it occurred or the quantities that were involved. Problem (a) arises because handlers are associated with program units, rather than individual statements. (For an example of the latter, see COBOL's treatment of overflow.) Problem (b) arises because the exceptions do not have parameters, and so the **signal** and **raise** statements cannot supply any information to the handlers about the cause of the exception. In this respect, a much better facility is provided by the language Clu (Liskov and Snyder, 1979). Clu uses a termination model very similar to Ada's, but allows its **signal** statement to pass one or more input parameters to the corresponding handler. The difficulty of doing this in Ada is that the values could get passed to a context in which their type is not valid.

These two models — resumption and termination — represent two different philosophies for the handling of exceptions. In cases where normal execution can sensibly be continued, the resumption model has an obvious advantage. However, the question must be asked: what sort of cases are these? To continue normal execution after (say) overflow or subscriptrange could be very hazardous. As for the program-defined exceptions, it was noted earlier that the **signal** statement treats them as procedures and so they offer nothing new. In short, the benefits of the resumption model are rather slim. The termination model accords more closely with the notion that an exception requires the program to change its course of action. Its underlying philosophy is therefore more attractive, even though its implementation in Ada may leave room for improvement.

A fuller discussion of the issues needs to be set in the context of procedures and tasks, where additional factors come into play. The role of exceptions also needs to be considered from the viewpoint of data abstraction: are they simply a coding device, or are they essential features of the objects that are being modeled? These issues will be considered further in the next three chapters.

8.16 REGULAR PROGRAMS

By way of review, it is appropriate to consider the general problem of program composition and, in particular, the status of the **goto** statement. As mentioned in Section 8.1, programmers are often urged to abandon the use of **goto** statements, along with any disguised **goto**s such as **exit** and **raise**. Instead, they are told to restrict their control structures to the basic three — sequencing, **if**, and **while**. A more tolerant critic might allow **case**, **repeat**, and **for**; but anything further is definitely frowned upon. Why is this so, and to what extent is it justified?

As remarked earlier, the three basic control structures correspond to the operations used in regular expressions — catenation, alternation, and repetition. Programs that use them as their only control structures can therefore be described as *regular programs*. They stand in contrast to the **goto** programs of Section 8.7, along with flowcharts and machine-code programs, all of which use a less structured style of programming. So the question is whether or not it is beneficial to restrict all programs to being regular ones.

An obvious point in favor of regular programs is simply that of clarity. At the lowest level, this is evident from a comparison of two pieces of code:

	Regular		*Non–regular*
	while x > 1 **do**	again:	**if** x ≤ 1 **then goto** done
	x := x / 2;		x := x / 2
	...		**goto** again
		done:	...

The two sequences do exactly the same thing and would doubtless compile into exactly the same machine code. Yet the regular version is much easier to understand. If this is the case with a small fragment, it will apply with greater force to large programs. Even so, is this always and absolutely the case? Are there not some situations where the use of a **goto** is in fact clearer?

Arguments about clarity tend to be rather subjective. A related issue, with more objective content, is that of correctness. The discussion of proof rules shows that in this respect the regular programs have all the advantages. Their proof rules are clear-cut and, with the inclusion of terminating functions for loops, are rules for total correctness: they ensure termination. By contrast, **goto**s require a strategy that is harder to formulate and that says nothing at all about termination.

For program composition, regular programs again have the advantages. Evidence for this is seen in the flowcharts of Figures 8-4, 8-5, and 8-8. Each of the three basic statements has exactly one entry point and one exit point, and the same is true of their substatements. As a result, the combination of these statements into larger units is relatively straightforward. There are no problems of having to interface each unit with several other units, as in unrestricted **goto** programs. This is also reflected in the proof rules, which provide a methodological basis for turning specifications into programs.

Another objective criterion is provided by the relative capabilities of the two kinds of program. It is clear from the flowcharts that any regular program can be easily converted to an equivalent **goto** program. Indeed, compilers are doing it all the time. But is the converse true? Can any **goto** program, however spaghetti-like, be rewritten as an equivalent regular program? If the answer were 'No', the **goto** supporters would have a clear-cut argument to strengthen their case. However, as shown below, the answer is 'Yes': with a reasonably pragmatic definition of 'equivalent', any **goto** program can be converted to an equivalent regular form.

Before going any further it is interesting to note the parallel with regular languages in this respect. Theorem 6.1 states that any type 3 grammar can be transformed into an equivalent regular expression. Since type 3 grammars are equivalent to finite automata and hence to skeleton flowcharts, we may reasonably expect a similar theorem for **goto** programs. Equally, since the conversion of type 3 grammars to regular expressions is not always simple and straightforward, we may expect the 'regularizing' of **goto** programs to involve occasional difficulties also. Indeed, the results will sometimes be more obscure than the original.

These conjectures are correct. However, as noted in Section 8.5, the correspondence between grammars and flowcharts is not close enough for inferring them directly. In a skeleton flowchart the decision boxes are empty and so there is an element of non-determinism. In a normal flowchart they are supplied with specific controlling conditions. This makes the situation more complicated, since a transformation has to preserve not only the possible action sequences but also the evaluation of the conditions. In fact, if the equivalence of two programs requires that they evaluate the same conditions, and execute the same actions, *and nothing else*, then the transformation is sometimes impossible. A case in point is the following loop:

```
while B1 loop
    S1 ;
    exit when B2 ;
    S2 ;
end loop ;
```

The **exit** command means that this is not a regular program as it stands. However, try as we may, we shall find that there is no way of transforming it into an equivalent regular program involving only *B1*, *B2*, *S1*, and *S2*. This was first postulated by G. Jacopini in a classic paper on the subject (Bohm and Jacopini, 1966), and was later proved by D. E. Knuth and R. W. Floyd (1971).

The transformation can be carried out only by introducing control variables of some sort or other. The minimum requirement appears to be one or more Boolean variables that act as *flags*. They record the value of a condition at one point — in the middle of a loop, for example — and can then be used for testing that condition at another point. With one such flag, the above loop can be transformed into the following regular program:

```
flag := true;
while flag and then B1 loop
    S1;
    if B2 then
        flag := false;
    else
        S2;
    end if;
end loop;
```

If the **and then** were regarded as 'irregular', it could be replaced by an ordinary **and**, but at the cost of evaluating *B1* one extra time when the loop terminates. This can be avoided by means of more elaborate rewriting, but the resulting code is considerably more obscure (Exercise 29).

Jacopini proved that any flowchart (and hence any **goto** program) can be converted into an equivalent regular program using flags in this way. Indeed, he established this conclusion under the following restrictions:

1.   When a flag has been set, it must subsequently be tested exactly once.

2.   In between the setting and testing of a flag, another flag may be set and tested.

3.   No other operations of the flowchart may be executed between the setting and testing of a flag.

From 1 and 3 it follows that the flags can be implemented by means of three simple operations on a stack of Boolean values:

pusht   load true on the stack;

pushf   load false on the stack;

popval   remove the top entry from the stack and make it available for immediate testing.

From 3 it follows that the stack can be implemented by any registers that happen to be available at the time. Using these three operations, the above loop can be expressed as follows:

```
    pusht;
    while popval and then B1 loop
       S1;
       if B2 then
          pushf;
       else
          S2;
          pusht;
       end if;
    end loop;
```

Taking 'equivalent' in the sense that includes these three operations, the desired theorem can be stated:

Theorem 8.1

[The *Structuring Theorem*] For each regular program there is an equivalent **goto** program; and for each **goto** program there is an equivalent regular program.

As anticipated above, the proof is rather cumbersome, so the reader is referred to Jacopini's paper for the details. With a weaker definition of 'equivalent', a much simpler proof can be given; but then the underlying structure of the program is liable to disappear from view (see Exercise 28). The use of flags preserves the structure as closely as can be expected and is the technique most commonly used in practice for the elimination of awkward **goto**s. An example will be given in the next section.

So much for the theory. The trouble is that although any program can be put into regular form, there is no guarantee that the result will be any easier to understand. On the contrary, as the above example indicates, the introduction of flags may make it *less* easy to understand and (correspondingly) more prone to error. In such cases it is worth looking deeper to determine whether it is the *program* that is causing the problem, or the underlying *algorithm*. If it is the latter, there is no point in fiddling around with flags. An awkward **goto** statement may indicate that the algorithm is poorly designed, and it challenges us to search for an improvement. Experience suggests that improvements can very often be found, and this constitutes one of the best arguments of all for abolishing **goto**s.

8.17   A CASE STUDY

This section examines a simple algorithm in order to see how some of the above principles work out in practice. Following Knuth (1974) and Atkinson (1984), it takes the task of searching through the elements of an array $A(1..n)$ for a value x. If x is found, the search terminates and the algorithm has to execute a statement $S1$; otherwise it has to execute $S2$. The process clearly involves a loop for scanning the elements. The question is: what form should the loop take?

For scanning an array $A(1..n)$, an obvious strategy is to use a **for** statement. If it finds an element that equals x, it executes $S1$ and jumps out, otherwise it goes through to the end and executes $S2$:

Version 1
```
for i in 1..n loop
    if A(i) = x then
        S1;                   -- x is in A(i)
        goto done;            -- stop the search
    end if;
end loop;
S2;                           -- x is not in A(1..n)
<<done>>
    . . .
```

The **goto** attracts our attention, and so also does the placement of *S1* inside the loop, which is not where it naturally belongs. A better approach might be to replace the **if** statement by an **exit**:

> **exit when** A(i) = x;

This not only disguises the **goto** statement but also removes *S1* from the loop. However, it runs into difficulties because, on completion of the loop, the value of i may be undefined (see Section 8.13). Worse still, in Ada it will have ceased to exist! This means that the choice between *S1* and *S2* cannot be made without introducing extra variables for the purpose. All things considered, this approach looks a bit tarnished.

The obvious alternative is to use a **while** statement. Since the condition A(i) = x terminates the search, a possible form is:

```
while A(i) ≠ x loop
    i := i + 1;
    . . .
end loop;
```

If x is found, the loop terminates normally and *S1* is executed; otherwise, when i becomes greater than n, the loop executes *S2* and terminates less elegantly:

Version 2
```
i := 1;
while A(i) ≠ x loop
    i := i + 1;
    if i > n then
        S2;                   -- x is not in A(1..n)
        goto done;
    end if;
end loop;
S1;                           -- x is in A(i)
<<done>>
    . . .
```

The pattern is similar to that of the previous version. The immediate advantage is that i is no longer local to the loop and so its own value is available on completion. On the other hand there is still a **goto** statement, and now *S2* has found its way into the loop instead of *S1*. More seriously, the algorithm does not behave correctly in the null case (n = 0). So this version is not looking too good either.

Both versions have a **goto** and neither is particularly good. What is the trouble? The answer, as indicated by the **goto**s, is that the loop can terminate under two different conditions. A better way to design it is therefore to build it around *both* of them:

while i ≤ n **and** A(i) ≠ x **loop** ...

Unfortunately, this has the drawback that if i reaches the value n + 1, there will be a reference to an element that may not exist, namely A(n+1). This can be avoided by using a conditional *and*, as described in Section 4.4:

Version 3
```
i := 1;
while i ≤ n and then A(i) ≠ x loop
    i := i + 1;
end loop;
if i ≤ n then
    S1;                    -- x is in A(i)
else
    S2;                    -- x is not in A(1..n)
end if;
```

The result is a regular program that is a definite improvement on the two previous versions. Its only niggling feature is the double test on i≤n.

If the conditional *and* were not available, the following would do instead:

```
i := 1;
while i ≤ n loop
    exit when A(i) = x;
    i := i + 1;
end loop;
    ...
```

To remove the disguised **goto**, we could introduce a flag, as described in the previous section. A Boolean variable called found would be appropriate:

Version 4
```
i := 1;
found := false;
while not found and i ≤ n loop
    if A(i) = x then
        found := true;
    else
        i := i + 1;
    end if;
end loop;
if found then
    S1;                    -- x is in A(i)
else
    S2;                    -- x is not in A(1..n)
end if;
```

This is more verbose than the previous version, but does have a minor advantage: the second occurrence of i ≤ n has disappeared.

An elaboration of this technique is to replace the two-valued flag by a three-valued state variable:

```
type state_type is
          (searching, found, missing);
state : state_type;
```

It is initialized to searching and the loop terminates when it becomes either found or missing:

Version 5
```
i := 1;
state := searching;
while state = searching loop
    if i > n then
        state := missing;
    elsif A(i) = x then
        state := found;
    else
        i := i + 1;
    end if;
end loop;
case state is
    when found =>
        S1;                 -- x is in A(i)
    when missing =>
        S2;                 -- x is not in A(1..n)
    when searching =>
        null;               -- cannot occur
end case;
```

The final **when** clause is required by Ada, even though it can never occur. Apart from that minor flaw, the overall structure is very attractive. It can be adapted to situations with any number of terminating conditions, and this makes it a powerful and versatile technique.

A similar version is provided by the use of exceptions, with the advantage that the final **when** clause can be omitted. The exceptions are the two conditions that can terminate the loop, corresponding to the states found and missing. In effect, they replace the state variable of the previous version by actual program states.

Version 6
```
declare
    found, missing : exception;
begin
    i := 1;
    loop
        if i > n then
            raise missing;
```

```
            elsif A(i) = x then
                raise found;
            else
                i := i + 1;
            end if;
        end loop;
    exception
        when found =>
            S1;                    -- x is in A(i)
        when missing =>
            S2;                    -- x is not in A(1..n)
    end;
```

This uses disguised **goto**s but in a constrained and systematic way. The method is similar to a proposal made by C. T. Zahn, as described by D. E. Knuth (1974), and is quite attractive. Even so, it seems like a large hammer for cracking rather small nuts.

So far, the general approach has been rather casual — try this, try something else, and see how it all turns out. A more disciplined approach is to begin with a formal specification of the problem and to use the techniques of loop construction that were described in Section 8.12. This is best done by leaving aside *S1* and *S2*, for which no specifications have been given, and concentrating on the search.

The precondition of the search is $n \geq 0$. This seems simple enough, though the inclusion of the null case, $n = 0$, is a significant factor. The postcondition is more complicated and is best considered in two parts. If the search is successful, the result must be an element $A(i)$ such that $A(i) = x$. More specifically, we shall require that $A(i)$ be the *first* such element (the previous algorithms took this for granted). This implies that x is not in $A(1..i-1)$ and so the postcondition *Q1* is

$$Q1 \quad \equiv \quad 1 \leq i \leq n \quad \wedge \quad x \notin A(1..i-1) \quad \wedge \quad A(i) = x$$

If the search is unsuccessful, the condition is simpler:

$$Q2 \quad \equiv \quad x \notin A(1..n)$$

However, this has the drawback that on completion there is no easy way of determining which of *Q1* or *Q2* is true. To provide a simple test, some possible tactics are:

- introduce a Boolean variable such as found;
- extend *Q2* with $i = n$ (implying $A(i) \neq x$);
- extend *Q2* with $i = n+1$.

The last of these has the attraction that *Q2* can be expressed as

$$Q2 \quad \equiv \quad i = n+1 \quad \wedge \quad x \notin A(1..i-1)$$

which has obvious similarities to *Q1*. Consequently, the combined postcondition $Q1 \vee Q2$ can be expressed as:

$$x \notin A(1..i-1) \quad \wedge \quad ((1 \leq i \leq n \wedge x = A(i)) \vee i = n+1)$$

To construct the loop, this must be put in the form $P \wedge \neg B$, where P is the invariant and $\neg B$ is the terminating condition.

Since '∉' is not a basic operation, there are obvious advantages in taking
$x \notin A(1..i-1)$ to be P. The postcondition $Q1 \lor Q2$ then becomes:

$$P \quad \land \quad ((i \neq n+1 \land A(i) = x) \lor i = n+1)$$

With the conditional *or*, this can be written as:

$$P \quad \land \quad (i = n+1 \text{ or else } A(i) = x)$$

In keeping with strategy 2 of Section 8.12 — 'deleting a conjunct' — the second term is
taken to be $\neg B$ and the following algorithm can then be derived:

Version 7

```
i := 1;
while i ≠ n+1 and then A(i) ≠ x loop
    i := 1 + 1;
end loop;
if i ≠ n+1 then
    S1;
else
    S2;
end if;
```

This is essentially the same as Version 3.

An alternative is to try strategy 1 instead — replacing a constant by a variable. The
constant n is replaced by a variable j, giving the postcondition:

$$P \quad \land \quad (i = j+1 \text{ or else } A(i) = x) \quad \land \quad j = n$$

The second term is then absorbed into the invariant, leaving $j = n$ as $\neg B$:

Version 8

```
j := 0;
i := 1;                          -- establish P ∧ i=j+1
while j ≠ n loop
    if A(i) = x then
        j := n;                  -- terminate
    else
        j := i;
        i := i + 1;              -- maintain P ∧ i=j+1
    end if;
end loop;
if i ≠ n+1 then
    . . .
```

As a regular program, this looks good, even though it is a little obscure. However, there
is a third strategy, due to J. H. Remmers (1984), that does even better. Instead of replacing the constant n by a variable, it replaces the variable i by a variable. Of course, there is
no advantage in doing this for *all* occurrences of i, otherwise it is simply a renaming
operation. So it leaves the ones in P but changes the others. If k is the new variable, this
produces the postcondition:

$$P \quad \land \quad (k = n+1 \text{ or else } A(k) = x) \quad \land \quad k = i$$

The resulting loop is:

Version 9

```
i := 1;
k := n + 1;                    -- establish P ∧ k=n+1
while i ≠ k loop
   if A(i) = x then
      k := i;                  -- terminate
   else
      i := i + 1;
   end if;
end loop;
if i ≠ n+1 then
   . . .
```

This is very neat and also quite different from any of the earlier versions. So it indicates the power of this more systematic approach.

Nine versions are surely enough. Nevertheless, there is a tenth which in some ways outperforms them all. A clue to its nature lies in the inconvenience of the clause:

$$\textbf{while } i \neq n+1 \textbf{ and then } A(i) \neq x \ ...$$

As in all nine versions, this involves two tests per iteration — one on i and one on x. How much better it would be if this could be reduced to only one! It would solve most of the difficulties in a single stroke. Since the test on x is essential, the test on i is the one that would have to be omitted. Is there some way of making it redundant? In other words, is there some way of ensuring that the test on x will eventually succeed?

With the more formal approach, the same clue can be found by considering the postcondition:

$$P \ \wedge \ ((i \neq n+1 \ \wedge \ A(i) = x) \ \vee \ i = n+1)$$

This would be much simpler if the last term were $i = n+1 \wedge A(i) = x$. In fact, since P includes the condition $1 \leq i \leq n+1$, it would then reduce to:

$$P \ \wedge \ A(i) = x$$

To produce this happy state of affairs, it is sufficient to set $A(n+1) = x$ initially. Provided that $A(n+1)$ is available for the purpose, this is easily done. The loop itself then becomes a model of simplicity:

Version 10

```
A(n+1) := x;
i := 1;
while A(i) ≠ x loop
   i := i + 1;
end loop;
if i ≠ n+1 then
   . . .
```

In programming jargon, the x in $A(n+1)$ acts as a 'sentinel' that stops the search from proceeding any further. What could be more regular, more elegant, and more efficient?

Admittedly, it is a little more *subtle* than the earlier versions. Also, to avoid even greater subtleties, $A(n+1)$ must be available for the purpose. In every other respect, though, the algorithm is attractive and well worth using.

What can we conclude from all this? The ten versions have illustrated an interesting variety of techniques — **goto**s, **exit**s, conditional **and**s, states, exceptions, specifications, invariants, sentinels, and so on. Some versions are undoubtedly better than others, but none is 'best' in any universal sense. Versions 3, 6, 9, and 10 all have merits that make them particularly noteworthy. They provide clear evidence for the benefits of abandoning **goto**s in favor of higher level control mechanisms. More importantly, they demonstrate the value of using systematic techniques for specifying and developing programs. This is what structured programming is all about. Good language features can assist the design process, but they are no substitute for a sound methodology.

FURTHER READING

Two books with the title *Structured Programming* are those by O-J Dahl, E. W. Dijkstra and C. A. R. Hoare (1972), and R. C. Linger, H. D. Mills, and B. I. Witt (1979). The former helped to create much of the interest in the subject and is still worth reading. The latter is more rigorous and systematic. For the wider literature an important reference point is *ACM Computing Surveys* **6:4** (December 1974), which was a special issue on programming. Particularly helpful is the rationale for structured programming presented by N. Wirth (1974) and the article by D. E. Knuth (1974) with the provocative title 'Structured programming with go to statements'. The latter includes an account of the early debate and attributes the first published criticism of **goto**s to Peter Naur (1963). Its bibliography has more than 100 references on the subject. Other collections of relevant papers and articles will be found in *Proceedings of the ACM National Conference* (August 1972), and in *Datamation* **19:12** (December 1973). A helpful study on the relative power of various control structures is given by H. F. Ledgard and M. Marcotty (1975). An extensive history of the 'structuring theorem' is given by D. Harel (1980a), who describes it as a 'folk theorem'.

Flowcharts are discussed at length in a tutorial by N. Chapin (1970), which sets out principles for structuring them properly. More recent work has been concerned with unraveling the bad ones — Williams and Ossher (1978), Prather and Guileri (1981), and for programs generally, Oulsnam (1982).

The notation for 'pure' **goto** programs, as used in Section 8.6, is taken from a book by R. Bird (1976). This gives a formal discussion of the relationship between flowchart programs and **goto** programs. It also examines the concepts of program equivalence, correctness, and termination.

The use of proof rules goes back to Floyd (1967) and Hoare (1969), where the notation is different and the rules do not address termination. They were regarded as axiomatic definitions of the language statements and gave rise to extensive studies on their form and their properties. A survey and assessment of the work in the 1970s is given in Harel (1980b), Apt (1981), and Mayer and Halpern (1982). For work on the total correctness of **goto** programs see Manna and Pnueli (1974), Wang (1976), and Lifschitz (1984).

The seminal paper by E. W. Dijkstra (1975) introduced the **if-fi** and **do-od** statements, with their guarded commands, in a language that became known as 'DIGOL' (Dijkstra's ALGOL). The language is a vehicle for exploring the concepts of total correctness, weakest preconditions, nondeterminacy, and the formal derivation of programs. It was followed by *A Discipline of Programming* (Dijkstra, 1976), which developed the ideas in more detail. Later books, including Gries (1981) and Backhouse (1986), give a more systematic presentation of the ideas and a good range of references.

Proof rules are by no means the only approach to defining the semantics of programming languages and proving the correctness of programs. The functional approach is an important alternative advocated by H. D. Mills (1975, 1980) and examined in Dunlop and Basili (1982). For a more wide-ranging review, see Grief and Mayer (1981).

Decision tables have been around for many years — for example, see Kirk (1965) and, for an early review of the literature, Pooch (1974). The book by J. R. Metzner and B. H. Barnes (1977) has a list of 191 references. For a more recent review see Moret (1982) and the extensive bibliography given there. See also Sethi and Chatterjee (1980) and McMullen (1984).

An early discussion of exceptions is given by J. B. Goodenough (1975). For more recent work see Yemini and Berry (1985), which has a good list of references. PL/I's exceptions are discussed in MacLaren (1977); Clu's are described in Liskov and Snyder (1979); a proposal for C is made in Lee (1983). Many proposals have been made for adding them to Pascal — see Cottam (1985) and Turba (1985). For other aspects see Cristian (1984) and Knudsen (1984).

EXERCISES

1   Section 8.2 discussed the trade-off between variables and program points. In general, the use of more program points results in more code but faster execution. A typical case occurs when a condition is tested at one point and then used to control a decision later on:

```
cond := x < y;
process (x, y);
if cond then
    S1;
else
    S2;
end if;
```

Show how cond can be eliminated by duplicating some of the code.

Another example occurs in the speeding up of loops. The basic idea is simple enough: a loop such as

```
for i in 1..100 loop
    S1;
end loop;
```

is rewritten as:

```
for i in 1..50 loop
    S1;
    S1;
end loop;
```

However, the statement *S1* will normally involve the value of i and so this is not quite equivalent. Moreover, there will be trouble if the number of iterations is, or could be, odd. Discuss these problems for some typical applications and investigate the gains in speed which may (or may not) be obtained.

2   The assertions in Section 8.3 show that the finite automaton of Figure 8-1 generates strings that always contain an odd number of a's. Add further assertions to show that the strings must also contain at least two characters. Prove that the automaton generates *all* strings having these two properties.

3   Construct a finite automaton that generates strings consisting of the letters a, b, and c, such that an a is never adjacent to a c. Prove that it generates these strings and no others.

4   Section 8.3 stated some properties of the predicate $S\{Q\}$. Consider the following:

$$\text{true} \;\Rightarrow\; S\{\text{true}\}$$
$$S\{\neg Q\} \;\Rightarrow\; \neg S\{Q\}$$
$$\neg S\{Q\} \;\Rightarrow\; S\{\neg Q\}$$
$$S\{Q\} \wedge S\{\neg Q\} \;\equiv\; \text{false}$$
$$S\{Q\} \vee S\{\neg Q\} \;\equiv\; \text{true}$$

If S is nondeterministic, are these true or false? What if it is deterministic? If true, can they be deduced from earlier properties, or should they be regarded as additional axioms?

5   Prove that the flowchart of Figure 8-2(b), with get(x) replacing x ← 13, has a smaller range of possible action sequences than the flowchart of Figure 8-2(a).

6   Read the note *'Go to statement considered harmful'* by E. W. Dijkstra (1968). Its main argument concerns the problem of summarizing the state of a computation: how far has the execution proceeded? With a regular program it is sufficient to point to the current statement and give the number of completed iterations of the surrounding loops. But if there are **goto**s, the problem is very much harder. In assessing the alleged harmfulness of the **goto** statement, would you agree with the claim that this strikes at the root of the matter? What other factors do you consider relevant?

7   The following program illustrates the sort of situation in which the switch comes into its own. The values of the switch variable have been written as labels to indicate that execution 'falls through' from one clause to the next. The program is freely adapted from an ALGOL 60 procedure Apiapt by C. J. Shaw, which sings that old Christmas favorite 'A Partridge in a Pear Tree'. The auxiliary procedure sing, we are told, 'simulates an *a cappella* choir and is an extraordinary procedure in that ... it usually knows the right tune, and when it doesn't, it fakes it. Altogether a triumph of heuristic programming.'

```
const which = ["first", "second", "third", "fourth",
                "fifth", "sixth", "seventh", "eighth",
                "ninth", "tenth", "eleventh", "twelfth"];

for day in 1..12 loop
  sing ("On the" which[day] "day of Christmas");
  sing ("My true love sent to me");
  switch on day into
      12 :   sing ("Twelve lords a-leaping");
      11 :   sing ("Eleven ladies dancing");
      10 :   sing ("Ten pipers piping");
       9 :   sing ("Nine drummers drumming");
       8 :   sing ("Eight maids a-milking");
       7 :   sing ("Seven swans a-swimming");
       6 :   sing ("Six geese a-laying");
       5 :   sing ("Five gold rings");
       4 :   sing ("Four colly birds");
       3 :   sing ("Three French hens");
       2 :   sing ("Two turtledoves, and");
       1 :   sing ("A partridge in a pear tree.");
  end switch;
end loop;
```

Can you think of any other examples where the switch proves better than the **case** statement? For the ALGOL 60 procedure and a picture of the sing mechanism, see *Datamation* **10:12**, pp. 48-49 (December 1964). For a complexity analysis of songs, see Knuth (1984b).

8   How would you implement a switch in a language such as Pascal or Ada?

9   Devise a proof rule for Dijkstra's **if-fi** statement (Section 8.10).

10   Devise a proof rule for the **case** statement (Section 8.10).

11   If you have access to a language with a **case** statement, investigate the way in which it is implemented. For example, what happens to a program in which the case constants are integers in the range 1 to 10,000?

12   Figure 8-7 shows a decision table containing an array of conditions 'yes', 'no', and 'don't care'. Write a procedure which, given a set of such values in an array C(1..m,1..n), tests the set for (a) completeness, (b) ambiguity, and (c) redundancy.

13   Devise a proof rule for the **repeat** statement (Section 8.12).

14   How would you implement Dijkstra's **do-od** statement (Section 8.12) in Ada or Pascal? Give two versions — one that always evaluates the guards *B1, B2, ...* in sequence, accepting the first that is true, and one that introduces an element of non-determinism. The latter should ensure 'fairness' in that repeated iterations give each guarded command an equal chance of being executed.

15   The following program implements integer division by repeated subtraction, setting q to be the quotient of i ÷ j and r to be the remainder:

```
        q := 0;
        r := i;
        while r ≥ j loop
            r := r - j;
            q := q + 1;
        end loop;
```

State (a) the precondition, (b) the postcondition, (c) the invariant, and (d) a suitable bound function.

16   Review the loop for calculating $\lceil \log_2 n \rceil$, as given in Section 8.12, and prove that it is correct (including termination).

Write a similar loop for evaluating $\lfloor \sqrt{n} \rfloor$. Give (a) the precondition, (b) the postcondition, (c) the invariant, and (d) a suitable bound function.

17   An alternative way of computing $\lfloor \sqrt{n} \rfloor$ is to use a binary search technique. This establishes a range a..b in which the value must lie, and successively halves the range until its length is 1. What is the invariant? What is a suitable bound function? Write the loop and prove that it is correct (including termination).

18   Exercise 4.7 discussed the problem of writing a loop to evaluate $x ** i$, where i is a non-negative integer. The simplest method is to use i multiplications. A faster method takes advantage of the fact that $x ** 2j = (x^2) ** j$. Give a formal specification of the problem and derive the corresponding algorithms.

19   The following loop simulates the repayment of a loan for which there is a certain monthly interest rate. Each month the interest is added and a repayment is made. The program counts the number of months to complete the repayment:

```
        months := 0;
        while debt > 0 loop
            debt := debt * (1 + rate/100) - repayment;
            months := months + 1;
        end loop;
```

How would you prove the correctness (or otherwise) of this program? What is the relevant precondition? What is the relevant postcondition? Can you prove that the loop will terminate? (If not, don't take out the loan!)

20   Revise the program of the previous exercise so that it prints out the debt at the end of every twelfth month. It should also print out the debt after the final repayment.

21   Let x be an integer variable whose initial value is in the range 0..100, and consider the following algorithm:

```
        -- assert x in 0..100
        y := 1;
        while y ≠ 0 loop
            if x ≤ 100 then
                x := x + 11;
                y := y + 1;
```

```
        else
            x := x − 10;
            y := y − 1;
        end if;
    end loop;
        -- assert x = 91
```

This is known as McCarthy's '91' function, after its originator J. McCarthy. Find a bound function that decreases by exactly 1 on each iteration. Use an inductive argument on its value to prove that the final value of x is always 91. (Hint: try a function of the form ax + by + c.)

22   The proof rule for the **for** statements is particularly useful for developing loops that process arrays. Given an array of integers A(1..n), what would be a suitable invariant for:

(a)   summing the elements;
(b)   finding the maximum element;
(c)   counting the number of 0s.

23   Let A(1..n) be an array of 0s and 1s. Devise a simple loop for determining the longest sequence of 1s. (Hint: find its invariant first.)

24   Let A(1..n) be an array of integers. The elements of A(i..j) constitute a *maximum subsequence* if their sum is the maximum over all such subsequences. For example, in the sequence

$$6 \quad 13 \quad −10 \quad 16 \quad −28 \quad 14 \quad 9 \quad 21 \quad −19 \quad 24 \quad −17 \quad 12$$

the subsequence 14 9 21 −19 24 has the sum 49 and no other subsequence is greater. Develop a simple, efficient program for finding a maximum subsequence of A(1..n). Hint: as for the previous exercise. For a good discussion of the problem, see Bentley, J. (1984), 'Programming Pearls', *Commun. ACM* **27:9**, 865-871.

25   In the programming language C, the **for** statement has the form

$$\textbf{for} \quad (S1; \; B; \; S2) \; S$$

which, by definition, is equivalent to:

```
S1;
while ( B )
    { S; S2 }
```

For example, since '=' is the assignment operator and i++ increments i by 1, the version

$$\textbf{for} \; (i = 1; \; i \leq n; \; i++) \; S$$

is more or less equivalent to:

$$\textbf{for} \; i := 1 \; \textbf{to} \; n \; \textbf{do} \; S$$

However, it is not *exactly* equivalent: why not? Discuss the merits of this construction from the viewpoint of (a) notational convenience, and (b) programming philosophy.

26   The statement

> **for** i := 1 **to** n **do** S

is equivalent (with certain constraints) to:

> i := 1;
> **while** i ≤ n **loop**
>   S;
>   i := i + 1;
> **end loop**;

Show that the proof rule for the former is equivalent to the proof rule for the latter.

27   The previous exercise defines the **for** statement in terms of a (more or less) equivalent **while** statement. This technique is used for giving the official definition of the **for** statement in several languages. And yet it runs into a problem if n is the highest value that can be assigned to i. Investigate the problem of finding an equivalent **while** statement that is more robust in this respect. For a detailed discussion of the problem, see Newey and Waite (1985).

28   The Structuring Theorem (Section 8.16) states that any **goto** program can be converted to an equivalent regular program. This can be proved almost trivially by using 'pure' **goto** programs, as described in Section 8.7. Without loss of generality, we may assume that they have the form:

> S :   *statement_0*
> L1 :   *statement_1*
>
>   . . .
>
> Ln :   *statement_n*
> F :   **halt**

The basic idea is to introduce a control variable, current say, whose value will be the label of the statement currently being executed. Every occurrence of **goto** L in the statements is replaced by:

> current := L

The program can then be rewritten in the following 'regularized' form:

> current := S;
> **while** current ≠ F **loop**
>   **case** current **is**
>   **when** S => *statement_0*;
>   **when** L1 => *statement_1*;
>
>   . . .
>
>   **when** Ln => *statement_n*;
>   **end case**;
> **end loop**;

In effect, current plays the role of an instruction pointer, similar to ip in machine-code programming (see Section 5.5). So this eliminates all the **goto** statements by calling them assignments to an instruction pointer instead! This is *reductio ad absurdum*. But does it prove anything interesting?

29   The 'regularized' program in Section 8.16 contains the line:

> **while** *flag* **and then** *B1* **loop**

But is the use of **and then** allowable in a regular program? Write an equivalent loop that avoids it.

30   As an exercise in eliminating **goto** statements, consider the following code:

```
<<state1>>
        -- assert B2 is false
    S1;
    if B1 then
        goto state2;
    else
        S2;
        goto state1;
    end if;
<<state2>>
    if B2 then
        goto done;
    else
        S3;
        if B3 then
            goto state2;
        else
            S4;
            goto state1;
        end if;
    end if;
<<done>>
```

Here are *five* **goto**s! Eliminate them all by using a variable state, with possible values state1 and state2, and a loop of the form:

> **while not** *B2* **loop**
>   **case** state **is**
>
>   . . .

Do you think that the result is an improvement? How would it be affected if the assertion on line 2 were not applicable?

For an actual program of this form see Aho *et al.* (1983, p.85). Consider their claim that it implements 'one of those awkward tasks that can be best described in terms of states and implemented by **goto**s between states.'

31   In the search algorithm of Section 8.17, versions 7–9 were derived from a specification with n≥0 by weakening the postcondition in various ways. Repeat the process, but starting with n≥1 instead.

32   Develop a search algorithm starting with a postcondition in which a flag, found say, indicates whether or not x was found.

33   Let $A(1..n)$ be an array of real numbers $(n \geq 1)$. Develop an algorithm for determining the maximum element in the array. Can you find a version that makes only one test per iteration?

34   Version 10 of the search algorithm requires the use of $A(n+1)$. Investigate ways of implementing the algorithm when $A(n+1)$ is not available.

35   In a letter headed '*GOTO Considered Harmful' Considered Harmful*, F. Rubin puts forward the following problem as an example of one that benefits from the use of **goto**s:

> Let X be an $N \times N$ matrix of integers. Write a program that will print the number of the first all-zero row of X, if any.

This may be regarded as a two-dimensional version of the search problem. Investigate possible solutions and comment on the extent to which they benefit from using **goto**s.

The letter was published in *Commun. ACM*, **30:3**, 195-196 (March 1987). The *Forum* section in the next five issues and the *Technical Correspondence* in the November issue show that the **goto** controversy is far from dead!

36   The game 'Greedy Pig' is played with two dice, each of which has a pig drawn on one face and the numbers 2 to 6 on the others. Contestants take it in turn to throw the dice, the object being to accumulate a score of 100 or more. A turn consists of as many throws as desired, subject to the following rules:

1.   A throw containing one pig cancels the player's score for that turn and ends the turn.

2.   A throw containing both pigs cancels the player's total score so far and ends the turn.

To decide when to stop throwing, a player chooses to adopt a third rule:

3.   Stop throwing when the score for the turn exceeds some fixed limit (such as 25).

Write a loop for playing a turn and investigate various ways of handling the three terminating conditions. Some possible ways are illustrated by the versions of the search algorithm in Section 8.17. Which is most suitable for this application?

37   Write a program to read a sequence of numbers and to store the first n distinct numbers successively in an array $A(1..n)$. You may assume that sufficient numbers are available. (Note: this example is taken from Wirth (1974). The challenge is to find the best structure for your program.)

38   Write a procedure to read a character from input. It should ignore blanks and new-line characters, and also any sequence beginning with '{' and continuing to the next '}'. (Note: as for the previous exercise.)

PROCEDURES AND FUNCTIONS

9.1 SUBPROGRAMS

Subprograms are the basic units of modularity. They allow a program to be divided into smaller, more manageable parts, each with its own specification and its own working environment. They therefore play a fundamental role in the design of any program that is more than a few lines long.

Historically, they were introduced as the high-level counterpart of subroutines (see Section 5.6). In the process a distinction was made between two basic kinds — the procedure and the function. The role of the former was to execute a group of statements, and syntactically a procedure call was defined to be a statement. The role of the latter was to compute a result, and syntactically a function call was defined to be an expression. For many years, the term 'procedure' was often used for both kinds. In ALGOL 60, for example, functions were declared as **integer procedure**, **real procedure**, or **Boolean procedure**, according to the type of their result, and they were known collectively as 'type procedures'. Thus the term 'procedure' had a wider sense that included functions, and a narrower sense that did not. The term 'subprogram' avoids any confusion in this respect, but it is not used so widely.

As the name suggests, a subprogram is similar to a main program, even though it plays a role which is in some sense subordinate. Its basic structure is more or less identical to a main program and its internal workings do not introduce any particularly novel features. Accordingly, this chapter will be mainly concerned with two other topics. The first is the way in which subprograms interface with the main program and with each other. The second is the device of recursion, whereby a subprogram calls itself. As with type 2 grammars, recursion provides a control mechanism that is radically different from the basic ones of sequencing, selection, and iteration. It is so powerful that, in principle, every program can be rewritten as a recursive function in which variables, assignments, and all the trappings of procedural programming have disappeared from view. Sections 9.7 – 9.13 examine it in detail, drawing on the analysis of recursion given in Chapter 6 to distinguish the various forms that it can take.

9.2 PROCEDURES

The simplest kind of subprogram is a nonrecursive procedure with no parameters. The following is an example, written in Ada, whose purpose is to read characters from input, skipping blanks until a non-blank character is found. It then assigns the non-blank character to a variable called ch:

```
procedure skip_blanks is
    blank : constant character := ' ';
    x : character;
begin
    get (x);
    while x = blank loop
        get (x);
    end loop;
    ch := x;
end skip_blanks;
```

The overall format was discussed in Section 7.2, where the procedure was taken to be the main program. The definition begins with a procedure *heading*, which gives the name of the procedure and a description of its parameters (if any). This is followed by an optional set of declarations and then by a **begin-end** statement sequence. The name of the procedure is repeated after the closing **end** to indicate what is ending at that point. Compared with a main program, the only novelty in skip_blanks is that there are two kinds of variable. The variable x is declared at the start of the procedure body and is therefore said to be *local* to the procedure. On the other hand, ch is assumed to be declared in a surrounding module and is therefore said to be *non-local*, or *global*, or *external*. This aspect of procedures will be considered more fully in Chapter 10.

The procedure *body* is usually taken to be the part following the heading. However, in Ada the terminology is slightly different. The heading is called the *specification* and the entire definition, including the heading, is called the *body*. The reason for this change in terminology is that Ada allows the specification to be given separately from the body. In that case the specification ends with ';' instead of **is**:

```
procedure skip_blanks;
```

The full definition has to be given later, including a repeat of the specification. This enables the intervening code to include calls on the procedure, even though it has not been fully defined. The facility is needed for supporting separate compilation and for giving specifications of packages (see Section 10.4). It is also needed for declaring two or more subprograms that are mutually recursive (see Section 10.3).

As with subroutines, a procedure *call* will cause the code to be executed. For a procedure with no parameters, the relevant statement is simply the procedure's name:

```
skip_blanks;
```

In such a simple case, the call could be implemented by the basic hardware instructions for subroutine entry and exit (see Section 5.6). More generally, though, it requires the use of a stack and, as shown in Chapter 12, it may involve several instructions for the entry and exit sequences. Since the overheads can prove quite significant, it is sometimes preferable to compile the procedure as *inline code*. This means that the calling sequence is replaced by the full code of the procedure body, with no entry or exit instructions being required. Ada has a pragma that can request this for specified subprograms:

pragma inline (skip_blanks);

If implemented, it provides valuable support for modular programming by removing the penalty that is otherwise inherent in the use of small procedures. It is regrettable that so few languages provide an option of this kind.

Execution of the procedure body normally continues through to the final statement. However, Ada provides for earlier termination either by the **return** statement or by the **raise** statement. The former is similar to the **exit** statement for loops, being a powerful form of **goto**. It is open to the criticism that it cuts across the normal one-entry/one-exit structure of regular programs, and so it should not be used too lightly. The latter was described in Section 8.14. If a suitable exception handler is not provided at the end of the procedure body, exit is made normally and the exception is then raised in the calling module. This process is continued, possibly through many levels, until eventually a handler is found. The trouble is that the further it goes, the harder it will be for the handler to do anything sensible. The general strategy should therefore be to deal with exceptions in the procedures where they occur.

9.3   PARAMETERS

The usefulness of procedures is greatly increased by the inclusion of *parameters*. These allow certain details to be left blank (so to speak) when the procedure is defined and to be supplied later when it is called. They can therefore be varied from one call to the next. Such details are denoted in the procedure by *formal* parameters, sometimes known as 'dummy variables'. They are then supplied at the point of call by *actual* parameters. As an example, consider a procedure report for reporting errors that are detected in a file of text. It prints a message that describes the error and then the number of the line where it occurred. For example:

```
***** error: illegal symbol
          - occurred in line 42
```

Since the procedure does not know in advance what the message and the line number will be, it specifies them by the formal parameters message and line:

```
procedure report (message : in string;
                      line : in line_number) is
begin
   new_line;
   put ("***** error: " & message);
   new_line;
   put ("          - occurred in line ");
   put (line, 1);
   new_line;
   errors := errors + 1;
end report;
```

The symbol **in** denotes that message and line are both *input* parameters — a term that will be described below. In other respects, the specification of the parameters is much like that of ordinary variables. However, since the parameters are 'dummy' variables, no storage is allocated for them. They are descriptions of things to come, rather than names of things that exist.

The actual parameters are supplied when the procedure is called and, as remarked earlier, they can be varied from one call to the next:

```
report ("illegal symbol", 42);
report ("missing parenthesis", current_line);
```

Normally, the actual parameters must match the formal parameters in number, order, and type — a convention known as *positional correspondence*. In Ada, an alternative is to use *named correspondence*, the names of the formal parameters being repeated in the call:

```
report (line => 42, message => "illegal symbol");
```

In this case, the parameters can be listed in any order. Furthermore, input parameters can be given default values in the specification, in which case the actual parameter can be omitted. This convention is used in Ada's standard input/output procedures — for example, in the provision of default field widths. It is also popular in the command languages of operating systems as a method of listing options.

The actual parameters are said to be *passed* to the procedure. What exactly does this mean? There are several possible answers, corresponding to various modes of transmission. The basic idea, as adopted from mathematics, is that the procedure body is executed with each occurrence of a formal parameter x replaced by the corresponding actual parameter e. However, variations arise in two respects. First, e is an expression and may therefore be subject to preliminary evaluation — either in data mode or in reference mode (see Section 7.8). Second, x is not replaced by e in any literal fashion: instead, it is either 'bound' to e in a way that is effectively equivalent, or it is linked to e in some less stringent sense.

Before examining the details, it is useful to look at some of the terminology. A helpful distinction is the one between *input* parameters and *output* parameters. The former pass values *into* a procedure. The latter receive values *out* of a procedure; they are variables to which results are assigned. Some parameters are used in both roles — the *input–output* parameters: their values are passed into the procedure at the start and new values are assigned back to them either during execution or at the end.

Next come the terms that describe the detailed mechanisms. Unfortunately, some of them are not well chosen. They frequently have the form *call*-by-something, even though it is the procedure that is called, not the parameters. A more appropriate wording is *pass*-by-something and we shall adopt this version in the following paragraphs. It should also be noted that terms such as 'call by value' and 'call by name' have been used in more than one sense, so there is a measure of ambiguity hanging over them. We shall attempt to follow the most common usage, but other interpretations may be encountered elsewhere.

The principal mechanisms for parameter transmission can now be listed. The first two evaluate the actual parameter e in data mode and so e can be any expression of the required type. However, since e produces a data value rather than a reference value, these first two mechanisms can only be used for input parameters — assignments to data values would not make sense.

1.   *Pass-by-constant.* The formal parameter x is treated as a constant whose value is the data value of e. Since it is a constant, assignments to x in the procedure body are illegal.

2.   *Pass-by-value.* The formal parameter x is treated as a local variable of the procedure and is initialized to the data value of e. Assignments to x are therefore legal, though their effects are local to the procedure body.

Of these, method 1 is conceptually cleaner, being a strict binding of x to the data value of e. Method 2 is rather more confusing, since it uses x for two different purposes; but it is allowed by many languages as a concession to convenience. It could better be described as 'pass-to-local-variable'. The reasoning behind the concession is largely pragmatic. In both methods, when the value of e has been passed to the procedure, it has to be stored in some location. But a location that is used for a constant, as in method 1, can equally well be used for a variable, as in method 2. So method 2 gains the use of a variable at no extra run-time cost.

The next two methods evaluate the actual parameter e in reference mode, producing a reference to a variable, v say. In some cases, the variable will be a simple scalar; in others it will be a large data structure, such as a record or an array. Since it is a variable, it is suitable for use as an output parameter.

3.   *Pass-by-reference.* The formal parameter x is bound to the reference value of e and hence to the variable v. This means that the value of x is the value of v, and assignments to x are assignments to v. In effect, x becomes an *alias* for v — that is, another name for referring to it.

4.   *Pass-by-result.* The reference to v is evaluated as in method 3, but it is not in fact passed to the procedure. Instead, x is treated as an uninitialized local variable which is used by the procedure for computing some sort of 'result'. On completion this result is passed out of the procedure and assigned back to v. (For a variation on this, see Exercise 5.)

These parallel the first two methods in the following respects. Methods 1 and 3 are conceptually the cleanest, reflecting the mathematical view of a parameter as described earlier: x is bound to a fixed entity in the calling environment — a data value in one case, a variable in the other. Methods 2 and 4 are pragmatic variations: x is a local variable and communication with the actual parameter is confined to the execution boundaries — on entry in one case, on exit in the other.

Method 2 is sometimes known as 'copy in', since the value of e is copied into the procedure as the initial value of x. Similarly, method 4 is known as 'copy out': the final value of x is copied back to v. The two methods can be combined to provide a fifth one, namely 'copy in/copy out'. This provides an alternative to method 3 for input–output parameters:

5.   *Pass-by-value-result.* The parameter x is treated as a local variable. Its initial value is supplied by v on entry and its final value is returned to v on exit.

With this method, x acts as a sort of local representative of v. It starts by taking v's value and then interacts with the procedure on v's behalf. On completion, it reports back to v with its result. (For a slightly different definition, see Exercise 5.)

To illustrate the different mechanisms, consider a procedure set_sum (Z, n, sum) that takes a one-dimensional array Z, computes the sum of its first n elements, and assigns the result to a variable sum:

```
procedure set_sum (Z : in vector;
                   n : in natural;
                   sum : out real) is
begin
    sum := 0;
    for i in 1..n loop
        sum := sum + Z(i);
    end loop;
end set_sum;
```

The following call uses it to add the first 1000 elements of an array A, assigning the result to a variable sigma:

```
set_sum (A, 1000, sigma);
```

Using named correspondence, an equivalent call would be:

```
set_sum (n => 1000, Z => A, sum => sigma);
```

We shall consider each of the parameters in turn.

The simplest one is the input parameter n, which takes the value 1000 and is never altered. The obvious mechanism for it is pass-by-constant. If this were not available, pass-by-value would do instead. In that case, n could be used as a local variable and so it would be possible, in principle, to dispense with i. However, as remarked previously, this would involve n in two different roles and so there would be a loss of clarity.

The parameter sum is an output parameter and so methods 1 and 2 are not appropriate. Since the actual parameter sigma has to be evaluated in reference mode, the obvious choice is method 3 — pass-by-reference. This has the effect that sum becomes an alias for sigma and so all the assignments to sum (and there are 1,001 of them) are, in fact, assignments to sigma. It works perfectly well, but it also incurs certain costs. The trouble is that unless set_sum is compiled as inline code, the assignments to sigma have to be implemented by indirect addressing — a slower process than ordinary direct addressing (see Section 5.9). Generally speaking, it would be more efficient to accumulate the sum in a local variable, assigning it to sum, and thereby to sigma, on completion. But this, of course, is precisely what happens with method 4, namely pass-by-result: sum plays the role of the local variable and its final value is assigned to sigma as required. Thus pass-by-result is more efficient than pass-by-reference in some cases.

Finally, there is the array parameter Z and its corresponding actual parameter A. Like n, this is an input parameter and so pass-by-constant would be appropriate. However, there is a new factor to be reckoned with: pass-by-constant supplies set_sum with a complete copy of A and so it has to make a copy of all 1,000 elements. It would be more efficient to pass a *reference* to A, as in method 3. This is all very well; but, as noted above, all accesses to A would then have to be made by indirect addressing and this might offset the savings on copying. So there is a trade-off between the passing mechanism and the accessing mechanism. In practice, the details will depend on (a) the number of accesses and (b) the code that is generated. In many cases, the indirection does *not* add to the cost of accessing arrays and so pass-by-reference is the best method. But there may occasionally be situations where pass-by-value or pass-by-value-result (despite its *two* copying operations) has the edge.

The question naturally arises: are pass-by-reference and pass-by-value-result equivalent in their ultimate effects? For most practical purposes the answer is Yes. However, there are certain unusual situations where they do in fact behave differently. For example, consider the parameter sum and its corresponding actual parameter sigma. With pass-by-reference sigma is active during the execution of set_sum, whereas with pass-by-value-result it is passive. So, if the loop inside set_sum contained the output statement

    put (sigma);

the resulting values would vary in the former case but would all be the same in the latter case. A similar divergence could be obtained by using sigma in any other way. The trouble arises because of the aliasing. With pass-by-reference, sum is an alias for sigma and so assignments that are made directly to sigma should change the value of sum. But with pass-by-value-result this does not happen. Of course, it is unusual to have a procedure that refers to a global variable (such as sigma) that has also been supplied to it as a parameter (such as sum). But it *can* happen, and on occasions it *does* happen, and so programmers need to be aware of the potential hazards.

For completeness, one other mechanism should be mentioned:

6.   *Pass-by-expression.* The actual parameter *e* is passed to the procedure as an unevaluated expression. Whenever the formal parameter *x* is encountered during execution, *e* is evaluated either in reference mode or in data mode, as the context requires.

The method is found in languages of the ALGOL 60 family, where it is known as 'call by name' — a rather unhelpful description. In many simple cases, it is equivalent to pass-by-reference. But if A is an array and *e* is the expression A(i), it has the effect that *x* can denote A(3) at one instance and A(4) at the next, depending on the current value of i (see Exercise 4). This is conceptually confusing and also costly to implement. The parameter has to be represented as a pair of procedures, sometimes known as *thunks* — one for evaluating *e* in reference mode and one for evaluating it in data mode. There are no worthwhile advantages to offset these overheads (though see Exercise 6) and so the method has passed from favor.

From these six methods, it seems that two languages seldom offer the same selection. APL relies on pass-by-constant; C is similar, except that the constant can be a reference. ALGOL 60 has pass-by-value and pass-by-expression; ALGOL 68 has pass-by-constant and pass-by-reference. COBOL also has pass-by-constant (which it calls by content) and pass-by-reference (the default). FORTRAN and PL/I use pass-by-reference and/or pass-by-value-result and therefore have conceptual problems with actual parameters that are constants. In particular, if a subroutine makes an assignment to a parameter that is a constant, the effect on the program is 'unpredictable'. It might even change the constant! Pascal uses pass-by-value and pass-by-reference, the former being the default and the latter being specified by the prefix **var**. This has the unfortunate effect that if **var** is accidentally omitted, assignments to the parameter become assignments to a local variable; consequently the error is not picked up by the compiler. If the default were pass-by-constant, some tedious bug-hunts would be avoided.

Ada is equally individualistic. Its modes are **in**, **out**, and **in out**, reflecting the possible roles of parameters that were described above. The default is **in**. Assignments are allowed to **out** and **in out** parameters, but **in** parameters are treated as constants — an improvement on Pascal. For scalar parameters the three modes have to be implemented by copy-in and/or copy-out and so they are equivalent to the following mechanisms:

in	—	pass-by-constant;
out	—	pass-by-result;
in out	—	pass-by-value-result.

The advantage of the copy-in and copy-out mechanisms is that, in the absence of global variables, the procedure interacts with the calling program only on entry and exit. In between, it can execute independently. On a distributed system, it therefore lends itself to implementation on a separate processor — a factor that was an important criterion in Ada's design. A minor benefit is that the copying mechanism has no problems with fields of packed records (see Volume II). However, on non-distributed systems, the copying of large arrays and records can be unnecessarily expensive and so for these parameters Ada allows pass-by-reference instead. As shown above, in certain circumstances this can produce different effects and so the program's behavior becomes dependent on the choice that the compiler makes. In such cases, Ada states that the program is 'erroneous'.

9.4 FUNCTIONS

A *function* is a subprogram that produces a result. It is like an expression — a set of rules for producing some value — and syntactically the call of a function *is* an expression. The idea is familiar enough from the standard functions of a language, such as abs or sqrt. For example, the Pascal assignment

    x := sqrt(y)

includes sqrt (y) as an expression. The function sqrt returns the appropriate result and this is duly assigned to x.

In the simplest cases a function can be defined by means of a single expression. For example, a function ρ might be defined mathematically as follows:

$$\rho(x, y) = \sqrt{(x^2 + y^2)}$$

In programming, it might look more like this:

    function rho (x, y : real) = sqrt (x * x + y * y);

Then any expression of the form sqrt $(E1*E1 + E2*E2)$ could be abbreviated to rho $(E1, E2)$. A facility of this kind is available in FORTRAN, where rho can be defined by the statement:

    rho (x,y) = sqrt (x * x + y * y)

Unfortunately, the notation looks exactly like an assignment to an array element. It has therefore caused considerable grief to unsuspecting programmers: they forget to declare their arrays and unwittingly define a function by mistake. Following this bad publicity, the idea has been omitted from most other languages. However, it has an alternative formulation in the *lambda calculus*:

$$\textbf{function } \text{rho} \ = \ \lambda\,(x, y \ : \ \text{real}) \ . \ \text{sqrt}\,(x * x \ + \ y * y)$$

The right-hand side is a *lambda expression* and denotes the function that is derived from the expression sqrt $(x*x + y*y)$ by treating x and y as parameters — a process known as *functional abstraction*. It reflects the understanding of a function as found in mathematics and is one of the main features of the programming language LISP 1.5 (see Volume II). It is also found in ALGOL 68.

The trouble with this approach is that expressions are a rather restrictive mechanism for describing computations. In theory they can define any computable function, but in practice it is often more convenient to use ordinary algorithmic means. So either there has to be a special form of expression for the purpose — one that allows a sequence of statements to produce a value; or functions have to be definable in much the same way as procedures. The former approach is found in BCPL and LISP; it also occurs in ALGOL 68 and C, where the distinction between statements and expressions is completely blurred. The latter is found in most other languages, including Pascal and Ada. In Ada, for example, with a suitable package for real arithmetic, the function rho would be defined as follows:

```
function rho (x, y : real) return real is
begin
    return sqrt (x * x  +  y * y);
end rho;
```

For trivial functions such as rho, the notation is rather more verbose than the previous versions. But since the function body can include declarations and statement sequences, the basic facility is much more powerful. It can be illustrated further by writing a function sum (Z, n) that gives the sum of the first n elements of an array Z. It is similar to the procedure set_sum of the previous section, except that the sum is not assigned to a parameter sum but is returned as a result:

```
function sum (Z : vector; n : natural) return real is
    partial_sum : real := 0;
begin
    for i in 1..n loop
        partial_sum := partial_sum + Z(i);
    end loop;
    return partial_sum;
end sum;
```

The **return** statement can occur anywhere in the function body and must be followed by an expression of the type that is specified in the heading. As with procedures, several such statements are allowed and execution terminates when the first of them is encountered. The value of its argument is the function's result. If no such statement is ever executed, the result is undefined. In some languages, including Pascal, the result is not specified by a **return** statement but is assigned to the function's name, which behaves as a write-only variable for the purpose. Execution continues to the end of the function body and the value of the name is then returned as the result. By preventing an earlier exit from the function body, this helps to enforce the one-entry/one-exit philosophy of structured programming. On the other hand, the function's name can also be used for calling the function recursively, and this can be rather confusing.

If functions are defined by ordinary statement sequences, they can cause problems by having *side effects* — that is, effects on the state of the computation other than those of returning a value. The most obvious way to produce a side effect is by assigning a value to an output parameter or to a global variable. The following is one of the early examples, adapted from ALGOL 60:

```
function Sneaky (z : real) return real is
begin
    W := z + 1;
    return z + (z − 2) ** 2;
end Sneaky;
```

Here W is a global variable and is altered by a call of Sneaky. The result of executing

```
Pip := Sneaky (k) + W;
```

therefore depends on whether W is evaluated before or after Sneaky (k). Since the order of evaluation is usually not specified (to encourage compiler optimization), the effect of the assignment is undefined. Other side effects can be obtained by reading data from input or, more dramatically, by executing a jump out of the function body.

Side effects create difficulties for language definition in every context where expressions can occur. Indeed, when their implications began to dawn on the ALGOL community, there was a strong reaction against them. One well-known author described it as 'quite unreasonable to allow the evaluation of expressions to induce side effects'. And two of the authors of the ALGOL 60 Report made a striking admission:

> Indeed, the idea of expressions having any effect but defining an actual value is so preposterous that it was not even considered by the ALGOL committee.

After all, they argued, it would allow conditions such as:

$$x + f(x) \neq f(x) + x$$

— which is clearly absurd. (See *ALGOL Bulletin* **10** : p3 and **12** : p7, 1960-61.) Some proposals were put forward for making side effects illegal, but they curtailed the language so drastically that they were never adopted. Instead, the Revised Report left the side effects of functions as one of the matters to be left for 'further consideration ... in the expectation that current work on advanced programming languages will lead to better resolution'.

The 'better resolution' has not materialized. Indeed, many people would argue that there are occasions where side effects are thoroughly desirable; so any attempt to eliminate them would be a *worse* resolution. At any rate, most subsequent languages have continued to allow them quite freely, including SIMULA 67, ALGOL 68, Pascal, and so on. In its preliminary form Ada decreed otherwise: functions were not to have side effects.

Assignments to global variables were disallowed, whether by direct assignment, or via **out** or **in out** parameters, or via pointers (access values), or via procedure calls. In the revised version, though, pragmatism won the day and side effects were admitted. The only surviving restriction is that functions cannot have **out** or **in out** parameters.

To illustrate the need for side effects, consider the case of a random number generator. A typical technique is to define a series of integers by means of the relations:

$$x_0 \quad = \quad \text{some initial integer (the 'seed')}$$
$$x_{i+1} \quad = \quad (a*x_i + b) \ \textbf{mod} \ m \qquad\qquad \ldots i \geq 0$$

Here a, b, and m are carefully chosen integer constants (see Exercise 10.4). The following procedure random replaces x by the next number in the series and produces the result x/m. This provides a distribution in the range $0 \leq x/m < 1$:

```
function random return real is
begin
    x := (a * x + b) mod m;
    return real (x) / real (m);
end random;
```

The assignment to the global variable x is a side effect that is essential to the technique, but it allows the use of 'Sneaky' expressions such as random + x. This can be avoided by hiding x from the calling program — for example, by putting it inside a package (see Section 10.4). Even so, there would still be ambiguity over expressions such as random / random; so the problem of side effects cannot be avoided completely.

A final point of interest from Ada is that function definitions can be used for giving new meanings to operators. An example of this was given in Section 4.9, defining the product of two length values to be an area value:

```
function "*" (a, b : length) return area is
begin
    return area (a * b);
end "*";
```

The only difference in the definition is the use of the operator symbol "*" instead of the function name. It means that the symbol can be applied to arguments of type length, using normal infix notation, and the result, instead of being a length, will be an area.

9.5   TYPES AS PARAMETERS

The following procedure swaps the values of two integer variables x and y:

```
procedure swap (x, y : in out integer) is
    temp : integer;
begin
    temp := x;
    x := y;
    y := temp;
end swap;
```

To swap two integer variables, A(i) and A(j), it can be called in the obvious way:

```
swap (A(i), A(j));
```

This is all very well for integer variables, but for swapping two complex variables (say) it is no help. For that, another procedure would have to be written, with every detail the same except for the type. Each occurrence of integer would be replaced by complex.

Clearly it would be helpful if a version could be provided in which the type itself were one of the parameters. It might go something like this:

```
procedure swap (t : type;
                     x, y : in out t) is
       temp : t;
  begin
       temp := x;
       x := y;
       y := temp;
  end swap;
```

To swap A(i) and A(j) the appropriate call would be:

```
swap (integer, A(i), A(j));
```

Similarly, to swap two complex variables, z1 and z2, it would be:

```
swap (complex, z1, z2);
```

Thus swap would provide a single, universal, swapping procedure, exactly as required.

This looks good, but unfortunately it runs into two problems — the first practical and the second theoretical:

1. On the practical side, the compiler writer asks: how can the universal swap procedure be implemented? The trouble is that there is no universal code for implementing assignments. Type integer will require one piece of code, complex another; arrays and records will be different again. So either the universal procedure will have to select the appropriate code at run-time, according to the value of t; or there will have to be a separate version of the procedure for each value of t that is used.

2. On the more theoretical side, the programmer should ask: what operations can legitimately be applied to t? The swap procedure assumes that assignment is legitimate and this, by and large, is a very reasonable assumption. However, other procedures may wish to use operators such as '*' and '<', or even functions such as pos and val. This means that there is an implied restriction on the value of t: the type must be legitimate for the operations that are applied to it. A procedure heading that fails to list the operations is therefore incomplete.

Because of these two problems very few languages have attempted to allow types as parameters. The language Model pioneered some of the issues, adopting an approach that was similar to the simple-minded scheme outlined above (Johnson and Morris, 1976). More recently, though, Ada has adopted a significantly different approach, based on the concept of program units that are *generic*. We shall consider the case of procedures, though functions and packages can be generic too.

A generic procedure is best regarded as a template for generating a family of other procedures. It has to be defined in two parts — first the specification and then the body. As an example, here is the specification for a generic version of swap:

```
generic
    type t is private;
procedure swap (x, y : in out t);
```

The first two lines are the *generic part*, with t being a *generic parameter*. The designation of t as **private** means that nothing is known about it other than its suitability for three standard operations: '=', '≠', and assignment. The specification of swap has the same form as that of an ordinary procedure, and so also does the body:

```
procedure swap (x, y : in out t) is
    temp : t;
begin
    temp := x;
    x := y ;
    y := temp;
end swap;
```

To swap two integer variables, a particular version of swap has to be generated, with t replaced by integer :

```
procedure swap_int is new swap (integer);
```

This process is known as *generic instantiation*. Similarly, to swap two complex variables, a second version has to be generated:

```
procedure swap_comp is new swap (complex);
```

The two instantiations can then do the required swapping:

```
swap_int (A(i), A(j));
swap_comp (z1, z2);
```

This two-stage process provides an explicit solution to problem 1. Each value of t requires a separate instantiation of swap and so, by implication, each one produces a separate body of code.

Problem 2 concerns the operations that can be applied to t. These are specified in the first instance by giving t a *generic formal type*. The simplest one is **private** which, as mentioned above, implies that the operations of equality, inequality, and assignment are all applicable. A more restricted version is **limited private**, which allows no operations at all. On the more liberal side, the range of operations can be extended by one of the specifications shown in Figure 9-1. For example, the specification (<>) means that the actual generic parameter will be a discrete type; consequently, entities of type t can be subjected to all the standard operations for discrete types — first, last, pos, val, succ, pred, width, image, and value. With **range** <>, they can be subjected to '+', '−', and so on. Also, if t has one of these specifications, the succeeding generic parameters can be array or record types with t as a type of their components.

Specification	Meaning
(<>)	any discrete type
range <>	any integer type
digits <>	any floating point type
delta <>	any fixed point type

Figure 9-1   Specifications for generic formal types

These possibilities provide only a partial solution to problem 2. For a complete solution, there must be a way of specifying any further operations that are required. Ada therefore allows them to be listed explicitly as a series of **with** clauses in the generic part. A simple illustration is provided by a function cube for producing the cube of an item x under some multiplication operator '*'. The type of x and the details of '*' are both generic:

```
generic
    type item is private;
    with function "*" (u, v : item) return item;
function cube (x : item) return item is
begin
    return x*x*x;
end cube;
```

The **with** clause states that the type item must be supplied with some sort of multiplying operator '*', whose result is also of type item. (Its formal parameters u and v are never actually referred to.) In the following instantiation,

```
function real_cube is new cube (real, "*");
```

the compiler checks that '*' is defined for real in the required way. However, the multiplying operator need not be '*'. For strings, it could be catenation:

```
function string_cube is new cube (string, "&");
```

And for type Rubik, it could be a programmer-defined function called twist:

```
function Rubik_cube is new cube (Rubik, twist);
```

This provides a complete solution to problem 2. Solutions to Rubik's cube, of course, are another matter.

9.6 SUBPROGRAMS AS PARAMETERS

The preceding sections have shown that parameters can be constants, variables, or types. This section considers one further possibility — parameters that can be subprograms. These occur quite commonly in numerical software. For example, a procedure find_root might be needed for finding the root of an arbitrary function f in an interval (a, b). In that case it is natural to make f a parameter of find_root. To what extent do languages cater for parameters of this kind?

The answer is that most general-purpose languages cater for them in a fairly natural way. An example is provided by the following version of find_root written in Pascal. It assumes that f is continuous over the interval, with $f(a) \leq 0$ and $f(b) \geq 0$, and it finds the root by means of *repeated bisection*: that is, it repeatedly halves the interval in which f changes sign, stopping when the size of the interval is less than a specified value epsilon. Note that a and b are pass-by-value parameters and can therefore be used as local variables:

```
procedure findroot (function f : real;
                          a, b, epsilon : real;
                          var root : real);
     var midpoint : real;
begin
     {assert a < b, f(a) ≤ 0, f(b) ≥ 0}
     while b − a > epsilon do begin
          midpoint := (a + b) / 2;
          if f (midpoint) ≤ 0
               then a := midpoint
               else b := midpoint
     end {while};
     root := midpoint
end {findroot};
```

If slope is a function with a real result and flatspot is a real variable, a typical call would be:

```
findroot (slope, 0, 1, 0.0000001, flatspot);
```

This version is based on the original definition of Pascal and it illustrates a potential problem. Although the procedure heading gives the type of f's result, it says nothing about its parameters. Under the original definition, the parameters had to be passed by value (and so slope, for example, could not have **var** parameters), but there was no requirement that they agree in number or in type. There was a gap in the run-time security at this point. If slope required three integer parameters (say), it would not respond kindly to its treatment within findroot. A sophisticated compiler might attempt to close the gap by analyzing the usage of f inside the procedure body. In practice, though, this is seldom done; and in any case, if the procedure body were supplied separately, it could not be done at all.

To close the gap properly, the Pascal Standard requires that the specification of f should have the form of an ordinary function heading:

```
procedure findroot (function f (x : real) : real;
                          ... );
```

This gives the number, mode, and type of f's parameters and even supplies them with names (which are never used). When findroot is called, the actual function must have parameters of the same kind (though their names can be different).

Most other general-purpose languages are like the original version of Pascal at this point: parameters such as f are not fully specified and so there are gaps in the security. Ada, with its policy of strong typing, is more like the Pascal Standard. However, it does not allow f to be treated as an ordinary parameter but insists that it be a generic one. The find_root example therefore has the following specification:

```
generic
    with function f (x : real) return real;
procedure find_root (a, b, epsilon : real;
                        root : out real) is ...
```

To find the roots of slope, a special instantiation is needed:

```
procedure slope_root is new find_root (slope);
```

Compared with the more conventional approach, this seems unnecessarily complicated. The **with** notation is also rather odd, since there is nothing that f actually goes *with*. The reasoning seems to be that the generic mechanism provides a method of passing subprograms as parameters, so why bother with anything else?

The impression may have been given that functional parameters are rather offbeat things that are needed only by the numerical analysts. However, it is worth noting that there are some languages in which they figure more prominently and in which they are used much more widely. The best known of these is LISP, whose applications are mostly non-numerical. One of its central features is that functions can be created dynamically by means of lambda expressions (see Section 9.4). They can then be passed around as arguments of other functions in ways that produce very powerful effects. Not surprisingly, the checking of parameter lists has to be done at run-time. LISP gives explicit recognition to another problem that arises with functional arguments. When they are passed around to other parts of a program, the functions may have to be executed in contexts that are different from those in which they were defined; so how are their global (or *free*) variables to be interpreted? This is known as the *funarg* problem and is a topic that will be considered further in Chapter 12.

9.7 RECURSIVE PROCEDURES

A procedure P is *recursive* if it can activate itself. It is *directly* recursive if it calls itself from within its own procedure body: that is, the definition of P includes one or more calls of P. It is *indirectly* recursive if it can activate itself via one or more other procedures: P calls Q, which calls R, ... which calls P. Either way, one activation of P can initiate another activation of P and so there may be two or more activations in existence at the same time. Procedures with this property are of great importance in computer programming, especially in fields such as compiler writing, symbolic algebra, and artificial intelligence. The rest of this chapter is devoted to the principles of their design.

By way of introduction, it is relevant to recall the basic features of recursion that were presented in Chapter 6. They were developed in the context of type 2 (context-free) grammars; but, as noted at the time, they have close parallels with the subroutines of a

program. The results of that chapter therefore carry over to procedures in the following
important ways:

1.   Procedures can be classified as nonrecursive, left-recursive, right-recursive, and
      self-embedding.

2.   Left-recursive or right-recursive procedures provide an alternative mechanism to
      loops for obtaining a repetitive action sequence; they are easily converted to
      equivalent loops.

3.   In a limited but significant sense, self-embedding procedures are more powerful
      than regular programs; if they are inherently self-embedding, they can be con-
      verted to equivalent regular programs only by the introduction of control vari-
      ables.

4.   In such cases the control variables will embody some sort of a stack.

These principles are particularly important for classifying the different forms of recursion
and for showing how they can be implemented by equivalent, nonrecursive loops (see
Sections 9.11 – 9.13).

    For an example of recursion it is useful to begin with a procedure Vprint (i, j) that
prints a large version of the letter V:

```
        *           *
          *       *
           *     *
            * *
             *
```

The parameters i and j give the positions of the asterisks on the first line and the asterisks
move one place inwards on each successive line. The implementation will be based on
the observation that once the first line has been printed, the remaining task is to print a
slightly smaller V. Since this is a task of the same kind as the original, it can be done by
calling Vprint recursively! If a procedure print_stars (i, j) is available for printing the first
line, the rest is almost trivial:

```
        procedure Vprint (i, j : integer) is
        begin
            print_stars (i, j);            -- print the first line
            Vprint (i+1, j−1);            -- the recursion
        end Vprint;
```

This is promising. However, it has a fatal flaw in that Vprint calls itself recursively *every
time*. Consequently, the first call will initiate a second call, which will initiate a third
call, which ... and the recursions will never end (except possibly with an error message
when time or space expires). The procedure therefore needs an *escape clause* that will
stop the recursions from continuing too far. In this case, the time to stop them is when i
becomes greater than j, at which point there is nothing left to do:

```
procedure Vprint (i, j : integer) is
begin
    if i > j then                  -- escape condition
        null;                      -- the escape action
    else
        print_stars (i, j);        -- the recursive part
        Vprint (i+1, j−1);         -- as before
    end if;
end Vprint;
```

Since the escape action is null, the code can be shortened by reversing the test and giving only the recursive part:

```
if i ≤ j then
    print_stars (i, j);
    Vprint (i+1, j−1);
end if;
```

However, this breaks with the normal convention of handling the escape condition explicitly at the start and so it makes the code slightly harder to follow.

Another alleged 'improvement' stems from the observation that it is a waste of time to call Vprint when its action is **null**. So why not remove the escape test from the point of entry and place it prior to the recursive call? To do this, the test has to be expressed in terms of the parameters of the recursive call. The condition $i \leq j$ is therefore replaced by $i+1 \leq j−1$, or equivalently $i < j−1$, and this leads to the following version:

```
procedure Vprint (i, j : integer) is
begin
    print_stars (i, j);
    if i < j−1 then                -- the revised test
        Vprint (i+1, j−1);         -- the recursive call
    end if;
end Vprint;
```

Like the previous revision, this is slightly harder to follow. More importantly, though, it has the serious drawback that it no longer handles the null case. For Vprint, this may not matter: after all, who would ever want to print a blank V? (But sooner or later, someone inevitably will.) In general, though, it is essential that the null case be included if the procedure is to work reliably. So, as with loops, it is best to test for termination at the start, rather than in the middle or at the end.

Is Vprint left-recursive, right-recursive, or self-embedding? In considering this question it is important to appreciate that it relates to the run-time action sequences: where within the execution of Vprint will the recursive call occur? The answer is that it will come at the end, as the last action before execution terminates. In this sense Vprint is right-recursive, or what is often called *tail-recursive*. In keeping with the principles given earlier, this indicates that it is basically a disguised form of repetition. Section 9.11 presents a standard transformation for converting it to an equivalent loop.

As an example of a self-embedding procedure consider the problem of printing an X instead:

```
      *    *
       *  *
        *
       *  *
      *    *
```

This can be done in the same way as the V, by printing the first line and then making a recursive call to print a smaller X. The only difference is that, on completion of the smaller X, a copy of the first line has to be added at the end:

```
procedure Xprint (i, j : integer) is
begin
    if i > j then
        null
    else
        print_stars (i, j);          -- first line
        Xprint (i+1, j-1);           -- smaller X
        print_stars (i, j);          -- last line
    end if;
end Xprint;
```

This time there is an escape clause, but is it the correct one? A quick experiment with i = 1 and j = 3 shows that the middle asterisk is printed twice. A better version might therefore add the phrase:

```
elsif i = j then
    print_stars (i, j);
```

However, even this may not be exactly what is wanted; so perhaps the problem needs formulating more carefully (Exercise 10).

Since the recursive call of Xprint has statements that are executed both before and after it, the procedure (like the X) is self-embedding. As shown in Section 9.12, there is a standard transformation that will convert it to a nonrecursive form that uses two loops. In this case there happens to be a transformation that results in only one loop; but it is feasible only because of certain special conditions (see Exercise 26).

These examples show that in designing a recursive procedure we have to address the following two questions:

1. What is the escape condition and, when it is satisfied, what actions (if any) must be taken?

2. In the other cases how can the procedure be used recursively to attain the overall goal?

A third question concerns the requirement that the recursive calls will eventually terminate — an issue that is considered in Section 9.9:

3. Is the recursion guaranteed to terminate? That is to say, will the parameters of the recursive calls eventually satisfy the escape condition?

Having answered these questions satisfactorily, we can write the procedure and leave the implementation to take care of the rest. Generally speaking, it is a mistake to try to visualize the execution as it plunges down through successive levels of the recursive calls, each with its own parameters and its own locus of control. Our human brains are not very good at this sort of activity. Instead, we need to focus our attention on the top level of control, writing the procedure on the assumption that the recursive calls work successfully. An inductive argument can then be used to prove that the procedure is correct. Further details are given in the chapter on recursive data structures (see Volume II).

9.8   RECURSIVE FUNCTIONS

We turn now to consider how recursion can be used in functions. A popular example is the function factorial (n) for computing n!. Mathematically, it can be defined by the following relations, of which the second is directly recursive:

$$0! \ = \ 1$$
$$n! \ = \ n \times (n{-}1)! \qquad\qquad \dots \ n \geq 1$$

If functions could be defined by expressions, as described in Section 9.4, a convenient definition would be the following:

```
function factorial (n : natural) =
    if n = 0 then 1
        else n * factorial (n−1);
```

As in most languages, though, a more roundabout route has to be taken, using a conditional statement. Here is the Ada version:

```
function factorial (n : natural) return natural is
begin
    if n = 0 then
        return 1;
    else
        return n * factorial (n−1);
    end if;
end factorial;
```

The correctness of the function follows almost trivially from the form of the original definition. A formal proof of termination will be given in the next section.

Another popular and instructive example is provided by the Fibonacci numbers 0, 1, 1, 2, 3, 5, 8, 13, ... Apart from the initial 0 and 1, each number is the sum of its two predecessors. The series can therefore be defined by the relations:

$$F_0 \ = \ 0$$
$$F_1 \ = \ 1$$
$$F_n \ = \ F_{n-1} + F_{n-2} \qquad\qquad \dots \ n \geq 2$$

As with factorial, the definition can be translated directly into Ada:

```
function Fib (n : natural) return natural is
begin
    if n = 0 then
        return 0;
    elsif n = 1 then
        return 1;
    else
        return Fib (n−1) + Fib (n−2);
    end if;
end Fib;
```

Since a single activation of the procedure body can initiate two recursive calls, the function is an example of *nonlinear* recursion. The reason for the name is evident from Figure 9-2, which shows the recursive calls for evaluating F_4. As can be seen, F_4 calls for the evaluation of F_3 and F_2; these call for F_2, F_1, F_1, and F_0; and the first of these calls for F_1 and F_0. So F_1 has to be evaluated three times and F_0 twice. The pattern is certainly very far from being linear. In general, since F_n is the sum of all the final values 1 and 0, it is clear that F_1 has to be evaluated F_n times. For F_{10} it would have to be evaluated 55 times; and for F_{100} ... well, an estimate of 1.6^{100} would be on the low side (see Exercise 14).

The method clearly leaves room for improvement. In this case, the improvement comes by a radical change of approach. Instead of starting with F_n and working *backwards*, it is much better to start with F_0 and F_1 and to work *forwards*. A simple loop evaluates F_2, F_3, ... F_n, recording the two most recent values at each stage (see Section 9.10). If required, the loop can be transformed to an equivalent right-recursive function whose behavior is linear in n. For even faster algorithms, see Exercise 15.

Another popular and instructive example is Ackermann's function:

$$
\begin{array}{llll}
\text{Ack} (0, n) & = & n+1 & \qquad ... \ n \geq 0 \\
\text{Ack} (m, 0) & = & \text{Ack} (m−1, 1) & \qquad ... \ m \geq 1 \\
\text{Ack} (m, n) & = & \text{Ack} (m−1, \text{Ack} (m, n−1)) & \qquad ... \ m, n \geq 1
\end{array}
$$

This is different in that one of the parameters of the recursion is itself a recursive call. In mathematical terms, it is an example of 'non-primitive' recursion — that is, recursion in which the parameters do not move linearly towards the escape condition. As a consequence, it is far from clear that the recursions will always terminate. In point of fact, Ack

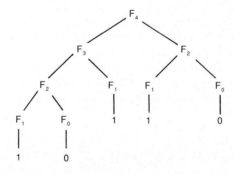

Figure 9-2   Evaluation of F_4 by recursion

does always terminate, though the number of recursive calls grows in an explosive manner as m and n increase. For example, Ack (4, 1) has the value 65,533 and involves the execution of 2,862,984,009 recursive calls. Ack (4, 2) is a number that does not bear repeating (it has 19,729 digits). The magnitude of the explosion is hard to grasp. In fact, a series of functions can be defined whose growth rates are successively linear, exponential, hyper-exponential, etc., and yet Ack (n, n) grows faster than any of them (see Exercise 20). As a result, it can be shown that Ack is *essentially* non-primitive: that is to say, primitive recursion is incapable of defining it. This gives the function a certain theoretical interest. Furthermore, its ultra-slow-growing inverse is relevant to the analysis of certain algorithms. On the more practical side, it has few applications except as a testbed for the calling mechanisms of procedures (Wichmann, 1976, 1977). Given its behavior, this is probably just as well.

The above examples are instructive and interesting, but in terms of practical applications it must be admitted that they are poor advertisements for recursion. Ack is not the sort of function that programmers need in practice and the others can all be written as simple, equivalent loops which make the recursion look rather heavy-handed. Where, then, are more realistic examples to be found? A popular answer is the problem of the Towers of Hanoi (see Exercise 12 and the references in the Bibliography), but this too is seldom needed except as a programming exercise. More convincingly, the answer is to be found in the programming of recursive data structures, especially those that are inherently self-embedding — lists within lists, trees within trees, and so on. These structures are described in Volume II and so most of the worthwhile applications of recursion will have to be deferred until the relevant places there. The chapter on recursive data structures is particularly important and introduces several other aspects of recursive programming.

9.9 TERMINATION

The basic rule has been enunciated that if a recursive procedure is to terminate it must have a nonrecursive escape clause. This is necessary; but it is by no means sufficient, as the following example shows:

```
procedure trap (n : integer) is
begin
    if n = 0 then
        put_line ("escape ! !");
    else
        trap (n);
    end if;
end trap;
```

The trouble, of course, is that the parameter of the recursive call is the same as the original one and so it does not make any progress towards the escape condition. If it were n−1 instead of n, it would represent progress towards n = 0 provided that n were positive; but if n were negative the recursions would again continue indefinitely.

To guarantee termination, we use the same techniques as for loops (see Section 8.13). The situation is simplest when there is a single parameter, *x* say, and a single recursive call, as in the above example. The escape condition B will be an expression involving x and so it can be written as $B(x)$. Similarly, the parameter of the recursive call will be an expression $E(x)$. The general intention is that if $B(x)$ is false, then $E(x)$ should in some sense be nearer to satisfying B than x itself.

As with loops we need an invariant $P(x)$ and a bound function, or terminating function, $t(x)$. The invariant is usually quite simple, being some condition that x must always satisfy. The bound function must decrease at each recursive call and must ensure termination by the time it becomes zero or negative. It must therefore have the following properties:

1. $$t(E(x)) < t(x)$$

2. $$t(x) \leq 0 \;\Rightarrow\; B(x) \;\vee\; \neg P(x)$$

A simple example is provided by factorial (n), for which B is $n = 0$ and E is $n-1$. The invariant P is $n \geq 0$ and the obvious choice for t is n itself. Property 1 is satisfied because $n-1 < n$, and property 2 is satisfied because:

$$n \leq 0 \;\Rightarrow\; n = 0 \;\vee\; \neg(n \geq 0)$$

Thus the proof formalizes our intuitive understanding: successive calls reduce the parameter n by 1 until it becomes 0, at which point the recursion terminates.

If there are two or more recursive calls termination requires that property 2 be satisfied for each. With Fib (n), for example, E is $n-1$ for one call and $n-2$ for another. The escape condition is $n = 0 \vee n = 1$, which caters for both. If a recursive call has two or more parameters, both properties have to be generalized. Thus, with two parameters x_1 and x_2, there will be two parameters for the recursive call, $E1(x_1, x_2)$ and $E2(x_1, x_2)$, and property 1 becomes:

1(a). $$t(E1(x_1, x_2), E2(x_1, x_2)) \;<\; t(x_1, x_2)$$

For example, consider the procedure Vprint (i, j) of Section 9.7. Its recursive call is Vprint $(i+1, j-1)$, and so $E1$ is $i+1$ and $E2$ is $j-1$. The appropriate choice for t is $j-i+1$. Substituting in 1(a) gives:

$$(j-1) - (i+1) + 1 \;<\; j-i+1$$

which reduces to $-2 < 0$. B is $i > j$ and so $\neg B$ is equivalent to $t \leq 0$. This establishes property 2 with no need for an invariant, and termination follows.

Ackermann's function is tougher since $E2$ involves the subsidiary recursive call Ack $(m, n-1)$, which becomes part of 1(a). The terminating function must therefore satisfy:

$$t(m-1, \; \text{Ack}(m, n-1)) \;<\; t(m, n)$$

Given the explosive behavior of Ack, this looks like a formidable task. Fortunately, most of the problems can be avoided by treating m and n independently. The key is to use induction on m, showing that if Ack (m, n) is total for any fixed value of m, then so is Ack $(m+1, n)$. The details are left as an exercise (Exercise 22).

9.10 TABULATION TECHNIQUES

Section 9.8 considered the problem of implementing the function Fib (n) as a simple-minded translation of the relations:

$$F_0 = 0$$
$$F_1 = 1$$
$$F_n = F_{n-1} + F_{n-2} \qquad \ldots n \geq 2$$

As shown in Figure 9-2, the evaluation of Fib (4) incurs two evaluations of Fib (2), three of Fib (1), and two of Fib (0). For higher values of n, the redundancy is much worse. This section describes a technique for evaluating such functions more efficiently.

A straightforward way of improving Fib is derived from the simple fact that, for $n \geq 2$, each F_n is the sum of its two immediate predecessors. It follows that if the numbers are evaluated in the order $F_0, F_1, F_2, F_3, \ldots$, the computation of each one is almost trivial. It is sufficient to set up an array F(0..n), with F(0) = 0 and F(1) = 1, and then do:

```
for i in 2..n loop
    F(i) := F(i-1) + F(i-2);
end loop;
```

The result would be a table of all the values up to F_n, computed in O (n) time. If a large enough version were retained permanently in memory, it would enable Fib to be implemented by direct look-up. The only drawback would be the cost in space. For Fib this would not be significant; but for other functions it could be more serious.

Instead of retaining the table in memory, another strategy is to make each call of Fib (n) evaluate $F_0, F_1, \ldots F_n$ from scratch. It could declare the table, execute the above loop, and return F(n) as its result. After that, the space for the table would be released for further use. In fact, since F(i) is no longer needed after F(i+2) has been calculated, it is possible to dispense with the table and to work with three simple variables. In the following function they are called x, x1, and x2, and they correspond to F_i, F_{i-1}, and F_{i-2}. They are carefully initialized for the case i = 0:

```
function Fib (n : natural) return natural is
    x : natural := 0;
    x1 : natural := 1;
    x2 : natural;
begin
        -- invariant: x = Fᵢ, x1 = Fᵢ₋₁
    for i in 1..n loop
        x2 := x1;
        x1 := x;
        x := x1 + x2;
    end loop;
    return x;
end Fib;
```

In fact, if parallel assignments are available, the three variables can be reduced to only two, the body of the loop being:

```
x, x1 := x + x1, x;
```

This technique can be generalized to a wide variety of functions. The number of variables is related to the solution of a 'pebbling' game, as described by R. Bird (1980).

A completely general approach is to take the function in its original, simple-minded form and to augment it with a table T for storing known values. Initially, T is empty (or, equivalently, all the values are marked 'unknown'). When the function is called with a parameter x, it looks up T to see if the value has been computed previously. If so, it returns immediately with that value; otherwise it computes the value and stores it in T. The method is called *exact* tabulation, because it computes the values that are needed and no others. If the table is designed with sufficient care, it can handle arbitrary values of x in ways that are economical both in space and in speed.

In conclusion, it is interesting to relate these techniques to the definition of a recursive function in mathematical theory. For example, consider the function n!, which was defined earlier by the relations:

$$
\begin{aligned}
0! &= 1 \\
n! &= n \times (n-1)! \qquad\qquad \dots n \geq 1
\end{aligned}
$$

In recursive function theory, the definition would be subtly different:

$$
\begin{aligned}
0! &= 1 \\
(n+1)! &= (n+1) \times n! \qquad\qquad \dots n \geq 0
\end{aligned}
$$

This form does not fit into the framework of ordinary procedural languages because n+1 cannot be used as a formal parameter. (Users of Prolog or of functional languages such as Miranda would feel more at home with it.) Theoretically, it has the advantage of using addition instead of subtraction (which is harder to define). It also reflects an interesting change of perspective. Given n, the programming definition is concerned with reducing it to the escape value 0. By contrast, the mathematical one is concerned with advancing it to n+1. Starting with 0!, the definition shows how to evaluate 1!, then 2!, then 3!, and so on. Thus, the values of n! are tabulated by repeated application of the recurrence relation.

A more interesting example is provided by Ackermann's function. Ack (0, n) is defined nonrecursively for all n and so, in principle, its values can be tabulated immediately. Using these values, a single application of the recursive rules fills in Ack (1, 0); a second one fills in Ack (1, 1); a third one fills in Ack (2, 0) and Ack (1, 2); and so on. Since Ack is total, every value of Ack (m, n) will eventually be filled in. (Remember: this is entirely theoretical!) Mathematically, a recursive function can be defined as the limit of this tabulation process. In other words, its value at any point is the number that is eventually filled in; or, if the position remains permanently blank, the value is undefined. This approach avoids the difficulties of trying to define functions in terms of themselves.

9.11   RECURSION AND LOOPS

The last three sections of this chapter develop a series of techniques for *recursion removal* — that is, for converting a recursive subprogram to an equivalent nonrecursive form. This will serve two purposes, one theoretical and one practical. On the theoretical side, it classifies the various forms that recursion can take and shows that in some cases the recursion is a disguised form of iteration (see Section 6.10). On the practical side, the techniques can improve the efficiency of the implementation by avoiding the overheads of the recursion mechanism. Indeed, considerable work has been done on writing compilers that will apply them automatically. Also, in a language such as FORTRAN where recursion is not allowed, the techniques are not merely an optimizing device but rather a practical necessity.

The strategy will be to present a number of *schemata* to which standard transformations can be applied. They will all have the general form:

```
procedure P ... is
begin
    if B then            -- escape condition
        S;               -- escape action
    else
        ...              -- recursive part
    end if;
end P;
```

The assumption is that B is a Boolean expression, usually involving the parameters of P, and S is any statement sequence that does not contain calls of P. This framework can be modified in one or two minor respects; but for most purposes it is the best one to work from.

This section considers procedures that are right-recursive or, to use the more popular term, 'tail-recursive'. As explained in Section 9.7, the property is not concerned with syntactic structure but with dynamic, run-time action sequences. It means that when the procedure body is executed the recursive call is the final action to be taken: once it has been completed, there is nothing more to do. The practical significance of this is that the recursive call can be converted quite simply into an equivalent looping mechanism.

The first schema deals with the case in which P has no parameters.

Schema 1
```
procedure P is
begin
    if B then
        S;
    else
        S1;
        P;               -- tail recursion
    end if;
end P;
```

In order to achieve termination $S1$ must eventually cause B to become true. The important feature of this simple, right-recursive schema is that, since the recursive call of P is the last action to be taken, there is no need to execute it recursively. It is quite sufficient to re-enter P by looping back to the start of its procedure body. This suggests the following alternative version, in which the recursive call is replaced by a **goto** statement that takes control back to the start:

```
procedure P is
begin
<<start>>
    if B then
        S;
    else
        S1;
            goto start;        -- re−enter P
    end if;
end P;
```

A little massage will then eliminate the **goto**, resulting in the following simpler form:

```
procedure P is
begin
    while not B loop
        S1;
    end loop;
    S;
end P;
```

The **goto** statement is a special case of the trick that was described in Exercise 5.6. If the last action of a subroutine P is to execute another subroutine Q, the call of Q can (in suitable circumstances) be replaced by a direct jump to the start of Q's code. In high-level languages this is not usually possible, since jumps into procedures are not allowed. However, in the case of a recursive call it *is* possible, since the jump is from the end of P back to its start.

Schema 1 can be extended to the more plausible case where P has one or more parameters. We shall use a single parameter x, but it represents as many parameters as necessary:

Schema 2
```
procedure P (x : T) is
begin
    if B(x) then
        S(x);
    else
        S1(x);
        P (E1(x));
    end if;
end P;
```

As in Section 9.9, the escape condition B and the recursive parameter $E1$ will be expressions involving x. For termination, $E1$ will have a value that is in some sense 'nearer' to satisfying B than x itself. S and $S1$ represent statement sequences that will also involve x. The basic transformation is the same as in Schema 1: instead of executing the recursive call, the code loops directly back to the start of the procedure body. The only difference is that x must first be replaced by its new value, $E1(x)$:

```
procedure P (x : T) is
begin
    while not B(x) loop
        S1(x);
        x := E1(x);        -- see note
    end loop;              -- re-enter P
    S(x);
end P;
```

Note   The assignment to x assumes that the parameter mechanism is pass-by-value (see Section 9.3). If it is pass-by-constant (as in Ada), the assignment is illegal and so x must be replaced by a local variable that is initialized to its value. This gives the same effect as pass-by-value. If the mechanism is pass-by-reference, the situation is more tricky. The viability of the technique depends on the availability of an assignment that updates the reference in the required way. If it is pass-by-result or pass-by-value-result, a combination of techniques will be required. If two or more parameters are involved, the parallel assignment may have to be separated into several ordinary ones.

An example is provided by the procedure Vprint (i, j) of Section 9.7. The nonrecursive version requires two local variables loc_i and loc_j, and the parallel assignment is split into two single ones:

```
procedure Vprint (i, j : integer) is
    loc_i : integer := i;          -- local variables
    loc_j : integer := j;          -- replacing i and j
begin
    while loc_i ≤ loc_j loop
        print_stars (loc_i, loc_j);
        loc_i := loc_i + 1;
        loc_j := loc_j - 1;
    end loop;
end Vprint;
```

The result is the simple loop that might well have been written in the first place. It demonstrates the fact that some forms of recursion are merely disguised loops.

As a final commentary on this schema, it is worthwhile returning to the function factorial of Section 9.8. The version given there contained the recursive call:

```
return n * factorial (n - 1);
```

Since the call of factorial $(n-1)$ has to be followed (dynamically) by a multiplication, the function is not tail-recursive. This is a little surprising, because n! can be computed by a simple loop and we might have expected Schema 2 to produce that loop. In response, we shall therefore construct the version that *does* correspond to the loop. This can be done by writing the loop and then applying the inverse of Schema 2, suitably modified for functions. A suitable loop was given in Section 8.12:

```
function factorial (n : natural) return natural is
    i : natural := 0;
    fac : natural := 1;
begin
        -- invariant: fac = i! ∧ i ≤ n
    while i ≠ n loop
        i := i + 1;
        fac := i * fac;
    end loop;
    return fac;
end factorial;
```

To convert the loop into a recursive function, the first step is to turn the body of the loop into a single, parallel assignment. This requires a little care:

```
    i, fac := i+1, (i+1) * fac;
```

The strategy is then as follows:

• The variables i and fac become the formal parameters.

• Their initial values 0 and 1 become the arguments of the initial call.

• The values assigned to them by the parallel assignment, namely i+1 and (i+1) * fac, become the arguments of a recursive call.

• The exit condition of the loop, namely i = n, becomes the escape condition of the recursion.

• The final action, **return** fac, becomes the escape action.

This creates a new function fact (i, fac) whose initial call has to be fact (0, 1). Since its escape condition refers to n, its definition has to be embedded in factorial:

```
function factorial (n : natural) return natural is

    function fact (i, fac : natural) return natural is
            -- assert    fac = i! ∧ i ≤ n
    begin
        if i = n then
            return fac;
        else
            return fact (i + 1, (i + 1) * fac);
        end if;
    end fact;

begin
    return fact (0, 1);
end factorial;
```

Since fact is right-recursive this achieves the objective of a function that is recursive but not self-embedding. Of course, the iterative version is simpler and more efficient, and so the transformation is of little practical value. However, the exercise has illustrated, from a different angle, the strong connection that exists between right-recursion and loops.

9.12 RECURSION AND STACKS

Having dealt with 'loop' recursion, we now turn to 'real' recursion — that is, to subprograms whose action sequences are self-embedding. As anticipated in Section 9.7, their conversion to nonrecursive form is not so straightforward, and in general it requires the use of a stack. Of course, stacks are needed for the recursive versions too, but they are concealed within the calling mechanism. The conversion to nonrecursive form merely brings them into the open.

The simplest version of 'real' recursion is provided by Schema 3. It is obtained from Schema 2 by the addition of a statement $S2(x)$ following the recursive call:

Schema 3

```
procedure P (x : T) is
begin
    if B(x) then
        S(x);
    else
        S1(x);
        P (E1(x));        -- self-embedding recursion
        S2(x);
    end if;
end P;
```

The procedure Xprint of Section 9.7 provides a typical example. In order to understand the relevant transformation it is helpful to consider the action sequences that P can perform. Initially it does the same as in Schema 2, repeatedly executing $S1$ until condition B is satisfied and then executing S. Let us suppose that this involves n executions of $S1$, at successively deeper levels of recursion. Having completed the escape action S, it then has to 'unwind' the recursive calls, executing $S2$ for each one in turn, until it is back at its original, outermost level. In the process it executes $S2$ the same number of times as $S1$, and so its overall action sequence is:

$$S1^n; \ S; \ S2^n$$

There is a familiar ring to this, because it is like the type 2 language whose sentences are $a^n x b^n$ (see Section 6.11). It expresses the fact that a self-embedding procedure executes a self-embedding series of actions.

The nonrecursive version reflects this pattern by having three parts:

1. A loop that executes $S1(x)$.
2. The escape action $S(x)$.
3. A loop that executes $S2(x)$.

In the simplest case, the first two parts are the same as before, with the addition that they record the number of iterations n. The value of n can then be used for controlling the third part. However, there is a serious problem if $S2$ uses any parameters or local variables. The trouble is that in the recursive sequence

$$S1(x); \; P(E1(x)); \; S2(x)$$

these values are not altered by the call of P (since x, we are assuming, can only be an input parameter). But in the nonrecursive version of Schema 2 they are changed by the inner levels of execution. What can be done to preserve them? The answer (of course!) is that they have to be put on a stack. They are loaded after each execution of $S1(x)$ and unloaded before each execution of $S2(x)$. Provided that the stack is initially empty, this has the additional advantage that there is no need for a variable to count the number n. Instead, the second loop terminates when the stack becomes empty again.

In order to implement the stack, we shall anticipate some of the material of the next chapter. In particular, we shall assume that there is a generic package stack_pack for handling stacks and that the following declaration instantiates a version called stack for items of type T:

> **package** stack **is new** stack_pack (T);

The following operations will then be available:

stack.empty	— tests whether the stack is empty
stack.load $(x : \textbf{in } T)$	— loads x on the stack
stack.unload $(x : \textbf{out } T)$	— unloads the top element into x

The stack is empty when first instantiated and is 'unbounded' in the sense that it can never become full. (For further details, see Volume II.) Using the three-part pattern anticipated earlier, we can now write the transformation as follows:

```
procedure P (x : T) is
    package stack is new stack_pack (T);
begin
    while not B(x) loop                       -- the loop for S1(x)
        S1(x);
        stack.load (x);
        x := E1(x);                           -- see note for Schema 2
    end loop;
    S(x);                                     -- the escape action
    while not stack.empty loop                -- the loop for S2(x)
        stack.unload (x);
        S2(x);
    end loop;
end P;
```

Since either $S1$ or $S2$ can be null, the Schema has two special cases. If $S2$ is null, of course, it reverts to Schema 2. If $S1$ is null, its effect is simply to load a series of values on the stack and then, using $S2$, to process them in reverse order.

A similar situation arises in the case of a recursive function, f say. If the recursive call stands by itself, it can be treated as in Schema 2 (Exercise 28). In general, though, it will be part of a larger expression. With factorial (n), for example, it is part of the expression n * factorial (n − 1). In the following Schema, $E1$ is the argument of the recursive call and $E2$ is the larger expression in which the call is embedded:

Schema 4

```
function f (x : T)  return T1  is
begin
    if B(x) then
        return E(x);
    else
        return E2(x, f (E1(x)));
    end if;
end f;
```

The notation indicates that the expressions E and $E1$ can include x but not f, whereas $E2$ can include both. Since the recursive call is embedded in $E2$, it is a case of 'real' recursion. This can be made clearer by splitting the evaluation of $E2$ into two parts, using a local variable term:

```
term := f (E1(x));
return E2(x, term);
```

The basic form is now similar to that of Schema 3, with $S1(x)$ being null. The corresponding transformation loads successive values of x on the stack and then processes them in reverse order:

```
function f (x : T)  return T1  is
    term : T1;
    package stack is new stack_pack (T);
begin
    while not B(x) loop
        stack.load (x);
        x := E1(x);                    -- see note for Schema 2
    end loop;
    term := E(x);                      -- escape action
    while not stack.empty loop
        stack.unload (x);
        term := E2(x, term);
    end loop;
    return term;
end f;
```

This handles the general case satisfactorily. However, for a simple function such as factorial (n) it is unnecessarily heavy-handed. The resulting algorithm solemnly loads n, n−1, ... 1 on the stack and then forms their product while taking them off again. It would clearly be better to dispense with the stack and to use a single loop. In the case of factorial, there are two conditions that make this possible. One retains the first loop, the other the second:

1. The expression *E2* is n * factorial (n−1). Since '*' is associative, the product can be formed during the forward loop instead of the backward one. This makes the stack and the second loop redundant.

2. From the parameter n it is easy to predict that the backward sequence will be 1, 2, ... n. These values can be computed directly by the second loop, making the stack and the first loop redundant.

In general, the first of these requires that *E2*, as a function of *x* and *f(E1)*, be associative. The second requires that the reverse sequence be computable: its initial value must be predictable and *E1*, as a function of *x*, must have an inverse. In either case, a single loop is sufficient and so there is no need for a stack.

9.13 NONLINEAR RECURSION

So far all the schemata have used *linear* recursion. The significance of this term is shown in Figure 9-3(a). The procedure *P* is called at level 0; it then executes a recursive call at level 1, which in turn executes a recursive call at level 2, and so on. The essential feature is that no activation of *P* makes more than one recursive call. The code may *contain* two or more such calls — for example, in different branches of a conditional statement — but when it is activated, only one of them is ever executed.

By contrast, Figure 9-3(b) shows the execution of a procedure that uses *nonlinear* recursion. It assumes that each activation of *P* can execute two recursive calls. There is therefore an exponential growth in the number of activations as the depth of recursion increases. Subprograms of this kind are very common in situations where a goal can be split into two smaller but similar subgoals. The strategy is known as 'divide and conquer' and can be illustrated by the well-known problem of the Towers of Hanoi (see Exercise 12).

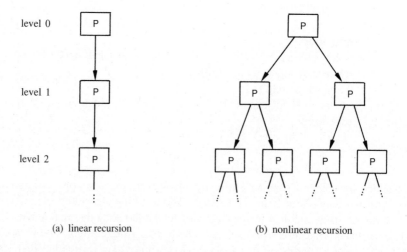

(a) linear recursion   (b) nonlinear recursion

Figure 9-3   Patterns of recursive activation

Schema 5 gives a typical outline for procedures of this kind. It is similar to Schema 3 except that *S2* has been replaced by the second recursive call:

Schema 5

```
procedure P (x : T) is
begin
    if B(x) then
        S(x);
    else
        S1(x);
        P (E1(x));          -- self-embedding recursion
        P (E2(x));          -- tail recursion
    end if;
end P;
```

The transformation to nonrecursive form requires a combination of strategies. For *P (E1)* it follows Schema 3 by using a stack; for *P (E2)* it follows Schema 2 by overwriting the parameter(s) and looping back to the start of the procedure body. The loop terminates when the stack becomes empty:

```
procedure P (x : T) is
    package stack is new stack_pack (T);
begin
    loop
        while not B(x) loop       -- as for Schema 3
            S1(x);
            stack.load (x);
            x := E1(x);           -- see note for Schema 2
        end loop;
        S(x);
        exit when stack.empty;
        stack.unload (x);
        x := E2(x);               -- as for Schema 2
    end loop;
end P;
```

The **exit** statement attracts our attention (a disguised **goto**!). If *E2* can be evaluated prior to the execution of *P (E1)*, the **exit** can be eliminated quite neatly (see Schema 6). Without this assumption, though, it turns out that there is no very satisfactory way of 'regularizing' the code. The ability to exit from the middle of the loop is therefore quite useful in this case.

Schema 6 extends the procedure body by including k recursive calls ($k \geq 2$):

Schema 6

```
procedure P (x : T) is
begin
    if B(x) then
        S(x);
    else
```

$$S1(x);$$
$$P(E1(x));$$
$$P(E2(x));$$
$$...$$
$$P(Ek(x));$$
$$\textbf{end if};$$
$$\textbf{end } P;$$

In this case, the simplest transformation is based on the assumption that *E1, E2, ... Ek* can all be evaluated immediately after the execution of *S1(x)*. In other words, their values are not affected by the recursive calls — a property that applies in most practical cases. The idea is to load them all on the stack, where each one records a commitment to execute *P* at some time in the future. If the order of execution is important, they must be loaded in reverse order; in other cases, they can be loaded in any order that is convenient. The recursions are then implemented by repeatedly re-entering the procedure body until the stack is empty. In order to set things going, *x* is placed on the stack initially:

```
procedure P (x : T) is
    package stack is new stack_pack (T);
begin
    stack.load (x);
    while not stack.empty loop
        stack.unload (x);
        if B(x) then
            S(x);
        else
            S1(x);
            stack.load (Ek(x));
            ...
            stack.load (E2(x));
            stack.load (E1(x));
        end if;
    end loop;
end P;
```

As usual, a local version of x may have to be declared in order to provide a variable. It will be noticed, of course, that the value of *E1* is loaded on the stack and then immediately unloaded. If the code is reorganized to avoid this, the result is similar to Schema 5 (Exercise 30).

The schemata could be made yet more complicated by introducing other features — for example, pass-by-reference parameters or recursive calls within loops. The nonrecursive versions would then require the stack to contain more sophisticated information, including something equivalent to a return address. However, there is little point in doing all this book-keeping, since the run-time system does precisely the same thing for the recursive version and probably does it more efficiently. It is only in the simpler cases that the transformation to nonrecursive form is worth considering.

FURTHER READING

Subprograms and, in particular, their parameter passing mechanisms are described in books on programming languages — for example, Tennent (1981), Pratt (1984), and Horowitz (1987). For a fuller discussion of parameters see Jones and Muchnick (1978).

An early book on recursive programming is Barron (1968), which catches the enthusiasm of its time, when the techniques were being explored in the context of LISP and ALGOL. A more recent text is *Recursion via Pascal* by J. S. Rohl (1984). This covers the standard examples, along with many other examples, in the context of Pascal. For a taste of purely functional programming, in which recursion is the only control mechanism see Henderson (1980). For something really original and entertaining, try *Gödel, Escher, Bach: An Eternal Golden Braid* by D. R. Hofstadter (1979).

More theoretical treatments of recursion are given in books by W. H. Burge (1975), M. Wand (1980), and F. L. Bauer and H. Wossner (1982). The analysis of recursive algorithms by means of recurrence relations is described by Rohl (*op. cit.*), and a survey of the relevant techniques is given in Lueker (1980). See also Greene and Knuth (1981), and other books on the analysis of algorithms.

Methods of recursion removal have been widely studied. Tabulation techniques are surveyed by R. Bird (1980); a more detailed study is Cohen (1983). For the transformation techniques see Bird (1977a), Auslander and Strong (1978), Arsac (1979), and Arsac and Kodratoff (1982). An automatic system for developing and transforming recursive programs is reported in Darlington and Burstall (1976) and Burstall and Darlington (1977). See also Bird (1977b) for the inverse operation — improving programs by the *introduction* of recursion.

The Fibonacci numbers have a long history and occur in a surprising variety of contexts. The original one was the breeding of rabbits (in AD 1202), as described in a helpful discussion of the numbers by D. E. Knuth (1973). Algorithms for computing them in $O(log\,n)$ time have been published in many places and have been extended to the order-k Fibonacci numbers, in which F_n is the sum of its immediate k predecessors ($n \geq k$). For recent versions, together with a good range of references, see Wilson and Shortt (1980), Er (1983a), and Martin and Rem (1984). The matrix methods can be applied to arbitrary linear recurrence relations. This was recognized in an early paper by J. C. P. Miller and D. J. Spencer Brown (1966).

Ackermann's function is discussed in Kleene (1952), which gives the reference to its German source (Ackermann, 1928). A good description of it is given in Rohl (*op. cit.*). Its use in testing the efficiency of procedure calls is described by B. A. Wichmann (1976, 1977). For an interesting discussion of induction and recursion see Buck (1963); this presents an attractive variation of the function (see Exercise 23) together with an alternative to the tabulation technique as a method of definition.

The problem of the Towers of Hanoi has been discussed many times in the literature, almost to the point of exhaustion. It comes with many embellishments, including 64 golden disks being moved by Buddhist monks as a prelude to the end of the world. A 'guided tour' of the literature is given by T. D. Gedeon (1986), with references going back to W. W. Rouse Ball (1892), who gave the recursive solution. An early discussion of removing the recursion is given in Partsch and Pepper (1976) and Hayes (1977). A more recent one is (Rohl, 1987). For something a little different, try Stone (1982).

EXERCISES

1 Why must an inline subprogram be nonrecursive? Could it be passed as a parameter?

2 Consider the following example of a procedure glug that uses a global variable g:

```
procedure glug (x : out integer) is
begin
    x := 2;
    g := 3;
end glug;
```

Now let us introduce some aliasing by calling it with g as the actual parameter. What will be the value of g on completion if the parameter mechanism uses (a) pass-by-reference, (b) pass-by-result? Which value does your version of FOR-TRAN give? What about Pascal or any other language available to you? What about Ada?

3 Here is another form of aliasing:

```
procedure slug (x, y : out integer) is
begin
    y := 2;
    x := 3;
end slug;
```

If the two actual parameters are the same, x and y become aliases for the one variable:

```
    slug (g, g);
```

What will be the value of g on completion if the parameter mechanism is (a) pass-by-reference, (b) pass-by-result? Which value does your version of FOR-TRAN give? What about Pascal or any other language available to you? What about Ada?

4 Consider the following example of a procedure inc (x) that increments its parameter x and also a global variable i:

```
procedure inc (x : integer) is
begin
    i := i+1;
    x := x+1;
end inc;
```

If A is an array of integers and i has the value 3, what is the effect of inc (A(i)) if the parameter is passed (a) by constant, (b) by value, (c) by reference, (d) by value-result, (e) by expression?

5 According to method 4 of Section 3, the pass-by-result mechanism evaluates an actual parameter *e* (in reference mode) on *entry* to a procedure. However, the resulting reference is not used until the final *exit*. An alternative definition can be given in which the evaluation of *e* is delayed until this point. Discuss the merits or otherwise of this approach.

If this is extended to the pass-by-value-result mechanism of method 5, it produces yet another variation. The parameter *e* is evaluated *twice* (in reference mode), once on entry and once on exit. How would this variation affect part (d) of the previous question?

As reported in Tai (1982), this definition of pass-by-value-result was formulated for ALGOL W and, historically, may claim to be the 'correct' one. Because of its drawbacks, several implementations of ALGOL W evaluated *e* only on entry, as in method 5. Most authors on the subject have interpreted the term in similar fashion and so method 5 is certainly correct in terms of popular usage.

6 [Jensen's device] The following Pascal procedure is designed to print out n numbers:

```
procedure print (e, i, n : integer);
begin
    for i := 1 to n do
        writeln (e)
end;
```

In ordinary Pascal, the default parameter mechanism is pass-to-local-variable and so the value of e never changes. For example, the effect of

```
k := 5;
print (2*k−1, k, 10);
```

is to print 10 occurrences of the value 9. If the default were pass-by-expression (as in ALGOL 60, where it is known as 'call by name'), the parameter 2*k−1 would be evaluated each time round the loop. Since the parameter k is used as the control variable, the output would be the values 1, 3, 5, ... 19. Similarly, the call

```
print (A[j], j, 100);
```

would produce the values of A[1], A[2], ... A[100].

Write a similar procedure (or function) that sums the values of e, rather than printing them out. Write statements that use it for the following:

(a) summing the squares of the first 50 integers;

(b) summing A[2], A[4], ... A[20];

(c) summing the elements on the main diagonal of an n×n matrix M.

This programming trick was a feature of ALGOL 60 (Rutishauser, 1967) and is generally credited to J. Jensen (*ALGOL Bulletin* **10**, p.13, 1960). Its essence is the use of two pass-by-expression parameters: the first actual parameter is an expression and the second is a variable that occurs within that expression. In effect, the device treats the first parameter as a function of the second; in other words, it does functional abstraction. What advantages (if any) does it have over the straightforward use of functions as parameters?

7 Write a generic procedure max for determining the maximum element of a one-dimensional array A. The elements of A have the generic formal type t, on which a comparison operator '>' is defined. The subscript range is A'range.

Use max to find the maximum integer in an array T. Use it to find the minimum real number in a vector V.

8 Suppose that a procedure P takes some other procedure Q as a parameter. As mentioned in Section 9.6, the original version of Pascal did not require it (or even allow it) to specify the types of Q's parameters. Its heading would simply be:

> **procedure** P (**procedure** Q) ...

It followed that P could be applied to itself: P (P). Show that if the specification of Q has to include the types of its parameters, this is no longer possible.

In fact, the need to specify the types of Q's parameters induces a hierarchy of procedure types:

> level 0 : those with no procedure parameters
> level 1 : those with level 0 procedure parameters
> level 2 : those with level 1 procedure parameters
> and so on.

The philosopher Bertrand Russell proposed that sets be restricted to a similar hierarchy in order to avoid self-referencing paradoxes. In particular, he wanted to disallow the question 'does the set of all sets that do not contain themselves contain itself?'.

What paradoxes follow if procedures can be applied to themselves? One curious consequence is that a recursive procedure need not be self-referencing. Thus the recursive procedure

> **procedure** P $(x : T)$;
>   **begin** ... $P(E(x))$ ... **end**;

can be rewritten as

> **procedure** P $(x : T)$;
>   **begin** $P1$ $(P1,x)$ **end**;

where $P1$ is the same as P except for the use of a procedure parameter Q:

> **procedure** $P1$ (**procedure** Q; $x : T$);
>   **begin** ... Q $(Q,E(x))$ ... **end**;

Neither P nor $P1$ is self-referencing. Yet the statement $P1$ $(P1,x)$ activates $P1$ recursively to an arbitrary number of levels.

Unfortunately this remarkable phenomenon appears to have no practical uses. As a means of providing recursion in languages where recursion is not available, it is almost certainly doomed to failure. Why?

9 Write the procedure print_stars (i, j) as required by Vprint and Xprint in Section 9.7. Its output should be a line with an asterisk in positions i and j. What is the precondition?

10 Consider the output of procedure Xprint in Section 9.7. What will the middle of the X look like? Rewrite the procedure so that the middle line is (a) never duplicated, (b) duplicated when it has two stars but not when it has one.

11 Write a recursive procedure int_print(n) that prints the positive integer n with no leading blanks or zeros.

12 A favorite example of recursion is the problem of the Towers of Hanoi. As shown in Figure 9-4, this involves n disks, all of different sizes, and three rods — A, B, and C. The disks are initially placed on rod A, in decreasing order of size, and the problem is to move them to rod C. The disks must be moved one at a time, from any rod to any other rod, subject to the condition that a larger one must never be placed on a smaller one.

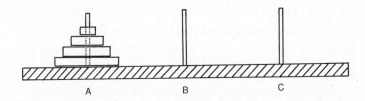

A   B   C

Figure 9-4 The Towers of Hanoi

Write a procedure to perform this task. Note that, in order to move the largest disk to rod C, the top n−1 disks must first be moved to rod B. Since this is a subproblem of the same kind, a recursive technique is a natural one to consider.

Is your procedure left-recursive, right-recursive, or self-embedding? Can you devise any rules that would enable the program to work nonrecursively but without using a stack?

Revise your procedure so that it will use four rods instead of three. What is the optimum strategy?

This problem has received extensive coverage in the literature. For details, see the Bibliography.

13 The following algorithm for catching lions has been proposed by A. van Wijngaarden:

> There are, of course, many ways to catch a lion, but the programmer's technique is recursive. The process is as follows. In order to catch a lion, first catch two lions and throw one away. In order to catch two lions, catch four lions and throw two away. If this process is continued recursively, it must terminate since there are a finite number of lions in the world. It follows that we have a lion-catching algorithm.

Surely there must be a catch somewhere; but where is it? (Quoted by T. B. Steel in *Datamation* **17**, February 1971, p.42.)

14　As stated in Section 9.8, the Fibonacci numbers are defined by $F_1 = 0$, $F_1 = 1$, and for $n \geq 2$:

$$F_n = F_{n-1} + F_{n-2}$$

Show that $F_n = \alpha^n$ is a solution of this relation if α is either Φ or $1 - \Phi$, where Φ is the 'golden ratio' $1.618\ldots$. Hence derive an expression for F_n in the form:

$$a\Phi^n + b(1 - \Phi)^n$$

Deduce that the ratio F_{n+1}/F_n tends to Φ as $n \to \infty$ and that F_n is $O(\Phi^n)$. For a fuller discussion of techniques for solving recurrence relations see Lueker (1980).

15　It was pointed out that the function Fib (n), as defined in Section 9.8, is very inefficient. Indeed, the previous exercise confirms that its evaluation takes $O(\Phi^n)$ time, where Φ is approximately 1.618. The version in Section 9.10 used a simple loop that takes $O(n)$ time. Less obviously, there are at least two ways of doing it in $O(\log n)$ time.

The first method is derived from the simple loop by observing that the parallel assignment

```
x, x1  :=  x + x1, x;
```

can be written as a matrix multiplication:

$$\begin{pmatrix} x \\ x1 \end{pmatrix} := \begin{pmatrix} 1 & 1 \\ 1 & 0 \end{pmatrix} \begin{pmatrix} x \\ x1 \end{pmatrix}$$

Repeating it n times is therefore equivalent to doing:

$$\begin{pmatrix} x \\ x1 \end{pmatrix} := \begin{pmatrix} 1 & 1 \\ 1 & 0 \end{pmatrix}^n \begin{pmatrix} x \\ x1 \end{pmatrix}$$

By using techniques for fast exponentiation (see Exercise 4.7), this can be reduced to $O(\log n)$ time, as required.

The second method makes use of the following two recurrence relations:

$$F_{2n} = 2F_{n-1}F_n + F_n^2$$

$$F_{2n+1} = F_n^2 + F_{n+1}^2$$

Implement an $O(\log n)$ function using one of these techniques. On the other hand, if speed is really important, why not tabulate F_0, F_1, ... F_n and obtain constant time? Investigate the problems of the tabulation approach.

The previous exercise gives a 'closed form' expression for F_n which, using fast exponentiation, could also be computed in $O(\log n)$ time. Would this be a suitable method?

The Bibliography gives references to some of the literature on this fascinating function.

16　Section 8.13 gave a loop for evaluating the greatest common divisor of two integers $m, n \geq 1$. Rewrite it as a recursive function gcd (m, n) and prove that it terminates.

Do the same for McCarthy's '91' function, as described in Exercise 8.21.

17 The following function, taken from Bird (1980), uses non-primitive recursion:

$$s(0) = 1$$
$$s(n) = s(s(n-1) - 1) + 1 \qquad \ldots\ n \geq 1$$

Implement it, obtain some values, and then prove the property that you observe.

18 The following function (source unknown) also uses non-primitive recursion, but its properties are not so obvious:

$$f(0) = 0$$
$$f(n) = n - f(f(n-1)) \qquad \ldots\ n \geq 1$$

Implement it, obtain some values, and verify that $f(F_n)$ is F_{n-1}, where F_n is the nth Fibonacci number. Prove that it terminates and investigate faster methods of implementation.

19 The following 'chaotic' function is taken from Hofstadter (1979):

$$q(1) = 1$$
$$q(2) = 1$$
$$q(n) = q(n - q(n-1)) + q(n - q(n-2)) \qquad \ldots\ n \geq 3$$

Implement it and see if you can observe any pattern in its behavior. Can you prove that it terminates? Investigate faster methods of implementation.

20 As stated in Section 9.8, Ackermann's function is defined by the relations:

$$Ack(0,n) = n+1 \qquad \ldots\ n \geq 0$$
$$Ack(m,0) = Ack(m-1,1) \qquad \ldots\ m \geq 1$$
$$Ack(m,n) = Ack(m-1, Ack(m,n-1)) \qquad \ldots\ m,n \geq 1$$

Let us devise a series of functions $A_0(n)$, $A_1(n)$, $A_2(n)$, ... by defining:

$$A_i(n) = Ack(i,n) \qquad \ldots\ i \geq 0$$

Show that they satisfy the relation

$$A_{i+1}(n) = A_i^{n+1}(1)$$

where $A_i^3(1)$, for example, means $A_i(A_i(A_i(1)))$. Hence show that:

$$A_0(n) = n + 1$$
$$A_1(n) = n + 2$$
$$A_2(n) = 2n + 3$$
$$A_3(n) = 2^{n+3} - 3$$

Note that $n+2 = 2 + (n+3) - 3$ and $2n+3 = 2*(n+3) - 3$. What is the pattern? Can you formulate A_4?

It is clear that A_2 is linear in n, A_3 is exponential, A_4 is hyper-exponential, and so on. But now consider the function:

$$Acker(n) = Ack(n,n)$$

The remarkable fact is that it grows faster than any of them! As mentioned in Section 9.8, Ackermann used this property to prove that, even though the function is total, it cannot be defined by means of primitive recursion.

21   In Section 9.8 it was asserted that to evaluate Ack $(4,1)$ from the above definitions would require 2,862,984,009 recursive calls. Verify this by defining a function Nack (m, n) whose value is the number of recursive calls required by Ack (m, n).

It was further asserted that Ack $(2, 4)$ has 19,729 digits. Investigate ways of verifying this.

22   Complete the proof that Ack (m, n) always terminates, as outlined in Section 9.9.

Investigate ways of evaluating Ack (m, n) that are not so expensive.

23   The following function, taken from Buck (1963), is closely related to Ackermann's:

$$
\begin{aligned}
\text{Buck } (0, 1) \ &= \ 2 \\
\text{Buck } (0, 2) \ &= \ 0 \\
\text{Buck } (0, n) \ &= \ 1 & \dots \ n \geq 3 \\
\text{Buck } (m, 0) \ &= \ m+1 & \dots \ m \geq 0 \\
\text{Buck } (m+1, n+1) \ &= \ \text{Buck } (\text{Buck } (m, n+1), n) & \dots \ m, n \geq 0
\end{aligned}
$$

Try it out for some small values of m and n. What is the behavior of Buck $(m, 5)$?

24   Revise the transformation of Schema 3 in Section 9.12 so that it does not execute the innermost pair of load–unload actions.

25   Devise a transformation for removing the recursion from Schema 2, with the addition of a statement $S0(x)$ immediately following **begin**.

Do the same for Schema 3.

26   Schema 3 involved a procedure P with a self-embedding sequence of actions

$$S1(x); \quad P (E1 (x)); \quad S2(x)$$

The transformation to nonrecursive form preserved the parameters of P on a stack. In some cases, though, it is possible to dispense with the stack and to recover them by computation instead. For example, suppose that the parameter x cannot be altered by $S1$ and that $E1$ is the expression $x + 1$. In the nonrecursive version, each iteration of the first loop will execute the assignment:

$$x := x + 1;$$

It is then sufficient for each iteration of the second loop to reverse the process by executing:

$$x := x - 1;$$

The iterations can terminate when x is back at its original value. Apply this transformation to the procedure Xprint of Section 9.7.

What conditions must be fulfilled if this approach is to be feasible? Give the general schema.

In fact, Xprint can be implemented as a single loop. What conditions make this possible? Give the general schema.

27   Convert the procedure int_print (n) of Exercise 11 to nonrecursive form. Which schema is relevant?

28 The following schema is a simplified version of Schema 4 of Section 9.12. The recursive call of the function is no longer embedded in a larger expression:

```
function f (x : T)  return T1  is
begin
    if B(x)  then
        return  E(x);
    else
        return  f(E1(x));
    end  if;
end  f;
```

Devise a simple transformation to nonrecursive form. Apply a suitably extended version to your gcd function of Exercise 16.

29 Apply the transformation of Schema 5 in Section 9.13 to the recursive version of your procedure for the Towers of Hanoi (Exercise 12).

30 Revise the transformation of Schema 6 so that *E1* is not loaded on the stack and then immediately unloaded.

31 Section 8.16 presented ten versions of an algorithm that searches for a value x in an array A(1..n). Write a *recursive* version, using either a procedure or a function. Apply a standard transformation to remove the recursion. Which of the ten (if any) do you obtain?

32 What practical evidence is there that *any* recursive subprogram can be converted to nonrecursive form?

OBJECTS AND PROCESSES

10.1 OBJECT-ORIENTED PROGRAMMING

An important principle in many areas of programming is that the structure of a program should match the structure of the situation with which it is dealing. If the program models the situation in a straightforward way, its correctness is more clearly seen and, if the situation should change, the necessary modifications are more easily made.

A limited version of the principle states that the program should reflect the structure of its data. For example, if it is processing a repetitive sequence of records, it should use a repetitive loop. Some well-known methodologies have been developed from this principle and have been widely used in conventional data processing (see Volume III). Beyond a certain point, though, they run into difficulties because the situation with which the program is dealing is not to be found in the data but in the real world (or possibly some imaginary world) from which the data come.

A more recent methodology, known as *object-oriented programming*, sets out to take the wider aspects more seriously. Its basic approach is to identify the objects in the real (or imaginary) world and to model them by means of program modules. A module defines either a single object or else a class of similar objects, where each object is characterized by the following features:

1. A set of *attributes*, either constant or variable, describing its current state;

2. A set of *operations* that can be applied to it;

A class with these two features can be regarded as a data type. The objects are passive, reacting to the operations but not initiating any actions of their own. They become much more interesting if a third feature is added:

3. A *statement sequence* that is executed as part of a parallel or quasi-parallel system;

Objects of this kind are sometimes called *processes*. The ongoing execution of their statement sequence, in parallel with other objects, gives them a life of their own and enables them to model real-world objects of a rather more active kind — for example, human beings.

Sometimes the modeling requires a class to be divided into two or more subclasses. For example, humans might be divided into males and females. The subclasses share features that are common to the 'parent' class, but are differentiated by having extra features of their own. Languages can support this in various ways, the basic mechanism being *inheritance*. It can be included as a fourth feature of the object-oriented approach:

4. A class can be defined as a *subclass* of some other class. It *inherits* all the features of its parent class and adds others of its own.

This feature enables the programmer to construct a hierarchy of classes and provides an additional, powerful tool for modeling the real world.

An *object-oriented language* is one that supports this general style of programming. The earliest such language was SIMULA 67, which uses the object-oriented approach as the basis for its discrete-event simulations. Its **class** module implements all of the above four features, including an attractively simple inheritance mechanism. It was, and still is, one of the great pioneering achievements of language design. Its successors have improved on some of its individual features, but few (if any) have managed to combine all of them in such an elegant and effective way.

One of its best known successors is the language Smalltalk, in which every aspect of the language is brought under one grand, object-oriented umbrella. A single object hierarchy covers everything, including a fully integrated programming environment. The standard version does not allow objects to be independent processes (feature 3), and so in this respect Smalltalk is less powerful than SIMULA 67. However, according to one view the only requirements of an object-oriented language are that it should support features 1, 2, and 4. On that basis Smalltalk is certainly object-oriented (Cardelli and Wegner, 1985; Wegner, 1987).

Ada supports features 1, 2, and 3 by means of two separate modules, namely packages and tasks, and has been used as the basis for an object-oriented methodology (Booch, 1987). On the other hand, it does not support inheritance, except in a limited form through its generic mechanism (see Section 10.7). So, according to the view mentioned above, it does not qualify as 'object-oriented'. The view can be challenged on the grounds that, for modeling objects in the real world, processes are more important than inheritance. The debate would raise some interesting issues, but this is not the place for canvassing them. We shall simply accept the fact that 'object-oriented' is sometimes used in a broad, general sense and sometimes in a narrower, more specific sense.

This chapter examines a range of modules which, in various combinations, provide a suitable basis for object-oriented programming. It begins by reviewing two important concepts, namely visibility and existence, within the framework of conventional block-structured languages. It then looks at modules that provide better control of these two features, starting with Ada's packages and working through to processes for quasi-parallel systems. These lead naturally into full parallelism, which is the subject of Chapter 11.

10.2 BLOCK STRUCTURE

A good starting point for any study of program modules is the 'classical' approach of block-structured languages. This was first devised for ALGOL 60 and, because of its elegance and effectiveness, it rapidly became a *de facto* standard for subsequent procedural languages. Object-oriented languages have extended it in various ways, but most of them have retained its basic framework.

A *block* can be defined as any program unit that alters the execution environment. On this basis a main program is a block, since its declarations extend the predefined environment of the language. So also are subprograms, whose parameters and/or local declarations extend the environment further. A subprogram with no parameters or declarations also qualifies, because at the very least it affects the interpretation of a **return** statement.

In ALGOL 60 there is one other unit that satisfies the criterion, and that is the unit known simply as a 'block'. To avoid confusion with 'block' in its more general sense, Ada calls it a *block statement*, reflecting the fact that syntactically it is a statement. Its role is to allow one or more declarations to be associated with an arbitrary statement sequence, and its general form in Ada is as follows:

```
identifier :                    -- optional name
   declare
      declarative_part          -- the declarations
   begin
      statement_sequence        -- the statements
   exception                    --  ) optional part
      exception_handlers        --  ) for exception handlers
   end identifier;              -- the same optional name
```

As can be seen, it is like a procedure whose heading has been replaced by the symbol **declare**. In fact, a block statement can be regarded as a special sort of procedure — one that is defined and called at the same point. As with a procedure, its execution goes through three stages. Initially, when it is entered, the declarations are elaborated and the declared entities are brought into existence. Next, the statement sequence is executed. Finally, when control reaches the **end** (or when exit is made by other means, such as a **goto** or a **return**), the declared entities are deleted.

The main advantage of a block statement is that it allows a program to introduce variables and other entities at the precise place where they are needed. For example, one was used in Section 8.17 for introducing an exception and its related handler. A simpler example is one for interchanging the values of two variables x and y of type any:

```
declare                   -- enter the block
   temp : any;            -- declare a local variable
begin
   temp := x;             -- swap x and y
   x := y;
   y := temp;
end;                      -- leave the block
```

The point is that the variable temp is introduced especially for the purpose of swapping x and y. It is created when the block is entered; it is deleted when the block is left; and it cannot be referred to from anywhere else. Thus, block statements support the general principle that variables and other resources should be available only at the place where they are needed, and that they should be protected against interference from other parts of a program.

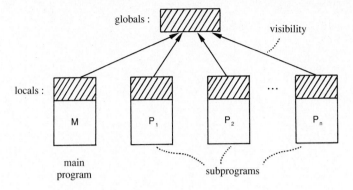

Figure 10-1   A 'flat' program structure

This very precise positioning of declarations can be overdone, of course, resulting in code that is unduly cluttered and difficult to follow. Why write seven lines when three will do? In any case, it is arguable that since a block statement is equivalent to a procedure, it would be better to define the procedure separately and reduce the statement itself to a one-line procedure call. This sort of reasoning explains why block statements were omitted from Pascal. Nevertheless, for declaring exceptions, dynamic arrays, and other such entities, they can prove very useful; and, since they fit naturally into the block-structured framework, there is much to be said for retaining them.

In languages such as FORTRAN (in all its varieties), the block structure is very limited. The subprograms have a 'flat' structure, as illustrated in Figure 10-1. The main program M has a set of subprograms P_1, P_2, ... P_n, with no further structure imposed on them. Each unit has its own set of local variables and all units have access to a common set of global variables. Any unit can call any subprogram, with the important proviso that in most such languages recursion is forbidden. The language C is an exception in this respect.

By contrast, a fully *block-structured language* is one in which blocks can be nested within blocks to arbitrary depth. The main program can declare subprograms; subprograms can declare sub-subprograms; and so on. Any unit can include a block statement, and any block statement can include other blocks. The result is a hierarchy of blocks, as illustrated in Figure 10-2. Compared with the 'flat' approach, the essential difference is that each unit can have its own local subprograms. P_3, for example, has subprograms P_{31} and P_{32} that are not available to M, P_1, or P_2. The details will be described more fully in the next section. The important advantage is that this more structured approach gives the user better facilities for dividing a program into separate, self-contained parts.

10.3   SCOPES AND LIFETIMES

It is important to appreciate that program modules have two distinct but complementary roles to play. One operates at the static level, being concerned with the grouping of resources in the program text and with the sharing and hiding of resources among different parts of a program. The other operates at the dynamic level, being concerned

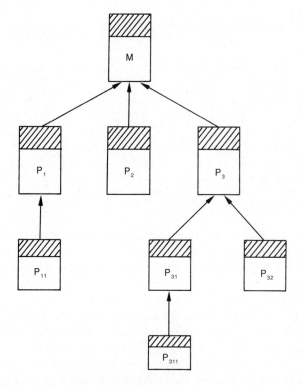

Figure 10-2   A block-structured program

with the run-time actions and the general flow of control. This section illustrates these roles by examining two particular concepts — the static concept of scopes and the dynamic concept of lifetimes. It discusses them with reference to the modules of a conventional block-structured language as described above. Later sections explore the ways in which this classical framework can be modified in order to handle other requirements.

The *scope* of a declaration is a purely textual concept, being the region of text in which the declared identifier refers to its associated entity. For example, the scope of the declaration

        x : integer;

is the region of text in which x refers to the integer variable. Throughout this region, the variable is said to be *visible*; outside the region, it either ceases to exist or it is *invisible*. If it exists but is invisible, it is said to be *hidden*.

In a block-structured language, the basic rule is that the scope of the declaration is the block in which it occurs. This has to be qualified in two ways. The first concerns earlier declarations in the same block. In ALGOL 60, the scope includes *all* the declarations: they can all refer to each other regardless of the order in which they are written. In later languages such as Pascal and Ada, the earlier declaration are excluded: the scope of x extends forwards but not backwards. In practical terms, this means that a name cannot be used until it has been declared. The rule is important for the elaboration of a sequence such as:

```
n : integer := 100;
n_squared : integer := n * n;
```

It is also helpful to one-pass compilers, and even to the human reader. However, it causes trouble when two subprograms A and B are mutually recursive, each referring to the other. Like two over-polite people entering a room, each requires the other to go first. To get round this difficulty, Pascal provides a 'forward' declaration. For example:

> **procedure** A (*formal parameters*); **forward**;
> **procedure** B (*formal parameters*); **forward**;

This can be followed by the complete definitions of A and B, except that their formal parameters are not repeated. A similar device is available in Ada, being a special case of the principle that the specification of a unit can be given separately from its full definition (see Section 9.2):

> **procedure** A (*formal parameters*);
> **procedure** B (*formal parameters*);

The use of the semicolon instead of **is** indicates that the full definitions will follow later. They have to repeat the procedure headings, including the formal parameters.

The second qualification concerns sub-blocks in which the name x is redeclared. In some languages the scope of the old x has to exclude the scope of the new one. The new meaning of x hides the old one, making it invisible. In Ada, though, it is possible to access the old x by means of an *expanded* name, as in the following example:

```
outer:                                  -- start of outer block
    declare
        x : integer;                    -- outer x
    begin
        x := 1;
    inner:                              -- start of inner block
        declare
            i : integer := x + 2;       -- the outer x
            x : integer := 3;           -- a new, inner x
            y : integer := x + 4;       -- the inner x
        begin
            y := outer.x + x;           -- outer x + inner x
        end inner;
        x := 5;                         -- the outer x
    end outer;
```

Here x is declared as an integer variable in block outer and as a real variable in block inner. Just prior to its redeclaration, it still refers to the former, but for the rest of block inner it refers to the latter. To refer to the former from inside inner, Ada provides the expanded name outer.x. A similar notation applies to identifiers of any program unit: their expanded form overrides any new meaning that might otherwise be given to them within textually nested subunits. With ordinary blocks the reverse is not possible: it is no use trying to refer to inner.x from block outer. However, there are other modules for which this *is* possible, as described in later sections.

The *lifetime* of an entity is the duration of its existence. It begins when the entity is created and ends when it is deleted. The term is not used so commonly as 'scope', but it represents an important concept and is related to scopes in a significant way. In practice, it normally refers to objects such as variables or constants that occupy storage space. The creation of the object means that storage is allocated to it, and its deletion means that the space is released for other purposes. There are three basic strategies for determining when these events should occur:

1.   *Static*. Storage is allocated to the object on a fixed, permanent basis and so the object exists throughout the execution of the program.

2.   *Automatic*. Storage is allocated when the object is declared and is released when execution of the associated block is complete.

3.   *Controlled*. Storage is allocated and released under the control of the program, by means of explicit operators such as **allocate** and **free**.

The terminology is taken from PL/I. We shall consider each method in turn.

The *static* method is the simplest, safest, and most efficient, being used by languages such as BASIC and FORTRAN to the exclusion of all else. It is normally associated with the 'flat' structure depicted in Figure 10-1. The shaded areas correspond to storage that is fixed at compile-time, not only for the common set of global variables, but also for the parameters and local variables of each subprogram. This is very inflexible and rules out some important programming facilities, including dynamic arrays and recursive procedures. On the other hand, it allows a procedure to retain its local variables from one activation to the next, which can occasionally be useful (see below).

The *automatic* method is the one used by conventional, block-structured languages of the ALGOL family. An object is brought into existence as soon as it is declared (though possibly with an undefined value — see Section 7.6), and continues to exist as long as its associated block is being executed. It is deleted when the block is finally left. Thus its lifetime is co-extensive with the execution of its block. For objects declared in the main program this is equivalent to the static method; but for those declared in inner blocks the implementation is rather more elaborate. As shown in Chapter 12, it is based on the use of a stack and, with sufficient care by the compiler, the extra costs can be kept quite low. Not surprisingly, the stack takes recursion in its stride.

In spite of its name the *controlled* method is dangerous. It allows the program to refer to objects before they have been created, or after they have been deleted, and it is much the most expensive to implement. However, it is useful for creating linked data structures and for certain other purposes where the amount of storage is unpredictable. Its uses and its implementation will both be described in Volume II.

Lifetimes are related to scopes in the sense that, if an object is visible, we may reasonably expect it to exist. We do not want ghosts, mirages, or hallucinations! For a static object this is easily guaranteed, since it exists permanently. With the automatic, block-structured approach it is also guaranteed: the object exists for the duration of its block and this is precisely the area in which it is visible (though the use of procedures complicates the situation — see Exercise 3). But for controlled objects, as already noted, there are no safeguards at all: scopes and lifetimes are divorced from each other and so references to non-existent objects become a serious hazard.

With the automatic, block-structured approach visible objects are guaranteed to exist, but the converse does not apply: existing objects are not guaranteed to be visible. This holds true even when expanded names are allowed. For example, consider the following block with its two procedures P and Q:

```
declare

    procedure Q is
    begin
        . . .                   -- P's local variable is invisible
    end Q;

    procedure P is
        x : integer;
    begin
        x := 1;                 -- P's local variable is visible
        Q;                      -- P calls Q
        x := 2;
    end P;

begin
    P;                          -- main block calls P
    Q;                          -- main block calls Q
end;
```

P has a local variable x which is visible to P but not to Q. So, when P calls Q, it becomes temporarily invisible even though it continues to exist. This, of course, is highly desirable: after all, when Q is later called from the main block, x no longer exists.

The conventional block-structured approach safeguards the programmer from referring to non-existent objects. However, there are other respects in which it is less satisfactory. In particular, it has the effect that objects declared in the main program are visible to everything else. In other words, the outermost block is totally unprotected: every sub-sub-sub-sub-block, however small and insignificant, has free access to all its variables. In terms of a human organization, this means that every member of the staff can raid the boss's filing cabinet! It is a very lax system and one that can lead to serious trouble. For example, in a large project, someone might use a variable called p in a block B, having mistakenly failed to declare it. Unknown to them, there is another variable called p in an enclosing block. So the block B unintentionally alters this other variable and the program continues blithely on its way. The results can be very mystifying.

A second problem concerns *own* variables. These are local variables of a procedure that retain their values from one call of the procedure to the next. In the static approach they do this anyhow. But with the automatic, block-structured approach local variables are deleted on exit and recreated when the procedure is next entered. To provide the option of retention ALGOL 60 allowed them to be designated as **own** (hence the name). However, the details raised some awkward problems of interpretation and so the idea was not generally adopted (see Exercise 4). In the absence of any other facility, the only alternative is to declare the variables in an outer block — even though the outer block never needs them. As with the previous problem, this cuts across the basic principle that objects should not be visible to modules that do not need them. It showed up the inadequacy of classical block structuring and helped to motivate the search for modules that are more flexible.

10.4 PACKAGES

In order to allow greater flexibility in the sharing and hiding of resources, several other language constructs have been designed. Their common feature is that they allow a group of facilities to be formed into a module that interfaces with the environment in a strictly controlled way.

In Ada the module is called a *package*. Here is an example that simply declares a collection of variables:

```
package group is
    i, j : integer := 0;
    A : array (1..10) of real;
end group;
```

This combines i, j, and A into a single unit called group, which is similar to an ordinary record. Its components can be referred to as group.i, group.j and group.A. Alternatively, following the declaration

```
use group;
```

they can be written simply as i, j, and A.

There is little merit in all this. The package wraps things up and the **use** clause unwraps them: but why bother with the wrappings at all? The advantages begin to emerge with the introduction of subprograms. At this point the definition of the package splits into two parts, known as the *specification* and the *body*. The former tells the outside world what the package has to offer — the types, variables, procedures, and so on; the latter describes how they are implemented. The separation of the two aspects supports several important principles of program design, including data abstraction (see next section) and independent compilation.

To illustrate the concept we shall take the random number generator that was first considered in Section 9.4 and shall put it in a package called ran_pack. The following specification states that the package contains a function seed for initializing the numbers and a function random for producing them. It also gives the constants that are used by the algorithm:

```
package ran_pack is
    procedure seed (z : integer);
    function random return real;
    a : constant integer := 421;
    b : constant integer := 2113;
    m : constant integer := 10000;
end ran_pack;
```

(For a discussion of the choice of constants, see Exercise 5.) The package body now gives the details of how seed and random are implemented:

```
package body ran_pack is

    x : integer;                              -- an "own" variable

    procedure seed (z : integer) is
    begin
        x := (abs z) mod m;
    end seed;

    function random return real is
    begin
        x := (a * x + b) mod m;
        return real(x) / real(m);
    end random;

begin
    x := 4321;                                -- default seed
end ran_pack;
```

The package not only groups the resources into a single, identifiable unit, but also allows the unit to use its own working variables. This is exemplified by the variable x, which is local to the package body. When the package declaration is elaborated, x is created and the statement part of the package body is executed, giving it an initial value of 4321. Subsequently, it retains its value between successive calls of seed and random, exactly as required, and it is not deleted until the execution of the enclosing block is complete. The important point is that, since it is local to the package body, it is hidden from outside interference — a technique known as *data encapsulation* or *information hiding*. The package can be contrasted with the original version of the function random as given in Section 9.4. Ideally, x should have been an 'own' variable of the function, as described at the end of the previous section. But it had to be implemented as a global variable instead, and this made it visible to all the calling routines. The package version is very much better in this respect, allowing 'own' variables to be shared by a group of related procedures in a safe and flexible way.

This shows how a package specification enables the programmer to list those entities that are to be visible to the outside world. However, it does not solve the converse problem — saying which entities of the outside world are to be visible to the package. One possibility, as found in the modules of Modula-2 (and also in some assembly languages), is to assume that all global entities are invisible to a package unless otherwise stated. The package then has to list the ones that it wants to use. Ada's packages have no facility of this kind: global entities are always visible. The preliminary definition allowed the range of visibility to be restricted; but this feature was dropped in the revision.

Packages are useful not only as units for grouping logically related resources but also as units for separate compilation. For top-down development the technique is to give the package specification and then to write:

```
package body some_pack is separate;
```

This treats the body as a 'stub' that is to be developed later. For bottom-up development the package is written and compiled first. It can then be made available to another unit by means of the **with** clause:

```
with some_pack;
procedure main is ...
```

Ada's standard input/output facilities are provided in this way:

package text_io;	— for input/output of text;
package sequential_io;	— for sequential files;
package direct_io;	— for direct access files.

An installation can provide libraries of other packages for various fields of applications — statistics, financial modeling, and so on. This extends the traditional concept of a sub-routine library in a very powerful way.

A further feature of Ada's packages is that they can be generic. As explained in Section 9.5, this means that they can be instantiated for a variety of data types, making them considerably more versatile. The concept will be considered further, along with several examples, in Section 10.7.

10.5 ABSTRACT DATA OBJECTS

Abstraction is concerned with separating the essential features of an idea from the concrete details of its specific instances. In abstract art, for example, an artist chooses to express the primary theme by deliberately divorcing it from its usual, recognizable form. The message comes across: 'This is what matters — forget the rest'.

When this principle is applied to data structures or data types it leads to a very important technique called *data abstraction*. The basic question is this: what are the essential features of a data structure or data type, and what are its secondary, incidental details? The answer was given in Section 4.1, where the concept of a type was first discussed. According to the view presented there, the essential features of a type are its values and the operations that can be applied to them. The secondary details are its representation and other aspects of its implementation. On this basis, a program that uses the type should be provided with a specification of the operations and should interact with the data only via those operations. It should then work correctly with any implementation of the type that satisfies the specifications and behaves in the required way.

The idea is familiar enough for types that are defined by a high-level programming language. For example, the type integer is used with no concern about the way in which integers are represented or processed. As long as the arithmetic is done correctly, programs should be able to run on any machine for which the language is available. In practice, of course, the range of integers is a limitation that varies from one machine to another and so, to that extent, the abstraction is not complete. Even so, the intention is clearly there.

More recently, programming languages have been designed that allow programmers to implement data abstractions of their own. The required facilities are embodied in a module known variously as a *class*, *cluster*, *capsule*, or some such, and its essential role is to do two things. On the one hand, it must enable programmers to define a new type in terms of the operations that are applicable to it. On the other hand, it must enable them to protect the implementation from other forms of access. The operations must be visible to the user; their implementation must be hidden. But this, of course, is familiar territory. Grouping concepts and hiding information — that is what packages are designed for! It follows that a class, cluster, capsule, or whatever, can be regarded as a special kind of package. Conversely, a well-designed packaging facility should be able to handle data abstraction.

This section examines a rather limited form of data abstraction — the *abstract data object* (ADO). As its name implies, it is concerned with abstraction for a single object, rather than a whole class of objects. The usual example is a stack, which illustrates the concept very nicely. However, in order to introduce some variety we shall develop a different example, based on Josephus' problem. This problem was presented earlier as an exercise in specification (Exercise 7.15), but its details are worth repeating.

> Some condemned criminals are made to stand in a circle, awaiting their execution. They are numbered 1, 2, ... n around the circle and a number k ($1 \leq k \leq n$) is then announced. Starting with criminal k, the executioner shoots every kth criminal, working round the circle and ignoring the gaps that are created, until only one remains. As a display of mercy, this last one is spared. A program is required which, given n and k, will determine the number of the survivor.

The problem can be solved by simulation. The program sets up a circle of prisoners and simulates the executions, one by one, until the final survivor is determined.

The ADO is the circle of prisoners and so the main design issue is to choose the set of operations that are to be performed on it. These can be pitched at various levels. At one extreme there could be a single operation, Josephus (n, k), that solves the entire problem. This is so abstract that it expresses nothing at all — rather like ultra-abstract art — and so it can be discarded as useless. At the other extreme there could be a set of low-level operations effectively defining the representation. However, this would defeat the purpose of abstraction by involving the user in matters of implementation; so it can be discarded too. The need is for something in between, a set of operations that separate essential features from secondary details. There is room for considerable debate about what constitutes the best selection, but here at any rate is one possibility:

insert (x)	— insert number x at the current position
advance (k)	— advance the current position by k places
current	— return the number in the current position
delete	— delete the number in the current position

These all involve the notion of a 'current position', which corresponds to the executioner aiming at a particular victim. The details need to be carefully spelt out, especially for insert and delete; but as a rough cut at the operations, this will do. Incidentally, it will be noticed that abstraction has been applied to some of the words that are involved. In particular, 'criminals' have become 'numbers' and 'shoot' has been sanitized to 'delete'. This smacks of the technique used by generals and politicians to describe casualties in war. If the ADO is to be of wider use, the abstraction has an obvious advantage. From the human angle, though, it could be regarded with some misgivings.

To implement the ADO in Ada the first step is to list the above operations in a package specification:

```
package circle_of_integers is
    procedure insert (x : integer);
    procedure advance (k : natural);
    procedure delete;
    function current return integer;
    empty_circle : exception;
end circle_of_integers;
```

The empty_circle exception is raised by advance, current, and delete if they are applied to an empty circle, and it should be regarded as an essential part of the abstraction. Admittedly, a correct solution to Josephus' problem will never need it; but it can be useful for trapping errors, and in other applications it may even have a more positive role to play.

The following version of the main program assumes that the package is provided separately. The initial **with** clause makes it available. The **use** clause avoids the need to qualify insert, advance, and so forth, by the package name:

```
with circle_of_integers; use circle_of_integers;
procedure Josephus (n, k : natural) is
begin
    for crim in 1..n loop          -- form the circle
        insert (crim);
    end loop;                      -- current position is n
    advance (k);                   -- aim at criminal k
    for i in 1..n-1 loop
        delete;                    -- shoot
        advance (k);
    end loop;
    write "the survivor is " current;
exception
    when empty_circle =>
        write "this should not occur!";
end Josephus;
```

As long as the operations behave in the required way, this provides a straightforward solution to Josephus' problem.

It is worth noting that the ADO itself does not appear as an argument of its operations. The reason is that the **use** clause makes this redundant. If the **use** clause were omitted an operation such as insert (crim) would have to be expanded to

```
circle_of_integers.insert (crim);
```

The ADO would then appear as a sort of prefixed argument. But since only one circle is involved, there is no ambiguity about the argument and so the simpler, more convenient notation is sufficient.

The next step in developing the ADO is to define the operations more precisely. In Volume II some techniques will be presented for specifying them algebraically, but for the time being a less formal description will have to do. The most important point is that the current position must be correctly set by each of the operations. In particular, insert (x) must insert x immediately after the current position and then advance the current position to x. Conversely, delete must delete the current element and then move the current position back one place. (Thus insert (x) followed by delete has a null effect.) If the circle is empty, the current position becomes undefined: insert treats this as a special case and the others raise the empty_circle exception.

The final step is to implement the ADO by choosing a representation and devising suitable algorithms for the operations. A simple representation for the circle of integers is an array. It is not ideal because it imposes a limit on the size of the circle; but it is typical of the compromises that are often made. To make the limit more explicit, we shall include it as a constant max_size in the package specification, together with an exception for when it is exceeded:

```
max_size : constant natural := 100;
full_circle : exception;
```

In the following version the variable size gives the number of items in the circle, these being held in the array elements A(0) to A(size−1). The variable pos gives the current position. Since it lies in the range 0..size−1, it can be moved around the circle by means of arithmetic modulo size (see Exercise 4.3):

```
package body circle_of_integers is

    subtype index is integer range 0..max_size−1;
    A : array (index) of integer;        -- the circle
    size : natural;                      -- the number of items
    pos : index;                         -- the current position

    -- assert (size = 0 ∧ pos = 0) ∨
    --            (size in 1..max_size ∧ pos in 0..size−1)

    procedure insert (x : integer) is
        -- insert x following pos and advance pos to x
    begin
        if size = max_size then          -- no more room
            raise full_circle;
        end if;
        if size > 0 then                 -- create a gap
            pos := pos + 1;
            A(pos+1..size) := A(pos..size−1);
        end if;
        A(pos) := x;
        size := size + 1;
    end insert;

    procedure advance (k : natural) is
        -- advance pos k places round the circle
    begin
        if size = 0 then                 -- nothing there
            raise empty_circle;
```

```
        else
            pos := (pos + k) mod size;
        end if;
    end advance;

    procedure delete is
        -- delete the item at pos and move pos back one place
    begin
        if size = 0 then                        -- nothing to delete
            raise empty_circle;
        end if;
        size := size - 1;
        if size > 0 then                        -- close the gap
            A(pos..size-1) := A(pos+1..size);
            pos := (pos - 1) mod size;
        end if;
    end delete;

    function current return integer is
        -- return the current element
    begin
        if size = 0 then                        -- nothing there
            raise empty_circle;
        else
            return A(pos);
        end if;
    end current;

begin                                           -- initialize
    size := 0;
    pos := 0;
end circle_of_integers;
```

An important feature of the package is the statement sequence enclosed between the concluding **begin ... end**. It is optional: that is to say, the **begin** and the statement sequence can be omitted. But if present, it is executed when the package is declared, allowing the ADO to be initialized. In this case it consists of two assignments that could equally well have been made in the declarations of size and pos. For data structures that cannot be initialized by the declarations, its role is more critical.

A final comment concerns the correctness of the implementation. For example, the code for insert does not assign a value to pos in the case where size = 0; so what can be said about pos at that point? More generally, what can be said about all the variables? The answer is given by the assertion that follows the declaration of the variables:

```
--    assert (size = 0 ∧ pos = 0) ∨
--                (size in 1..max_size ∧ pos in 0..size-1)
```

When size = 0 this asserts that pos = 0 also; otherwise pos is in the range 0 .. size−1. It is called an *invariant* of the representation (Hoare, 1972) and is the ADO equivalent of the invariants that were used earlier for loops and recursive functions. To prove that the implementation is correct, the strategy is to show that the invariant is established by the initialization and preserved by each of the operations. The former is usually trivial; the latter can be done by standard proof techniques. The terms of the formal specification are then mapped into expressions within the representation and, using the invariant, the required relations are verified.

10.6 ABSTRACT DATA TYPES

An abstract data object (ADO) is a single data object on which certain specified operations can be performed. By contrast, an *abstract data type* (ADT) defines a whole class of such objects. It provides a type that can be used in the same way as any other type. In particular, this means that the program can have variables of that type, arrays with elements of that type, records with components of that type, and so on. Furthermore, the resulting objects can be passed around by means of assignments and can be used as parameters of subprograms. ADTs are therefore much more flexible than one-off ADOs. Their only drawback is that, for simple ADO purposes, their definition, initialization, and usage tend to be less convenient.

As an example, we shall develop the circle_of_integers package a stage further. For Josephus' problem, one circle is enough; but if several circles were needed it would be better to introduce a new data type for the purpose. The following package specification calls it int_circle:

```
package circle_of_integers is
    type int_circle is private;
    max_size : constant natural := 100;
    procedure insert (C : int_circle; x : integer);
    procedure advance (C : int_circle; k : natural);
    function current (C : int_circle) return integer;
    procedure delete (C : int_circle);
    empty_circle, full_circle : exception;
private
    . . .
end circle_of_integers;
```

This makes the type int_circle visible to the user, along with its associated operations. Following the declaration

```
use circle_of_integers;
```

it is now possible to declare three circles of integers simply by writing:

```
C1, C2, C3 : int_circle;
```

Apart from the inclusion of int_circle, the main difference in the specification is that the four operations all have to be given an extra int_circle parameter. This is necessary because there is no longer a unique int_circle object and so the operations have to say which one is required. For example:

```
insert  (C1,  crim);
advance  (C2,  10);
delete  (C3);
```

This is a little less convenient than for the ADO, but not a serious hardship.
    As usual, the line

type int_circle **is private**;

states that objects of type int_circle are subject to the three standard operations of '=', '≠',
and assignment. To prohibit these, it could be **limited private** instead. Informally, the
term **private** suggests that any information about the representation of int_circle is hidden
from the user. However, there is a third party that certainly *does* need to know something
about it, namely the compiler. In particular, when the compiler creates int_circle objects,
it must know how much storage to allocate for them. Since the specification has to supply all the information that is needed for separate compilation, Ada adds an extra component especially for the compiler's benefit. As indicated in the above example, it is
inserted just prior to the concluding **end**. It begins with the word **private** and is therefore
known as the specification's *private part*. Its basic role is to provide the type definitions
that the compiler needs to know, but it may in fact contain other declarations as well. In
the case of int_circle, for example, it could go as follows:

```
private
    subtype index is integer range 0..max_size−1;
    type int_circle is
        record
            size : natural := 0;              -- current  size
            pos : index := 0;                 -- current  position
            A : array (index) of integer;     -- the  elements
        end record;
```

Using this information, the compiler would allocate each int_circle object enough storage
for holding size, pos, and A.
    The information in the private part is available to the compiler and to the package
body, but not to the user program. If it were necessary to hide the representation more
completely, an access type could be used instead (effectively a pointer):

```
private
    type hidden_type;
    type int_circle is access hidden_type;
```

Ada allows hidden_type to be specified in the package body. So, at the cost of an extra
indirection, the representation can be relegated to the package body. In Modula-2 all data
abstraction is done in this way, using the extra pointer. Since the change is limited to the
private part, it might be thought that it does not affect the abstraction. However, this is
not the case: the introduction of the pointer affects the behavior of the ADT under assignment and equality (see Exercise 9).
    Inside the package body there is no longer any need to declare size, pos, and A as
local variables. Instead, they have to be accessed as fields of the int_circle parameters —
in this case, the parameter C. For example, here is the revised version of advance:

```
procedure advance (C : int_circle; k : natural) is
begin
    if C.size = 0 then
        raise empty_circle;
    else
        C.pos := (C.pos + k) mod C.size;
    end if;
end advance;
```

A final problem concerns initialization. The concluding statement sequence of the package body is not executed for each object that is created and so it cannot be used for initializing them. Initial values can be set for fields of records in the type definition, as in the above example; but anything more complicated would have to be done by means of a special initializing procedure.

The example of int_circle does not show ADTs to their full advantage. As a better demonstration of their potential, here is the specification of a simplified package for doing complex arithmetic. The ADT is called complex and the main operations are '+' and '*'. The package also provides constants for zero and i (the square root of -1):

```
package complex_arithmetic is
    type complex is private;
    zero, i : constant complex;

    function "+" (z1, z2 : complex) return complex;
    function "+" (z1 : complex; x : float) return complex;
    function "+" (x : float; z2 : complex) return complex;

    function "*" (z1, z2 : complex) return complex;
    function "*" (z1 : complex; x : float) return complex;
    function "*" (x : float; z2 : complex) return complex;

    function real_part (z : complex) return float;
    function imag_part (z : complex) return float;

private
    type complex is
        record
            real, imag : float;
        end record;
    zero : constant complex := (0.0, 0.0);
    i : constant complex := (0.0, 1.0);
end complex;
```

Some features of particular interest are the multiple versions of '+' and '*', and the definition of zero and i as *deferred constants*. The constants are visible to the user, but their values have to be given in terms of the implementation and so they are deferred to the private part. Using this package, a program can declare:

```
a, sum : complex := zero;
Z : array (1..n) of complex;
```

It can then do things like:

```
a := 3.5 * i + 2.5;
for i in 1..n loop
    sum := sum + Z(i);
end loop;
```

It can also pass complex numbers as parameters to subprograms and receive them back as the results of functions. In short, they are treated as 'first class citizens'. With a suitably extended package they would appear exactly as if they were a standard, predefined type. Languages that provide facilities of this kind are known as *extensible languages*.

10.7 GENERICS

The abstraction of the type circle_of_integers is helpful as far as it goes, but its potential usefulness can be greatly increased by taking it one step further and defining the pure concept of a circle. In this more abstract version, the type of the elements is relegated to a secondary feature that can vary from one instance to another. Indeed, the idealized circle is so abstract that it never actually exists. Each instance has to be a circle of *something*; so one may be a circle of integers, another a circle of people, another a circle of stones, and so on.

In Ada, abstractions of this kind are provided by the *generic* facility ('generic' = general, not specific or special). This was described in the previous chapter, where it was used as a mechanism for allowing types to be parameters of subprograms. For example, a generic swap procedure expressed the abstract idea of swapping the values of two variables, independently of their type (see Section 9.5). The same technique can be used for packages, where its application is one of the key features of Ada's philosophy. By way of practical example, it was used at the end of the previous chapter as a means of generating stacks for elements of some arbitrary type T:

```
package stack is new stack_pack (T);
```

The result was an ADO for elements of type T, with operations load, unload, and empty. This section explains how such packages are written, taking stack_pack as its example.

As with subprograms the specification begins with a generic part, listing the factors that are to be 'genericized'. These constitute the generic formal parameters and in the case of stack_pack there is only one of them — the type of the elements. The rest of the specification follows the standard form:

```
generic
    type element is private;           -- the generic type
package stack_pack is
    procedure load (x : in element);
    procedure unload (x : out element);
    function empty return boolean;
    underflow : exception;
end stack_pack;
```

This introduces element as a generic formal type and specifies it as **private**, meaning (as usual) that it is subject to assignments and equality tests. It then lists the required operations, using the generic type element for the parameters of load and unload, and concludes with the underflow exception.

The package body is written in exactly the same way as for an ordinary ADO. Here is its outline:

```
package body stack_pack is

    ...                       -- declaration of local entities

    procedure load (x : in element) is
    begin
        ...                   -- implementation of load
    end load;

    procedure unload (x : out element) is
    begin
        ...                   -- implementation of unload
    end unload;

    function empty return boolean is
    begin
        ...                   -- implementation of empty
    end empty;

begin
    ...                       -- initialize to empty
end stack_pack;
```

Since the stack is unbounded, having no maximum size and no overflow exception, an appropriate implementation would be a linked list. Further details are given in Volume II.

Suppose now that a data type has been declared called plate. To create a stack of plates, a particular version of the package is instantiated with plate as the actual type:

```
package plate_stack is new stack_pack (plate);
```

A plate variable p can then be used in statements such as:

```
plate_stack.load (p);
while not plate_stack.empty loop
    plate_stack.unload (p);
    ...
end loop;
```

As usual, the declaration **use** plate_stack would allow the prefix plate_stack to be omitted.

To convert the generic ADO to a generic ADT, the strategy is the same as in the previous section — introduce the abstract type stack (say) and add a parameter of that type to each of the operations:

```
generic
    type element is private;
package stack_adt is
    type stack is limited private;
    procedure load (S : in out stack; x : in element);
    procedure unload (S : in out stack; x : out element);
    function empty (S : in stack) return boolean;
    underflow : exception;
private
    ...                        -- the representation
end stack_adt;
```

To create stacks for plates the first step is to instantiate the required type:

```
package stack_of_plates is new stack_adt (plate);
use stack_of_plates;
```

The stacks can then be declared:

```
S1, S2 : stack;
```

Finally, they have to be initialized. As explained in the previous section, the **private** part of the specification can include some initialization by giving values to fields of a record. However, the statement sequence at the end of the package body is not executed for each object and so, if further initialization is required, a special procedure, init say, has to be defined and called. This has the advantage that the calling program can provide the initial values:

```
S1.init ( ... );
S2.init ( ... );
```

The three-stage process — instantiation, declaration, initialization — shows once again that it is easier to work with Ada's ADOs than with Ada's ADTs. The ADOs are therefore preferable if only one or two objects are needed. In other more object-oriented languages, the ADT option is often the only one provided, but it is correspondingly easier to use.

If a generic formal type requires other operations besides '=', '≠', and assignment, the specification **private** can be replaced by one of the alternatives listed in Section 9.5. For example, if the type index were to be used for indexing arrays, it would have to be specified as a discrete type:

```
type index is (<>);
```

If it also needed an addition operator this would have to be specified as an extra generic parameter:

```
type index is (<>);
with "+" (x, y : index) return index;
```

An instantiation would then have to provide two actual generic parameters — a discrete type and a function (not necessarily called '+') that operates on the type in the required way. The Ada reference manual gives a list of rules concerning the formal-actual association of generic parameters; but most of them state the obvious and so there is no advantage in repeating them here.

In conclusion, it should be pointed out that generic parameters are often plain integers or other simple, scalar values. For example, if stacks were to be implemented with a maximum size, a generic parameter max_size could be included; then each instantiation could have its own specified maximum size. The significance of this is that it allows packages to implement *dynamic* data structures — that is, structures whose size and implementation are determined at run-time. Generics make this possible even for packages that are compiled separately, thus adding further to their power and flexibility.

10.8   CLASSES, HIERARCHIES, AND INHERITANCE

As noted in Section 10.1, objects in the real world are often classified into some sort of hierarchy. They are divided into classes, with subclasses, sub-subclasses, and so on. Figure 10-3 shows a classification of this kind for drinks. The two main subclasses are alcoholic and non-alcoholic, and each of these is divided into three sub-subclasses. The classification can be continued to as many levels as necessary.

With object-oriented programming the first requirement in modeling such a hierarchy is to identify the properties that characterize the different classes. A property can be either a descriptive attribute or an operation. For example, a drink might have the attribute *quantity* and the operations of being *served* and *consumed*. An alcoholic drink also has an attribute known as its *proof* — that is, its alcoholic strength. A wine has the further attribute of its *vintage*, and a white wine needs the operation of being *chilled*. All this is indicated in the diagram of Figure 10-3.

An important feature of such hierarchies is that each class *inherits* the properties of its ancestors in the hierarchy. Thus an alcoholic drink inherits *quantity*, *serve*, and *consume*, to which it adds *proof*. A wine inherits *quantity*, *serve*, *consume*, and *proof*, to which it adds *vintage*. A white wine inherits all of these and adds *chill*.

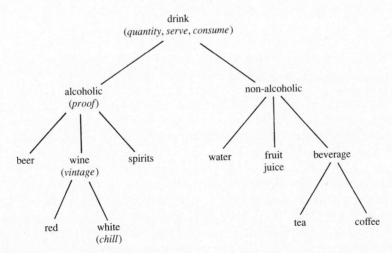

Figure 10-3   A classification of drinks

It is clear that each class can be modeled by an ADT that makes its attributes and operations visible to the user. However, in a fully object-oriented language it is desirable to have facilities that also support the modeling of class hierarchies, with particular reference to the concept of inheritance. Since such facilities are not provided by Ada, we shall illustrate them from SIMULA 67. As stated previously, this language pioneered the concepts in a remarkably elegant way.

In SIMULA 67, the relevant module is called (very appropriately) a **class**. The following is a simple example that illustrates its main features. For convenience, the comments are written in Ada's notation:

```
class A (x, y);                    -- class name
    real x, y;                     -- its formal parameters
begin
    integer i, j;                  -- its local variables
    procedure zig (g); ...         -- a local procedure
    statement_sequence             -- the class body
end;
```

This declares a class A having formal parameters x and y, local variables i and j, and a procedure zig. The parameters are 'call by value' — that is, pass-to-local-variable (see Section 9.3). Together with the local variables they constitute A's *attributes* and are accessible both to the procedure zig and to the class body. An object of class A is created by evaluating an expression of the form

$$\textbf{new} \; A \; (tic, \; tac)$$

where tic and tac are actual parameters of the appropriate type. The operator **new** creates an object with components x, y, i, and j, and initializes x and y to the values of tic and tac. It then executes the *statement_sequence*, which can be used for initializing i and j in the same way as for packages. Finally it returns a pointer to the object as its result (though see Section 10.10 for further possibilities).

The pointer can be assigned to a variable of type **ref** (A) using the symbol ':−' to denote a pointer assignment. Thus, the declaration

$$\textbf{ref} \; (A) \; p;$$

introduces a variable p for pointing to A-type objects, and the statement

$$p \; :− \; \textbf{new} \; A \; (tic, \; tac);$$

assigns it a specific object with attribute values tic and tac. Its attributes can then be referenced as p.x, p.y, p.i, and p.j, just as if they were fields of a conventional record. Furthermore, the statement p.zig (w) calls zig with the actual parameter w. Any references to x, y, i, or j within zig will then refer to the corresponding components of p's object.

A class can implement an ADT in a straightforward way. Each object of the class is initialized with the specified parameters, is represented by the local variables, and is processed by the defined procedures. The only problem is that the local variables are visible to the user and so the representation is not hidden. Some implementations provide an option for making the attributes either read-only or completely hidden. This enables the abstraction to be completed.

To support hierarchies, SIMULA 67 allows a class to be used as a *prefix* to another class. For example, the class A can be used to prefix a new class B as follows:

```
A class B (z);
    real z;
begin
    integer k;
    procedure zag (h) ... ;
    ...
end;
```

The effect is that B inherits all the attributes and operations of A. An object of class B has to be created by an operation of the form

$$\text{new B (tic, tac, toe);}$$

where tic and tac match the formal parameters of A and toe matches the extra parameter z of B. If the resulting pointer is assigned to a **ref** (B) variable q, the following features of the B-type object become accessible: the variables q.x, q.y, q.z, q.i, q.j, and q.k, and the procedures q.zig and q.zag.

Inheritance can be extended over several levels. For example, SIMULA's files have a hierarchy that is defined as follows:

```
        class file (name); ...
    file class infile; ...
    file class outfile; ...
outfile class printfile; ...
```

Every file has a name and some related attributes such as a buffer; it also has standard operations such as open and close. An infile object has additional operations for reading data and for testing the end-of-file condition. An outfile object has operations for writing data; its subclass printfile has operations for controlling lines and pages.

Suppose now that the classes A, B, C, and D have the following simple hierarchy:

Suppose further that the following declarations provide variables a, b, c, and d for accessing members of each class:

```
ref (A) a;
ref (B) b;
ref (C) c;
ref (D) d;
```

The question arises: what values can be assigned to these variables? The basic principle is that a variable can be assigned objects from its own class or from any of its descendant classes. Thus a can be assigned objects from A, B, C, and D, and b can be assigned objects from B, C, and D. The following assignments are therefore legal:

> a :– b;
> a :– c;
> b :– d;

On the other hand, the assignment

> c :– d;

is illegal, because D-class objects cannot belong to C. The case

> c :– b;

is less clear-cut. The point is that b's object might belong to B, C, or D, and if it happens to belong to C the assignment should be allowed. This suggests that the assignment should be subject to a run-time check on b's class. To make this explicit, SIMULA requires it to be written in the form:

> c :– b **qua** C;

In general, an expression of the form p **qua** X must be used whenever the class of p is an ancestor of the class X that the context requires. If the check fails there is a run-time report. To check the class more cautiously, SIMULA provides the tests p **is** B and p **in** B. The former requires p's object to be of class B but not C or D; the latter allows any of them. There is also a special form of conditional statement:

> **inspect** p
> > **when** C **do** *statement_1*
> > **when** D **do** *statement_2*
> > **otherwise** *statement_3*

This tests for p **in** C and then p **in** D before settling for the default. In Smalltalk the variables are not typed: they can be assigned any value and so the problems do not arise.

   An important feature is that a class can specify one or more of its operations as being **virtual**. This means that the operation is common to all the members of the class but that each of the subclasses uses a different implementation. The full definition is therefore given separately for each class at the lower levels. When the operation is applied to a specific object, the system scans the hierarchy, starting at the object's class and working upwards, until it finds a definition. For example, the class file specifies that open and close are **virtual**. It provides a basic version for itself, but infile and outfile define more extensive versions as required by their specific devices. In Smalltalk, all operations are treated in this way and every application of an operation involves a search of this kind. As with the untyped variables, this adds considerably to the run-time overheads.

10.9   SEMICOROUTINES

It is time now to look at modules that provide greater power over the run-time flow of control. Packages can collect resources together and restrict their availability, but as far as the flow of control is concerned, they offer nothing new: they operate only at the static level. The rest of this chapter will be concerned with modules whose effects are more

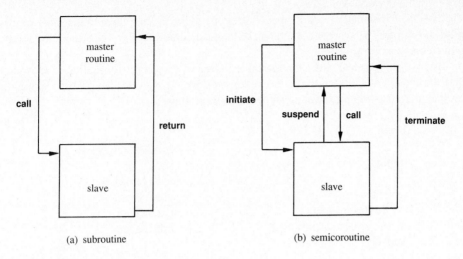

(a) subroutine   (b) semicoroutine

Figure 10-4   Calling sequences

dynamic, allowing objects to be developed into independent processes (see property 3 of Section 10.1).

As a starting point, it is relevant to note the following two rules that are obeyed by an ordinary subprogram:

1.   It must complete its task in a single call;

2.   It must return control to the calling program.

These rules give it the status of a subroutine — that is, a subordinate routine controlled by the module that defines it. As shown in Figure 10-4(a), there is a master–slave relationship between the two: the master can call the slave, but the slave cannot call the master. The slave can only complete its task and then disappear from view.

Conventional subroutines have always had this simple, straightforward, subservient role. But might there be advantages in emancipating them? The answer is: Yes, indeed! Nevertheless, it is wise to proceed in stages. So we shall begin by looking at the *semicoroutine* which, as its name implies, is only half emancipated. It can break rule 1 but not rule 2. The next section considers the full coroutine — or 'cooperating' routine — which can break rule 2 as well. In both cases we shall illustrate the concepts by means of the **class** module of SIMULA 67. Its body can be written as a coroutine and this allows the class objects to be components of a quasi-parallel system (see Section 10.11). We shall take the liberty of making some minor changes to the notation, as set out in Figure 10-5.

SIMULA Notation	Revised Notation
detach	**suspend**
call (P)	**call** P
resume (P)	**resume** P

Figure 10-5   Control operators of coroutines

The effect is to highlight the principal control operators, treating them in the same way as **goto** or **return**. The symbol **detach** has been renamed **suspend** in order to remove some of its more technical overtones.

By abolishing rule 1, the semicoroutine is free to suspend its execution at any point that it chooses; it then waits for the calling routine, or maybe some other routine, to resume it. In its simplest form, it can be written as follows:

```
class C ( ... );
    ...                            -- formal parameters
begin
    ...                            -- local variables
    statement_sequence_1;          -- initialization
    suspend;                       -- suspension
    statement_sequence_2;          -- continuation
end C;
```

An object of this class is created by the operator **new** and the resulting pointer can be assigned to a **ref** (C) variable in the usual way:

```
p :- new C ( ... );
```

As stated in the previous section, the **new** operator causes the body of C to be executed and this can be used for initializing the variables. In this case, though, execution does not go through to the end. On reaching the **suspend** command it is temporarily stopped and so p is assigned a pointer to an object that still has statements to be executed. To resume it, the calling program executes:

```
call p;
```

The body of p's object will then be resumed at the point following the **suspend**. Execution continues either until it again encounters a **suspend** or until it reaches the concluding **end**. In either case it returns control to the calling program in the traditional master–slave style, as illustrated in Figure 10-4(b).

From all this it will be seen that the execution of a semicoroutine involves four distinct operations:

1. *Initialization*. This was carried out by **new**. In some languages, though, it is done automatically when the coroutine, or coroutine object, is declared.

2. *Suspension*. This was done by **suspend**.

3. *Resumption*. The **call** mechanism is non-standard in SIMULA 67, though it is available in some versions. The more usual method is to use **resume**, as described in the next section.

4. *Termination*. This happens automatically when control reaches the **end** of the coroutine body, at which point it executes an implied **suspend**. Some systems provide an explicit command for the purpose.

Following termination any attempt to resume the coroutine will cause an error. However, the object continues to exist and its attributes can still be accessed in the normal way. It is not finally deleted until exit is made from the block in which its class is declared.

Before going any further it is worth noting the restriction on C's parameters. For procedures, SIMULA 67 allows parameters to be passed in three ways — by value, by reference, and by expression. For classes, though, they can only be passed by value. The reason for this can be seen in the following code:

```
class C (x); real x;            -- a class
    begin ... end C;
ref (C) p;                      -- a pointer
...
begin                           -- enter an inner block
    real z;                     -- a local variable
        p :- new C (z);         -- create an object
end;                            -- leave the inner block
p.x := 0;                       -- what is x?
```

Here p is assigned an object whose actual parameter z has been declared in an inner block. The question is: in the final assignment, following the inner block, what does its formal parameter x refer to? With pass-by-reference or pass-by-expression, it would refer to a variable that had ceased to exist. The only way to avoid this problem is to restrict parameters to one of the 'copy in' mechanisms.

A common application of semicoroutines is the *value-producing* routine. This is rather like a vending machine: it is switched on by the **new** button and a value can then be obtained by pressing the **call** button. A simple example is provided by our old friend the random number generator, last seen in Section 10.4. Unfortunately, because of the restriction on parameters, the values have to be assigned to a global variable. In this case it is a **real** variable called rand:

```
class random (seed);
    integer seed;
begin
    integer a, b, m, x;
    a := 421;                   -- initialization
    b := 2113;
    m := 10000;
    x := seed;
    suspend;                    -- wait for the first call
    while true do begin         -- infinite loop
        x := mod (a * x + b, m);
        rand := x / m;
        suspend;                -- deliver the value
    end;
end random;
```

The main program can declare a variable rangen of type **ref** (random) and initialize it by:

```
rangen := new random (4321);
```

This 'seeds' the generator with the number 4321. Repeated execution of

> **call** rangen

will then set rand to a series of pseudo-random numbers in the range $0 \leq \text{rand} < 1$.

As can be seen, the coroutine sits inside an endless loop, waiting at the end of each iteration for the next call. The variable x is local and retains its value between each execution of **suspend** and the subsequent call. If random were an ordinary procedure, x would not retain its value in this way and so it would have to be global. As noted earlier, this would be less secure. So here is the first advantage of the coroutine:

- It preserves the values of its working variables from one active phase to the next, without having to make them global.

Of course, as shown in Section 10.4, the package provides an alternative mechanism for the purpose. So, if this were the only advantage of coroutines, there would be little need for them. The package, being simpler, would always be preferred.

The second major advantage of the semicoroutine is that it can suspend itself at any point in its execution and be resumed later on. The benefits of this are not very great in the case of random, so let us consider an example adapted from the paper in which coroutines were first described (Conway, 1963). The problem is to devise a module that reads successive characters from input and assigns them to a variable called ch. The only catch is that any occurrence of the sequence '**' must be replaced by '↑'. The following coroutine does this very neatly:

```
class readchar;
begin
    character next;
    suspend;                          -- wait for the first call
    while true do begin               -- infinite loop
        inchar (next);
        if next = '*' then begin
            inchar (next);            -- look for '**'
            if next = '*' then
                next := '↑'           -- found
            else begin
                ch := '*';            -- not found
                suspend;              -- return '*'
            end else;
        end if;
        ch := next;
        suspend;                      -- return ch
    end;
end readchar;
```

The point of the example is that the coroutine has two **suspend** commands, each requiring different action sequences on resumption. The coroutine has no trouble in handling this, since each **suspend** command has its own resumption point. On the other hand, an ordinary procedure can only use the **return** command followed by re-entry at its start. So it would have to merge the two action sequences together and then separate them out again. This would require the setting and testing of flags (and global ones at that), all of which makes for obscurity and inefficiency. So here is the second major advantage of the semicoroutine:

- It preserves the continuity of its operation, from one active phase to the next, in the simplest and most natural way.

This second advantage shows up to even better effect if **suspend** is executed from a routine that is recursive. A typical example arises in a program that has to traverse a tree structure, applying some process to each of the nodes in turn. The standard way of doing this is to use a recursive procedure. In the following SIMULA version the tree is a conventional binary one, with each node having two branches left and right, possibly null. For the purposes of this illustration there is no need to describe it further:

```
procedure traverse (t);
    ref (tree) t;
begin
    if t =/= none then begin
        process (t);
        traverse (t.left);
        traverse (t.right);
    end;
end traverse;
```

This is all very well except that the traversal calls process as a subsidiary routine. The principle of abstraction suggests that it should be defined independently of the processing. One way of achieving this is to implement the traversal as a coroutine that suspends itself at each node, allowing the calling program to do the processing. In effect, it becomes a value-producing routine, the values being the nodes of the tree. To do this, there has to be a global variable node (say), and the statement process (t) has to be replaced by:

```
node :- t;
suspend;
```

However, **suspend** can only be done from a coroutine. The traverse procedure therefore has to be embedded in a coroutine as follows:

```
class traverser (root);             -- the coroutine
    ref (tree) root;
begin

    procedure traverse (t);         -- the recursive procedure
        ref (tree) t;
    begin
        if t =/= none then begin
            node :- t;
            suspend;                -- supply the node
```

```
                    traverse  (t.left);
                    traverse  (t.right);
              end  if;
        end  traverse;

        suspend;                       -- wait for the first call
        traverse  (root);             -- traverse the tree
        node  :-  none;               -- signal completion
    end  traverser;
```

After waiting for the first call the coroutine enters traverse (root) to do the traversal. The **suspend** commands are then executed from arbitrary levels of the recursion without affecting its overall progress. When traverse finishes the coroutine signals completion by setting node to **none** and then terminates.

To process a tree x, the calling program first creates the traverser:

```
        trav  :-  new  traverser  (x);
```

It then does:

```
        call  trav;
        while  node  =/=  none do begin
            process  (node);
            call  trav;
        end;
```

This separates the traversal from the processing in the required way. The traversal is still subsidiary to the main program. Nevertheless, from its own viewpoint it might be excused for seeing itself as the master, the main program being its slave. Its **suspend** command says: 'Deal with this value and then return control to me.' So, which one really *is* the boss?

It should be remarked that SIMULA 67 does not allow the **suspend** command (which it calls **detach**) to be executed from a procedure and so the above coroutine is illegal. The reasons for the restriction are not clear. The **resume** command, to be described next, is not restricted in this way, even though it has a very similar effect. In order to make the above technique work, we would therefore have to replace the **call–suspend** mechanism of the semicoroutine with the **resume–resume** mechanism of the full coroutine.

The traverser coroutine allows the calling program to iterate over successive nodes of the tree and is therefore known as an *iterator*. Routines of this kind are useful for almost every kind of data structure, including arrays, queues, lists, trees, and files. There are several techniques for implementing them (see Exercise 19), but semicoroutines are certainly one of the best. The only trouble is that very few languages provide them. One way of proceeding is therefore to write the coroutine and then carry out a transformation to some equivalent, non-coroutine form — rather like the recursion removal of the previous chapter. The general technique is described by M. A. Jackson (1975), who calls it 'program inversion'. As indicated in the discussion of readchar, it involves the setting and testing of flags and other variables; also the local variables may have to be turned into globals (see Exercise 16). The resulting code is messy and prone to error, but in the absence of coroutines it may have to be endured.

10.10 COROUTINES

The full coroutine — or 'cooperating' routine — is freed from both the restraints that were mentioned in the previous section. Like the semicoroutine, it can suspend its execution and be resumed later; but besides that, it can pass control to other coroutines and they in turn can resume it later. No longer does it have to report back to the master program, nor is it dependent on the master program for its resumption. So in these respects its freedom from authority is increased.

The calling scheme is illustrated in Figure 10-6, which shows a typical system consisting of a master routine and three cooperating coroutines — a total of four 'components'. The rules are as follows:

1.   Any component can initiate a new coroutine. The latter joins the system at the same level as all the others: it is a cooperating routine, not a subordinate one.

2.   Any component can resume a non-terminated coroutine, thereby suspending its own execution.

3.   A coroutine can suspend itself with control returning to the master routine.

4.   When a coroutine reaches the end of its code, its execution is terminated and control returns to the master routine. An attempt to resume it would cause an error.

If a component Q wants to pass control to a component P referenced by p, it executes the statement:

> **resume** p;

This is similar to **call** p except that, if P then does **suspend**, control does not go back to Q. Instead, it returns to the master routine. More usually, though, P will suspend itself by resuming one of the other coroutines, the general intention being that the coroutines should operate autonomously. They are responsible for resuming each other and control returns to the master routine only when some form of monitoring action is required or when the system has completed its task.

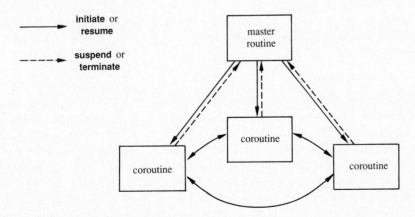

Figure 10-6   A cooperating system

As a simple example of a cooperating system, we shall develop a program to simulate n people playing a game of Greedy Pig (see Exercise 8.36). They will be numbered 1 to n and they will each be given a parameter limit that determines their playing strategy (if their score for a turn reaches the limit, they end their turn). They will also be told the number of the player to whom they should pass the dice next:

```
class play (limit, next);
    integer limit, next;
begin
    integer score;
    score := 0;                              -- initialize
    suspend;                                 -- wait for first turn
    while true do begin

        . . .                                -- play a turn
        if score ≥ 100                       -- have I won?
            then goto exit;                  -- yes!
            resume player[next];             -- no: pass the dice
    end loop;
exit :
    shout ("I've won!");
end play;                                    -- implied suspend
```

The master routine declares an array of references to the players:

```
ref (play) array player [1:n];
```

It then creates the players with the required parameters, reading the values of their limits from input:

```
for i := 1 step 1 until n do begin
    inint (limitval);
    nextval := if i < n then i + 1 else 1;
    player[i] :- new play (limitval, nextval);
end;
```

At this point the players all have zero scores and are waiting in suspense for play to begin. The master routine starts the game by resuming the first of them (or whichever one it chooses):

```
resume player[1];
```

Play continues, with each player resuming the next, until eventually one of them scores 100 and shouts 'I've won'. The **suspend** command then returns control to the master routine which must decide how to finish off.

As usual, a trivial application does not demonstrate the power of the mechanism at all adequately. In this case the program could be written equally well using semicoroutines instead. The **resume** statement inside play would be replaced by **suspend** and the master routine would resume each player in turn until one of them reached 100. The coroutines come into their own only when the master program would otherwise be very much more complicated. In such cases they offer substantial advantages by allowing the control to be decentralized. They work particularly well in simulations where there are processes of several kinds interacting in irregular fashion, and it is to this situation that we now turn.

10.11 QUASI-PARALLEL SYSTEMS

A system is *quasi-parallel* if it uses sequential processing to simulate one that is truly parallel. Such systems are commonly used for simulating real-world situations where a collection of independent objects are interacting with each other at discrete points in time. This section outlines the version that is used for this purpose in SIMULA 67. It considers it mainly from an abstract point of view, leaving aside the details of the implementation.

The basic components of a simulation are *processes* that model the real-world objects. A process in this context is an ADO whose **begin–end** code is a coroutine. This means that it is not simply a passive object whose role is to react to external operations. Instead, it has a life of its own: it executes a series of statements which, by means of **suspend** and **resume** commands, can extend over (simulated) time.

At any instant, each process will be in one of four possible states:

1. *Active*. It is the *current* process — that is, the one being executed.

2. *Scheduled*. It has executed **suspend** and its resumption has been scheduled for some specified future time.

3. *Passive*. It has executed **suspend**, but its resumption has not yet been scheduled (for example, it might be waiting in a queue).

4. *Terminated*. It has completed its execution and any attempt to resume it will cause an error.

For each active or scheduled process there is an *event notice* indicating the time for which it has been scheduled. The event notices are placed on a list, known as the *event set* (or in SIMULA 67 as the *sequencing set*), where they are held in ascending order of scheduled time. The one at the head of the list is the notice for the current process and its time is taken to be the current (simulated) time. The simulation package provides a function current that returns a pointer to this process and a function time that returns its time. The remaining notices act as a calendar of future events. The situation is illustrated in Figure 10-7, where n processes are scheduled for times $t_1, t_2, \dots t_n$ with

$$t_1 \leq t_2 \leq \dots \leq t_n$$

The first process is the active one, with t_1 being the current time; the remainder are the scheduled ones, awaiting their turn.

In SIMULA 67 the simulation package includes a class called process which provides basic facilities for this purpose. It is used as a prefix to the particular subclasses required by an application, as illustrated below. Among other things, it provides each process with a pointer to an event notice and with operations for joining and leaving queues. Although the processes are coroutines they do not explicitly execute **suspend** or **resume**. Instead, they use the scheduling facilities of the simulation package, which call **suspend** and

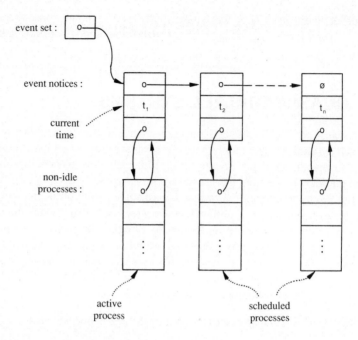

Figure 10-7   A simulation event set

resume in ways that preserve the integrity of the system. The facilities consist of five basic operations which, when executed by the currently active process, have the following effects:

passivate   Suspend the process by removing its event notice from the front of the event set. The process 'goes to sleep' and is therefore dependent on some other process to 'wake it up' by calling activate (see below). Meanwhile, the second event notice becomes the first one and its process is therefore resumed.

wait (q)   This is similar to passivate, except that the suspended process is placed at the end of the queue q. The process that wakes it up will normally be the one that is serving the queue.

hold (t)   Suspend the process and reschedule it for t time units later. As with passivate, its event notice is removed from the front of the event set; but in this case its scheduled time is increased by t and the event notice is inserted at the appropriate point further down the list.

cancel (x)   Remove the event notice of process x from the event set. (If a process cancels itself, the effect is equivalent to passivate.)

activate x ...   Schedule the process x either for immediate resumption or for action at some time in the future.

The last of these is provided by a special **activate** statement or, if x is already scheduled, by an equivalent **reactivate** statement. It has the following five versions:

> [re]**activate** x
>
> [re]**activate** x **at** t [**prior**]
>
> [re]**activate** x **delay** t [**prior**]
>
> [re]**activate** x **before** y
>
> [re]**activate** x **after** y

The parts in brackets are optional. The first version causes immediate activation and so the current process is suspended. The next two cause activation at a future time, with **delay** t being equivalent to **at** time + t. The **prior** option specifies that x is to have priority over any other processes that are already scheduled for that time. The last two versions schedule x for the same time as process y, either immediately before it or immediately after it.

As a simple application of these operations, consider customers at a small store with a single checkout point. They arrive at irregular intervals and are characterized by two parameters, shoptime and checktime, that determine the times required for choosing the goods and for paying at the checkout. This can be modeled by representing each customer as an object of class customer and the checkout as an object called checkout of class check. The latter will have an associated queue, whose type in SIMULA is denoted by **ref** (head).

The following definition of the customer process expresses the sequence of actions that a real-life customer might perform:

```
process class customer (shoptime, checktime);
    real shoptime, checktime;
begin                                   -- enter the store
    hold (shoptime);                    -- choose the goods
    if checkout.idle then               -- alert the checkout
        activate checkout after current;
    wait (checkout.queue);              -- join the queue
    out;                                -- leave the queue
    passivate;                          -- receive service
end customer;                           -- terminate
```

The hold operation suspends the process while the customer is (notionally) shopping. At the end of this period the system resumes the process, which then joins the checkout queue. Prior to joining, though, it looks to see if the checkout is 'idle' (that is, passive or terminated) and, if so, it arranges for it to be activated next. Sooner or later it reaches the front of the queue and is woken up by the checkout (see below). At this point it leaves the queue, notionally entering the checkout point, and passivates itself a second time while it is being served. When next woken, it reaches the **end** symbol and, from the definition of its parent class process, this causes it to terminate in an orderly fashion.

The checkout process, of class check, must be written in a way that interacts appropriately with this sequence of events. In a selfless dedication to duty it executes an infinite loop, serving customers if and when they arrive:

```
process class check;
begin
    ref (head) queue;                -- the head of the queue
    ref (customer) cust;             -- a customer
    queue :- new head;               -- initially empty
    while true do begin              -- an endless loop
        if queue.empty then
            passivate;               -- wait for a customer
        cust :- queue.first qua customer;
        activate cust;               -- cust leaves the queue
        hold (cust.checktime);       -- do the checking out
        activate cust;               -- cust leaves the shop
    end;
end check;
```

The process iterates around an endless loop, serving the customers in the queue. If the queue becomes empty it passivates itself and is therefore dependent on the next customer to wake it up (see above). In serving a customer it uses its variable cust to record who the customer is, assigning it the value queue.first **qua** customer — that is, a pointer to the first customer in the queue. The phrase **qua** customer is needed because, in principle, the queue could contain objects from other classes (see Section 10.8). The first **activate** allows the customer to leave the queue and the second one allows him/her to terminate. It would be simpler to keep the customer in the queue while being served; but the code divides the waiting and serving into two distinct stages in order to be more realistic.

The full simulation package provides several other facilities that are not relevant here — for example, random number generators and procedures for accumulating statistics. Its construction is very elegant, illustrating the great power of the class concept. Similar packages have been written in languages such as Ada, using facilities for parallel processing. However, this results in a certain amount of overkill. For quasi-parallel systems, where time is not real but simulated, a coroutine structure is more appropriate.

FURTHER READING

Object-oriented programming has been discussed extensively in recent literature, as witnessed by the special issue of *Byte* for August 1986 (*Byte* **11:8**). It has also been the theme of an annual OOPSLA Conference (Object-Oriented Programming Systems, Languages and Applications). The proceedings of the first two have been published in SIGPLAN Notices (Meyrowitz, 1986, 1987). A good introduction is the book by B. J. Cox (1986). Cardelli and Wegner (1985) discuss some of the issues involved and state the view that inheritance is an essential feature. Booch (1986, 1987) presents an object-oriented methodology with real-time processes but no inheritance, based on Ada. Meyer (1988) uses a language called Eiffel. The standard work on Smalltalk is Goldberg and Robson (1983); see also Kaehler and Patterson (1986) and Budd (1987). Danforth and Tomlinson (1988) give a helpful review of type theories in the context of ADTs and object-oriented programming, with special reference to inheritance.

Block structure goes back to the original ALGOL 60 Report (Naur, 1960), and is described by textbooks on programming languages. A minor variation on the ALGOL scheme is proposed by R. T. House (1986). For further discussion and criticism see Hanson (1981), Tennent (1982), Cormack (1983), and Winkler (1984).

A standard reference on program modularity is Parnas (1972). For a later discussion of the topic see Meyer (1982). For a study of encapsulation constructs in programming languages see Appelbe and Ravn (1984). Ada's packages are described in textbooks on Ada — for example, Barnes (1989); and Modula's modules in books on Modula-2 — for example, Sale (1986). For Clu see Liskov *et al.* (1981).

The literature on data abstraction is far too great to list in detail. The proceedings of an early conference are contained in a special issue of the ACM SIGPLAN Notices (Volume 11, 1976). For some recent reviews see Bertziss and Thattle (1983) and Shaw (1984). The Clu language was one of the first to provide major support for data abstraction. Its philosophy is outlined in Liskov *et al.* (1977) and described more fully in a book by B. Liskov and J. Guttag (1986). Ada's approach is similar, having been influenced by Clu and by papers such as Thatcher *et al.* (1978). Its early version is explained in the rationale by Ichbiah *et al.* (1979) and its subsequent development in a monograph by P. Hilfinger (1983). For its application see Hibbard *et al.* (1981) and the textbook by J. Bishop (1986).

The standard book on SIMULA 67 is Birtwhistle *et al.* (1979); a more recent text is Pooley (1987). There has been little else. Many of the ideas in Sections 10.8 – 10.11 were presented in a paper by Dahl and Hoare (1972) which forms the third part of the book *Structured Programming* (Dahl *et al.*, 1972). As mentioned at the end of Chapter 8, this book still makes good reading.

Coroutines are the subject of a book by C. D. Marlin (1980). The basic idea was first put forward in a paper by M. E. Conway (1963), from which several of the classic examples have been derived, and is discussed by D. E. Knuth (1973). Coroutines were incorporated in SIMULA 67 and in Bliss (Wulf *et al.*, 1971). They have also been implemented as non-standard extensions to several other languages. For example, their inclusion in BCPL is described by Moody and Richards (1980), and in Pascal by Horton and Turner (1986). For further discussion of coroutines see Wang and Dahl (1971), Grune (1977), Bezivin *et al.* (1978), and Lindstrom and Soffa (1981).

Quasi-parallel systems are discussed in Hoare *et al.* (1976) with special reference to their application to simulation. See also Kriz and Sandmayr (1980), where coroutines are added to Pascal for the purpose. A recent book by W. Kreutzer (1986) gives a thorough review of languages and techniques for system simulation.

EXERCISES

1   The Report on the Algorithmic Language ALGOL 68 (Van Wijngaarden *et al.*, 1975) introduces its Section 2.1.3.2 on Names with a famous quotation from *Romeo and Juliet*:

>   What's in a name? that which we call a rose
>   By any other name would smell as sweet.

Do you agree? What in fact does ALGOL 68 mean by a 'name'?

Suppose that in a conventional block-structured language an entity is declared with the name rose. If every occurrence of rose throughout the scope of the declaration is replaced by some other identifier, would the program necessarily smell as sweet? Would it behave in the same way?

2   In a conventional block-structured language, the declaration of an entity x temporarily hides any previous entity called x. However, some languages allow x to retain both of its meanings, and in such cases Ada says that x is *overloaded*.

As in natural languages, the potential ambiguity can be resolved either by qualifying x or by considering the context. An example of the former was given in Section 10.3, where the x declared in a block called outer was referenced from an inner block by the expanded name outer.x. An example of the latter is the ability to overload the names of procedures and functions, including operator symbols such as '+', by having different versions for different parameter types. In this case the ambiguity is resolved by choosing the version that matches the type of the actual parameters.

Investigate the extent to which overloading is allowed in any suitable language that is familiar to you, with particular reference to the following features:

(a)   The names of enumerals in type declarations:

> **type** primary_color **is** (red, yellow, blue);
> **type** traffic_light **is** (red, amber, green);

(b)   The names of fields of records;

(c)   The names of procedures and functions.

Why is overloading important if generics are available?

3   Prove that in a conventional block-structured language, such as ALGOL 60 or Pascal, an entity x exists whenever it is visible. (Note: it is important to show that if a procedure P can refer to x, then P cannot be called after the execution of x's block is complete. Allow for the case where P is an actual parameter of some other procedure.)

4   In ALGOL 60 an 'own' variable is one whose declaration begins with the symbol **own**. It differs from ordinary variables in that it retains its value from one execution of its block to the next. The idea seems simple enough, and yet it raises several problems:

(a)   The first execution of the block has to be treated differently from all the subsequent ones since it is the only one in which the **own** variable does not already have a value. (This could be remedied by allowing an initial value to be specified.)

(b)   If a procedure body contains **own** variables it is not clear whether different calls of the same procedure should share the same set of **own** variables or not. The different calls could be from repeated execution of the same statement, or from recursive execution of the same statement, or from execution of several different statements.

(c) If an array A[m:n] is specified as **own** there is a problem of interpretation and/or implementation if m and n can change from one execution of the block to the next.

In Ada, the variables declared within a package body are said to be 'own' variables. To what extent do they provide a similar facility and in what ways do they avoid the above problems?

5 The package ran_pack in Section 10.4 uses the 'mixed congruential' method for generating random numbers:

$$x_0 = \text{initial value (the 'seed')}$$
$$x_{i+1} = (a * x_i + b) \ \textbf{mod} \ m \qquad \ldots \ i \geq 0$$

This generates a series of integers x_1, x_2, x_3, ... in the range 0 to $m-1$. The constants a, b, and m must be chosen so that the numbers are distributed uniformly over the range and so that the series does not repeat itself too soon.

For a discussion of how to choose a, b, and m, see Knuth (1981). In particular, pp.170–1 give a summary in the form of seven rules. The second rule is that the number m should be large, say at least 2^{30}. On the other hand, to avoid overflow it should satisfy $a * (m - 1) + b \leq \text{integer'last}$. If the word size is n bits, a good strategy is to take $m = 2^{n-1}$ and to do double-length multiplication (probably using assembly code). The constants in Section 10.4 were chosen for use on a seven-digit pocket calculator. For further discussion see Park and Miller (1988).

As an example of a bad choice consider $a = 43$ and $m = 100$. Regardless of the values of b and x_0 the series will repeat itself almost immediately. Investigate this behavior and prove the related result.

6 Another problem with the mixed congruential method is that the rightmost bits of the integers are non-random. Show why this must always be so. This, of course, is why the result of random is returned as a fraction rather than an integer: the rightmost bits are then comparatively insignificant. What would you do to x_i if you wanted to generate a random series of 0s and 1s? (Note: there are other methods of generating random bit sequences. See Knuth, *op. cit.*, pp.29-31.)

7 Exercise 7.14 described a program for playing the game Mastermind. Define a package, or equivalent module, for handling the pegs and for counting cows and bulls.

8 Prove that the implementation of the ADO circle_of_integers in Section 10.5 establishes and maintains the stated invariant.

9 In Section 10.6 the package circle_of_integers specified an ADT int_circle and, in the **private** part of the specification, represented it as a record. It was mentioned that the representation could also be given as a pointer to hidden_type, with hidden_type being defined in the package body. If C1 and C2 are two int_circle objects, show that the effect of

```
C2 := C1;
insert (C2, x);
```

will depend on which representation is used. Might it be better (or safer?) to specify int_circle as **limited private** instead of **private**?

Explain why similar considerations apply to the other operations on private types, namely '=' and '≠'.

10   Suppose that person has been defined as an enumerated type. For example:

> **type** person **is** (Ted, Fred, Jed, Ned, Ed, Zed);

Define an ADO called club for representing a set of persons with the associated operations join, leave, belongs, and size. Initialize it with no members (club.size = 0). Provide exceptions for any irregular conditions. What is its invariant?

Define an equivalent ADT called club_type.

Define a generic version of the ADO in which person is a generic formal type.

Define a generic version of the ADT.

11   Specify and implement a package, or equivalent module, for histograms. A histogram records the frequency with which samples of some variable x fall within certain intervals. The intervals are defined by a sequence of increasing real numbers $z_1, z_2, ... z_n$ for some $n \geq 1$:

$$\text{interval } 0: \quad x \leq z_1$$
$$\text{interval } i: \quad z_i < x \leq z_{i+1} \qquad ... \, 1 \leq i \leq n\text{-}1$$
$$\text{interval } n: \quad z_n < x$$

Initially all the frequencies are zero. The operation *tabulate (x)* records a sample. The operation *frequency (i)* returns the frequency with which x has occurred in interval i ($0 \leq i \leq n$). It equals the number of readings for interval i divided by the total number of readings.

Define the histogram as a generic ADO. Which factors should be 'genericized' and what are their generic operations?

12   Specify and implement an ADT for doing arithmetic of one or more of the following special kinds. The operations should include addition, negation, subtraction, multiplication, input, output, and appropriate type conversions. What problems would be caused by division?

(a)   Complex arithmetic (as outlined in Section 10.6);

(b)   Circular arithmetic — that is, integer arithmetic modulo m for some constant m (preferably generic);

(c)   Infinite precision integer arithmetic (the integers could be represented as linked lists of base-b digits for some suitable value of b);

(d)   Integer arithmetic in which each integer is represented by a pair of ordinary integers (i, j) representing the value $i * 10^j$;

(e)   Interval arithmetic, in which each number is represented by an interval (x, y) in which it is known to lie.

13 In what ways, and to what extent, do the following features of Ada provide an inheritance mechanism?

- subtypes;
- derived types;
- variant records;
- generics.

For a detailed comparison of generics and the inheritance mechanism see Meyer (1986, 1988).

14 A package is required for drawing and manipulating geometric figures on a screen. The figures include points, lines, circles, triangles, rectangles, polygons, etc., and the operations include drawing, moving, rotating, etc. Define a suitable hierarchy of objects together with their attributes and operations. Which operations are 'virtual'? How would you implement the hierarchy in one or more of (a) SIMULA 67, (b) Smalltalk, (c) Ada, (d) other?

15 In Section 10.9, it was pointed out that a value-producing semicoroutine has to return its values in a global variable. This is not ideal, and it may well be asked: why not let it return its result in the same way as a function does, by making it an argument of **suspend**? Corresponding to procedures and functions there would then be two kinds of coroutine — the *coprocedure* and the *cofunction*. Draw up a proposal along these lines and rewrite random accordingly.

16 Use 'program inversion' on the coroutine readchar of Section 10.9 to turn it into an ordinary procedure, preserving its underlying logic. Since it has three **suspend** statements, use a three-way switch at the start and do not hesitate to use **goto**s into the branches of a conditional statement. The result may be messy, but it makes explicit what would otherwise be done implicitly by the **suspend**–**call** mechanism.

17 Write a recursive procedure partition (n) that lists all the partitions of the positive integer n — that is, all sequences $(x_1, x_2, \ldots x_k)$ with

$$x_1 + x_2 + \ldots + x_k = n$$

Note that for each value of x_1 the choice of $x_2, \ldots x_k$ constitutes a subproblem of the same kind — hence the recursion.

Rewrite the procedure as a value-producing semicoroutine, as in the example of traverse (Section 10.9).

(Remember: there are 2^{n-1} partitions of n. To reduce the number, try imposing the condition that the x_i be strictly increasing.)

18 A similar problem to partitions is a procedure permutations for listing the permutations of the integers 1, 2, ... n. Write a value-producing semicoroutine for this. (For a discussion of the problem see Dahl and Hoare (1972). For more efficient methods see Exercise 3.9.)

19 An *iterator* is a facility that allows a procedure to be applied iteratively to all the members of some data structure. If the set is an array, the **for** statement provides a suitable facility for the purpose. If it is a binary tree, the semicoroutine of

Section 10.9 provides a possible mechanism, and this technique can be applied to any other data structure for which a traverser can be written.

In general, suppose that an ADT called structure has been defined and that an iterator mechanism has to be added to it. If S is one such structure, and if the procedure P is to be applied to each of its members, it would be convenient if we could write a statement such as:

iterate (S, P);

Or possibly:

S.iterate (P);

Suggest a way of doing this in Ada or in any other suitable language available to you.

20   Complete the coroutine play of Section 10.10 for playing Greedy Pig and embed it in a suitable master routine. Revise it so that play continues until all players have scored 100, each player dropping out after reaching or passing that score. At the end, the master routine should list the players, giving the limit and the number of turns for each.

21   This classic example of coroutines comes from Conway (1963). It involves three coroutines:

(a)   disassembler — reads 80-column cards from input and, on each resumption, assigns the next character to a global variable ch1. It inserts a blank between successive cards.

(b)   squasher — this is basically the same as readchar in Section 10.9. It reads characters from ch1, as supplied by disassembler, and passes them over to ch2, except that "**" is replaced by "↑".

(c)   assembler — takes successive characters from ch2, as supplied by squasher, and prints them in lines of 132 characters.

The overall flow of information is shown in Figure 10-8

Write the three coroutines so that they interact in the required way and place them in a master program that initiates the system. Assume that a procedure readcard (A) is available for reading a card into the 80-character array A and that printline (B) is available for printing a line of output.

Revise the programs so that they terminate correctly on reading a card with a '$' in column 1.

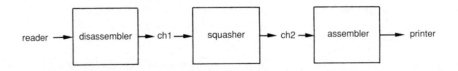

Figure 10-8   Three cooperating routines

22   In the shopping simulation of Section 10.11 the customer's action on finding the checkout to be idle was:

>   **activate** checkout **after** current;
>   passivate;

Explain exactly what these statements do. The customer then goes through the charade of joining and leaving an empty queue. Investigate an alternative scheme in which the customer does

>   **activate** checkout;

and never joins the empty queue.

23   Write a coroutine for generating customers at intervals of t time units, where t has a negative exponential distribution with mean avtime. This distribution can be obtained by generating a pseudorandom number x in the range $0 \le x < 1$ and evaluating $- \text{avtime} * \ln(1-x)$. Each customer should be generated with parameters shoptime and checktime. The former can be drawn from a normal distribution, as described in Knuth (1981, p.117), or from any other plausible sample; simulation languages provide procedures for doing this. The latter could be derived from it by some simple formula (for example, checktime = $0.1 *$ shoptime + 1.0). Arrange for the customers to stop arriving after closetime. (Note: avtime and closetime will be parameters of the simulation.)

24   Revise the simulation to handle n checkouts, with a separate queue for each. Customers go to any idle checkout or else join the shortest queue. (If q is a queue, its length in SIMULA 67 is given by q.cardinal.)

PARALLEL PROCESSES

11.1 THE CHALLENGE

Parallel processing presents one of the biggest challenges in the history of computing. With hardware becoming so cheap, the goal is to build a machine with a large number of processors and, by making them execute in parallel, to obtain a major increase in performance. It holds out the prospect of relief from the 'von Neumann bottleneck' — the constraint of having to funnel all activity through a single processor.

The idea seems so simple: with n processors a machine should provide n times the throughput. In reality, it never turns out that way. Some applications are inherently non-parallel and so the gains are negligible. Others are well suited to parallelism, but the organizational overheads prevent the factor of n from being attained, or even approximated. Additional processors tend to yield less and less advantage and eventually, if the overheads are too great, they may even become counterproductive. A scenario can be envisaged where the processors spend their entire time looking after each other and never do any useful work — a phenomenon that has occasionally been observed in the human context (see, for example, Exercise 1).

The computers that offer the greatest potential for speed-up are the *array processors*. They take advantage of the parallelism that is inherent in array operations — for example, the multiplication of two matrices. An obvious possibility is to make the n processors operate on n-element subarrays with a very strict form of parallelism, applying a single instruction to all the elements in unison. This is known as 'tight coupling'. By crunching the numbers in blocks of n, the machines achieve an n-fold speed-up for short periods of time. In a typical array-processing algorithm the factor becomes diluted by more mundane activity; even so, the overall performance can be quite impressive. The details will be considered further in the chapter on arrays (see Volume II).

This chapter examines a more flexible form of parallelism, one with a wider area of application but with less potential for dramatic speed-up. The main difference is that the processors operate independently: each one executes a separate *process* — that is, a separate sequence of instructions with its own locus of control. The processes are similar to the coroutines of the previous chapter, but instead of being quasi-parallel — merely *imitating* parallel behavior — they are truly parallel.

Parallel processes were pioneered during the 1960s within the context of operating systems. The first steps were concerned with allowing the central processor to operate in parallel with the input/output devices, as described in Section 5.14. The next requirement was that two or more programs should be able to execute in interleaved fashion, so that if one were held up by an input/output operation, another could make use of the processor. The technique was known as *multiprogramming*, and it opened up the way for the time-shared operating systems in which many users can interact with the machine from online terminals. Their programs appear to operate simultaneously; in reality, on a single-processor machine, the system attends to them one at a time, giving a short 'time-slice' to each one in turn, as the need arises. The writers of such systems have to ensure that the different programs do not interfere with each other and that resources of memory, processor time, and so on, are equitably shared. It was against this background that most of the early work on parallel processing was done.

Time-shared systems changed the programming environment in some far-reaching and beneficial respects, but still left the users with what appeared to be an ordinary, sequential von Neumann computer. More recently, with multiprocessor machines becoming widely available, the reverse situation has become important. Instead of having several programs executing on a single processor, the aim is to have one program executing on several processors. How can this be achieved?

If programmers still write ordinary, sequential programs, the only way is for the compiler to determine where parallel processing is possible. For example, it might discover that the following two statements can be executed independently:

```
x   :=   a * b;
y   :=   c * d;
```

It could therefore arrange for two processors to execute them in parallel. An elaboration of this principle is provided by the dataflow machines, which have been the subject of considerable research (Treleaven *et al.*, 1982).

The alternative is to allow programmers to specify the parallelism themselves, using a language with special facilities for the purpose. During the 1970s, there was a burst of activity in the design of such languages. The challenge was to formulate a simple, robust mechanism that would be natural and convenient for all the applications that might arise. Many different proposals were made and they were applied to a variety of problems that circulated as informal test cases (Welsh and Lister, 1981). Unfortunately, an approach that worked well for some of them usually turned out to be less suitable for others. However, some valuable principles were developed and the new languages were generally much easier and safer to use. One of the most important is CSP, which takes its name from the paper 'Communicating Sequential Processes' by C. A. R. Hoare (1978). It provides a clear, conceptual model for a theoretical study of parallel processing, and it has also had a major influence on other more pragmatic languages, notably Ada and occam. The following sections use it in discussing the basic principles of parallel processing; they then move on to Ada for some more extensive examples.

11.2 FORK AND JOIN

Figure 11-1 uses *process flowgraphs* to depict the parallel execution of some simple processes. They are directed acyclic graphs in which each arc represents the execution of a process (Shaw, 1974). The rule is that the processes entering a node must all be completed before the ones leaving it can begin. The first flowgraph shows simple parallelism between three processes, p1, p2, and p3. The second starts in the same way, but then p2

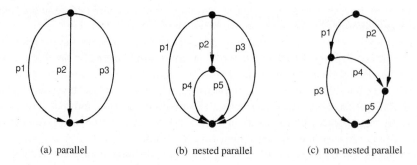

(a) parallel   (b) nested parallel   (c) non-nested parallel

Figure 11-1   Process flowgraphs

divides into two subprocesses, p4 and p5: it is an example of *nested* parallelism. The third is more complicated: p3 and p4 are parallel processes, but the parallelism is not properly nested since one of them joins up with p2 and the other does not. (For an alternative way of depicting such dependencies, see Exercise 2.)

A typical application for such parallelism is in the execution of a series of assignments. For example, consider the following:

```
a  :=  x + 1;
b  :=  y + 2;
c  :=  a + 3;
d  :=  a + 4;
e  :=  b + d;
```

The first two can be executed in parallel, but the third and fourth must wait for the results of the first one; similarly, the fifth must wait for the second and fourth. The dependencies are, in fact, equivalent to those of Figure 11-1(c). As mentioned in the previous section, an optimizing compiler could detect the opportunities for parallelism and, on a multiprocessor machine, might generate code that takes advantage of them.

It is interesting to speculate on the sort of code that it might produce. The details, of course, will depend on the number of processors available and on the way in which they are activated. But a possible answer can be given by introducing the **fork** and **join** operations (Conway, 1963; Dennis and van Horn, 1966):

fork p   initiate a process, in parallel with the current one, whose execution starts at address p;

join n   subtract 1 from n and, if this reduces n to zero, continue execution; otherwise, terminate the process.

With these operations the flowgraph of Figure 11-1(a) can be implemented as follows:

```
        n := 3;
        fork P2;
        fork P3;
P1 :    code for p1; goto L;
P2 :    code for p2; goto L;
```

```
P3 :    code for p3;
  L :    join n;
         . . .
```

The original process begins by setting n = 3, in preparation for the three-way join later on. It then spawns two other processes, one for p2 and one for p3, before entering on the code for p1 itself. In due course each process completes its code and, having branched to L, executes **join** n. The first to arrive reduces n to 2 and then terminates. The second reduces it to 1 and terminates also. The third reduces it to 0 and therefore continues execution. Since the relative speeds of the processes are (in principle) quite arbitrary, any one of the three could turn out to be the 'survivor'. This is a potential drawback of the **fork–join** operations (Exercise 3).

An important aspect of **join** is that it must be executed as an indivisible count-and-test operation; otherwise it is conceivable that the three processes would each subtract 1 from n before any of them tested n = 0. If this were to happen, they would all find n = 0 to be true and would all continue execution. To avoid this hazard, a single hardware instruction is needed that carries out the count and the test as a single, uninterruptible operation.

It is readily verified that **fork** and **join** are sufficient for implementing any flowgraph, including those of Figure 11-1 (Exercise 4). Equally, it is clear that flowgraphs and **fork**s are the parallel equivalent of flowcharts and **goto**s and that they are therefore open to the same sorts of criticism. Higher-level constructs are needed if parallel programming is to be carried out in any sort of structured way.

11.3   PARALLEL COMMANDS

The first requirement for 'structured parallelism' is a notation for the parallel execution of two or more code segments. In CSP, the construct is called a *parallel command* and has the following simple form:

$$[\quad process\_1 \quad || \quad process\_2 \quad || \quad \ldots \quad || \quad process\_n \quad]$$

An elementary example is provided by the assignments from Section 11.1:

$$[\; x := a * b \; || \; y := c * d \;]$$

The processes execute in parallel and the combined command terminates successfully if and when each of its components has terminated successfully.

The case n = 3 corresponds to the flowgraph of Figure 11-1(a). Since parallel commands can be nested, it is easy to model Figure 1(b) also. However, it can be shown that parallel commands are not sufficient in themselves to model Figure 11-1(c). In this respect they are less powerful than the more primitive **fork–join** operations (Exercise 5). Later sections describe synchronizing mechanisms that overcome this deficiency.

Although there is a clear intention that the n processes should execute in parallel, there is no guarantee that they will in fact do so. Indeed, if n processors are not available, full parallelism will be impossible. So, even when programs are written with parallel constructs, an implementation is free to reduce the parallelism to fit within its hardware constraints. Furthermore, even if the processes *are* executed in parallel, there is no requirement that they should in any sense progress at the same rate. Some may go much faster than others; it may even happen that some finish before others begin. In the absence of explicit synchronization the implementation can do what it likes in this respect.

An important limiting case occurs on a conventional, single-processor machine, where real parallelism is impossible. As in a time-shared operating system, the processor has to divide its attention between the competing processes under the control of a scheduling algorithm. Ideally, it should do *time-slicing*, giving a small amount of time to each process in turn. In that case, their operations are said to be *interleaved*. With small enough slices, the quasi-parallel behavior can be almost indistinguishable from real parallelism. On the other hand, as already indicated, the implementation is free to go to the other extreme, taking each process through to completion before attending to the next.

Parallel commands of this kind look fairly innocuous. In fact, though, their implementation is liable to open up a can of rather unpleasant worms. For example, suppose that a variable i has the value 3 and that the following command is then executed:

$$[\ i := i + 1 \ \ || \ \ j := i \ ]$$

If the two assignments are executed more or less simultaneously, they will be equivalent to the parallel assignment

$$i, j := i + 1, i$$

and so j will be assigned the value 3. However, it is possible — and with a single processor it is highly probable — that the first assignment will be completed before the second is begun, in which case j will be assigned the value 4. Since the implementation is free to take either course, the outcome may be different from what the programmer intended.

For double trouble there is the case described in Section 5.14:

$$[\ i := i + 1 \ \ || \ \ i := i - 1 \ ]$$

If i is initially 3 its final value may be 2, 3, or 4, depending on the way in which the accesses to i are interleaved. This is known as the *concurrent update* problem — two or more processes updating a common variable at the same time. It occurs on a larger scale when multiple users can update a common database. The variable could be someone's bank balance and the concurrent updates could be a deposit and a withdrawal. If the concluding balance were unpredictable, the bank manager would be heading for trouble.

To emphasize the far-reaching nature of the problem consider the even simpler command:

$$[\ i := i + 1 \ \ || \ \ \textbf{null} \ ]$$

According to Section 8.4, the proof rule for **null** is

$$\{P\} \ \ \textbf{null} \ \ \{P\}$$

which states that if P is true before the execution of **null** it will also be true afterwards. But if P contains a reference to i, the parallel execution of $i := i + 1$ could change its value to false. So the proof rule for **null** cannot be relied on. Nor, similarly, can any of the other proof rules that were presented in Chapter 8. Thus parallelism threatens to undermine the entire foundations of structured programming.

These problems have a common cause, namely a variable that is updated in one process but used by another. A simple solution is therefore to forbid the use of shared variables (except possibly in read-only mode). Accordingly, CSP imposes the restriction that parallel processes must be *disjoint*, in the sense that a variable that is updated by one process must not be referenced by any of the others. Sharing can only be carried out indirectly, by means of message passing (see Section 11.6). If this restriction is applied to assertions as well as to the commands themselves, the proof rules for conventional commands will remain valid.

A more flexible, but potentially more dangerous, policy is to allow direct access to shared variables but to control it in certain ways. Section 11.5 examines some possible mechanisms. For the time being, the lesson is clear enough: parallel programming has several pitfalls that are waiting to trap the unwary.

11.4 SYNCHRONIZING

As already noted, parallel processes are basically *asynchronous*. They are not like the members of an orchestra, with a conductor to keep them all in time. Instead, they are more like the staff of an office, each person proceeding at a different pace, often in rather stop-start fashion.

This is all very well for processes that are totally independent of each other. In practice, though, they usually have to cooperate in various ways and this involves synchronizing particular actions at certain critical points. In the simplest case, action A1 in one process has to be executed *after* action A2 in some other process. With full synchronization, A1 and A2 have to be executed simultaneously ('synchronous' = 'at the same time'). In practice, strict simultaneity is not always possible; after all, there may be only one processor. So the less stringent condition is imposed that both processes must arrive at the relevant instructions before either is allowed to execute them. One may have to wait while the other catches up.

To express these requirements, we shall use a statement of the form

wait until *condition*

which prevents a process from proceeding until the given condition becomes true. For example, to ensure that process_1 does not execute A1 until process_2 has executed A2, the condition can be a Boolean variable A2_done, initialized to false. The parallel processes then proceed as follows:

process_1	process_2
. . .	. . .
wait until A2_done;	A2;
A1;	A2_done := true;
. . .	. . .

If process_1 arrives at the **wait until** statement and finds that A2_done is false, it is said to be *blocked*. It is essential that A2_done be initialized prior to either process being started, otherwise process_1 could find itself blocked permanently (Exercise 6). With that proviso, it is clear that A1 will not be executed until after A2, as required. For full synchronization we can work the same trick twice, using two variables and two **wait until** statements. Care is needed to avoid deadlock, with each process waiting for the other in the notorious 'deadly embrace' (Exercise 7).

The question now arises: what does a process do when it is waiting? The simplest answer is that it executes a *busy loop*, repeatedly testing the condition until it becomes true (see Section 5.14). The **wait until** statement is therefore equivalent to:

while not *condition* **do null**;

The technique has the obvious advantage that it is very easy to implement. However, it suffers from several drawbacks:

1.   It wastes processor time in the busy loop.

2.   On an implementation with a single processor and no time-slicing, process_1 can become stuck in its busy loop, with process_2 having no opportunity to proceed.

3.   For more complicated situations the programming becomes very tricky.

To counter the first two objections, the only alternative is for the process to suspend its execution, releasing its processor for use by others. It goes to sleep hoping that, when the condition becomes true, it will be woken up either by some other process or by the run-time system. For example, with this interpretation the **wait until** statement of process_1 says, in effect: 'If A2_done is true, allow me to proceed; but if it is false, suspend my execution and resume me when it becomes true.'

There are several ways in which a strategy of this kind might be effected, but the most basic one is to restrict the condition to being a two-valued variable known as a *semaphore*. As its name suggests, this is similar to a railway signal and so we shall define its two values to be red, meaning 'you must wait', and green, meaning 'you may proceed'. When a semaphore S is declared, it is initialized with a default setting of green. The following two operations can then be applied to it:

wait (S)   if S is red, suspend execution and wait to be resumed; on resumption, or if S is already green, set it to red and proceed;

signal (S)   set S to green; if any processes are waiting on it, resume one of them.

Implicit in the operations is the fact that several processes may be waiting on S at the same time and that each execution of signal allows only one of them to proceed. The next section illustrates the advantages of this convention.

With these operations simple synchronization can be implemented by setting S to red and then executing the following:

process_1	process_2
. . .	. . .
wait (S);	A2;
A1;	signal (S);
. . .	. . .

Provided that no other processes are using S, the wait operation will delay process_1 until process_2 has executed signal, thus achieving the required effect. Full synchronization can be implemented by using two semaphores in a similar way (Exercise 7).

In order to implement wait and signal the run-time system associates with each semaphore S a queue of waiting processes, initially empty. If a process executes wait (S) when S is red, the system adds it to the queue. If it executes signal (S), the system selects a process from the queue (unless empty) and resumes its execution. The queuing discipline will normally be first-in/first-out (FIFO), though this is not essential.

Semaphores were first introduced by E. W. Dijkstra (1965), who called the two operations P and V (from the Dutch words *proberen* and *verhogen* for 'test' and 'increment', or possibly *passeren* and *vrygeven* for 'pass' and 'release' — the literature offers both explanations). The above example is a *binary* semaphore, having the two values 0 for red and 1 for green. A more general kind is the *integer* semaphore: its value can be any non-negative integer i, with $i = 0$ being equivalent to red and $i \geq 1$ to green. When it is non-zero, a *wait* operation decreases it by 1; a *signal* operation increases it by 1 and allows a waiting process to proceed. Some languages have included semaphores of this kind as a predefined type — for example, ALGOL 68. The preliminary version of Ada included them in its package standard; but they were dropped from the final version, presumably on the grounds that they could be implemented sufficiently well by means of tasks (see Section 11.14).

11.5 SHARING

Section 11.3 commented on the hazards of allowing parallel processes to use shared variables (except in read-only mode, which makes them effectively constants). The hazards extend not just to the sharing of simple variables, but to the sharing of almost anything at all — arrays, files, databases, peripheral devices, and so on. Furthermore, if any of these things can be accessed via a subprogram, then sharing the subprogram is hazardous also. Its local variables are created separately for each call and therefore cause no problems; but its global ones are shared and are therefore exposed to all the same risks.

In spite of these difficulties, there are many situations where it is essential that parallel processes be allowed to share resources. For example, they might be updating a common database or reading from a common device. Mechanisms are therefore needed that enable the sharing to be done as securely as possible. This section examines some of the more primitive ones, in which direct access to shared variables is still allowed. They can be used as stepping stones to some higher-level alternatives, as described later.

The basic strategy is to ensure that a shared resource is used by only one process at a time. The rule is therefore made that when a process wants to use a resource, R say, it first has to *seize* it and then, on completion, *release* it:

```
seize  R;
  ...              -- code for using  R
release  R;
```

The code between *seize* and *release* is called a *critical section*. It could be a single access to R, or else a series of accesses during which other processes have to be excluded. If every reference to R is enclosed in a critical section of this kind, the strategy translates into the requirement that only one process at a time may execute in a critical section. This policy is known as *mutual exclusion*. If a second process wants to enter a critical section, the *seize* operation must force it to wait; and if several processes are waiting to use R, they must proceed on a strict, one-at-a-time basis.

Several higher-level constructs have been devised that express the strategy more clearly and help to enforce its observance. In one such proposal (Brinch Hansen, 1972) a resource R can be designated as **shared** and its use then has to be restricted to statements of the form:

region R **do** *statement_sequence*

The compiler encloses the *statement_sequence* between the appropriate *seize/release* protocols. An extension of the idea is the *conditional critical region*, which has the form:

region R **when** *condition* **do** *statement_sequence*

The *condition* acts as a guard that has to be true before the process can enter its critical region. As long as it is false, other processes will be allowed to use R instead. Whenever they leave their critical regions the system re-evaluates the condition to see if it has become true.

If the *seize* and *release* protocols are to control access to the resource in a reliable and equitable way, it is important that they satisfy three requirements (Peterson and Silberschatz, 1985):

1. *Mutual exclusion.* As already stated, two processes may not execute their critical sections at the same time.

2. *Progress.* If the resource is free, one of the waiting processes (if any) must be allowed to proceed, the choice being made independently of the non-waiting processes.

3. *Bounded waiting.* A waiting process must be sure of proceeding within a fixed number of turns.

The first is fundamental to the whole strategy. The second rules out various forms of deadlock. The third states that a waiting process should not be 'starved' — either deliberately, because other processes always have precedence, or by sheer bad luck, through leaving the choice to chance. Of course, 2 and 3 cannot *guarantee* progress and non-starvation: after all, a process might go into an infinite loop inside its critical section. They merely state that deadlock and starvation should not be caused by the protocols.

The implementation of *seize* and *release* is basically a matter of synchronizing events so that the two operations are executed alternately. This can be done either by flags and busy loops or by semaphores, as described in the previous section. Semaphores are particularly well suited for the purpose — so well suited, in fact, that *seize* and *release* can be implemented directly by the *wait* and *signal* operations. A semaphore, S say, is associated with the shared resource and initialized to 1, indicating that the resource is free. The critical sections then take the form:

```
wait (S);
    critical section
signal (S);
```

The *wait* operation automatically queues processes if necessary, and *signal* allows one of them to proceed. Provided that S is not used for any other purposes, requirements 1 and 2 will clearly be satisfied. If the queuing discipline is first-in/first-out, the third one will be satisfied also.

If semaphores, or something equivalent, are not available, we might try using flags and busy loops instead. However, it is surprisingly difficult to implement *seize* and *release* in a way that satisfies the three requirements. Even the simplest, two-process case is a tough nut to crack. As a starting point, here is an attempt that uses a variable turn to indicate which of the two processes can proceed:

process_1

loop

. . .

   turn := 2;

   wait until turn = 1;

      critical section

. . .

end loop;

process_2

loop

. . .

   turn := 1;

   wait until turn = 2;

      critical section

. . .

end loop;

The loops indicate that both processes want to access the resource on a recurring basis. It is easily verified that when process_1 is in its critical section, turn must have the value 1; similarly, with process_2 it must have the value 2. Since it cannot have both values at once, mutual exclusion is assured. On the other hand, the progress requirement is *not* assured: process_1 depends on process_2 to set turn = 1 and may therefore have to wait in its busy loop even though the resource is free.

To get round this difficulty a good technique is to introduce two Boolean variables, critical_1 and critical_2, which are true when their corresponding processes are either in their critical sections or else trying to enter them. Initially, both are false. The *seize* protocol for process_i begins by setting critical_i to true; the *release* protocol resets it to false. The point of all this is that if critical_2 is false, process_1 can enter its critical section even though turn ≠ 1. Similarly for process_2:

process_1

loop

. . .

   critical_1 := true;

   turn := 2;

   wait until turn = 1

         or not critical_2;

      critical section

   critical_1 := false;

. . .

end loop;

process_2

loop

. . .

   critical_2 := true;

   turn := 1;

   wait until turn = 2

         or not critical_1;

      critical section

   critical_2 := false;

. . .

end loop;

With this arrangement neither process can be delayed when the other one is not competing for the resource, and so the progress requirement is satisfied. The use of turn ensures that the third requirement is also satisfied (no 'starvation'). Less obvious is the first one — mutual exclusion. To prove that this is satisfied, it is easiest to assume that it is *not* satisfied and to derive a contradiction. So let us assume that both processes are executing in their critical sections and, without loss of generality, that turn = 1. For turn to have the value 1 it is clear that process_1 must have executed

```
critical_1 := true;
turn := 2;
```

before process_2 executed:

```
turn := 1;
```

Since process_2 then managed to enter its critical section, there must have been a subsequent assignment either setting critical_1 to false or setting turn to 2. Inspection of the code shows that for this to be possible process_1 must have completed its critical section — contrary to the hypothesis. If follows that the two processes cannot be in their critical sections together and so mutual exclusion is guaranteed.

The above algorithm was published by G. L. Peterson (1981). It is simpler than an earlier one by T. Dekker that was used by E. W. Dijkstra in his paper on 'Cooperating Sequential Processes' (Dijkstra, 1965). It is very neat and also quite subtle (see, for example, Exercise 9). Similar techniques can be used for the *n*-process case (Eisenberg and McGuire, 1972), but the protocols are considerably more elaborate. An alternative approach has been presented by L. Lamport (1974) using the 'bakery' algorithm. This is based on the simple idea that when a process wants to use the resource it obtains a sequence number; it then executes a busy loop until all processes with earlier numbers have had their turn. As always, though, the coding has to be done with great care.

11.6 MESSAGE PASSING

If parallel processes are to cooperate it is important that they be able to communicate. Process X must be able to send information to process Y, and Y must be able to send information back again.

A rudimentary mechanism for the purpose is to use a shared variable, v say. X writes values to v and Y reads them, or vice-versa. For once-only communication, this requires simple synchronization — the *write* must precede the *read* — and so a semaphore, or something similar, has to be used. For repeated communication the problems are more severe: X must not overwrite an old value before Y has read it, nor may Y try to read a new value before X has written it. So two semaphores are needed and the programming is harder. For more complex situations the programming can become very tricky and errors are easily made.

An alternative, higher-level strategy is to use *message passing*. X sends information to Y via some communication channel and Y (if it is behaving cooperatively) receives it. This avoids the problems of shared variables and is therefore easier to program. It is also much more suitable for *distributed* processes — that is, processes not sharing a common memory. Typical messages are:

'Deal with this value.'

'Event *E* has just occurred.'

'What state are you in?'

The communications can be either *synchronous* or *asynchronous*. The former is like calling someone on the telephone: the sender of the message has to wait until the recipient is ready and then the send/receive operations are executed simultaneously. It is sometimes called *blocking* mode, because the sender is blocked until the recipient is ready. The latter is more like mailing a letter: having sent the message, the sender continues execution and never knows at what moment the message is received.

A restricted form of message passing is provided by one of the most useful and distinctive features of the Unix operating system, namely *pipes*. In Unix each process has a standard input file from which it reads information (usually in character form), and a standard output file to which it writes information. A pipe is a mechanism that allows the standard output of a process X to be used as the standard input of a process Y. It is represented by the notation:

$$X \quad | \quad Y$$

In a typical application, a series of processes P1, P2, ... Pn can be connected in this way, as shown in Figure 11-2. They are known as *filters*, since each one processes the characters in some way before passing them on. The following is a simple example:

$$ls\ -l \quad | \quad grep\ "\hat{\ }d" \quad | \quad more$$

The command ls −l lists the current directory, one line per entry; its output is passed to grep "^d", which picks out the lines beginning with the letter 'd' (the subdirectories); these are then passed to more, which displays them one page at a time.

As the notation 'X | Y' suggests, the pipe mechanism allows X and Y to execute in parallel. A possible implementation is to use an intermediate buffer, capable of holding *n* values, as described in Section 11.11. X writes values to the buffer and is delayed if it becomes full. Y reads them out again and is delayed if it becomes empty. In the special case *n = 0*, there is no buffer and so X is forced to communicate directly with Y, with full synchronization of the read/write operations. At the other extreme, if *n* is effectively infinite, X and Y can be executed sequentially: X writes its entire output to a temporary file, which is then read by Y. Thus, there is a spectrum of possibilities: the coupling between X and Y can be anything from very tight to very loose. However, since there is no feedback from Y, the outcome is always the same.

For general-purpose, parallel programming, pipes are inadequate: they only provide a single, one-way channel of communication. Several other mechanisms have therefore been devised for implementing a more versatile form of message passing. One of the best

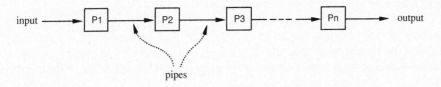

Figure 11-2   Pipes

known is CSP, whose name comes from a paper on 'Communicating Sequential Processes' by C. A. R. Hoare (1978). It may be contrasted with the 'Cooperating Sequential Processes' of E. W. Dijkstra (see Section 11.5). As the name indicates, CSP takes communication between sequential processes as its primary concern. In its original version, a process X can send a message to a process Y by executing an *output command* with one of the following forms:

> Y ! *expression*
> Y ! *name* (*expression_list*)

In order to receive the message Y must execute a corresponding *input command* with one of the forms:

> X ? *variable*
> X ? *name* (*variable_list*)

The *name* (if present) must be the same in both cases, and the variable(s) must match the expression(s) in number and in type. The communication is synchronous and its effect is to assign the values of the expressions from X to the corresponding variables in Y. The particular case where X executes

> Y ! *name* ()

and Y responds with

> X ? *name* ()

corresponds to synchronization without any message passing.

As an example, consider a message from X to Y, asking it to compute the cube of some value, x say. Y returns the result by sending a message back to X:

process X	process Y
x, x3 : integer;	y, n, yn : integer;
...	...
Y ! power (x, 3);	X ? power (y, n);
...	... -- compute yn = y^n
Y ? x3;	X ! yn;
...	...

The synchronization means that when X sends the message power (x, 3) to Y, it may have to wait until Y is ready to receive it. Alternatively, Y may have to wait until X is ready to send it. When the message has been passed, X and Y proceed independently until the result is sent back.

When a process is receiving messages from several different sources, it may not know the order in which to expect them. A facility is therefore needed for allowing it to choose any message that happens to come in. In CSP this is provided by the *alternative command*, which is modeled on Dijkstra's **if-fi** command (see Section 8.10). It has the form

$$[\quad ... \quad \square \quad ... \quad \square \quad ... \quad] \qquad\qquad ... \text{ (1)}$$

where each '...' is a guarded command. A guard is a list of declarations and/or Boolean expressions, optionally followed by an input command. For example:

$$n < 10, \ X ? \text{deposit} \ (x) \quad \rightarrow \quad command\_sequence$$

If $n < 10$ is false, or if X has terminated, the guard fails and so the corresponding *command_sequence* cannot be considered for execution. But if $n < 10$ is true and X has not terminated, the guard succeeds when X is ready to execute a corresponding output command. To accept an integer from either X or Y, a process can therefore execute:

$$[\ X ? i \quad \rightarrow \quad \ldots \quad \text{\char"0F} \quad Y ? i \quad \rightarrow \quad \ldots \ ]$$

This will be delayed, if necessary, until at least one of the input commands becomes executable — that is, until X and/or Y is ready to execute a corresponding output command. If both are executable, it makes a nondeterministic choice between them. In other cases, the normal intention is that the first one to become executable should be selected. However, the term 'first' is meaningless in principle and its precise determination may be difficult to implement in practice; so the system is free to choose either alternative provided that it becomes executable. If X and Y are both terminated, the alternative command fails.

The concept is extended to the *repetitive command*, which is obtained by prefixing (1) with an asterisk. For example, the following command repeatedly reads an integer from either X or Y:

$$* \ [\ X ? i \quad \rightarrow \quad \ldots \quad \text{\char"0F} \quad Y ? i \quad \rightarrow \quad \ldots \ ]$$

When X and Y have both terminated the repetition terminates also.

With these facilities CSP can provide solutions to a wide range of problems, including many of the 'classical' ones which, as mentioned in Section 11.1, are used as test cases (Hoare, 1978). In a subsequent book (Hoare, 1985) the notation has been altered in some minor ways and communication is made by using a *channel*. This enables a process to receive a message without having to nominate the sender and is an essential feature for the construction of general-purpose process libraries.

11.7 TASKS

In Ada parallel processes are not simply statement sequences embedded in some larger, parallel construct. Instead, they are separate units, called *tasks*, which are more akin to subprograms, each having a specification and a body. This makes them better suited for modeling objects in the real world. Their inclusion in a fully-fledged high-level language raises several issues that are not addressed in more restricted languages such as CSP. We shall consider the main ones as we proceed, but shall not attempt to cover all the details.

Tasks can be created in four different ways:

1. The main program, by definition, is a task.

2. A task can be declared by giving its specification and its body.

3. A task *type* can be introduced by a declaration that begins **task type** ... . Tasks can then be created by declaring objects of that type. They can also be declared as elements of an array or components of a record.

4. Given a task type, a program can create tasks dynamically by means of the alloca-
    tor **new**. This is similar to the creation of coroutine objects, as described in Sec-
    tion 10.9.

An important concept is that, apart from the main program, every task has a *master* on
which it *depends*. In the case of 2 and 3 the master is the subprogram, task, or block
statement in which the task object is declared. The case of 4 is different, but it will not be
considered here.

    The following program shows how tasks provide parallelism in its simplest form. A
procedure M (for 'master') declares two tasks X and Y, which then operate in parallel with
M itself. They assume that a procedure print_chars (ch, r) is available, which prints r
copies of the character ch on a single line.

```
procedure M is
   task X;                              -- specification of X
   task Y;                              -- specification of Y

   task X is                           -- body of X
   begin
      for i in 1..10 loop
         print_chars ('x', 3);
      end loop;
   end X;

   task Y is                           -- body of Y
   begin
      for i in 1..20 loop
         print_chars ('y', 5);
      end loop;
   end Y;

begin                                  -- statements of M
   for i in 1..8 loop
      print_chars ('m', 7);
   end loop;
end M;
```

Task X prints 10 lines, each containing "xxx"; similarly Y prints 20 containing "yyyyy",
and M prints 8 containing "mmmmmmm". Notionally, they operate in parallel, sending
their output to a common device via print_chars. As with CSP, though, nothing is stated
about their relative rates of progress and so the interleaving of the lines and/or characters
will (in principle) be unpredictable. It may vary from one implementation to another and
even from one run to another (Exercise 13).

    In considering the details more closely we shall look first at initiation, then at execu-
tion, and finally at termination.

    As the example shows, Ada does not initiate tasks in any explicit way. Its prelim-
inary version had an **initiate** statement; but in the final version initiation is carried out
automatically. To be more specific, the tasks are initiated when control reaches the
begin–end statement sequence of their master. At that point their declarations (if any)

are elaborated, so that they too reach the start of their **begin–end** statement sequences. When all their entities have been successfully created the master and its dependants can proceed in parallel.

The execution phase follows the principles that were discussed in Section 11.3. For example, if X, Y, and M are run on three separate processors, they execute in parallel and, as already mentioned, the interleaving of their output will to some extent be unpredictable (Section 11.10 discusses this point further). On the other hand, if there is only one processor, their execution will be quasi-parallel: the system will attempt to behave in parallel fashion, even though execution will be restricted to one task at any given time. A run-time *scheduler* is responsible for deciding when each task is to have its turn (see Section 12.10). If some tasks need precedence over others, they can each be given a *priority*. This is done by means of a pragma in their specification. For example:

```
task X is
    pragma priority (10);
end X;
```

Other things being equal, tasks of higher priority will always be given precedence. In the absence of any priorities, Ada allows the scheduler to do what it likes. Ideally, it should use some form of 'time-slicing', as described in Section 11.3. On the other hand, a crude version might run X to completion, then Y, then M. To enforce some interleaving, a **delay** statement can be included in their loops:

```
for i in ... loop
    print_chars ( ... );
    delay 0.01;
end loop;
```

A delay of 0.01 suspends their execution for a minimum of 0.01 seconds, allowing the other tasks to take over. By varying the delays we can vary the output that is produced.

Finally, the tasks have to terminate. The basic rule is that a master must not terminate until all its dependants have terminated. For instance, M must not terminate until X and Y have. The reason is clear enough: X or Y might refer to entities declared in M and so these must not be deleted until X and Y have finished with them. When M reaches its concluding **end** it must therefore check the status of its dependants and, if any of them are still active, it must mark itself as 'ready to terminate' but defer termination until later. In this case, Ada states that the task is *completed* but not *terminated*. There are two attributes that can be used for testing these conditions — M'callable and M'terminated. If M is completed but not terminated, they are both false. When it has terminated, the latter becomes true. Other facilities for handling termination are described in Section 11.10.

11.8   THE RENDEZVOUS

The tasks X, Y, and M are very simple in that each executes independently of the others. If they are to cooperate they need facilities that allow them to synchronize, share, and communicate, as described in Sections 11.4 – 11.6. Ada provides a single mechanism for the purpose, which is an elaboration of CSP's message-passing system and is called the *rendezvous* — a reminder, perhaps, of Ada's origins in France. (Plural, *rendezvous*; also verb intransitive, he/she *rendezvouses*, we are *rendezvousing*, they *rendezvoused*.)

To set the scene we shall take a second look at task specifications which, like all specifications, describe the interface with potential users. In the case of tasks the interface is very restricted. Unlike subprograms, tasks cannot have parameters; unlike packages, they cannot provide types or variables or subprograms. All that they can offer are *entries*. The following example specifies one called *send* and one called *receive*:

```
task T is
    entry send (x : in item_type);
    entry receive (y : out item_type);
end T;
```

From the viewpoint of the user the entries look like procedures. Their specification has the same form; they can have parameters of the same kinds; and they are called in the same way. Thus, if alpha and beta are item_type variables, T's entries can be called as follows:

```
T.send (alpha);
T.receive (beta);
```

Both in their appearance and in their behavior, these could be either procedure calls or entry calls. It is only in their implementation that the differences begin to appear.

In order to execute its entry calls the body of T must contain one or more **accept** statements. In the following outline, there is one for send and one for receive:

```
task body T is
    ...                              -- local entities
begin
    ...
    accept send (x : in item_type) do
        statement_sequence
    end send;
    ...
    accept receive (y : out item_type) do
        statement_sequence
    end receive;
    ...
end T;
```

As can be seen, an **accept** statement echoes the specification of the entry that it is accepting and then has a **do-end** part. The latter is optional; but if it is included it consists of an arbitrary sequence of statements and is the only place where the parameters of the entry can be referred to. The **accept** statement is executed when a corresponding entry call has been made by some other task (recursive calls by the same task are not allowed). When this happens the calling task and the accepting task have their rendezvous. For a brief moment their execution sequences coincide. They exchange information by means of the parameters and perform other actions as necessary. Then, on completion of the **do-end** statement sequence, they part company and resume their separate ways.

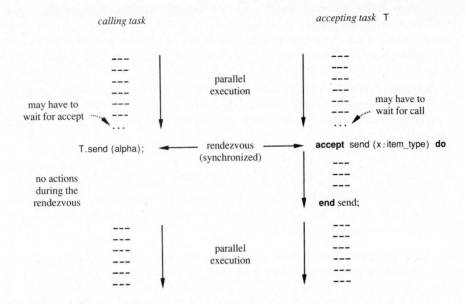

Figure 11-3 A rendezvous

Figure 11-3 depicts the sequence of events in more detail. It starts with the calling task performing a sequence of actions on the left, while the accepting task T performs another sequence of actions on the right. In principle, these execute in parallel. In due course, the calling task arrives at the entry call T.send (alpha) and T arrives at its statement **accept** send (x), and so the rendezvous takes place. Of course, it is highly unlikely that the two parties will arrive simultaneously. In practice, one will arrive first and will have to wait for the other. Either the calling task issues its request and has to wait for acceptance, or T reaches its **accept** and has to wait for the call. As the figure shows, when the rendezvous is executed, the calling task suspends itself until the **do–end** part of the **accept** statement has been executed. This prevents the two processes from having access to the parameters simultaneously, with all the problems of shared variables that this would entail. In fact, it may be regarded as a form of mutual exclusion, with the **do–end** statement sequence being a critical region. On its completion the calling task can resume its execution and so the two tasks continue in parallel.

The synchronizing of the two tasks is the main feature that distinguishes an entry call from a procedure call. It carries the risk that one party may fail to arrive at the rendezvous and so the other becomes permanently hung up. Indeed, if the calling task attempts to call send while the accepting one is waiting for receive, they will *both* be hung up — a typical example of the 'deadly embrace'. As shown in Section 11.10, Ada provides several facilities for alleviating the problem. In the final analysis, though, it remains as one of the major pitfalls of parallel programming.

Things become slightly more complicated if an entry is called by several tasks at about the same time. To handle this situation each entry E has an associated queue, similar to the one for the *wait* operation of a semaphore (see Section 11.5). The competing tasks have to wait in the queue for their turn, the number of them — that is, the length of the queue — being given by the attribute E'count. They are served on a strict first-in/first-out (FIFO) basis, with no priorities or other facilities for jumping to the front. (The priorities mentioned in Section 11.7 are used by the scheduler but carry no influence in entry queues.) On reaching the front a task makes its rendezvous in the same way as before, with no indication that it has been competing with other tasks for that entry.

In its basic concept the rendezvous is clearly similar to the message-passing facility of CSP. The calling and accepting have to be synchronized and information can be passed from one process to the other. In its details, though, the rendezvous has some important differences:

1.   The accepting task does not name the calling task and so it will accept entry calls from all tasks without distinction. As mentioned at the end of Section 11.6, this is important for building process libraries. On the other hand, there are some applications where the calling task needs to identify itself and then the coding is more complicated.

2.   The communication at a rendezvous can be two-way. Parameters can be **in**, **out**, or **in out**, and this allows information to be passed in either direction.

3.   The accepting process can execute an arbitrary statement sequence during the rendezvous. This simplifies the coding in some cases.

As in CSP, several **accept** statements can be provided for the same entry. Ada restricts them to the body of the task that declares the entry and further stipulates that they may not occur in any inner unit (subprogram, package, or task), nor within another **accept** statement for the same entry. However, an **accept** statement for one entry can contain **accept** statements for *other* entries, and this is sometimes quite useful.

11.9 TASK PARAMETERS

In Section 11.7 tasks X and Y had the obvious drawback that each was tied to a particular character ('x' or 'y') with a particular repeat factor (3 or 5) for a particular number of lines (10 or 20). A more flexible arrangement would allow them to be initialized with these values as parameters. More generally, it would be useful if tasks could have parameters in the same way as ordinary subprograms.

Unfortunately, Ada does not allow this — at least, not in any clear, simple way. As noted earlier, the only things that can appear in a task specification are entries. Parameters are excluded, partly through lack of an **initiate** statement for providing their values, but more importantly because of the problem that was described for the case of coroutines. If an actual parameter is a variable, the task may outlive the variable and leave the formal parameter referring to an entity that no longer exists (see Section 10.9). This applies not only to **out** parameters but also to **in** parameters that are passed by reference (arrays and other large structures). The danger is particularly acute for tasks that are created dynamically by means of **new** (see Section 11.7, method 4).

Tasks cannot have parameters, but entries can; so it is interesting to consider the extent to which this provides an adequate alternative. The basic idea is simple enough. If a task has to be initialized with some parameters it is given an entry, init say, and the parameters are passed to init as soon as the task starts executing. To show how this works in detail, we shall apply it to the tasks X and Y. The resulting code will illustrate a simple rendezvous and several other tasking features.

The first thing to note is that, apart from their three parameters, X and Y are identical. It is therefore appropriate to declare them by means of a common task type, with the three parameters appearing in the specification of init.

```
task type char_printer is
    entry init (ch : character;
                    r, n : natural);
end char_printer;

X, Y : char_printer;
```

The body of char_printer acquires the parameters by accepting init and copying them to local variables. It then continues in the same way as before:

```
task body char_printer is
    local_ch : character;
    local_r, local_n : natural;
begin
    accept init (ch : character;          -- accept the parameters
                    r, n : natural) do
        local_ch := ch;                   -- make local copies
        local_r := r;
        local_n := n;
    end init;
    for i in 1..local_n loop              -- print the lines
        print_chars (local_ch, local_r);
    end loop;
end char_printer;
```

The master routine M begins by rendezvousing with X and Y in order to set the parameters. It then executes its own loop in parallel with the others:

```
begin
    X.init ('x', 3, 10);
    Y.init ('y', 5, 20);
    for i in 1..8 loop
        print_chars ('m', 7);
    end loop;
end M;
```

As an alternative, it could transfer its loop to a third task, Z say, and then remain idle while X, Y, and Z do the work.

This technique provides a 'copy in' facility by implementing a very explicit form of pass-to-local-variable. In the same way, another entry could be executed at the end of the task, using **out** parameters to provide a 'copy out' facility. As a means of handling task parameters this is better than nothing. Even so, it must be admitted that the coding is very clumsy. In the case of init, each parameter has to be copied across to a local variable so that it can be used by the rest of the task. The code would be simpler if the **for** statement were included in the **accept** statement, where it could refer to the parameters directly. But the trouble with this is that M would be prevented from continuing until the **for** statement had been completed and so there would be no parallel execution! The more elaborate version is therefore necessary.

11.10   THE SELECT STATEMENT

The **select** statement is Ada's facility for allowing a task to choose between various courses of action, depending on the readiness of other tasks to engage in a rendezvous. It has three basic forms:

- the conditional entry call;
- the timed entry call;
- the selective wait.

The first two are provided for the benefit of the *calling* task; the third is used by the *accepting* task.

The *conditional entry call* allows a task to call an entry with the proviso that the entry must be accepted immediately. It has the form:

> **select**
> > *entry_call*
> > *statement_sequence_1*
>
> **else**
> > *statement_sequence_2*
>
> **end select**;

If the entry call can be accepted immediately the rendezvous is made and then *statement_sequence_1* is executed; otherwise *statement_sequence_2* is executed. Some applications will be given in later sections.

With a *timed entry call* the proviso is that the entry call must be accepted within a specified time. Its form is:

> **select**
> > *entry_call*
> > *statement_sequence_1*
>
> **else**
> > **delay** *t*;
> > *statement_sequence_2*
>
> **end select**;

The expression *t* gives the maximum number of seconds for which the task is prepared to wait. In other respects the interpretation is the same as for the conditional entry call. If $t = 0$, it is in fact identical.

The *selective wait* is considerably more complicated. It allows a task to accept an entry without knowing in advance which particular entry will be called first. It is similar to CSP's alternative command (see Section 11.6), but is elaborated in several important, practical ways. Its basic form is as follows:

```
select
    when condition_1 =>
        accept entry_1 (...) do
            ...
        end entry_1;
        statement_sequence_1
or
    when condition_2 =>
        accept entry_2 (...) do
            ...
        end entry_2;
        statement_sequence_2
or
    ...
or
    when condition_n =>
        accept entry_n (...) do
            ...
        end entry_n;
        statement_sequence_n
end select;
```

Like CSP's command, it is modeled on Dijkstra's **if-fi** statement (see Section 8.10), and in recognition of this the conditions are called *guards*. The **when** clauses can be omitted, in which case the guards are assumed to be true. The implementation begins by evaluating the guards and determining which ones are true: the corresponding alternatives are said to be *open*. It then chooses between the open alternatives as follows:

- If exactly one has a waiting request, it executes that one.

- If two or more have waiting requests, it executes any one of them (a nondeterministic choice).

- If none has a waiting request, it waits until a request comes in.

If none of the alternatives are open, an error is assumed and the program_error exception is raised.

All this can be regarded as an intelligent transliteration of the CSP alternative command, with the usual difference that **accept** statements do not have to nominate the tasks that call them and that communication is two-way. However, Ada goes further by providing three options for handling special situations. A **select** statement can include at most one of them:

1.   A final clause of the form

else *statement_sequence*

This is executed if there are no open alternatives or if none of the open alternatives has a waiting request. It guarantees that the **select** statement will never have to wait.

2.   One or more **delay** alternatives, having the form:

or when *condition* =>   -- optional guard
    delay *t*;
        statement_sequence

This is similar to the **else** option, except that the task is prepared to wait for a maximum of *t* seconds before defaulting to the *statement_sequence*. If there are two or more such alternatives, the one with minimum *t* will be the default; if their delays are equal, the choice is arbitrary.

3.   A **terminate** alternative, having the form:

or when *condition* =>   -- optional guard
    terminate;

If no open **accept** alternatives have waiting requests, it may be that the master task and all its other dependants are ready to terminate. In that case an open **terminate** alternative causes the task to terminate, and the rest of the system will then terminate also.

It will be appreciated that options 1 and 2 are the accepting task's equivalent of conditional and timed entry calls. The **terminate** alternative serves an entirely different purpose. As the next section shows, it is particularly important for any **select** statement that is executed inside an infinite loop. Without it, the loop would continue to wait for entry calls even when all the other tasks in the system had finished, and this would prevent the system from terminating.

11.11 MONITORS

The tasks X, Y, and M of Section 11.7 all make calls on a procedure print_chars, which is available to them globally. They therefore *share* the procedure; and this, as explained at the start of Section 11.4, can be a hazardous business. For one thing, if print_chars uses global variables, it raises all the usual problem of shared variables. For another, it is not clear how the different calls of print_chars will interact in their output. The intention is that each call should print a line of characters, the interleaving of the lines corresponding to the interleaving of the calls. In principle, though, the calls by X, Y and M can all execute simultaneously and so it may turn out that the characters themselves are interleaved. This could occur even when there is only one processor: if time-slicing is used, the printing of one line could be interrupted by the printing of another.

A *monitor* is a mechanism that is designed to make the sharing of a resource much safer, guarding it against the perils described in Section 11.5. It consists of the resource itself and the subprograms for using it, with access being subject to two rules:

1.   Access can be made only by calling the subprograms.

2.   Only one subprogram can execute at a time.

Rule 1 states that a monitor is, in effect, an abstract data object (ADO) — one that is designed for use by parallel processes. Rule 2 states that the subprograms are treated like critical regions, being subject to mutual exclusion. The combination of the two policies produces a very valuable concept for the design of parallel systems. It emerged from an evolutionary process in the early 1970s and a particular version was described in a paper by C. A. R. Hoare (1974).

In Ada a monitor can be written as a task, its subprograms being converted to entries. The task executes an endless loop, accepting the entry calls one at a time as they come in. As a simple example we shall write one called printer, which provides an entry for print_chars. It uses the standard package text_io, which includes a procedure put for printing a character and new_line for terminating a line:

```
task printer is
    entry print_chars (ch : character; r : natural);
end printer;

task body printer is
    local_ch : character;
    local_r : natural;
begin
    loop
        accept print_chars (ch : character; r : natural) do
            local_ch := ch;
            local_r := r;
        end print_chars;
        for i in 1..local_r loop
            put (local_ch);
        end loop;
        new_line;
    end loop;
end printer;
```

At the start of the loop the task waits for a call on print_chars. When this comes in, it copies the parameters to local variables and then ends the rendezvous so that the calling task is free to resume execution. Continuing (hopefully) in parallel, it prints the required line of characters and then returns to the start of the loop, ready for the next call to come in. If the calls come in faster than it can handle them, they are automatically placed on the entry queue where they are served in FIFO order. The comment might be made that the task uses the global procedures put and new_line, and so the problem of shared subprograms still remains. If other tasks were also using put and new_line this would indeed be the case. However, if all calls on put and new_line are confined to the task printer, all will be well.

As a second example we shall take the classical problem of the *bounded buffer*. The problem arises when one task wants to send items to another task but without having to wait for a rendezvous. For example, the tasks might be two filters connected by a pipe, as shown in Figure 11-2. The sending task is commonly known as the *producer* and the receiving task as the *consumer*. Instead of synchronizing their actions, they communicate asynchronously via a buffer. The producer puts items into the buffer and the consumer takes them out again. The buffer is 'bounded' in that it can hold a maximum of n items, where n is some constant. If it becomes full the producer has to wait until an item has been removed; if it becomes empty the consumer has to wait until one has been deposited.

In the absence of tasking the bounded buffer would be represented as an ADO, using a package with two procedures, deposit and remove. Inside the package, there could be an array for holding n items and a variable called count to keep track of how many items are present. However, if deposit and remove are called in parallel, they run into the problem of shared variables. For example, if deposit tries to increment count at the same time as remove tries to decrement it, the effects are unpredictable (see Section 11.3). The correct approach is therefore to represent the ADO as a monitor instead, which prevents deposit and remove from executing in parallel.

Since the task cannot predict the order in which the deposit and remove requests will arrive, it uses a **select** statement, as described in the previous section. The deposited items are held in an array box (0..n−1), with the variable count to indicate how many there are. Variables d and r indicate which box is to be used next by deposit and remove. The guards ensure that a deposit can occur only when count < n and that a removal can occur only when count > 0:

```
task buffer is
    entry deposit (x : in item_type);
    entry remove (x : out item_type);
end buffer;

task body buffer is
    n : constant integer := 100;              -- number of boxes
    subtype index is integer range 0..n−1;
    box : array (index) of item_type;         -- the boxes
    d : index := index'first;                 -- next box for deposit
    r : index := index'first;                 -- next box for remove
    count : integer range 0..n := 0;          -- number of items held
begin
    loop
        select
            when count < n =>                 -- is there a free box?
                accept deposit (x : in item_type) do
                    box(d) := x;              -- place x in it
                end deposit;
                d := (d + 1) mod n;
                count := count + 1;
        or
```

```
        when count > 0 =>                       -- is there a full box?
            accept remove (x : out item_type) do
                x := box(r);                     -- take x from it
            end remove;
            r := (r + 1) mod n;
            count := count - 1;
    or
        terminate;
    end select;
    end loop;
end buffer;
```

Several points are worth noting. First, the **select** statement has no **else** clause and so it is essential that the guards cannot both be false. Since count lies in the range 0..n, this is easily guaranteed. Second, the possible combinations of conditions are all handled correctly — free boxes, full boxes, waiting deposits, and waiting removals — with an arbitrary choice when both entries are acceptable. Third, the parameters (as usual) are handled inside the critical regions; but d, r, and count, being local variables, can be handled outside them.

Finally, the **terminate** alternative is included to ensure that the buffer does not prevent its users from terminating when they want to. The same should have been done for the task printer above. Indeed, it should be done almost as a matter of routine for any task of this form.

11.12   ENTRY FAMILIES

In modeling real-world systems a task sometimes needs an array of entries, all of one kind. For example, suppose that it is modeling an elevator that services the floors of a building. The floors could be numbered by a discrete type such as:

```
        subtype floor_type is integer range 1..8;
```

The elevator has to service requests from any floor and at first sight it seems that this could be modeled by an entry that takes the floor number as a parameter:

```
        subtype floor_type is integer range 1..8;
        type direction is (up, down);

        task elevator is
            entry service (f : floor_type; d : direction);
        end elevator;
```

However, since the entry has only one queue, this implies that the users of the elevator all wait in a common queue — which is absurd! A more realistic model would have a queue for each floor, each handled by a separate entry.

Ada provides for this by allowing a task to have a *family* of entries. This is similar to an array in that the entries are indexed by a discrete type. For elevator the discrete type is floor_type:

```
task elevator is
    entry service (floor_type) (d : direction);
end elevator;
```

This specification creates eight entries, namely service (1), service (2), ... service (8), each with its own queue. A passenger who wants to go from level 3 to level 8 might therefore call:

```
elevator.service(3) (up);
```

The 3 is an index and up is an actual parameter. The notation can be a bit confusing because in a call such as

```
any_entry (i);
```

it is not clear whether i is an index or a parameter. This can only be determined by reference to the specification.

The eight entries have the same status as any other entry and can be accepted in the same way. For example, the body of elevator might accept a request from the first floor:

```
accept service (floor_type'first) (d : direction) do
    ...
end service;
```

Similarly, if f is a floor_type variable,

```
accept service (f) (d : direction) do ...
```

accepts one for floor f. The attribute service(f)'count gives the number of people waiting at level f.

In order to service an arbitrary entry — whichever happens to be called — it would be convenient if the **select** statement had a version in which

```
accept service (f) ...
```

accepted a call to any entry of the family, setting f to the corresponding index. This would require the statement to scan all of the entries, looking for one that was ready, and if necessary it would wait until one was called. CSP provides a statement that does precisely this. In Ada, however, the programmer has to code the requirement explicitly. If the number of entries is known in advance and is not too large, the simplest strategy is to use a **select** statement with a separate **accept** for each entry. The alternative is to write a loop that inspects each entry in turn until it finds one that is ready:

```
    f := floor_type'first;
    while service(f)'count = 0 loop        -- test entry f
        if f = floor_type'last then        -- increment f
            f := floor_type'first;
        else
            f := floor_type'succ (f);
        end if;
        delay 0.01;                        -- force time-slicing
    end loop;
```

This polls the entries at regular intervals and is therefore less efficient than the **select** statement, which waits for the system to wake it up. For further discussion of the 'polling bias' in Ada, see Gehani and Cargill (1984).

11.13 INTERRUPTS

Interrupts are an important feature of real-time programming, being needed for the control of peripheral devices and for other interfaces to the external world. They were described at machine level in Section 5.7 and were used for controlling low-level input/output in Section 5.14. It is now time to see how they can be incorporated into a high-level, real-time language.

As pointed out previously, interrupts are similar to subroutine calls. The main difference is that they are initiated by events rather than instructions. Also, they have to be linked to particular hardware addresses and, if several interrupts can occur at the same time, a priority system may be needed for handling them. In response to these requirements Ada allows interrupts to be handled by a special sort of task entry. The entry is distinguished by having an *address specification* that links it to the required hardware address. The idea is illustrated in the following task, which is designed for drawing a line on a plotter and accepting an interrupt when the job has been done:

```
task draw_line is
    entry draw (x : line_type);
    entry end_of_draw;
        for end_of_draw use at 16#80#;
end draw_line;
```

Here draw is an ordinary entry, but end_of_draw has an address specification of 80_{16} and is therefore an interrupt entry. The choice of the address, of course, will depend on the implementation.

The corresponding task body is written with **accept** statements in the usual way. The following is a possible outline:

```
task body draw_line is
begin
    loop
        accept draw (x : line_type) do
            ...                              -- initiate the drawing
        end draw;
        accept end_of_draw;
    end loop;
end draw_line;
```

The end−of_draw interrupt prevents the task from initiating a second line before the previous one has been completed. For some low-level applications this sort of control may be important.

As far as priorities are concerned, the system automatically gives interrupts higher priority than the user-defined tasks. The interrupts may also have their own pecking order, but this cannot be controlled by the Ada program.

11.14 CONTROLLERS

As a final excursion into parallel processing, this section looks at ways in which tasks can control the execution of other tasks. A simple example is provided by a task type for implementing binary semaphores. Its specification is:

```
task type semaphore is
    entry wait;
    entry signal;
end semaphore;
```

The task body repeatedly accepts wait followed by signal:

```
task body semaphore is
begin
    loop
        select
            accept wait;
            accept signal;
        or
            terminate;
        end select;
    end loop;
end semaphore;
```

Its form is similar to a monitor, but its function is rather different. Instead of providing a service, it simply controls the execution of wait and signal by other tasks, ensuring that they alternate in the required fashion. The entry mechanism automatically queues waiting tasks as described for semaphores in Section 11.5.

The task illustrates an important technique for the control of parallel processes. If tasks T1 and T2 are executing independently, their actions are interleaved in arbitrary fashion. However, if specific points in their execution have to be synchronized with a controlling task T, the interleaving can be forced to follow particular patterns. If the patterns are written as regular expressions they are called *path expressions*. For example, using P to denote wait and V to denote signal, the pattern for legitimate executions of P and V is the path expression $(P V)^*$ — that is, repetition of the sequence P-then-V for nought, one, or more times..

Path expressions were developed in the context of monitors as a means of specifying the sequences in which their operations could be executed (Campbell and Habermann, 1974). In Ada the control is provided by embedding the relevant **accept** statements inside the statement sequence of the task body, as illustrated above for semaphore. This achieves the same effect in a more powerful and flexible way. In the case of semaphores this is the *only* function of the monitor: it controls the sequence in which competing tasks can execute P and V, but beyond that it does nothing else.

For controlling real-life objects a process can follow the same object-oriented approach as in a simulation. Its sequencing structures model the behavior pattern of the object, initiating the control operations in the required way. A popular example is a process for controlling an elevator. Its basic operations could be the following:

open_doors	—	open the doors
close_doors	—	close the doors
ascend	—	move upwards
descend	—	move downwards
stop_at (f)	—	stop at floor f

The basic operational cycle is given by the following path expression:

(close_doors; (ascend | descend); stop_at (f); open_doors) *

This in turn can be modeled by a loop of the form:

```
loop
    close_doors;
    if ... then
        ascend;
    else
        descend;
    end if;
    stop_at (f);
    open_doors;
end loop;
```

The main decisions can all be slotted into this framework. In practice, the operation stop_at (f) might simply consist of setting an indicator at level f which would cause the elevator to stop when it next arrived there. If this were the case, the stop_at requests could be executed independently of the main cycle. For example, a simple strategy would be to execute stop_at (f) as soon as a request for floor f were made. However, the decision to stop at floor f can depend on other factors as well and so there are advantages in delaying it for as long as possible — preferably until the elevator has almost arrived there. The controller can then behave more 'intelligently', basing its decision on the most recent information. The above loop can accommodate this strategy and is therefore a suitable one to work from.

The decision-making information comes primarily from the various buttons that can be pressed by the users — an 'up' button on each floor except the top one, a 'down' button on each floor except the bottom one, and in the elevator itself a 'stop' button for each floor (not to mention various emergency buttons as well). These buttons can be pressed at any point in the main cycle and require an immediate response, possibly causing them to light up. Consequently, it is best to handle them independently of the main cycle, treating them as a separate object with a parallel process of its own. This second process is basically a simple monitor that responds to the buttons as soon as they are pressed, either by polling them or (preferably) by accepting interrupts. It provides information to the main controller on the current set of requests. When a particular request has been serviced, the main controller calls the monitor to unset the corresponding button, turning off its light and noting that it is no longer active.

These considerations provide a suitable framework for writing the controller. They illustrate an object-oriented approach by providing one process for the elevator and one for the buttons. The former is an *actor* in that its main task is to call entries rather than to accept them; it is implemented by modeling the elevator's operational cycle. The latter is a *server* with the more passive role of simply accepting calls; it is implemented as a conventional monitor. The combined system can be tested by introducing two other processes — a server for simulating the elevator and an actor for simulating the people who use it. (For further considerations see Exercises 27 - 28.) The resulting program provides an interesting mixture of simulation and real-time control.

This example illustrated the design of a relatively simple (though not entirely trivial) controller. With more processes the interactions become harder to handle and issues of priority can add to the complications. A reliable methodology is needed for designing and implementing such systems. Unfortunately, the literature on this subject is rather meager, though a few references are given below. Some applications involve control theory and sophisticated numerical computations. These take real-time programming into a whole new ball park and offer some of the most challenging problems in computing.

FURTHER READING

As remarked at the start of the chapter, parallel processing is rooted historically in the development of operating systems and, until recently, most of the relevant literature appeared in that context. For the material of this chapter some good introductions are given in Deitel (1984), Lister (1984), and Peterson and Silberschatz (1985). The last of these provides a comprehensive bibliography. Some classical papers are Strachey (1959) which first suggested the concept of time-sharing; Dijkstra (1965) which introduced semaphores; Hoare (1974) which was a focus for work on monitors; and Hoare (1978) which introduced CSP.

Andrews and Schneider (1983) is a good review of the concepts described in the first few sections of this chapter, and describes some additional notations for expressing them. For an earlier review see Brinch Hansen (1973). Perrott (1987) compares ten languages for parallel processing, including Modula-2, Pascal-Plus, Ada, occam, and some array-processing versions of FORTRAN. Welsh, Lister, and Salzman (1980) compares CSP with a notation devised by Brinch Hansen (1978). Welsh and Lister (1981) provides a similar comparison of CSP with Ada. These two papers include most of the standard problems which have been used in assessing languages for parallel processing. Wegner and Smolka (1983) makes a similar comparison of processes in CSP, tasks in Ada, and monitors. The book by Burns, Lister, and Wellings (1987) gives a very detailed review of Ada's tasking facilities followed by a bibliography of 234 references. See also Gehani and Cargill (1984).

Several books have been written on concurrent programming in Ada, including Gehani (1984) and Burns (1985). These present a good range of short, sample programs, but are not so helpful in providing a methodology for developing larger ones. Nielsen and Shumate (1987) presents a methodology using the Process Abstraction Model. See the references there and also Ben-Ari (1982), Downes and Goldsack (1982), Buhr (1984), and Shumate (1987). Welch (1986) concludes that occam is better for the purpose than Ada. Jackson (1983) provides a detailed methodology in a wider context.

This chapter has not attempted to give a formal definition of the concepts that it describes, nor to develop any associated theory or proof techniques. Nevertheless, there has been plenty of activity in the area. One approach extends the use of assertions and proof rules, as described in Chapter 8, usually taking the base language to be either CSP

(Apt *et al.*, 1980; Apt, 1983) or Ada (Barringer and Mearns, 1986). Barringer (1985) gives a survey of these techniques. A second approach develops a mathematical theory of communicating processes, as found in Milner (1980) and Hoare (1981, 1986). A third approach addresses the issues of timing by using some form of *temporal logic* (Lamport, 1983). Galton (1987) provides a good starting point for this. Barringer (1987) uses one such logic to develop a formal specification of a controller for multiple elevators. Readers who relish a challenge may care to read the specification and derive a working program. Users of the elevators would doubtless be reassured to know that the controllers have been developed by such rigorous means.

EXERCISES

1   Adding processors to a multiprocessor system involves the law of diminishing returns. There comes a point where further additions make no improvement at all, and they may even start to degrade performance. Discuss this phenomenon as it applies to teams of programmers attempting to complete a task. For an entertaining/sobering account of it see Brooks (1975).

2   Consider the process flowgraphs of Figure 11-1. The rule is that, if p_i enters a node and p_j leaves it, then p_i must be completed before p_j can begin. This induces a partial ordering $p_i < p_j$ on the processes which can be represented by a *precedence graph*. Each process is a node of the graph and an arc from p_i to p_j corresponds to the situation described above. Draw precedence graphs for the three flowgraphs in Figure 11-1.

3   As remarked in Section 11.2 the **fork–join** operations have the property that the 'survivor' of a **join** is unpredictable. What troubles might this cause? Suggest some alternatives that avoid the problem.

4   Write **fork–join** programs for the process flowgraphs of Figure 11-1(b) and (c).

5   Write parallel commands for implementing the flowgraphs (a) and (b) of Figure 11-1. Prove that flowgraph (c) cannot be implemented in this way.

6   Section 11.4 gives a simple method of ensuring that process_1 does not execute A1 until process_2 has executed A2. It uses a flag A2_done that has to be initialized before either process begins. What could go wrong if (a) process_1 initializes it, and (b) process_2 initializes it?

7   Rewrite process_1 and process_2 in Section 11.4, using **wait until** statements, so that A1 and A2 are fully synchronized.

Rewrite them using semaphores instead.

8   A process producer executes a loop in which it 'produces' an item and places it in a bounded buffer with n slots. At the same time a process consumer executes a loop in which it takes an item from the buffer and 'consumes' it. Show how integer semaphores can be used for controlling access to the buffer, giving the *seize* and *release* protocols for each process.

9   Section 11.5 gave protocols for two processes to execute critical sections without using semaphores. They used an integer variable turn and two flags critical_1 and critical_2. A previous version omitted the flags but failed to satisfy the progress requirement. The following version omits turn instead:

process_1   process_2

loop   **loop**

   . . .   . . .

   critical_1 := true;   critical_2 := true;
   wait until not critical_2;   **wait until not** critical_1;
    critical section   *critical section*
   critical_1 := false;   critical_2 := false;

   . . .   . . .

end loop;   **end loop;**

What is wrong with this 'solution'?

Perhaps it would be better to place the first assignment after the **wait** statement, instead of before it. But this does not work either. Why not?

For a discussion of this example, see Peterson and Silberschatz (1985, pp.328–333).

10 Show how binary semaphores can be used for implementing integer semaphores.

11 Show how binary and integer semaphores can be implemented in CSP. Assume that the semaphore is to be used by processes X and Y.

What difficulties arise if the semaphore is to be shared by an unspecified set of processes? (See also Exercise 21.)

12 Exercise 10.21 describes a set of three coroutines called disassembler, squasher, and assembler that communicate via the global variables ch1 and ch2. Show how the processes can be implemented in CSP, with particular reference to their method of communication, and compare the two techniques.

13 Use the tasks X, Y, and M of Section 11.7, with parameters as described in Section 11.9, to investigate the implementation of tasks in your version of Ada. For example:

  (a)   Does the system do time-slicing or must the tasks enforce it by means of **delay** statements?

  (b)   What sort of scheduling algorithm is used for the tasks?

  (c)   The lines from each task should be interleaved, but what about individual characters? What does this imply?

14 Investigate the use of tasks for solving some simple 'divide-and-conquer' algorithms. For example, to sum the elements of an array $A(1..n)$, a possible strategy is to sum $A(1..k)$ and $A(k+1..n)$ separately, where $k = n/2$. Write a task that uses one or more subtasks to sum them in parallel. Consider the problem of applying the same strategy recursively to the subarrays.

15   Show how a task can be used for implementing a semicoroutine with the **call-suspend** mechanism, as described in Section 10.9. What advantages are available through the use of entry parameters?

16   Show how tasks can implement a system of coroutines using the **resume-resume** mechanism, as described in Section 10.10. Note that when one task resumes another it must suspend its own execution; in other words, full parallelism must be reduced to quasi-parallelism.

17   Design a simulation package that offers facilities similar to those of SIMULA 67, as described in Section 10.11. For one such design, see Shore (1987).

Note   The next three exercises are classical problems in the field of concurrent programming. They all involve two or more processes wanting access to resources under certain constraints. The applications add some attractive color to the problems and have doubtless contributed to their popularity.

18   [Readers and writers]   A resource (such as a database) is being used by two groups of people — readers and writers. Several readers can use it at once; however, when a writer is using it, all other readers and writers must be excluded. A task is required for controlling access to the resource on the basis that each reader executes specified *start_read* and *end_read* protocols and that each writer executes specified *start_write* and *end_write* protocols.

There are many ways of achieving the basic objective. Here are some of them:

(1)   Allow only one reader or writer at a time, not necessarily in FIFO order.

(2)   As in (1), except that when the controller allows a reader to start, it allows all other waiting readers to start also.

(3)   As in (2), except that new readers can join existing readers at any time.

(4)   As in (3), except that new readers may not join existing readers if this means overtaking a waiting writer.

(5)   Strictly FIFO, one at a time.

(6)   Strictly FIFO, but with concurrent readers where possible.

In each case, state whether (a) readers can starve, (b) writers can starve, (c) both, or (d) neither.

This problem was first posed by Courtois *et al.* (1971). For an analysis of its many variations, see Gerber (1980).

19   [The cigarette smokers]   Three cigarette smokers, P, T, and M, are seated round a table. P has some cigarette papers; T has some tobacco; and M has some matches. Each needs all three items in order to have a smoke, but they are not willing to pool their resources. Fortunately for them, three suppliers SP, ST, and SM are ready to assist. SP can contribute papers, ST tobacco, and SM matches. The procedure is that two suppliers place two items on the table — for example, a paper and a match — whereupon the appropriate smoker grabs the items and has a smoke. The cycle is then repeated.

Investigate various strategies for implementing a system of this kind. Each smoker and supplier should be represented by a separate task. Can you devise a suitable path expression that could be enforced by a controller, as described at the start of Section 11.14?

This version of the problem uses 'concurrent' suppliers. The original version, formulated by S. Patil (1971), uses a single 'sequential' supplier. For a discussion of the earlier version see Parnas (1975).

20   [The dining philosophers]   Five philosophers share a circular dining table that has a place allocated to each. In the center is a communal bowl with an infinite supply of spaghetti from which they feed. To help themselves, they each need two forks. Unfortunately, there are only five forks available, one being placed between each pair of adjacent seats (see Figure 11-4).

The life of each philosopher can be described very simply as an infinite loop with the following essential components:

```
loop
     think;
     pick up the two adjacent forks;
     eat;
     put down the two adjacent forks;
end loop;
```

The problem is to model the philosophers by tasks or processes in a way that avoids the fatal deadlock — each picking up a fork and waiting. Investigate various strategies that avoid not only deadlock, when all the philosophers would perish, but also any unfairness, from which an individual philosopher might perish. Can the philosophers organize themselves or do they need some sort of controller?

The problem was posed by E. W. Dijkstra (1965) and is discussed in almost every book on concurrent programming. The details, of course, can be varied according to taste. Spaghetti and forks have other connotations for programmers, and so some authors prefer rice and chopsticks. (Also, the need for *two* chopsticks is rather

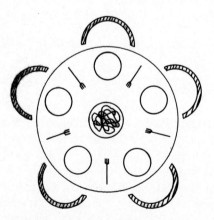

Figure 11-4   The dining philosophers

more convincing!) The five philosophers give the problem an air of erudition, but there is nothing critical about the number five. In fact, in keeping with the adage 'solve a simpler problem first', it might be helpful to start with only two.

21 Investigate the concept of a *channel* in the later version of CSP (Hoare, 1985). How does it solve the problem described in Exercise 11. Compare it with the entry calls of Ada's tasks.

22 With an array of processes (or tasks), a common requirement is that each process should know its own index number. This acts as an identifier for itself that it can pass to other processes.

Investigate ways of providing the numbers to an array of *n* tasks in Ada. Can parallelism be used, or must the *n* operations be carried out sequentially? Comment on the significance of this question.

How is the same problem solved in CSP?

For a discussion of the problem, see Wegner and Smolka (1983).

23 As stated in Section 11.8, task priorities are not considered by **select** statements. However, suppose that a monitor with an entry E needs to handle calls on a priority basis, each call having one of the following priority values:

> **type** priority_type **is** (low, medium, high);

One way of handling this requirement is to turn E into a family of three entries. The entry calls could then have the form:

> E (low) (...);
> E (medium) (...);
> E (high) (...);

Give the specification for a task T, and the outline of a **select** statement in its task body, so that calls on E are treated according to their priorities.

If the priorities are drawn from a much larger range of values, it is impractical to handle each one in a separate branch of the **select** statement. Write an alternative statement that uses polling to accept the highest priority waiting entry (if any). What is the drawback of this technique for a monitor?

For a discussion of this problem, see Burns (1987).

24 In some applications, a task T needs to allocate its own priorities to entry calls, based on the values of one or more parameters. In other words, it wants to do some scheduling. For example, T might be a disk server that schedules read/write requests on the basis of their disk address.

Outline a strategy for doing this on the assumption that the calling tasks do not have to wait for their requests to be serviced.

Outline an alternative strategy for the case where the calling tasks *do* have to wait for their requests to be serviced. Assume that there are no output or input/output parameters. If necessary, change the calling protocol.

Suggest a method of handling output parameters as well.

25   Suppose that a controller has to schedule itself to take some action X in t seconds time. A simple implementation would be:

       delay t;
       X;

However, if it is committed to regular polling of various conditions, it cannot afford to suspend itself in this way. Investigate ways of achieving the same effect without stopping the polling, and discuss their relative merits.

26   A control program requires a facility that plays the role of one or more alarm clocks. It sets an alarm by supplying three parameters — hours, minutes, and a message. The hours must be in the range 0..23 and the minutes in 0..59. The message M is any string. If the designated time is earlier than the current time, it should be interpreted as a time for the following day. In other words, the alarm can be set for any time within the next 24 hours.

The facility is an independent task that accepts the request and, at the designated time, executes:

       put (ascii.bel);
       put_line (M);

Write an appropriate task, or task type, for the purpose.

This example is taken from Gehani (1984). It requires a detailed understanding of how times and dates are handled. In Ada, the relevant information is in the predefined package calendar.

27   Write a controller for the elevator described in Section 11.14. Assume that the elevator has five operations as listed and that it provides feedback to the controller in two ways. First, when it comes to a halt after moving up or down, it gives an end-of-movement interrupt. Second, when it reaches or passes floor f, it sets the value f in some agreed location. When the elevator is moving, the controller can poll this location in order to track its progress. (Alternatively, on reaching or passing floor f, the elevator could give an interrupt.)

The controller should accept 'up' and 'down' requests from each floor and 'stop at floor *x*' requests from passengers on board. It records the requests immediately, but does not necessarily service them in FIFO order. Instead, it keeps moving up as long as there are requests for boarding or leaving higher up; it then reverses direction and keeps moving down as long as there are requests for further down. (A similar method of operation is often used by disk controllers.) Choose a suitable strategy for times when the elevator is idle. (Should its doors be open or shut? Should it move to a predetermined floor?)

In order to test the controller, write a process to simulate the elevator itself. There should be a mechanism to ensure that the doors operate safely and that the elevator always stops on reaching the top or bottom floor. Warnings should be given if the controller attempts to make it do otherwise.

Finally, write a process for simulating people who want to use the elevator. Generally speaking, they should behave in a rational fashion. However, realism requires that people who press an 'up' button sometimes decide that they would prefer to go downwards, or vice-versa. Having pressed a button, they must either require the elevator to wake them up when it reaches the required floor (corresponding to a bell ringing), or they must poll the lift's progress.

The program should display the behavior of the system on a screen, preferably in color graphics.

28 Revise the program of the previous exercise so that it handles multiple elevators working together in an intelligent and harmonious way. Begin by giving an informal specification of the strategy that they should follow for handling requests.

29 Another common application is the control of traffic lights. The problems can vary from a simple crossing to complex, multi-lane, multi-way intersections. Choose any intersection known to you, specify the requirements, and write a controller for the lights. As in the previous exercise, testing has to be done by adding extra processes to simulate the lights and the vehicles.

For a specification of a simple intersection and a corresponding Ada program, see Wheeler (1986, 1987).

12 RUN-TIME STRUCTURES

12.1 BLOCK INSTANCES

This chapter examines the structures that are used by the run-time support system of a typical block-structured language. Its purpose is to provide some feel for what goes on behind the scenes. What is involved in accessing a local variable or a global variable? What are the overheads of entering and leaving a procedure? And so on. In the final analysis, of course, the details will depend heavily on the nature of the compiler that is used and on the quality of the code that it generates. Nevertheless, underlying all implementations there are certain concepts and techniques that are relevant to the practising programmer.

If every feature of the program text had a unique counterpart in the run-time representation, the support system would be relatively simple. Each segment of code would have precisely one instantiation and each variable could be allocated a fixed area of memory. The trouble is that with higher-level languages this one-to-one correspondence seldom lasts long. It therefore becomes necessary to make the important distinction between a *block* and a *block instance*.

As shown in Section 10.2, a block is a static concept, being a program unit of a particular kind — one that alters the execution environment, usually by introducing parameters and/or variables. By contrast, a block instance is a dynamic concept, being a particular activation of a block at run-time. Since a block can be the body of a procedure, function, coroutine, or task, the two concepts have the following important differences:

1.   The place where a block appears in the text is usually different from the places where its block instances are activated.

2.   A block appears only once in the program text but it can be activated on many different occasions at run-time — either from different places in the program text or repeatedly from the same place.

3.   In some cases, several instances of a block can exist simultaneously. For example, the block could be the body of a recursive subprogram, or of a task type from which several similar tasks have been created.

In short, block instances are both more numerous and more transient than the blocks to which they correspond.

To illustrate some of these differences, consider the following program:

```
procedure M is                    -- the main program

    procedure P is                -- a procedure P

        ...
    begin
        ...
    end P;

    procedure Q is                -- a procedure Q

        ...
    begin
        P;                        -- Q calls P
        B: declare                -- a sub-block of Q

            ...
        begin
            P;                    -- Q calls P again
        end B;
    end Q;

begin
    Q;                            -- M calls Q
end M;
```

The block structure of the program text is shown in Figure 12-1(a) and, as can be seen, it is a tree. At the root lies the environment N, in which the main program M is conceptually embedded. M textually *encloses* the two procedures P and Q, and Q encloses the sub-block B. Conversely, B is *nested* in Q, and P and Q are both nested in M.

Figure 12-1(b) shows the structure of the block instances that are created when the program is run. A suffix *n* indicates the *n*th instance of the corresponding block. The

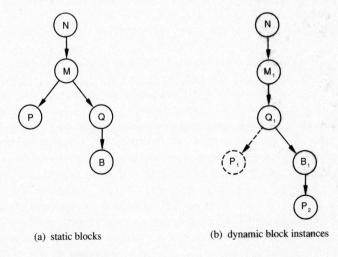

(a) static blocks   (b) dynamic block instances

Figure 12-1   Static and dynamic block structures

diagram assumes that M has called Q, which has executed P and then entered B; from within B it has then called P a second time. The block instance P_1 has therefore completed its execution and can be deleted — as indicated by the dotted lines. On the other hand, the block instances M_1, Q_1, B_1, and P_2 are still active. If the deleted block instance is included, the structure is again a tree. By themselves, though, the active block instances constitute a simpler structure — a single sequence of block instances, each of which has activated its successor. In this structure, M_1 *dynamically encloses* Q_1; similarly Q_1 dynamically encloses B_1, and B_1 dynamically encloses P_2.

In comparing the two structures it is helpful to focus on the procedure P, whose block instance P_2 is currently being executed, and on the path by which it is reached. In the static structure the path is the sequence N - M - P, which can be described as P's *nesting sequence*. It is the sequence of blocks that enclose P in the program text. Successive members are at levels 0, 1, 2, ... in the tree, the one at level i being nested $i - 1$ levels deep in the program text. If the maximum depth in the program text is d, the nesting sequences will have at most $d+2$ members, including the environment N.

By contrast, the block instance P_2 is reached by a longer path, $N - M_1 - Q_1 - B_1 - P_2$. This can be described as the *calling sequence*, since it gives the sequence of block instances that have led to the creation of P_2. Each block instance called its successor and will continue execution after its successor is complete. If the program is recursive, the sequence can contain several instances of the same block and, unlike the nesting sequence, it can be arbitrarily long.

The importance of the calling sequence is easily appreciated. It shows not only how P_2 came into being but also what to do when P_2 is complete. A **return** from P_2 takes control back to the execution of B_1; the completion of B_1 takes it back to Q_1; and so on. However, it should be noted that the situation is not always as simple as this. If the program includes coroutines or tasks, the active (partially executed) block instances need no longer form a linear sequence. Instead, they can form a tree structure and the different parts can interact in more complex ways. We shall return to this possibility later (see Section 12.9).

The importance of the nesting sequence is that it governs the interpretation of global variables and other global entities. Section 10.3 explained how this works at the level of the program text: a non-local identifier, z say, is interpreted by finding the nearest textually enclosing block that contains a declaration of z. If the current block is at nesting level i, and z is found further out at level j, then z is k levels out, where $k = i$-j. At run-time, though, the situation is considerably more complicated. The block structure ensures that z's block will be somewhere in the calling sequence (see Exercise 3), but its precise position cannot always be predicted. In any case, the calling sequence may contain several instances of z's block and therefore several instances of z. Which one should be used? Normally it is the one created most recently, which means that it is the one furthest down the calling sequence. However, there are some situations where this is not the case — for example, when the current procedure has been passed as a parameter — and so a different answer must be given. In general, it requires each block instance to be associated with an *environment*. This can be defined as the instance of its textually enclosing block that provides the correct interpretation of its global entities. The entities one level out belong to this block instance; those that are two levels out belong to the environment of the environment; and so on. Section 12.7 shows how this can be handled by the run-time system.

12.2   ACTIVATION RECORDS

The implementation of a block instance can be divided into two parts — the static and the dynamic. The static part handles the information that is common to all instances of the block and that can be shared between them. The most obvious component is the code for executing the block: provided that it cannot modify itself in any way, it can be used by all the instances even though several may be operating simultaneously. Such code is said to be *reentrant*. Besides the code, the static part includes static, or 'manifest', constants (see Section 7.4) and also static variables — that is, variables whose storage is permanently allocated by the compiler (see Section 10.3).

The dynamic part is known as an *activation record* and is created separately for each block instance. It has three main components:

- control information;
- the parameters;
- the local entities.

It is created when the block is first entered and it continues to exist until the execution of the block is complete. In the simplest case it is then released for further use (see Section 10.2); but in the case of a coroutine or task it has to be retained until there are no references to it from elsewhere.

As an example, consider the following procedure P:

```
procedure P (x, y : real) is
    n : constant integer := 10;
    i, j, k : integer;
begin
    ...
end P;
```

Let us suppose that it is called by the statement:

```
P (1.2, 3.4);
```

The implementation of the resulting block instance is shown in Figure 12-2. The static

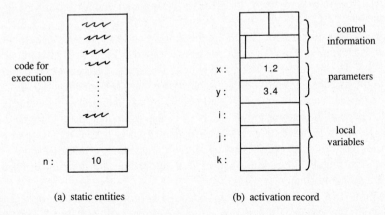

(a) static entities   (b) activation record

Figure 12-2   Representing a block instance

part contains the code for executing P and also the static constant n. The activation record contains the control information (see Section 12.4), the parameters x and y, and the local variables i, j, and k.

Each block instance has an activation record of this kind and so the structure of Figure 12-1(b) is implemented as a collection of such records. The dotted components correspond to records that have been created and later deleted. The others are records whose activation is still proceeding. When the active ones are depicted in full, they provide a 'snapshot' of the state of the computation. The next few sections explore some of their details.

12.3   STACKS AND HEAPS

When a block instance is created, an area of memory has to be allocated for its activation record. A system must therefore be provided for making the allocation and for enabling the code to determine the relevant address. There are three main possibilities.

The simplest method is the *static* one, as used by languages of the FORTRAN family. In these there are no recursive procedures and no coroutines or tasks; consequently, only one instance of a block can ever be active at a time. A sufficient strategy is to allocate the activation records at compile-time, one for each function or routine. This is very efficient because (a) there are no overheads in allocating and releasing storage at run-time, and (b) the variables all have fixed locations and so they can be accessed by direct addressing.

If procedures can be recursive the static method is inadequate. The second method therefore uses a *stack*, following the principles described in Section 5.11 and Section 6.13. At any one time, the active block instances are those of the calling sequence and their activation records are stored as the elements of a stack. Figure 12-3 depicts them for the calling sequence $N - M_1 - Q_1 - B_1 - P_2$ of Figure 12-1(b). The record for the environment N has been omitted, since its entities have a special status and are best handled by other means. As usual, the stack is shown growing upwards: the activation record of the main program M is at the bottom, with succeeding records placed above it. If P_2 were to activate another block instance, a new record would be added at the top. Conversely, when P is completed, its record is abandoned and so the top of the stack becomes B_1.

The record areas on the stack are commonly known as *stack frames*, the top one being the *current* stack frame. There is a pointer ap, as shown in Figure 12-3, which gives the base address of the current stack frame and which therefore gives access to the parameters and local entities of the currently executing block instance. When a new block is entered the space for its activation record is created simply by adjusting ap to the address of the first location beyond the current frame. A check is also made that the new frame does not exceed the limits of the stack area. The old value of ap is preserved in the new stack frame and so, when the new block is eventually left, the frame is 'deleted' simply by restoring ap to that value. Thus, the overheads of allocating and deleting the activation records are reasonably small.

As mentioned in Section 12.2, the introduction of coroutines and tasks makes life more difficult. The trouble is that the active (partially executed) block instances no longer form a linear sequence that simply grows and contracts at one end, and for which a

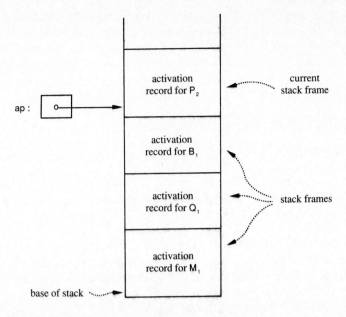

Figure 12-3   A stack of activation records

stack works so well. Instead, they form a tree structure in which growth can occur at any point at all. To handle this a third method is needed — one in which the activation records can be handled more flexibly. The basic idea is to use a general-purpose storage area called the *heap* and to provide a mechanism that allows records of arbitrary size to be allocated and released at random. A similar mechanism is needed for creating dynamic data structures, so it may be a simple matter to use it for activation records also. The only trouble is that heaps tend to be much less efficient than stacks. Considerable attention has been given to devising good algorithms for managing them; but even with the best ones the overheads can be quite significant. The details will be described in Volume II.

It will be appreciated that these three methods of handling the activation records correspond to the three kinds of variable that were considered in Section 10.3 — static, automatic, and controlled. The static variables can be allocated storage by the compiler; the automatic ones can be put on the stack; and the controlled ones are handled by the heap. Figure 12-4 shows the resulting correspondence between storage mechanisms, variable types, and module types. In practice, some compilers use a stack for static

Storage mechanisms	Variable types	Module types
static	static	nonrecursive
stack	automatic	recursive
heap	controlled	coroutines/tasks

Figure 12-4   Storage mechanisms

entities as well as for automatic ones, and for nonrecursive procedures as well as for recursive ones. This may add to the overheads, but the extent of the increase will depend very heavily on the details of the implementation and on the nature of the program involved.

12.4 CONTROL INFORMATION

The preceding discussion shows that, in general, the execution of a block instance B requires the use of three pointers. We shall refer to them as ap, ep, and ip:

1.   ap is the base address of B's activation record and is needed for accessing its parameters and local entities;

2.   ep points to the environment — that is, to an instance of the block that textually encloses B — and so it too is the base address of an activation record; as explained in Section 12.1, it is needed for accessing the global entities;

3.   ip points to the instruction of B's code that is to be executed next.

If the activation records are all allocated statically, the addresses of all parameters and variables will be known to the compiler and so there is no need to maintain ap and ep at run-time. But with a stack-based or heap-based system all three pointers have to be available. As long as B is executing, ap will normally be held in a register and ep in the activation record itself; ip, of course, is the instruction pointer of the machine (see Section 5.5)

Now let us suppose that B calls a subprogram P. What happens to the three pointers? The answer is that their current values are preserved by the calling mechanism and new values are set up for the execution of P. In order to preserve the old values each activation record has three fields. Their positions within the record will be denoted by the values afield, efield, and ifield. It is best if the fields can be accessed by single instructions, without the need for any packing or unpacking. So, if p is a pointer to the record, we shall assume that we can refer to them by means of the indexed indirect addresses p!afield, p!efield and p!ifield. There may be other fields also — for example, one or more bits to assist in the storage allocation — but they will not be considered here.

Figure 12-5 shows the activation record of Figure 12-2 with these details filled in. It assumes that the record has been allocated on a stack and therefore shows it growing upwards, rather than downwards: the control information is at the bottom and the variables have been added at the top. As can be seen, the three pointers are known by the following names:

$$
\begin{array}{lll}
\text{p!afield} & - & \text{the } \textit{dynamic link}; \\
\text{p!efield} & - & \text{the } \textit{static link}; \\
\text{p!ifield} & - & \text{the } \textit{return address}.
\end{array}
$$

The dynamic link gives the address of the dynamically enclosing block instance (the old value of ap). The static link gives the address of the appropriate textually enclosing block instance — that is, of P's environment (the current value of ep). And the return address,

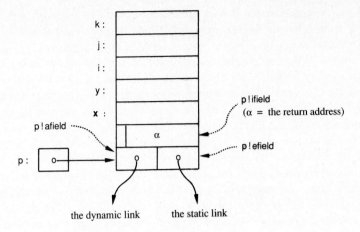

Figure 12-5 Preserving control information

of course, indicates the instruction that is to be executed when control returns to B (the old value of ip). The calling mechanism is responsible for initializing the record in this way and for establishing the new values of ap, ep, and ip. A typical calling sequence is as follows:

1. Create an activation record for P (as described in Section 12.3); let p be its base address.

2. Evaluate the parameters and place them in the relevant fields of the record (see Section 12.5).

3. Preserve ap in p!afield.

4. Calculate the new value of ep and store it in p!efield (see Section 12.7).

5. Set ap to p.

6. Make a subroutine jump to the start of P's code.

The last step preserves the old value of ip in some standard location, as described in Section 5.6, and sets ip to the starting address of P's code. The old value, of course, is the return address, α say. On being entered, P's first action is to preserve this address in its activation record:

7. Preserve α in ap!ifield.

It then proceeds to elaborate its declarations and to execute its statements. On completion, it returns control to B by means of the sequence:

8. Recover α from ap!ifield.

9. Reset ap from ap!afield, so that it now points to B's activation record.

10. Execute a jump to α.

This resumes the execution of B with ap and ip restored to their original values. By implication, ep also has its original value, as found in ap!efield. It should be noted that with a stack-based mechanism Step 9 has the effect of releasing the storage space of P's activation record. With a heap-based mechanism this would require extra work.

There are several variations on the basic formulation, some of which will be discussed in the succeeding sections. With coroutines, for example, it is important that ip be stored in B's activation record, not P's. Other variations are aimed at speeding up the execution of P by making better use of the registers. When all is said and done, though, certain minimum overheads are necessarily incurred by this approach. Most machines require at least eight instructions for entering and leaving each block instance, and in some cases they may need many more. For a small procedure that is frequently used the costs can be uncomfortably high. The only way of avoiding them is to abandon the calling mechanism and to compile the procedure as inline code instead — inserting the full procedure body, with suitable parameter substitution, at each place of call (see Section 9.2). This eliminates the overheads and may also speed up the code in other ways. As mentioned previously, it is unfortunate that so few languages provide it as an option.

12.5 PASSING PARAMETERS

One of the tasks of the calling mechanism is to pass the parameters of P (if any) to the new block instance. The previous section assumed that this is done by placing the values of the parameters in P's activation record. It is now time to take a closer look at what these values are. The details can be listed for the six methods of passing parameters described in Section 9.3.

1. *Pass-by-constant*. The parameter is evaluated in data mode and the resulting value is placed in the appropriate field of the record. It is then treated as if it were a local constant of P. The details for accessing it will be discussed in the next section.

2. *Pass-by-value* (that is, pass-to-local-variable). As for method 1, except that the field of the record is treated as a local variable.

3. *Pass-by-reference*. The parameter (which must be a variable) is evaluated in reference mode and the resulting reference is placed in the record. In its simplest form it will be an address; for a structure such as an array it may be a rather more elaborate descriptor (see Volume II). References to the variable have to be handled indirectly via this value.

4. *Pass-by-result*. The easiest case is where the parameter is a simple variable, with no subscripts or other expressions that require evaluation. There is then no need to pass any value to P; instead, the field of the record is treated as an uninitialized local variable and the exit mechanism assigns its final value to the variable. If the parameter *does* require evaluation, the resulting address or descriptor can be stored in the activation record prior to the execution of P.

5. *Pass-by-value-result*. This is a combination of methods 2 and 4.

6.   *Pass-by-expression*. As stated in Section 9.3, this is much the most complicated. The parameter consists of two code segments, known as 'thunks' (Ingermann, 1961), one for evaluating the expression in reference mode and one for evaluating it in data mode. Their two entry points are stored in the activation record. When the value of the parameter is required, the appropriate code segment is executed with ap pointing to the activation record of the calling block instance. (By implication, this sets ep to ap!efield.) Fortunately, the required value of ap is available as P's dynamic link and so there is no need to set aside any extra storage for it.

All this assumes that the parameters are passed to P by being placed in its activation record. However, there is an alternative strategy: the calling module can place them in the central registers (provided that there are enough of them), leaving the creation of P's activation record to P itself. This has the advantage that P may prefer to keep the parameters in the registers, where they are much more readily accessible. It transfers them to the activation record only when the registers are needed for other purposes — typically, for calling another procedure. For small, self-contained procedures there is a good chance that this will never be necessary. In such cases the use of the registers leads to a very efficient implementation.

A special point of interest arises with parameters that are themselves procedures or functions (see Section 9.6). In Ada they have to be treated as generic parameters and the formal–actual correspondence is handled at compile-time. In other languages, though, the calling module must supply the necessary information at run-time. So let us suppose that a procedure Q is passed as a parameter to a procedure P and that it is subsequently called from within P. What values are needed for its execution? The answer is that ap must point to the activation record that is created for the call; ep must indicate the environment that was applicable when Q was passed to P; and ip, of course, must be the start of its code. It follows that the parameter Q must consist of an (ep, ip) pair. The method for determining ep will be described in Section 12.7.

Similar remarks apply to parameters that are labels (if allowed). Thus, suppose that a procedure P has a formal parameter L which is a label, and that it executes:

   goto L;

If the actual parameter is a label AA, it is not sufficient to supply the address of AA and to have the procedure execute a direct jump to that address. Instead, the calling module must supplement the address with a pointer to the block instance to which AA belongs, this block instance being determined at the time when AA is passed to P. In effect, the value of the label is an (ap, ip) pair. The **goto** statement is executed by working backwards through the calling sequence, leaving each block instance in turn, until the current block has the required ap value. Only then can the direct jump be performed.

12.6   ACCESSING LOCAL ENTITIES

If the current activation record has to be accessed via a pointer ap, it might be thought that the cost of using its components will be unnecessarily high. Is it not more efficient to use static storage so that they can be accessed directly? To answer this question the costs of dynamic storage have to be examined in some detail.

As a start, let us assume that the run-time system is executing the procedure P of Section 12.2 using the activation record shown in Figure 12-5. The pointer ap gives the base address of the record and, as stated earlier, it will normally be held in one of the high-speed registers; so let us assume that it is in R1. How, then, does the system access a local variable such as i? With static storage it can determine the address of i in advance and use direct addressing. But with dynamic storage it can only predict the position of the variable within the record — that is, its *offset* from the base address. According to Figure 12-5, this is 4c cells, where c is the number of cells per word. On a word-addressing machine, c is 1 and so this simplifies to an offset of 4. To access i, the system therefore has to use the address R1!4 (that is, R1↑.4). The indirection might appear inefficient; but in fact, as shown in Section 5.10, R1!4 is equivalent to 4.R1 which is an ordinary indexed address. So in this simple case the dynamic allocation is no problem.

The procedure P has parameters x and y. If these are pass-by-constant or pass-by-value, they are treated as local constants or variables and are therefore accessed in the same way as i. A more interesting situation arises if x (say) is pass-by-reference, its value being the address of an external variable v. With static storage the system can access v by treating x as an indirect address. According to Figure 12-5, x has an offset of 2 in the activation record and so the indirect address is (R1!2)↑, which can be rewritten as (2.R1)↑. As with i, accessing 2.R1 is no harder than accessing a fixed address; so once again there is no advantage in using static storage. In either case two memory references are needed instead of one.

Now let us complicate things by adding an array A to the local variables of P:

$$A : \textbf{array } (1..n) \textbf{ of } \text{integer};$$

Since n was defined to be a constant with the value 10, this requires an extra 10 words in the activation record, having offsets from 7 to 16. An element of A can be accessed very easily provided that its index is known in advance. For example, A(3) has the offset 9 and can be accessed in the same way as i or j. To access A(i), using the local variable i as an index, requires more work. With static storage the system can compute in advance the address B of the notional element A(0). It can then fetch i into R2 and access A(i) as the indexed address B.R2. With dynamic storage the address of A(0) is R1!6 and so the address of A(i) is (R1!6).R2. This is equivalent to 6.R1.R2 and therefore requires double indexing — one index for ap and one for i. Since most machines provide only for single indexing, it has to be treated as 6.(R1+R2), with R1+R2 being computed by an extra register-to-register addition. This adds a small percentage to the access time. An alternative approach is to begin by computing the address of the notional element A(0):

$$
\begin{array}{lll}
\text{R2} & \leftarrow \ \text{R1} + 6 & \quad \text{-- load @ A(0)} \\
\text{R3} & \leftarrow \ 4.\text{R1} & \quad \text{-- load i}
\end{array}
$$

Then the required address is R2!R3 or, equivalently, 0.R2.R3. Once again, this normally requires an extra register-to-register addition. The advantage of the method is that once @A(0) has been established in R2 it is available for further use. Even so, in the absence of double indexing the static system has a slight advantage.

As a final example, consider what happens if the array A has dynamic bounds — that is, bounds that are not fixed until run-time. For example, the constant n might be declared as

$$n : \textbf{constant} \text{ integer} := 2*m + 1;$$

where m is a variable in a surrounding block. This means that the upper bound of A is unpredictable. The first effect is that, since the value of n is no longer static, it cannot be shared among all the instances of the block; so, instead of being stored permanently with the static entities, it must be held in the activation record. Secondly, and more significantly, the array A now occupies an unpredictable number of words. Consequently, if any entities are stored in the area following it, their positions will be unpredictable. To get round this difficulty A could be placed last. However, this trick can only be worked once: any further structures of unpredictable size will have to be stored in unpredictable positions. So, in general, the following policy has to be adopted:

- In the design of an activation record structures of unpredictable size are allocated fixed-size fields that point to their representation elsewhere.

In the case of the array A the pointer field will be in position 8 and will contain the address of the notional element $A(0)$. The 'elsewhere' could be either at the end of the activation record or on the heap. Either way, there is an extra level of indirection and therefore an extra memory reference:

```
R2  ←  8.R1          -- load @ A(0)
R3  ←  4.R1          -- load i
```

The address of $A(i)$ is then given by R2!R3 which is equivalent to 0.R2.R3. As before, the best strategy is to establish @ A(0) in R2 so that the initial step need not be repeated. If this can be done, the extra memory reference is avoided and so the overheads of the dynamic bounds become negligible. With static storage the details might be slightly simpler. In practice, though, languages with static storage do not usually provide for arrays with dynamic bounds and so the analysis is irrelevant.

The above details would require minor modifications for a byte-addressing machine (Exercise 5). A more serious variation would be to consider a machine where only one register is available for indexing (Exercise 6). In general, though, the conclusion is that the costs of using dynamic storage are not at all high. The most serious case arises with an array element such as $A(i)$, where the extra register-to-register addition could add 15–30% to an individual accessing operation. However, such figures are no cause for alarm. For one thing, as a proportion of the entire execution time they will be considerably smaller. And for another, if the operations occur inside loops, an optimizing compiler can often succeed in eliminating the overheads entirely. So, when the final reckoning is made, the extra costs of using dynamic storage are unlikely to be significant.

12.7 ACCESSING GLOBAL ENTITIES

The next problem is how to access global variables from a procedure P. We shall assume that P is at nesting level i and that some global entity z is at nesting level j, where $j < i$. How can P access z?

With static storage the answer is very simple. Each block in the program text has an activation record that is permanently allocated to it. The position of z is therefore known to the compiler and so z can be accessed directly.

With dynamic storage the position is more complicated and the costs may well be higher. However, there is one case that is particularly simple, namely when z is part of the standard program environment $(j = 0)$. It can then be given static storage, as described above. Similar considerations apply if z is declared in the outermost level of the main program $(j = 1)$. On the assumption that there can only be one instance of the main program, it too can be handled statically.

A third possibility arises when a program is compiled as a single unit. By suitable analysis of the text, the compiler can determine which modules are unaffected by recursion, coroutines, or tasks. Such modules never require more than one instance to be active at a time and so, in principle, they too can be handled statically. Unfortunately, Ada does not have a unit called a main program; nor does it require that a program be compiled as a single unit. So it is less likely to make these optimizations.

In the general case the variable z is k levels out from the text of P, where $k = i-j$. To see how it can be accessed, consider a 'snapshot' of the sample program as depicted in Figure 12-6. This shows the activation records of Figure 12-3 with each one containing

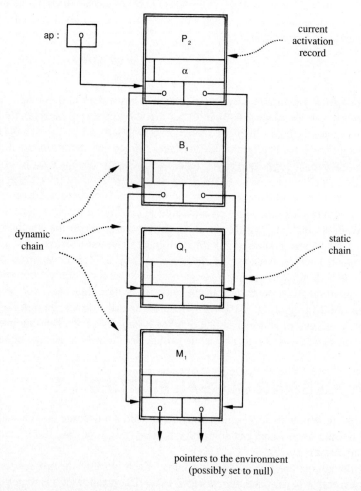

pointers to the environment
(possibly set to null)

Figure 12-6   A program snapshot

the control information of Figure 12-5. The records could be allocated on a stack or from a heap — the details do not matter. As usual, ap points to the current record and this contains the parameters and other local entities, together with a return address, dynamic link, and static link. Its dynamic link points to the dynamically enclosing block instance and, as shown, it initiates a series of such links known as the *dynamic chain*. In effect, the chain represents the reverse of the calling sequence, leading back through the blocks P_2-B_1-Q_1-M_1 until it reaches the standard program environment. In a similar way the static link points to an instance of the textually enclosing block and, as shown, it initiates a series of such links known as the *static chain*. The first link is the environment pointer ep that was described in Section 12.5. The full chain represents the reverse of the nesting sequence, leading back through the blocks P_2-M_1 until it too reaches the standard program environment.

The pointer ep is chosen so that it gives the correct environment for interpreting global variables, as described in Section 12.2. The method of accessing z, in a block that is k levels out from the current one, is therefore quite straightforward. The system follows k links of the static chain and accesses the required field of the resulting activation record. For example, if $k = 2$ and the field has an offset of 7, it accesses ap!efield!efield!7.

How are the static links calculated? If the system is executing procedure P at level i and has to enter a block B at level b $(b \leq i+1)$, the correct environment for executing B is the textually enclosing block at level $b-1$. To determine the appropriate instance of this block, the system follows $i-b+1$ links of the static chain and takes the final link as the new static link for B. In the particular case where B is local to P, b is $i+1$ and the new static link is the same as the new dynamic link: it is the pointer to P's activation record as provided by ap. The only variation on this basic theme is when B is a procedure parameter: in that case the environment is calculated when B is passed to P, as described in Section 12.6, and so the new static link is obtained from the representation of B as an (ep, ip) pair.

Accessing z is simple enough, but if k is at all large, tracing through the links can be rather time-consuming. To speed it up, an obvious possibility is to keep ep in a register, thereby saving one memory access each time. This has to be offset against the cost of tying up the register and of maintaining its value even when it is not needed.

Taking the principle a step further, the system might keep ep in one register and the next link, namely ep!efield, in another. This saves a second memory reference when $k \geq 2$, but is no help for the case $k = 1$; so the benefits are not so great. If the idea is taken to its logical conclusion it leads to the concept of a *display vector*, D say, which holds a copy of *all* the links in the static chain. To access a global entity at level j $(j < i)$, the system simply uses the activation record indicated by the element $D(j)$. To implement the technique it dispenses with the static chain and concentrates on maintaining D instead. However, this involves a non-trivial amount of work. The trouble is that if it is executing at level i and enters a block at level b, with $b < i$, it has to preserve the top $i-b+1$ elements of D before they are overwritten. It can put them on the stack and reinstate them on leaving the block; but storing and retrieving them involves more overheads than the setting of a single link.

Since the display vector involves more complications and more overheads than the static chain, its use must be justified by the gains in access speed. In comparison with the case where ep is kept in a register, these begin to accrue only when $k \geq 3$. If (as suggested above) the entities of the main program are handled statically as a special case, this limits the gains to the cases $3 \leq k < i$. These are likely to be a small proportion of the global accesses, which in turn are usually less than 5% of the total accesses. In such circumstances there is little to be said in support of maintaining the display vector. Nevertheless, it has been adopted by many compilers and has even been incorporated in the architecture of some computers.

12.8 IMPLEMENTATION OF BLOCK STATEMENTS

The preceding sections have used the term 'block' in its wider sense, meaning any program unit that alters the execution environment. This section considers the implementation of blocks in their narrower sense — that is, the block statement, as described in Section 10.2. The following is the example that was used at that time:

```
declare
    temp : any;
begin
    temp := x;
    x := y;
    y := temp;
end;
```

Since this construction is a block it might be thought that its execution involves all the overheads that are required for procedures and functions:

- allocating an activation record;
- creating a static link;
- storing and retrieving the dynamic link;
- storing and retrieving the return address.

If this were the case it would discourage the use of block statements. In fact, though, it is reassuring to know that a block statement can usually be implemented very much more efficiently.

The crucial point is that a block statement does not need a separate activation record. Instead, its local entities can be added to the activation record of the surrounding block. The extra space is allocated when the surrounding block is entered and comes into use when the block statement is executed. The effect is exactly the same as if the program had added the declarations to those of the surrounding block.

If there are two or more block statements within the one block, they share the same space in the extended activation record. They can do this because they can never be active simultaneously. So, if one requires m cells and the other requires n cells, the extension need only provide for the maximum of m and n, not for their sum. As noted in Section 10.2, this is one of the advantages of the block statement.

From all this it can be seen that the strategy incurs no costs for allocating an activation record nor for setting up static and dynamic links. Moreover, since the code for the block statement is embedded in the code for the surrounding block, it does not have to store and retrieve a return address. In short, it completely eliminates the above overheads.

12.9   IMPLEMENTATION OF COROUTINES

The mechanisms of Section 12.4 work well for entering and leaving ordinary subprograms, but they need several modifications for coroutines. Taking the semicoroutine first, as described in Section 10.9, we shall consider the execution of

p :– **new** C (...)

followed by the effects of **suspend**, **call**, and **terminate**. The coroutine object does not have a name in the program, so we shall refer to it simply as 'C's object'. (For convenience, this ignores the possibility that there may be other objects also of class C.)

The **new** operation can be implemented in the same way as a function call. It creates an activation record, which is C's object, and uses it for holding the control information and the attributes. As with a function call, the control information consists initially of the dynamic link, the static link, and the return address. The only novelty is that since coroutines do not operate on a last-in/first-out basis, C's object cannot be allocated from the stack: instead, it must be taken from the heap. This is a point that we shall return to later.

When C does **suspend**, it must preserve the value of ip as its *resumption address* — that is, the address to which control returns when it is next called. The obvious way to do this is simply by swapping ip with the return address. This preserves ip in C's object and returns control to the calling routine M. A subsequent execution of **call** p can then swap them back again. However, this works only on the assumption that C executes **suspend** from its own coroutine body. If it can do **suspend** from one of its procedures the situation is more complicated. The system must preserve not only the current value of ip but also the current value of ap. Moreover, since the command **call** p refers to the coroutine rather than the procedure, this (ap, ip) pair must be put in C's object. As before, ip can replace the return address and ap, very conveniently, can replace the dynamic link.

The effect of all this is illustrated in Figure 12-7, which gives a 'snapshot' of a suspended coroutine instance. The coroutine C has called a procedure B, which has then called A, which has then done **suspend**. As can be seen, their dynamic links form a circular chain, leading from C to A to B and back to C. Their return addresses form a similar chain. C has the resumption address α for A; A has the return address β for B; and B has the return address γ for C. With this arrangement, M can execute **call** p by swapping its current (ap, ip) pair with the one in C. This will automatically cause the procedure A to be resumed.

In principle, A can execute **suspend** by swapping the (ap, ip) pairs back again, so that M's becomes the current one. However, in order to do this it first has to locate C — the activation record of its enclosing coroutine. The record will be somewhere on the dynamic chain, but A cannot know in advance how many links to follow. The system therefore has to include a marker that distinguishes coroutines from ordinary routines. In Figure 12-7 it is denoted by the symbol '#'. The **suspend** operation begins by scanning the dynamic chain for the first occurrence of the marker; it can then interchange the (ap, ip) pairs in the way described. This is more elaborate than the ordinary **return** mechanism, and if it is done from within a deeply nested recursive procedure it can also be rather slow (though see Exercise 10).

The **call** operation involves another problem. If C has completed its execution, an attempt to call it should raise an exception or cause a report. Its object should therefore

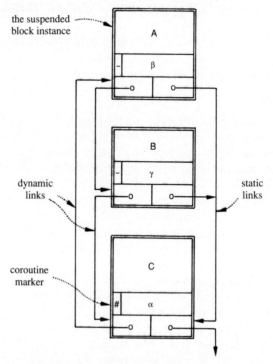

the suspended
block instance

dynamic
links

static
links

coroutine
marker

Figure 12-7   A suspended coroutine

include a flag that is set when C is terminated (normally by reaching its **end**). The **call** operation checks the flag and takes appropriate action if it is set. An alternative strategy is to dispense with the flag and to arrange for termination to set the resumption address to the start of an error-handling routine. An attempt to resume C would then activate the routine.

With full coroutines (see Section 10.10) there is a further difficulty in the execution of **suspend**. This arises because C can be initiated and resumed by other coroutines. Since it is not necessarily entered from the master routine M, how can its **suspend** operation determine the (ap, ip) pair of M to which it must return control? The answer is that M must preserve its (ap, ip) pair in its own activation record. In fact, M must operate in the same way as the coroutines themselves, having a structure similar to that of Figure 12-7. C executes **suspend** by preserving its current (ap, ip) pair in C and then finding the activation record of M. This will be on its static chain, the details depending on how the 'master' is defined. (In SIMULA 67 it is the nearest enclosing 'prefixed block' and so the static chain is searched until a 'prefixed' tag is found.) When the record has been found, its (ap, ip) pair is reinstated as the current one and this causes the execution of M to be resumed.

From all this it will be apparent that coroutines add significant complications to the run-time structures of a program. In terms of efficiency, though, the most important difference does not lie in the details of the calling mechanisms but in the fact that the activation records can no longer be allocated on a stack. Instead, they are taken from the heap and they form a structure that is known as a *branching stack* (or sometimes a

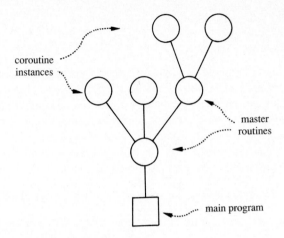

coroutine
instances

master
routines

main program

Figure 12-8   A branching stack (or cactus)

cactus). Figure 12-8 shows a typical example: the circles represent currently active
coroutines or master routines, and each one corresponds to a linked set of one or more
activation records similar to that of Figure 12-7. As far as the costs are concerned, the
real problem lies not so much in the extra work that has to be done by **suspend** and
resume, but in the handling of the space from the heap. The mechanisms for this are
described in Volume II and are likely to account for most of a coroutine's overheads.

12.10   IMPLEMENTATION OF TASKS

This section outlines the main features of a run-time system for handling Ada's tasks. It
is derived from the Ada Workbench Compiler Project at York University (Briggs *et al.*,
1982), which uses a coroutine model similar to that of SIMULA 67. Much of it
corresponds to Section 11.5 of 'Rationale for the Design of the Ada Programming
Language' (Ichbiah *et al*, 1979b), which sketches an implementation of tasks for the preliminary version of Ada. Doubtless there are many ways in which the details can be
varied; but the main features follow almost inevitably from the nature of tasks themselves. The only significant assumption made here is that the implementation is for a
machine whose processors share a common memory. Modifications would be needed for
a distributed system, in which processors had to communicate by message passing.

   Not surprisingly, each task has an activation record that is created when the task is
declared (or, for a task access type, when the **new** allocator is applied). To cater for the
execution of subprograms the record must provide a private stack in the same way as for
coroutines (see Figure 12-6). To access global variables it has the usual static link; and to
handle termination, it has references to its parent task and its own subtasks (if any). The
remaining information varies according to the task's state, but fields must be provided for
the following:

- state information;
- a link for placing the task on a queue;
- a descriptor for each entry;

- a priority;
- a wake-up time;
- a pending exception.

The first three are described below. A priority is set by a pragma, as described in Section 11.7, and is consulted when the task is scheduled to be run. The wake-up time is set by a **delay** statement and indicates the time at which the task should be resumed. The 'pending exception' refers to the possibility that an exception might be passed to the task while it is suspended, as the result of an unsuccessful rendezvous.

A task T must be in one of three basic states — *running*, *waiting*, or *terminated*. If it is waiting there are four main possibilities to be considered:

1. It is 'runnable' and is waiting for a processor to become available.

2. It has made a call to an entry in some other task and is waiting for the call to be accepted.

3. It is waiting at an **accept** statement for one of its own entries to be called. Within a **select** statement there are further complications because several **accept** statements could be open; a **delay** statement or a **terminate** statement could also be involved.

4. It has completed the execution of its task body but cannot terminate until all of its subtasks have terminated (or are ready to terminate).

For each of these conditions, there must be some mechanism that causes T to be resumed:

1. If T is waiting for a processor, it is placed on the *ready queue*. The tasks on this queue are held in order of priority and are reactivated by a routine called the *scheduler*. In the simplest implementation a running task must return control to the scheduler whenever it suspends its execution. The scheduler then selects the next task to be run. If the ready queue is empty the scheduler idles in a loop, waiting either for an interrupt or, in the case of a multiprocessor system, for a task to be put on the ready queue by another processor.

2. If T has called an entry X.E of some other task X, it is placed on E's *entry queue* where it awaits its turn on a FIFO basis. It becomes runnable when it reaches the head of the queue and X executes **accept** E. On completing the **accept** statement X must execute a routine set_run (T) in order to make T runnable. If T has higher priority than X, set_run suspends X (by putting it on the ready queue) and then resumes T.

3. If T has to wait on one or more **accept** statements, it sets their corresponding entry descriptors to indicate that the entries are 'open' and to give the position of the waiting **accept**s. If two or more **accept**s refer to the same entry, one is chosen at random. It then suspends itself (by returning control to the scheduler) and waits for some task, C say, to call one of the entries. C checks the entry descriptor and, on finding that it is 'open', it calls set_run (T). On resumption, T determines which of the entries to accept and resets all of the open entries to 'closed'. The handling of **delay** and **terminate** statements is described below.

4. If T has completed its execution it is waiting for its subtasks to terminate. So, when a subtask terminates or executes a **terminate** alternative, it must call a routine check_term to check whether its parent task (in this case T) can now terminate.

These mechanisms enable T to be resumed, but they do not guarantee that it ever *will* be resumed. On the contrary, there are many conditions that could leave T suspended indefinitely. Some of them are easily checked — for example, an entry to a blocked task; but others, such as the 'deadly embrace' (where A is waiting for B and B is waiting for A) are much harder to detect. The topic has been extensively discussed in the literature on operating systems.

  T executes a **delay** statement by evaluating its wake-up time and then placing itself on the *delay queue*. The tasks on this queue are held in order of their wake-up times, the earliest one being at the front. If the **delay** is an alternative to one or more **accept**s, and if one of the **accept**s is activated first, T has to remove itself from the queue; otherwise it remains there until its wake-up time occurs. If time is advanced by clock interrupts, the responsibility for reactivating T lies with the interrupt handler: it checks the front of the delay queue and calls set_run for any tasks whose delays have expired. If the clock is a read-only register, the responsibility lies with the scheduler which has to compare the clock with the delay queue whenever it is called. If there is no clock the system can use simulated time: when the ready queue becomes empty, the scheduler advances the simulated time to the wake-up time of the first task on the delay queue and then activates that task.

  T executes a **terminate** statement by setting its state to 'waiting on terminate'. It then calls check_term (P) to determine whether its parent task P has completed its execution and, if so, whether all the tasks dependent on P are either terminated or in the 'waiting on terminate' state. If these conditions are satisfied the entire system of tasks is terminated. Otherwise T has to wait for some other task to trigger the termination process. If in the meantime it receives an entry call, it resumes execution and ceases to be in the 'waiting on terminate' state.

  From this outline we can infer the specific actions that have to be taken in the execution of various operations. For example, when T executes a (non-selective) **accept** statement it has to do the following:

1. It inspects the queue in its corresponding entry descriptor.

2. If the queue is empty, it marks the entry as 'open' and suspends itself (by returning control to the scheduler). It waits for a task to join the queue and make it runnable. On being resumed, it marks the entry as 'closed'.

3. It takes the first task off the entry queue, marks it as having been accepted, and creates an activation record for the parameters and control information (though see below).

4. If the priority of the calling task is higher than its own, it saves its previous priority and takes the higher one *pro tem*.

5. It executes the body of the **accept** statement.

6. It releases the activation record, restores its own priority, and executes set_run for the calling task.

Compared with a conventional procedure call, as described in Section 12.4, this is considerably more complicated. On the other hand, some published figures suggest that in many cases it actually runs faster (Clapp *et al.*, 1986). The explanation for this rather surprising result may lie in the allocation mechanisms that are used for the activation records. Since **accept** statements cannot occur in subprograms of a task, it is possible to preallocate their activation records as part of the task's. As with block statements, this means that the overheads of entering and leaving them are almost negligible (see Section 12.8). If this explanation is correct, it underlines the high costs of dynamic storage allocation when compared with other aspects of the run-time system.

12.11 IMPLEMENTATION OF INTERRUPTS

The run-time system maintains an *interrupt table* that indicates the entry (if any) that is associated with an interrupt. When the interrupt occurs, the entry is called and any values provided by the interrupt are passed to it as input parameters. (The parameters of the entry must agree with the implementation at this point.) If the call cannot be handled immediately it is placed on the entry queue in the usual way. However, since the call is not issued by a task, it cannot be represented by an activation record. Instead, it is represented by a record containing its parameters. If there are no parameters, the queue can be reduced to a single integer giving the number of occurrences of the interrupt that are waiting to be accepted.

FURTHER READING

An excellent book for the study of run-time structures is *Programming Language Structures* (Organick *et al.*, 1978). This gives detailed accounts of the structures for ALGOL, FORTRAN, LISP, SNOBOL, and Pascal. Many of the concepts can be traced to papers by P. Wegner (1971) and J. B. Johnston (1971) in a symposium on 'Data Structures in Programming Languages' (Tou and Wegner, 1971). Briefer accounts are given in books on compilers. For block-structured languages most of the techniques were developed for the early ALGOL compilers. For example, the stack and the display vector were described by E. W. Dijkstra (1960b) and thunks by P. Z. Ingermann (1961). A standard work is *ALGOL 60 Implementation* (Randell and Russell, 1964), which contains most of the references. For more recent work, see De Prycker (1982) on the accessing of variables in block-structured languages and Er (1983b) on optimizing procedure calls.

The implementation of coroutines in Section 12.9 is derived from the techniques used for SIMULA 67 as described in Nybo (1974). The implementation of tasks in Section 12.10 is influenced by the outline given in Ichbiah *et al.* (1979b), but is taken more specifically from the version used for the York workbench compiler (Briggs *et al.*, 1982). For other accounts see Burns (1985) and Riccardi and Baker (1985). A study on the efficiency of the tasking mechanism, along with other Ada operations, is presented in Clapp *et al.* (1986).

EXERCISES

1 How efficient are various languages (and implementations) at handling subprograms? One way of investigating this is to time calls of Ackermann's function, as described in Section 9.8. Choose two or more languages that allow the function to be defined recursively and compare their execution times for calling it. For a discussion of this methodology see Wichmann (1976, 1977).

2 By timing suitable programs, obtain estimates of the time taken for the following operations:

  (a)   entering and leaving a parameterless procedure;

  (b)   accessing a local variable of a procedure;

  (c)   accessing a simple output parameter (pass by reference);

  (d)   accessing an element of a local array;

  (e)   accessing a global variable that is k levels out (plot the time against k);

  (f)   accessing a global variable that is declared in the outermost level of the main program;

  (g)   allocating a record from the heap (the figure may vary greatly according to the overall pattern of requests).

Comment on the results. Are the figures roughly what you would expect? What do they suggest about the details of the implementation?

3 Prove that in the execution of a block-structured program the calling sequence always contain at least one instance of the nesting sequence.

4 Why should a procedure parameter be passed as an (ep, ip) pair, whereas a label parameter requires an (ap, ip) pair? If a procedure is passed as a parameter at some point X and then called at some point Y, why do its global entities have to be interpreted in the context of X rather than Y? If your language allows procedure parameters, can you verify that this is indeed the way in which they are handled? Can you do the same for label parameters?

5 Revise the details of Section 12.6 for a byte-addressing machine with four bytes per word. What difference does this make to the overall conclusions?

6 Revise the details of Section 12.6 for a machine with only one register for doing arithmetic (the 'accumulator') and one for indexing. What difference does this make to the overall conclusions?

7 Section 12.7 describes two methods of accessing global variables. A third possibility is to treat them as though they were pass-by-reference parameters. In other words, if a block uses a global variable g, the address of g is computed on entry to the block and then stored as a local entity; g can then be accessed via this stored address. Discuss the merits and drawbacks of this proposal. Does it mean that the static links or display registers are no longer needed? How can the programmer obtain the same effect explicitly?

8   Using a language that allows block statements (Section 12.8), time a suitable program in order to determine whether or not there are any overheads in entering and leaving them.

9   Since coroutines are not executed on a last-in/first-out basis, it was stated that their activation records could not be allocated from the stack. Suggest a set of language restrictions that would allow the use of a stack after all.

10   Give a step-by-step algorithm for executing the **suspend** operation from a coroutine. According to Section 12.9 it is necessary to follow the dynamic chain in order to determine the activation record of the master coroutine. It would be faster to use the static chain, especially from deep inside a recursive procedure. Unfortunately, though, this method would not always work. Why not? What language restriction(s) would be necessary to make it work?

11   List the different queues on which a task T can be placed. For each of them state:

    (a)   the conditions that cause T to be put there;

    (b)   the queue discipline (FIFO or whatever);

    (c)   the conditions that cause T to be removed.

Show that T never has to be on more than one queue at a time.

12   According to Section 12.10 each entry descriptor of a task activation record contains an address field: if the task is suspended while waiting for that entry, the field holds the address of the relevant **accept** statement. Why could the address not be stored as an ordinary resumption address in the ifield of the activation record?

13   Investigate the cost of making an entry call in your implementation of Ada and compare it with that of an ordinary procedure call. How do your results compare with published figures — for example, Clapp *et al.* (1986)?

Investigate the cost of polling a family of *n* entries when none of them is waiting (see Section 11.12). Which is faster: using conditional entry calls or testing entry (i) 'count = 0 ?

14   From the description of a run-time system for tasks that was given in Section 12.10 state the actions required for executing the following operations:

    (a)   an entry call;

    (b)   a conditional entry call;

    (b)   a timed entry call.

APPENDIX

FURTHER READING ON PROGRAMMING LANGUAGES

The preceding chapters have mentioned a variety of programming languages. The following is a brief list of references giving their defining documents (if any) and some additional reading.

Several books provide good introductions to the field of programming languages, including overviews of the more popular ones. For a good coverage of the early languages see Sammet (1969). Some more recent books are Horowitz (1984), Pratt (1984), Wilson and Clark (1988), Sethi (1989), and Sebesta (1989). Some of the classic papers are reprinted in Rosen (1967) and Horowitz (1987). For a history of programming languages, see Wexelblat (1981).

Ada

The preliminary version of Ada and its detailed rationale are described in Ichbiah *et al.* (1979a, 1979b). The standard definition is ANSI/MIL-STD-1815A (January 1983), which is available free of charge from some sources. It is reprinted as *Lecture Notes in Computer Science* **155** (Springer-Verlag, 1983), and also as *The Ada Reference Manual* (Silicon Press, 1986). An updated version of the Rationale is given by Ichbiah *et al.* (1986). Barnes (1989) is an excellent introduction to the language. Booch (1987) describes it with an emphasis on software engineering, using an object-oriented approach. Watt, Wichmann, and Findlay (1987) covers both the language and its related methodologies. Burns, Lister, and Wellings (1987) reviews the tasking facilities. Gehani (1984) and Shumate (1987) give examples of their use.

ALGOL 60

The original report is Naur (1960); the revised report is Naur (1963). Good introductions are Dijkstra (1960a) and Rutishauser (1967).

ALGOL 68

The original report is van Wijngaarden *et al.* (1969); the revised report is van Wijngaarden *et al.* (1975). As an aid to interpreting these somewhat obscure reports, try Peck (1972). For more general introductions see Pagan (1976) or Lindsey and van der Meulen (1977).

APL

APL was first described in the book *A Programming Language*, from which it derives its name (Iverson, 1962). The final draft of the international standard is presented in ISO DIS 8485 (June 1986). A popular textbook is Gilman and Rose (1984). For APL2 see Brown, Pakin, and Polivka (1988).

BASIC

The language BASIC (Beginner's All-purpose Symbolic Instruction Code) comes in some form or other on almost every computer, big or small. In Kemeny and Kurtz (1985), its designers review its development and its future, and in Kemeny, Kurtz, and Elliott (1985) they provide a reference manual for 'True BASIC'. There are countless other textbooks on 'BASIC for machine X'.

BCPL

The definitive source is Richards and Whitby-Strevens (1980).

C

The second edition of Kernighan and Ritchie (1988) is based on the draft ANSI standard for C and serves both as a textbook and as an informal reference book. Many other textbooks are also available.

COBOL

The 1974 standard is defined by ANSI X3.23-1974, *American National Standard Programming Language COBOL*. A new standard was approved in 1985 but, because it was incompatible with the earlier version, its enforcement ran into legal difficulties. Nevertheless, most of its features are provided by modern compilers and described in modern textbooks. Among the latter are Philippakis and Kazmier (1986) and, for a very thorough coverage, the massive Stern and Stern (1988).

CSP

CSP was first described in Hoare (1978). A modified version is presented and rigorously defined in Hoare (1985). The language was designed primarily for theoretical study and so it is not generally available for practical programming. However, it was the primary influence on the design of occam (*q.v.*).

FORTRAN

The most common version is known as FORTRAN 77. It is defined in ANSI X.39-1978, as described by Brainerd (1978). Numerous programming texts are based on FORTRAN 77, including Koffman and Friedman (1987). Programmers who already know Pascal may prefer Terry (1987).

LISP

For many years the standard version was LISP 1.5, as defined in McCarthy and Levin (1965). Many other versions have followed with various degrees of acceptance. Danicic

(1983) is a slim introduction to LISP 1.5. For something more substantial, based on Common LISP, see Winston and Horn (1984).

Modula-2

The first version of Modula was described in Wirth (1977a). For an up-do-date description of Modula-2 see Wirth (1988). A good textbook is Sale (1986).

occam

The first version of occam is defined in Inmos (1984) and occam 2 in Inmos (1988). A good introduction to the latter is Burns (1988).

Pascal

Pascal was originally defined in Wirth (1971). After much debate, the ISO standard was split into two levels. Level 0, which is equivalent to ANSI X3.97-1983, differs little from the original. Level 1, which is the same as the British standard BS 6192 and the ISO draft proposal 7185, includes conformant arrays. Jensen and Wirth (1974) contains the original report and also a user manual; the 1985 edition is based on the standard. Cooper (1987) is a popular textbook.

PL/I

The IBM reference manual for PL/I is GC26-3977. A good introduction is provided by Clarke, Green, and Teague (1986). There is surprisingly little else.

Prolog

Prolog suffers from having a wide variety of versions and extensions. Clocksin and Mellish (1987) provides an excellent introduction: it is based on Edinburgh Prolog but describes other versions as well. Malpas (1987) discusses the language and its applications. Stirling and Shapiro (1986) covers more advanced techniques.

SIMULA 67

The reference manual is Dahl, Myhrhaug, and Nygaard (1970). A well-known textbook is Birtwhistle *et al.* (1979). For something more recent see Pooley (1987).

Smalltalk

The authoritative source for Smalltalk is Goldberg and Robson (1983). Some recent textbooks are Budd (1987) and Kaehler and Patterson (1986).

BIBLIOGRAPHY

Abraham, P.W. (1966), 'A final solution to the dangling else of ALGOL 60 and related languages', *Commun. ACM* **9:9**, 679–82.

Ackermann, W. (1928), 'Zum Hilbertschen aufbau der reellen zahlen', *Mathematische Annalen* **99**, 118–33.

Aho, A.V., Hopcroft, J.E., and Ullman, J.D. (1983), *Data Structures and Algorithms*, Addison-Wesley.

Aho, A.V., Sethi, R., and Ullman, J.D. (1986), *Compilers: Principles, Techniques, and Tools*, Addison-Wesley.

Ahrens, W. (1918), *Mathematische Unterhaltungen und Spiele* **2**, chapter 18, Teubner, Leipzig.

Andrews, G.R. and Schneider, F.B. (1983), 'Concepts and notations for concurrent programming', *ACM Comput. Surv.* **15:1**, 3–43.

Appelbe, W.F. and Ravn, A.P. (1984), 'Encapsulation constructs in systems programming languages', *ACM Trans. Program. Lang. Syst.* **6:2**, 129–58.

Apt, K.R. (1981), 'Ten years of Hoare's logic: a survey — Part I', *ACM Trans. Program. Lang. Syst.* **3:4**, 431–83.

Apt, K.R. (1983), 'Formal justification of a proof system for communicating sequential processes', *J. ACM* **30:1**, 197–216.

Apt, K.R., Francez, N., and de Roever, W.P. (1980), 'A proof system for communicating sequential processes', *ACM Trans. Program. Lang. Syst.* **2:3**, 359–85.

Arsac, J.J. (1979), 'Syntactic source to source transforms and program manipulation', *Commun. ACM* **22:1**, 43–54.

Arsac, J.J. and Kodratoff, Y. (1982), 'Some techniques for recursion removal from recursive functions', *ACM Trans. Program. Lang. Syst.* **4:2**, 295–322.

Atkinson, L.V. (1984), 'Jumping about and getting into a state', *Comput. J.* **27:1**, 42–6.

Auslander, M.A. and Strong, H.R. (1978), 'Systematic recursion removal', *Commun. ACM* **21:2**, 127–34.

Backhouse, R.C. (1979), *Syntax of Programming Languages: Theory and Practice*, Prentice Hall.

Backhouse, R.C. (1986), *Program Construction and Verification*, Prentice Hall.

Backus, J. (1978), 'Can programming be liberated from the von Neumann style? A functional style and its algebra of programs', *Commun. ACM* **21:8**, 613–41.

Barnes, J. (1989), *Programming in Ada*, 3rd edition, Addison-Wesley.

Barringer, H. (1985), *A survey of verification techniques for parallel programs*, Lecture Notes in Computer Science 191, Springer-Verlag.

Barringer, H. (1987), 'Up and down the temporal way', *Comput. J.* **30:2**, 134–48.

Barringer, H. and Mearns, I. (1986), 'A proof system for Ada tasks', *Comput. J.* **29:5**, 404–15.

Barron, D.W. (1968), *Recursive Techniques in Programming*, McDonald, London.

Bauer, F.L. and Wossner, H. (1982), *Algorithmic Language and Program Development*, Springer-Verlag.

Bell, C.G. and Newell, A. (1971), *Computer Structures*, McGraw-Hill.

Ben-Ari, M. (1982), *Principles of Concurrent Programming*, Prentice Hall.

Bertziss, A.T. and Thattle, S. (1983), 'Specification and implementation of abstract data types', *Advances in Computers* **22**, 295–353, Academic Press.

Bezevin, J., Nebut, J-L., and Rannou, R. (1978), 'Another view of coroutines', *SIGPLAN Notices* **13:5**, 23–35.

Biggs, N. L. (1985), *Discrete Mathematics*, Oxford University Press.

Bird, R. (1976), *Programs and Machines: an Introduction to the Theory of Computation*, John Wiley & Sons Ltd.

Bird, R. (1977a), 'Notes on recursion elimination', *Commun. ACM* **20:6**, 434–9.

Bird, R. (1977b), 'Improving programs by the introduction of recursion', *Commun. ACM* **20:11**, 856–63.

Bird, R. (1980), 'Tabulation techniques for recursive programs', *ACM Comput. Surv.* **12:4**, 403–17.

Birtwhistle, G., Dahl, O-J., Myhrhaug, B., and Nygaard, K. (1979), *Simula Begin*, 2nd edition, Van Nostrand Reinhold.

Bohm, C. and Jacopini, G. (1966), 'Flow-diagrams, Turing machines, and languages with only two formation rules', *Commun. ACM* **9:5**, 366–71.

Booch, G. (1986), 'Object-oriented development', *IEEE Trans. Soft. Eng.* **12:2**, 211–21.

Booch, G. (1987), *Software Engineering with Ada*, 2nd edition, Benjamin/Cummings.

Braffort, P. and Hirschberg, D. eds. (1963), *Computer Programming and Formal Systems*, North-Holland.

Brainerd, W. ed. (1978), 'FORTRAN 77', *Commun. ACM* **21:10**, 806–820.

Brent, R. (1982), 'An idealist's view of semantics for integer and real types', *Aust. Comput. Sci. Commun.* **4:1**, 130–40.

Briggs, J.S., Forsyth, C.H., Johnson, C.W., Murdie, J.A., Pyle, I.C., Runciman, C., Walker, I., Wand, I.C., and Williams, A.J. (1982), 'Ada Workbench Compiler Project 1981', York Computer Science Report No. 48.

Brinch Hansen, P. (1972), 'Structured multiprogramming', *Commun. ACM* **15:7**, 574–8.

Brinch Hansen, P. (1973), 'Concurrent programming concepts', *ACM Comput. Surv.* **5:4**, 223–45.

Brinch Hansen, P. (1978), 'Distributed processes: a concurrent programming concept', *Commun. ACM* **21:11**, 934–41.

Brooks, F. (1975), *The Mythical Man-Month*, Addison-Wesley.

Brown, J.A., Pakin, S., and Polivka, R.P. (1988), *APL2*, Prentice Hall.

Brown, W.S. (1977), 'A realistic model of floating-point computation', in *Mathematical Software III*, ed. Rice, J., pp. 343–60, Academic Press.

Buck, R.C. (1963), 'Mathematical induction and recursive definitions', *Amer. Math. Monthly* **70**, 128–35.

Budd, T. (1987), *A Little Smalltalk*, Addison-Wesley.

Buhr, R.J.A. (1984), *System Design with Ada*, Prentice Hall.

Burge, W.H. (1975), *Recursive Programming Techniques*, Addison-Wesley.

Burks, A.W., Goldstine, H.H., and Von Neumann, J. (1946), 'Preliminary discussion of the logical design of an electronic computing instrument', also 2nd edition (1947), Institute for Advanced Study, Princeton, reprinted in Traub (1963) volume 5, pp. 34–79, and in Bell and Newell (1971), pp. 92–119.

Burns, A. (1985), *Concurrent Programming in Ada*, Cambridge University Press.

Burns, A. (1987), 'Using large families for handling priority requests', *Ada Lett.* **7:1**, 97–104.

Burns, A. (1988), *Programming in occam 2*, Addison-Wesley.

Burns, A., Lister, A.M., and Wellings, A.J. (1987), *A Review of Ada Tasking*, Lecture Notes in Computer Science 262, Springer-Verlag.

Burstall, R.M. and Darlington, J. (1977), 'A transformation system for developing recursive programs', *J. ACM* **24:1**, 44–67.

Campbell, R.H. and Habermann, A.N. (1974), 'The Specification of Process Synchronisation by Path Expressions', *Lecture Notes in Computer Science* **16**, 89–102, Springer-Verlag.

Cardelli, L. and Wegner, P. (1985), 'On understanding types, data abstraction, and polymorphism', *ACM Comput. Surv.* **17:4**, 471–522.

Chang, A.P. (1985), 'A note on the modulo operation', *SIGPLAN Notices* **20:4**, 19–23.

Chapin, N. (1970), 'Flowcharting with the ANSI standard: a tutorial', *ACM Comput. Surv.* **2:2**, 119–46.

Chomsky, N. (1959), 'On certain formal properties of grammars', *Inf. Control* **2:2**, 137–67.

Clapp, R.M., Duchesneau, L., Volz, R.A., Mudge, T.N., and Schultze, T. (1986), 'Toward real-time performance benchmarks for Ada', *Commun. ACM* **29:8**, 760–78.

Clark, R.L. (1973), 'A linguistic contribution to GOTO-less programming', *Datamation* **19:12**, 62–3.

Clarke, G.R., Green, S.J., and Teague, P.R. (1986), *Practical PL/I*, Cambridge University Press.

Clocksin, W.F. and Mellish, C.S. (1987), *Programming in Prolog*, 3rd edition, Springer-Verlag.

Cloutier, M.J. and Matthew, J. (1983), 'Precision averaging for real-time analysis', *Commun. ACM* **26:7**, 525–9.

Cohen, N.H. (1983), 'Eliminating redundant recursive calls', *ACM Trans. Program. Lang. Syst.* **5:3**, 265–99.

Conway, J.H. (1971), *Regular Algebra and Finite Machines*, Chapman and Hall.

Conway, M.E. (1963), 'Design of a separable transition-diagram compiler', *Commun. ACM* **6:7**, 396–408.

Cooper, D. (1987), *Condensed Pascal*, W.W. Norton & Co.

Cormack, G.V. (1983), 'Extensions to static scoping', *SIGPLAN Notices* **18:6**, 187–91.

Cottam, I.D. (1985), 'Extending Pascal with one-entry/multi-exit procedures', *SIGPLAN Notices* **20:2**, 21–9.

Courtois, P.J., Heymans, F., and Parnas, D.L. (1971), 'Concurrent control with readers and writers', *Commun. ACM* **14:10**, 667–8.

Cox, B.J. (1986), *Object-oriented Programming*, Addison-Wesley.

Cristian, F. (1984), 'Correct and robust programs', *IEEE Trans. Soft. Eng.* **10:2**, 163–74.

Dahl, O-J. and Hoare, C.A.R. (1972), 'Hierarchical program structure', in Dahl, Dijkstra, and Hoare (1972).

Dahl, O.-J, Dijkstra, E.W., and Hoare, C.A.R. (1972), *Structured Programming*, Academic Press.

Danforth, S. and Tomlinson, C. (1988), 'Type theories and object-oriented programming', *ACM Comput. Surv.* **20:1**, 29–72.

Danicic, I. (1983), *LISP Programming*, Blackwell Scientific Press.

Darlington, J. and Burstall, R.M. (1976), 'A system which automatically improves programs', *Acta Inf.* **6:1**, 41–60.

Deitel, H.M. (1984), *An Introduction to Operating Systems*, 1st edition revised, Addison-Wesley.

Denning, P.J. (1970), 'Virtual memory', *ACM Comput. Surv.* **2:3**, 153–89.

Denning, P.J., Dennis, J.B., and Qualitz, J.E. (1978), *Machines, Languages, and Computation*, Prentice Hall.

Dennis, J.B. and Van Horn, E.C. (1966), 'Programming semantics for multiprogrammed computations', *Commun. ACM* **9:3**, 143–155.

De Prycker, M. (1982), 'A performance analysis of the implementation of addressing methods in block-structured languages', *IEEE Trans. Comput.* **31:2**, 155–63.

Dijkstra, E.W. (1960a), *A Primer of ALGOL 60 Programming*, Academic Press.

Dijkstra, E.W. (1960b), 'Recursive programming', *Numer. Math.* **2**, 312–8.

Dijkstra, E.W. (1965), 'Cooperating sequential processes', Report EWD-123, Technological University, Eindhoven, The Netherlands, reprinted in Genuys (1968), pp. 43–112.

Dijkstra, E.W. (1968), 'Go to statement considered harmful', *Commun. ACM* **11:3**, 147–8, 538, 541.

Dijkstra, E.W. (1975), 'Guarded commands, nondeterminacy and the formal derivation of programs', *Commun. ACM* **18:8**, 453–7.

Dijkstra, E.W. (1976), *A Discipline of Programming*, Prentice Hall.

Doerr, A. and Levasseur, K. (1985), *Applied Discrete Structures for Computer Science*, Science Research Associates.

Doran, R.W. (1976), 'Virtual memory', *IEEE Computer* **9:10**, 27–37.

Downes, V.A. and Goldsack, S.J. (1982), *Programming embedded systems with Ada*, Prentice Hall.

Dunlop, D.D. and Basili, V.R. (1982), 'A comparative analysis of functional correctness', *ACM Comput. Surv.* **14:2**, 229–44.

Eisenberg, M.A. and McGuire, M.R. (1972), 'Further comments on Dijkstra's concurrent programming control problem', *Commun. ACM* **15:11**, 999.

Er, M.C. (1983a), 'A fast algorithm for computing order-k Fibonacci numbers', *Comput. J.* **26:3**, 224–7.

Er, M.C. (1983b), 'Optimizing procedure calls and returns', *Softw. Pract. Exper.* **13:10**, 921–39.

Eve, J. and Kurki-Suonio, R. (1977), 'On computing the transitive closure of a relation', *Acta Inf.* **8**, 303–14.

Fateman, R.J. (1982), 'High-level language implications of the proposed IEEE floating-point standard', *ACM Trans. Program. Lang. Syst.* **4:2**, 239–57.

Fleck, A.C. (1984), 'A proposal for comparison of types in Pascal and associated semantic models', *Comput. Lang.* **9:2**, 71–87.

Flegg, G. (1983), *Numbers: Their History and Meaning*, Schoken Books.

Floyd, R.W. (1963), 'Syntactic analysis and operator precedence', *J. ACM* **10:3**, 316–33.

Floyd, R.W. (1967), 'Assigning meaning to programs', *Proc. AMS Symp. Applied Mathematics* **19**, 19–32, American Mathematical Society, Providence, R.I.

Forsythe, G.E. (1969), 'What is a satisfactory quadratic equation solver?', in *Constructive Aspects of the Fundamental Theorem of Algebra*, ed. Dejon, B. and Henrici, P., pp. 53–71, John Wiley & Sons Ltd.

Forsythe, G.E. (1970), 'Pitfalls in computation, or why a math book isn't enough', *Amer. Math. Monthly* **77:9**, 931–56.

Forsythe, G.E., Malcolm, M.A., and Moler, C.B. (1977), *Computer Methods for Mathematical Computations*, Prentice Hall.

Freeman, P. and Wasserman, A.I., eds. (1980), *Tutorial on Software Design Techniques*, 3rd edition, IEEE Computer Society.

Galton, A. ed. (1987), *Temporal logics and their applications*, Academic Press.

Gedeon, T.D. (1986), *SIGPLAN Notices* **21:6**, 11–12, letter to the editor.

Gehani, N. (1984), *Ada: Concurrent Programming*, Prentice Hall.

Gehani, N. and Cargill, T.A. (1984), 'Concurrent programming in the Ada language: the polling bias', *Softw. Pract. Exper.* **14:5**, 413–27.

Genuys, F. ed. (1968), *Programming Languages*, Academic Press.

Gerber, A.J. (1980), 'Modelling the readers and writers problem with inhibitor nets', *Aust. Comput. Sci. Commun.* **2:1**, 157–71.

Gilman, L. and Rose, A.J. (1984), *APL — an Interactive Approach*, John Wiley & Sons Ltd.

Goldberg, A. and Robson, D. (1983), *Smalltalk-80: the Language and its Implementation*, Addison-Wesley.

Goldstine, H.H. (1972), *The Computer, from Pascal to von Neumann*, Princeton University Press.

Goodenough, J.B. (1975), 'Exception handling: issues and a proposed notation', *Commun. ACM* **18:12**, 683–96.

Greene, D.H. and Knuth, D.E. (1981), *Mathematics for the Analysis of Algorithms*, Birkhauser, Boston.

Grief, I. and Mayer, A.R. (1981), 'Specifying the semantics of while programs', *ACM Trans. Program. Lang. Syst.* **3:4**, 484–507.

Gries, D. (1981), *The Science of Programming*, Springer-Verlag.

Grimaldi, R. P. (1985), *Discrete and Combinatorial Mathematics: an Applied Introduction*, Addison-Wesley.

Grune, D. (1977), 'A view of coroutines', *SIGPLAN Notices* **12:7**, 75–81.

Hamacher, V.C., Vranesic, Z.G., and Zaky S.G. (1984), *Computer Organization*, 2nd edition, McGraw-Hill.

Hamilton, D.E. (1986), 'Fast integer powers for Pascal', *Dr Dobb's Journal* **11:2**, 36–41.

Hanson, D.R. (1981), 'Is block structure necessary?', *Softw. Pract. Exper.* **11**, 853–66.

Harel, D. (1980a), 'On folk theorems', *Commun. ACM* **23:7**, 379–89.

Harel, D. (1980b), 'Proving the correctness of regular deterministic programs: a unifying survey using dynamic logic', *Theor. Comput. Sci.* **12**, 61–81.

Hayes, I. ed. (1987), *Specification Case Studies*, Prentice Hall.

Hayes, P.J. (1977), 'A note on the Towers of Hanoi problem', *Comput. J.* **20:3**, 282–5.

Henderson, P. (1980), *Functional Programming: Applications and Implementation*, Prentice Hall.

Hibbard, P., Hisgen, A., Rosenberg, J., Shaw, M., and Sherman, M. (1981), *Studies in Ada Style*, Springer-Verlag.

Hilfinger, P. (1983), *Abstraction Mechanisms and Language Design*, MIT Press.

Hoare, C.A.R. (1964), 'Case expressions', *ALGOL Bulletin* **18**, 20.

Hoare, C.A.R. (1969), 'An axiomatic basis for computer programming', *Commun. ACM* **12:10**, 576–80, 583.

Hoare, C.A.R. (1972), 'Proof of correctness of data representations', *Acta Inf.* **1**, 271–81.

Hoare, C.A.R. (1974), 'Monitors: an operating system structuring concept', *Commun. ACM* **17:10**, 549–57, erratum in **18:2**, p.95.

Hoare, C.A.R. (1978), 'Communicating sequential processes', *Commun. ACM* **21:8**, 666–77.

Hoare, C.A.R. (1981), 'A calculus of total correctness for communicating processes', *Sci. Comput. Program.* **1:1**, 49–72.

Hoare, C.A.R. (1985), *Communicating Sequential Processes*, Prentice Hall.

Hofstadter, D. (1979), *Gödel, Escher, Bach: An Eternal Golden Braid*, Basic Books Inc.

Hopcroft, J.E. and Ullman, J.D. (1969), *Formal languages and their relation to automata*, Addison-Wesley.

Hopcroft, J.E. and Ullman, J.D. (1979), *Introduction to Automata Theory, Languages, and Computation*, Addison-Wesley.

Horowitz, E. (1984), *Fundamentals of Programming Languages*, 2nd edition, Springer-Verlag.

Horowitz, E. ed. (1987), *Programming Languages: A Grand Tour*, Computer Science Press.

Horton, I.A. and Turner, S.J. (1986), 'Using coroutines in Pascal', *Softw. Pract. Exper.* **16:1**, 45–61.

House, R.T. (1986), 'Alternative scope rules for block-structured languages', *Comput. J.* **29:3**, 253–60.

Ichbiah, J.D., Barnes, J.G.P., Firth, R.J., and Woodger, M. (1986), *Rationale for the Design of the Ada Programming Language*, Silicon Press.

Ichbiah, J.D., Barnes, J.G.P., Heliard, J.C., Krieg-Brueckner, B., Roubine, O., and Wichmann, B.A. (1979a), 'Preliminary Ada reference manual', *SIGPLAN Notices* **14:6**, Part A.

Ichbiah, J.D., Barnes, J.G.P., Heliard, J.C., Krieg-Brueckner, B., Roubine, O., and Wichmann, B.A. (1979b), 'Rationale for the design of the Ada programming language', *SIGPLAN Notices* **14:6**, Part B.

IEEE Microprocessor Standards Committee Task Force P754 (1981), 'A proposed standard for binary floating-point arithmetic', *IEEE Computer* **14:3**, 51–62.

IEEE Microprocessor Standards Committee Task Force P754 (1985), 'IEEE Standard for Binary Floating-Point Arithmetic', ANSI/IEEE Standard 754-1985, IEEE Inc., New York, reprinted in *SIGPLAN Notices* **22:2**, 9–25 (February, 1987).

Ingermann, P.Z. (1961), 'Thunks', *Commun. ACM* **4:1**, 55–8.

INMOS Limited (1984), *occam Programming Manual*, Prentice Hall.

INMOS Limited (1988), *occam 2 Reference Manual*, Prentice Hall.

Iverson, K. (1962), *A Programming Language*, John Wiley & Sons Ltd.

Jackson, M.A. (1975), *Principles of Program Design*, Academic Press.

Jackson, M.A. (1983), *System Development*, Prentice Hall.

Jensen, K. and Wirth, N. (1974), *Pascal User Manual and Report*, also 3rd edition (1985) revised by Mickel, A. and Miner, F., Springer-Verlag.

Johnson, R.T. and Morris, J.B. (1976), 'Abstract data types in the Model programming language', *SIGPLAN Notices* **11:3**, 36–46.

Johnston, J.B. (1971), 'The contour model of block structured processes', *SIGPLAN Notices* **6:2**, 55–82.

Jones, C.B. (1986), *Systematic Software Development using VDM*, Prentice Hall.

Jones, N.D. and Muchnick, S.S. (1978), *TEMPO: A Unified Treatment of Binding Times and Parameter Passing Concepts in Programming Languages*, Lecture Notes in Computer Science 66, Springer-Verlag.

Kaehler, T. and Patterson, D. (1986), *A Taste of Smalltalk*, W.W. Norton & Co.

Kalmanson, K. (1986), *An Introduction to Discrete Mathematics and its Applications*, Addison-Wesley.

Kaubisch, W.H., Perrott, R.H., and Hoare, C.A.R. (1976), 'Quasiparallel programming', *Softw. Pract. Exper.* **6:3**, 341–56.

Kemeny, J.G., Kurtz, T.E., and Elliott, B. (1985), *Reference Manual for True BASIC*, Addison-Wesley.

Kemeny, J.G. and Kurtz, T.E. (1985), *Back to BASIC*, Addison-Wesley.

Kernighan, B.W. and Ritchie, D.M. (1988), *The C Programming Language*, 2nd edition, Prentice Hall.

Kirk, H.W. (1965), 'Use of decision tables in computer programming', *Commun. ACM* **8:1**, 41–3.

Kleene, S.C. (1952), *Introduction to metamathematics*, Van Nostrand.

Kleene, S.C. (1956), 'Representation of events in nerve nets and finite automata', in *Automata Studies*, pp. 3–42, Princeton University Press.

Knudsen, J.L. (1984), 'Exception handling — a static approach', *Softw. Pract. Exper.* **14:5**, 429–50.

Knuth, D.E. (1973), *The Art of Computer Programming, Volume I : Fundamental Algorithms*, 2nd edition, Addison-Wesley.

Knuth, D.E. (1974), 'Structured programming with go to statements', *ACM Comput. Surv.* **6:4**, 261–301.

Knuth, D.E. (1981), *The Art of Computer Programming, Volume II : Seminumerical Algorithms*, 2nd edition, Addison-Wesley.

Knuth, D.E. (1984a), 'Literate programming', *Comput. J.* **27:2**, 97–111.

Knuth, D.E. (1984b), 'The complexity of songs', *Commun. ACM* **27:4**, 344–6.

Knuth, D.E. and Floyd, R.W. (1971), 'Notes on avoiding go to statements', *Inf. Process. Lett.* **1:1**, 23–31, 177.

Koffman, E.B. and Friedman, F.L. (1987), *Problem-Solving and Structured Programming in FORTRAN 77*, Addison-Wesley.

Kreutzer, W. (1986), *System Simulation — Programming Styles and Languages*, Addison-Wesley.

Kriz, J. and Sandmayr, H. (1980), 'Extension of Pascal by coroutines and its application to quasi-parallel programming and simulation', *Softw. Pract. Exper.* **10**, 773–89.

Kurki-Suonio, R. (1971), *Computability and Formal Languages*, Auerbach.

Lamport, L. (1974), 'A new solution of Dijkstra's concurrent programming problem', *Commun. ACM* **17:8**, 453–5.

Lamport, L. (1983), 'What good is temporal logic?', in *Information Processing 83*, pp. 657–68, North-Holland.

Ledgard, H.F. and Marcotty, M. (1975), 'A genealogy of control structures', *Commun. ACM* **18:11**, 629–39.

Lee, P.A. (1983), 'Exception handling in C programs', *Softw. Pract. Exper.* **13:5**, 389–405.

Lehmer, D.H. (1964), 'The machine tools of combinatorics', in *Applied Combinatorial Mathematics*, ed. Beckenbach, E.F., pp. 5–31, John Wiley & Sons Ltd.

Lifschitz, V. (1984), 'On verification of programs with goto-statements', *Inf. Process. Lett.* **18:4**, 221–5.

Lindsey, C.H. and van der Meulen, S.G. (1977), *Informal Introduction to ALGOL 68*, revised edition, North-Holland.

Lindstrom, G. and Soffa, M.L. (1981), 'Referencing and retention in block-structured coroutines', *ACM Trans. Program. Lang. Syst.* **3:3**, 263–92.

Linger, R.C., Mills, H.D., and Witt, B.I. (1979), *Structured Programming: Theory and Practice*, Addison-Wesley.

Liskov, B. (1981), *CLU Reference Manual*, Lecture Notes in Computer Science 114, Springer-Verlag.

Liskov, B. and Guttag, J. (1986), *Abstraction and Specification in Program Development*, MIT Press.

Liskov, B. and Snyder, A. (1979), 'Exception handling in CLU', *IEEE Trans. Soft. Eng.* **5:6**, 546–58.

Liskov, H., Snyder, A., Atkinson, R., and Schaffert, C. (1977), 'Abstraction mechanisms in Clu', *Commun. ACM* **20:8**, 564–76.

Lister, A.M. (1984), *Fundamentals of Operating Systems*, 3rd edition, Macmillan.

Lueker, G.S. (1980), 'Some techniques for solving recurrences', *ACM Comput. Surv.* **12:4**, 419–36.

MacLaren, M.D. (1977), 'Exception handling in PL/I', *SIGPLAN Notices* **12:3**, 101–4.

Malpas, J. (1987), *Prolog: a Relational Language and its Applications*, Prentice Hall.

Manna, Z. and Pnueli, A. (1974), 'Axiomatic approach to total correctness of programs', *Acta Inf.* **3**, 243–63.

Manner, R. (1986), 'Strong typing and physical units', *SIGPLAN Notices* **21:3**, 11–20.

Marcotty, M. and Ledgard, H. (1986), *The Programming Language Landscape: Syntax, Semantics, and Implementation*, 2nd edition, Science Research Associates.

Marlin, C.D. (1980), *Coroutines*, Lecture Notes in Computer Science 95, Springer-Verlag.

Martin, A.J. and Rem, M. (1984), 'A presentation of the Fibonacci algorithm', *Inf. Process. Lett.* **19**, 67–8.

Mayer, A.R. and Halpern, J.Y. (1982), 'Axiomatic definition of programming languages: a theoretical assessment', *J. ACM* **29:2**, 555–76.

McCarthy, J. (1961), 'A basis for a mathematical theory of computation', in *Proc. WJCC*, May 1961, pp. 225–38, reprinted in Braffort and Hirschberg (1963), pp. 33–70.

McCarthy, J. and Levin, S. (1965), *LISP 1.5 Programmer's Manual*, 2nd edition, MIT Press.

McMullen, B. (1984), 'Structured decision tables', *SIGPLAN Notices* **19:4**, 34–43.

McNaughton, R. and Yamada, H. (1960), 'Regular expressions and state graphs for automata', *IEEE Trans. Comput.* **9**, 39–47.

Menninger, K. (1969), *Number Words and Number Symbols: A Cultural History of Numbers*, MIT Press.

Metropolis, N., Howlett, J., and Rota, G-C., eds. (1980), *A History of Computing in the Twentieth Century*, Academic Press.

Metzner, J.R. and Barnes, B.H. (1977), *Decision Table Languages and Systems*, Academic Press.

Meyer, B. (1982), 'Principles of package design', *Commun. ACM* **25:7**, 419–28.

Meyer, B. (1986), 'Genericity versus inheritance', in Meyrowitz (1986), pp. 391–405.

Meyer, B. (1988), *Object-oriented software construction*, Prentice Hall.

Meyrowitz, N., ed. (1986), 'OOPSLA '86 Conference Proceedings', *SIGPLAN Notices* **21:11**.

Meyrowitz, N., ed. (1987), 'OOPSLA '87 Conference Proceedings', *SIGPLAN Notices* **22:12**.

Miller, J.C.P. and Spencer Brown, D.J. (1966), 'An algorithm for the evaluation of remote terms in a linear recurrence sequence', *Comput. J.* **9**, 188–90.

Mills, H.D. (1975), 'The new math of computer programming', *Commun. ACM* **18:1**, 43–8.

Mills, H.D. (1980), 'Functional semantics for sequential programs', in *Information Processing 80*, ed. Lavington, S.H., pp. 241–50, Elsevier.

Milner, R. (1980), *A Calculus of Communicating Systems*, Lecture Notes in Computer Science 92, Springer-Verlag.

Minsky, M.L. (1967), *Computation: Finite and Infinite Machines*, Prentice Hall.

Moody, K. and Richards, M. (1980), 'A coroutine mechanism for BCPL', *Softw. Pract. Exper.* **10:10**, 763–72.

Moore, R.E. (1966), *Interval Analysis*, Prentice Hall.

Moret, B.M.E. (1982), 'Decision trees and diagrams', *ACM Comput. Surv.* **14:4**, 593–623.

Morgan, C. (1988), 'The specification statement', *ACM Trans. Program. Lang. Syst.* **10:3**, 403–19.

Nassi, I. and Shneiderman, B. (1973), 'Flowchart techniques for structured programming', *SIGPLAN Notices* **8:8**, 12–26.

Naur, P. (1963), 'Go to statements and good ALGOL style', *BIT* **3:3**, 204–8.

Naur, P. (1969), 'Proofs of algorithms by general snapshots', *BIT* **6**, 310–16.

Naur, P. ed. (1960), 'Report on the algorithmic language ALGOL 60', *Commun. ACM* **3:5**, 299–314.

Naur, P. ed. (1963), 'Revised report on the algorithmic language ALGOL 60', *Commun. ACM* **6:1**, 1–17, and also *Comput. J.* **5:4**, 349–367 (January 1963).

Newey, M.C. and Waite, W.M. (1985), 'The robust implementation of sequence-controlled iteration', *Softw. Pract. Exper.* **15:7**, 655–68.

Nielsen, K.W. and Shumate, K. (1987), 'Designing large real-time systems with Ada', *Commun. ACM* **30:8**, 695–715.

Nybo, R. (1974), 'NDRE SIMULA implementation: central run-time system', Teknisk notat S-374, Norwegian Defence Research Establishment.

Organick, E.I., Forsythe, A.I., and Plummer, R.P. (1978), *Programming Language Structures*, Academic Press.

Oulsnam, G. (1982), 'Unravelling unstructured programs', *Comput. J.* **25:3**, 379–87.

Pagan, F.G. (1976), *A Practical Guide to ALGOL 68*, John Wiley & Sons Ltd.

Park, S.K. and Miller, K.W. (1988), 'Random number generators: good ones are hard to find', *Commun. ACM* **31:10**, 1192–1201.

Parnas, D.L. (1972), 'On the criteria to be used in decomposing systems into modules', *Commun. ACM* **15:12**, 1053–8, reprinted in Freeman and Wasserman (1980), pp. 220–5.

Parnas, D.L. (1975), 'On a solution to the cigarette smoker's problem (without conditional statements)', *Commun. ACM* **18:3**, 181–3.

Partsch, H. and Pepper, P. (1976), 'A family of rules for recursion removal related to the Towers of Hanoi problem', *Inf. Process. Lett.* **5:6**, 174–7.

Patil, S. (1971), 'Limitations and capabilities of Dijkstra's semaphore primitives for coordination among processes', Memo 57, Project MAC, MIT.

Peck, J.E.L. (1972), *An ALGOL 68 Companion*, University of British Columbia Press.

Perrott, R. H. (1987), *Parallel programming*, Addison-Wesley.

Peterson, G.L. (1981), 'Myths about the mutual exclusion problem', *Inf. Process. Lett.* **12:3**, 115–6.

Peterson, J.L. and Silberschatz, A. (1985), *Operating System Concepts*, Addison-Wesley.

Philippakis, A.S. and Kazmier, L.J. (1986), *Structured COBOL*, 3rd edition, McGraw-Hill.

Pooch, U.W. (1974), 'Translation of decision tables', *ACM Comput. Surv.* **6:2**, 125–51.

Pooley, R.J. (1987), *An Introduction to Programming in SIMULA*, Blackwell Scientific Press.

Prather, R.E. and Giuleri, S.G. (1981), 'Decomposition of flowchart schemata', *Comput. J.* **24:3**, 258–62.

Pratt, T.W. (1984), *Programming Languages: Design and Implementation*, 2nd edition, Prentice Hall.

Randell, B. and Russell, L.J. (1964), *ALGOL 60 Implementation*, Academic Press.

Remmers, J.H. (1984), 'A technique for developing loop invariants', *Inf. Process. Lett.* **18**, 137–9.

Riccardi, G.A. and Baker, T.P. (1985), 'A runtime supervisor to support Ada tasking: rendezvous and delays', *Ada Lett.* **5:2**, 329–42.

Richards, M. and Whitby-Strevens, C. (1980), *BCPL — the Language and its Compiler*, Cambridge University Press.

Rohl, J.S. (1984), *Recursion via Pascal*, Cambridge University Press.

Rohl, J.S. (1987), 'Towers of Hanoi: the derivation of some iterative versions', *Comput. J.* **30:1**, 70–6.

Rosen, S. ed. (1967), *Programming Systems and Languages*, McGraw-Hill.

Rouse Ball, W.W. (1892), *Mathematical Recreations and Essays*, Macmillan, frequently reprinted.

Rutishauser, H. (1967), *Description of ALGOL 60*, Springer-Verlag.

Sale, A.H.J. (1986), *Modula-2: Discipline and Design*, Addison-Wesley.

Salomaa, A. (1973), *Formal Languages*, Academic Press.

Salvadori, A. and Dumont, C. (1979), 'Some inconsistencies in programming language implementation', *SIGPLAN Notices* **14:11**, 107–9, see also **15:6**, **15:9**, and **18:4**.

Sammet, J.E. (1969), *Programming Languages: History and Fundamentals*, Prentice Hall.

Scott, N.R. (1985), *Computer Number Systems and Arithmetic*, Prentice Hall.

Sebesta, R.W. (1989), *Concepts of Programming Languages*, Benjamin/Cummings.

Sedgewick, R. (1977), 'Permutation generation methods', *ACM Comput. Surv.* **9:2**, 137–64.

Sethi, I.K. and Chatterjee, B. (1980), 'Conversion of decision tables to efficient sequential testing procedures', *Commun. ACM* **23:5**, 279–85.

Sethi, R. (1989), *Programming Languages: Concepts and Constructs*, Addison-Wesley.

Shaw, A.C. (1974), *The Logical Design of Operating Systems*, Prentice Hall.

Shaw, M. (1984), 'Abstraction techniques in modern programming languages', *IEEE Software* **1:4**, 10–26.

Shore, R.W. (1987), 'Discrete-event simulation in Ada: concepts', *Ada Lett.* **7:5**, 105–12.

Shumate, K. (1987), *Understanding Concurrency in Ada*, Harper and Row.

Shurkin, J. (1984), *Engines of the Mind: a History of the Computer*, W.W. Norton & Co.

Siewiorek D.P., Bell C.G., and Newell A. (1982), *Computer Structures: Principles and Examples*, McGraw-Hill.

Skvarcius, R. and Robinson, W. B. (1986), *Discrete Mathematics with Computer Science Applications*, Benjamin/Cummings.

Smith, A.J. (1982), 'Cache memories', *ACM Comput. Surv.* **14:3**, 473–530.

Sterling, L. and Shapiro, E. (1986), *The Art of Prolog*, MIT Press.

Stern, N. (1980), 'John von Neumann's influence on electronic digital computing, 1944–1946', *Ann. Hist. Comput.* **2:4**, 349–62.

Stern, N. and Stern, R.A. (1988), *Structured COBOL Programming*, 5th edition, John Wiley & Sons Ltd.

Stone, R.G. (1982), 'Points recurring: the history of a railway problem', *SIGPLAN Notices* **17:9**, 88–94.

Strachey, C. (1959), 'Time sharing in large fast computers', in *Proceedings of the International Conference on Information Processing*, pp. 336–41, UNESCO, Paris.

Strachey, C. (1966), 'Towards a formal semantics', in *Formal Language Description Languages for Computer Programming*, ed. Steel, T.B., pp. 198–220, North-Holland.

Tai, K.C. (1982), 'Comments on parameter passing techniques in programming languages', *SIGPLAN Notices* **17:2**, 24–7.

Tanenbaum, A.S. (1984), *Structured Computer Organization*, 2nd edition, Prentice Hall.

Tennent, R.D. (1981), *Principles of Programming Languages*, Prentice Hall.

Tennent, R.D. (1982), 'Two examples of block structure', *Softw. Pract. Exper.* **12:4**, 385–92.

Terry, P. (1987), *FORTRAN from Pascal*, Addison-Wesley.

Thatcher, J.M., Wagner, E.G., and Wright, J. (1978), 'Data type specification: parameterization and the power of specification techniques', in *Proceedings of the 10th SIGACT Symposium on the Theory of Computing*, pp. 119–32.

Tou, J.T. and Wegner, P., eds. (1971), 'Proceedings of a Symposium on Data Structures in Programming Languages', *SIGPLAN Notices* **6:2**.

Traub, A.H. ed. (1963), *The Collected Works of John von Neumann*, Macmillan.

Treleaven, P.C., Brownbridge, D.R., and Hopkins, R.P. (1982), 'Data-driven and demand-driven computer architecture', *ACM Comput. Surv.* **14:1**, 93–143.

Turba, T.N. (1985), 'The Pascal exception handling proposal', *SIGPLAN Notices* **20:8**, 93–8.

Van Wijngaarden, A. (ed.), Mailloux, B.J., Peck, J.E.L., and Koster, C.H.A. (1969), 'Report on the algorithmic language ALGOL 68', *Numer. Math.* **14:2**, 79–218.

Van Wijngaarden, A. (ed.), Mailloux, B.J., Peck, J.E.L., Koster, C.H.A., Sintzoff, M., Lindsey, C.H., Meertens, L.G.L.T., and Fisker, R.G. (1975), 'Revised report on the algorithmic language ALGOL 68', *Acta Inf.* **5**, 1–236, reprinted in *SIGPLAN Notices* **12:5**, 1–70 (May 1977).

Wand, M. (1980), *Induction, Recursion and Programming*, Elsevier.

Wang, A. (1976), 'An axiomatic basis for proving total correctness of GOTO-programs', *BIT* **16**, 88–102.

Wang, A. and Dahl, O-J. (1971), 'Coroutine sequencing in a block-structured environment', *BIT* **11**, 425–49.

Warren, A.S. (1977), 'Functions realizable with word-parallel logic and two's complement addition instructions', *Commun. ACM* **20:6**, 439–41.

Warshall, S. (1962), 'A theorem on Boolean matrices', *J. ACM* **9:1**, 11–12.

Watt, D.A., Wichmann, B.A., and Findlay, W. (1987), *Ada: Language and Methodology*, Prentice Hall.

Wegner, P. (1971), 'Data structure models for programming languages', *SIGPLAN Notices* **6:2**, 1–54.

Wegner, P. (1987), 'Dimensions of object-based language design', in Meyrowitz (1987), pp. 168–82.

Wegner, P. and Smolka, S.A. (1983), 'Processes, tasks, and monitors: a comparative study of concurrent programming primitives', *IEEE Trans. Soft. Eng.* **9:4**, 446–62.

Welch, P.H. (1986), 'A structured technique for concurrent systems design in Ada', in *Ada: Managing the Transition*, ed. Wallis, P.J.L., pp. 261–72, Cambridge University Press.

Welsh, J., Lister, A., and Salzman, E.J. (1980), 'A comparison of two notations for process communication', *Lecture Notes in Computer Science* **79**, 225–54, Springer-Verlag.

Welsh, J., Sneeringer, W.J., and Hoare, C.A.R. (1977), 'Ambiguities and insecurities in Pascal', *Softw. Pract. Exper.* **7**, 685–96.

Welsh, J. and Lister, A. (1981), 'A comparative study of task communication in Ada', *Softw. Pract. Exper.* **11**, 257–90.

Wexelblat, R. ed. (1981), *History of Programming Languages*, Academic Press.

Wheeler, T.J. (1986), 'An example of the developer's documentation for an embedded computer system written in Ada, Part I', *Ada Lett.* **6:6**, 61–71.

Wheeler, T.J. (1987), 'An example of the developer's documentation for an embedded computer system written in Ada, Part II', *Ada Lett.* **7:1**, 40–8.

Whitehead, A.N. and Russell, B. (1910), *Principia Mathematica*, Cambridge University Press.

Wichmann, B.A. (1976), 'Ackermann's function: a study in the efficiency of calling procedures', *BIT* **16:1**, 103–10.

Wichmann, B.A. (1977), 'How to call procedures, or second thoughts on Ackermann's function', *Softw. Pract. Exper.* **7:3**, 317–29.

Wilkinson, J.H. (1963), *Rounding Errors in Algebraic Processes*, Prentice Hall.

Williams, M.H. and Ossher, H.L. (1978), 'Conversion of unstructured flow diagrams to structured form', *Comput. J.* **21:2**, 161–7.

Wilson, L. and Clark, R. (1988), *Comparative Programming Languages*, Addison-Wesley.

Wilson, T.C. and Shortt, J. (1980), 'An O(log n) algorithm for computing general order-k Fibonacci numbers', *Inf. Process. Lett.* **10**, 68–75.

Winkler, J.F.H. (1984), 'More on block structure: using Ada', *Ada Lett.* **3:6**, 48–56.

Winner, R.I. (1984), 'Unassigned objects', *ACM Trans. Program. Lang. Syst.* **6:4**, 449–67.

Winston, P.H. and Horn, B.K.P. (1984), *LISP*, 2nd edition, Addison-Wesley.

Wirth, N. (1971), 'The programming language Pascal', *Acta Inf.* **1**, 35–63.

Wirth, N. (1974), 'On the composition of well-structured programs', *ACM Comput. Surv.* **6:4**, 247–59.

Wirth, N. (1977a), 'Modula: a language for modular multiprogramming', *Softw. Pract. Exper.* **7**, 3–35.

Wirth, N. (1977b), 'What can we do about the unnecessary diversity of notation for syntactic definitions?', *Commun. ACM* **20:11**, 822–3.

Wirth, N. (1988), *Programming in Modula-2*, 4th edition, Springer-Verlag.

Wulf, W.A., Russel, D.B., and Haberman, A.N. (1971), 'Bliss: a language for systems programming', *Commun. ACM* **14:12**, 780–90.

Yemini, S. and Berry, D.M. (1985), 'A modular, verifiable exception-handling mechanism', *ACM Trans. Program. Lang. Syst.* **7:2**, 214–43.

Yoder, C.M. and Schrag, M.L. (1978), 'Nassi-Shneiderman charts: an alternative to flowcharts for design', in *Proceedings ACM SIGSOFT/SIGMETRICS Software and Assurance Workshop*, November 1978, reprinted in Freeman and Wasserman (1980), pp. 386–93.

INDEX